The best of **Britain**

Peak District

Roly Smith & Janette Sykes

Contents

THIS BOOK IS DEDICATED
TO THE MEMORY OF SIR MARTIN DOUGHTY (1949-2009),
A REAL CHAMPION OF THE PEAK

The Guide

06 Heather moorland

Three-quarters of the world's heather moorland is in the UK – and a large proportion of that is in the Peak District National Park. It is of global ecological and conservation importance, supporting rare and endangered plants and animals, p. 148

07 Bakewell Market

There's probably been a market at Bakewell for a thousand years, and farmers still flood into the Wye-side town every Monday to buy and sell their stock, p. 100

08 Arbor Low

Sometimes dubbed 'the Stone-henge of the North', the ancient stone circle and henge of Arbor Low, west of Youlgrave, puts its Wiltshire contemporary to shame with its air of untouched mystery and enchantment, p. 95

09 Derwent dams

The three huge reservoirs of Howden, Derwent and Ladybower which flood the Upper Derwent Valley are a massive visitor attraction, and their still waters and surrounding forests constitute the Peak District's Lake District, p. 169

10 Buxton Opera House

Frank Matcham's 1905 ornate rococo white and gilded masterpiece is the scene of the annual Buxton Festival of the Arts, and the glorious centrepiece of the cultural life of the Peak District, p. 200

Secret
Peak District
Local recommendations

01 Castleton Garlanding

A strange, pagan custom involving a flower-decked 'King' and his 'Queen', held annually on Oak Apple Day (29 May), p. 28

02 No. 6 The Square Tea Room, Buxton

Award-winning tea room in a beautiful Georgian-style building in the centre of Buxton, p. 212

03 Tindalls Bakery & Delicatessen, Tideswell

A cornucopia of locally-produced and homemade food, from bread and cakes to original pork pies and home-cooked local meats, p. 130

04 World Toe Wrestling Championships

Toe-curlingly bizarre competition held annually in August at the Bentley Brook Inn, Fenny Bentley, near Ashbourne, p. 116

05 Freshfields Donkey Village, Peak Forest

The kids will love this sanctuary for abused and neglected donkeys, supported by the stars, p. 126

06 Lud's Church
Follow in the footsteps of Sir Gawain to this secret chasm near Gradbach, p. 223

07 Lemon Grass Restaurant, Matlock
An exotic taste of Vietnamese cuisine in the heart of the Derbyshire Dales, p. 85

08 Manifold Valley
Escape the crowds of Dovedale and admire the quieter pleasures of the Manifold, including Thor's Cave (pictured), p. 105

09 Druid Inn, Birchover
Drinkers and diners can sample the best of both worlds at this 17th-century establishment, beneath Row Tor Rocks, p. 101

10 Riley Graves
Near Eyam, discover the true meaning of the tragedy of the Plague village in this poignant graveyard for a family of seven, p. 121

Factfile

01   The Peak District National Park was Britain's first, established on 17 April 1951

02   It covers 555sq miles/1,438sq km, from Ashbourne in the south to Meltham in the north, and from the outskirts of Sheffield in the east to the Staffordshire Moorlands in the west

03   With around 22 million day visitors, it is the second most visited National Park in the world (after Mount Fuji in Japan)

04   Although it is often mistakenly known as the 'Derbyshire Peak District', the National Park actually covers parts of six different counties

05   The highest point of the Peak District is the moorland plateau of Kinder Scout, at 2,088ft/636m

06   There are over 50 reservoirs in the Peak District, and no real natural lakes

07   About 38,000 people live within the National Park, and Bakewell is the largest town with a population of just under 4,000

08   Tourism is now the biggest single industry in the Peak District, worth around £450 million annually and employing over 14,000 people

09   It is the only British National Park to be awarded the Council of Europe's Nature Conservation Diploma

10   It is the northernmost home of many southern species, such as the hobby and nettle-leaved bellflower, and the southernmost home of many northern species, such as the mountain hare and cloudberry

THE FACTS

WHEN TO GO

The Peak District National Park has often been described as a 'park for all seasons'. And it is true that there are good reasons to visit the area at any time of the year.

Spring

Wildflowers are at their best during a Peakland spring. In the woodlands, the first to appear are usually the celandines, closely followed by the wood anemones and then the smoky mist of bluebells, while in the dales, the early purple orchids thrust their spears through the greensward to decorate many of the steeper slopes.

The Easter holiday is traditionally the time when the tourist season gets into full swing, as more visitors descend on Peak District villages and towns after their winter 'hibernation'. The well dressings traditionally start at Tissington on Ascension Day, quickly followed by other villages in the White Peak as spring moves into summer.

Summer

Summer still remains the busiest and most popular holiday season, when the car parks in popular places such as Bakewell, Castleton and Dovedale are likely to fill up quickly. Coach tours are becoming increasingly popular, and attractions and visitor centres note pulses of activity as they disembark their passengers. Regular events, such as Bakewell Market (every Monday); the Bakewell Show (first week in August) and the various well dressings throughout the summer period can also create traffic and parking problems.

But summer also sees the Peak District wildlife burgeoning, when the limestone dales of the White Peak are at their loveliest, full of wildflowers, loud with birdsong and buzzing with insect life. And towards the end of August, the gritstone moors of the Dark Peak gradually start to blush into warm swathes of purple, as the heather comes into flower.

Autumn

Autumn tints colour the deciduous woodlands of the Peak in a display which can rival the famous Fall colours of New England. This is the time to enjoy the late sunshine of the frequent Indian summers, which can extend well into October in a good year. It's also the time for several sheepdog trials, where the telepathic skills of man and dog can be observed at close hand.

On the heights, for example on the Eastern or Western Edges of gritstone, autumn is also the season for those magical days of temperature inversion, when the valleys are blanketed in a swirling white mist, while up above you are still bathed in glorious sunshine. And the red deer in the parks of Chatsworth and Lyme are in full voice for their annual rut.

Winter

Thanks to global warming, continuous days of snow lying in the Peak are rare, except on the highest points of Kinder, Bleaklow and Black Hill. But when the snow does fall, the A57 Snake Road between Sheffield and Manchester is still one of the first to be blocked and last to clear, such is its high altitude.

A crisp winter's day is a fine time for a walk in the Peak, when the grass crunches under your feet and the vegetation is coated with a tinsel-like covering of frost. Although there are usually fewer visitors about, this is the time for Christmas lights, carol singing and shopping in places such as Chesterfield, Matlock, Bakewell and Castleton.

GETTING THERE

Located at the heart of England, the Peak District is easily accessible for travellers, whether you are using road, rail, coach, bus or air. The website www.transportdirect.info has useful information to help you plan your journey.

By road

The Peak District is effectively bracketed by motorways. Coming from the south, the M1 from London to Leeds passes to the east of the district, which can be easily accessed from junction 28 (Ripley and Matlock) via the A6, or junction 29 (Chesterfield) via the A619. To the west, the M6 junctions 17, 18 (Congleton) and 19 (Knutsford) give easy access to the western side of the Peak via the spectacular A537 (Cat and Fiddle road) or A54 roads. To the north, the M62 cross-Pennine motorway linking the A1 (M) and Leeds with Manchester gives access to the north of the area via junction 22 (Oldham). The M60 Manchester orbital motorway gives easy access to Glossop and New Mills via the M67.

By rail

The pretty Derwent Valley Line links to the main line at Derby and takes you via Belper, to Cromford and Matlock Bath. The East Coast main line passes through Derby, Chesterfield and Sheffield, where there are bus links to the Peak.

The scenic Hope Valley Line cross-park service between Manchester and Sheffield stops at Grindleford, Hathersage, Bamford, Hope, Edale and New Mills, and the Manchester to Buxton line stops at Disley, New Mills, Whaley Bridge and Chapel-en-le-Frith. For further information on any of these services either call ☎ 08457 48 49 50 or visit www.nationalrail.co.uk.

By coach

The National Express coach service number 440 between London and Manchester travels through the Peak District, stopping at Derby, Belper, Matlock, Matlock Bath, Bakewell and Buxton. For further information either call ☎08705 80 80 80 or visit www.nationalexpress.com.

The low cost inter-city bus service megabus.com (www.megabus.com) operates services to Sheffield and Manchester, from where a local bus or train can be caught into the Peak District.

By bus

There are frequent links from neighbouring towns and cities into the Peak District. The most popular is the frequent Transpeak bus service (www.transpeak.co.uk).

The best sources of bus travel advice are the Peak District, Mid and South Derbyshire, and North East Derbyshire bus timetables, which are published twice a year by Derbyshire County Council (DCC). They are available from any tourist information centre in the area or by sending a cheque for £1.60 per booklet (payable to DCC) to The Public Transport Unit, Derbyshire County Council, County Hall, Matlock, Derbyshire DE4 3AG. Telephone ☎01629 580000 (ext 6738) to order with a Visa/Mastercard debit or credit card.

For further information either call ☎0871 200 2233 or visit www.derbyshire.gov.uk/buses or visit Peak Connections.

By air

Both Manchester and Nottingham East Midlands airports offer easy links to the Peak District for the air traveller. The 199 Skyline bus runs daily between Manchester Airport and Buxton, from 3am until 11pm (usually twice or three times an hour but exact times vary so please consult the timetable for details). The service also calls at a number

10... places to avoid in the Peak District

1 **Langsett** – if ever a village deserved a by-pass, it's this one. Dissected by the never-ending stream of heavy traffic on the A616 between Sheffield and Manchester, you wonder how local people ever manage to get across the road.

2 **Matlock Bath on a summer Sunday afternoon** – unless you like admiring leather-clad bikers and their motorbikes! This truly is the Blackpool of the Peak, full of tacky candy floss, amusement arcades and fish and chip shops.

3 **Dove Holes** – just outside Buxton on the A6 is not to be confused with the Dove Holes caves in beautiful Dovedale. Dubbed by a BBC Radio 5 poll as *'the ugliest village in Britain'*, this bleak settlement high on the limestone plateau is surrounded by quarries and always seems to have a thoroughly depressing air about it.

4 **The Cat and Fiddle road (A537)** – between Buxton and Macclesfield, which has been labelled 'Britain's most dangerous road'. Not only is it treacherous in fog, ice and snow, it can be a nightmare on clear days and at weekends, when some bikers use its challenging contours and sharp bends as a racetrack.

5 **Stoney Middleton** – should be an attractive village, hemmed in as it is by the steep limestone crags of Middleton Dale below Eyam. But it is scarred by active quarries and threaded by the constant roar, dust and mud of heavy quarry traffic on the busy A623.

6 **Dovedale on a summer weekend** – when you'll have to queue up to cross the Stepping Stones. And when you've eventually crossed the river, you'll find yourself in a continuous chattering crocodile of walkers, filing up the path and queuing at every stile.

7 **Bakewell on Market Day (Monday)** – where you'll be at your wits end in trying to find somewhere to park. The town gets clogged with livestock lorries too, going to and from the market, and it gets even worse on the two days of the Bakewell Show (the first week in August).

8 **Castleton on a Bank Holiday weekend or at Christmas time** – when it seems as if the whole of the population of Sheffield has decamped into the tiny village. It shares the same problem with parking as Bakewell does on a Market Day.

9 **Kinder Scout, Bleaklow or Black Hill in bad weather** – these can be dangerous and desolate places in fog, snow or heavy rain, especially if you're not adequately prepared with appropriate clothing and equipment.

10 **Longdendale** – another beautiful valley destroyed by a busy road, in this case, the trans-Pennine A628. But that's not the only indignity that Longdendale has had to suffer. There's also a marching army of disfiguring high-voltage power lines and although the railway has gone now, you actually wish it was still there to take some of the traffic off the road.

of towns and villages in the Peak District. Services from Manchester Airport can be checked at www.manchesterairport.co.uk.

A half-hourly bus service – the AirLine Shuttle – runs day and night from Nottingham East Midlands airport into Derby. There are regular train and bus services from the city into the Peak District. The Nottingham East Midlands Airport website is at www.eastmidlandsairport.com.

GETTING AROUND

The Peak District boasts one of the best rural public transport networks in Britain, with frequent buses or trains from neighbouring towns, cities and airports.

Most of the visitor attractions and walking areas are easy to get to, and with a little planning and travelling one way by public transport, many interesting linear walks can also be enjoyed. The major attractions, such as Chatsworth, especially when there is an event such as the Game Fair, or Bakewell at Bakewell Show time, can become very busy at peak times, and the roads can become very congested.

The Peak District, Mid and South Derbyshire, North East Derbyshire bus timetables and Derbyshire train timetables are excellent sources of travel information and are available from Peak District visitor centres and Derbyshire tourist information centres.

The **Derbyshire Wayfarer Day Rover Ticket** is a bargain, and provides travel on buses and trains throughout the county, plus discounts at some of the county's top attractions. These ticket are also valid on journeys across the county border, including Leek, Macclesfield and Sheffield city centre, and within Staffordshire on services 42, 442 and 443, and from the East Midlands Airport on service SDL. Wayfarer tickets are available from bus or train travel offices or tourist information centres.

Peak connections guides

Peak Connections is a partnership scheme about getting everyone to think about how they travel around the Peak District, and considering how they can travel in a more sustainable manner. The scheme aims to make using public transport as easy as possible. There are lots of ideas and information to show you just how easy it is to travel by bus or train to see many of the spectacular sights or visit the great attractions of the area.

The guides offer ready-made day out itineraries for bus or rail travel to and around the Peak District. Full details of each guide, together with a downloadable PDF of each, can be found at www.visitpeakdistrict.com/html/travel/peak-connections/peak-connections-guides; printed copies of some of the guides are also available free of charge from Peak District tourist information centres. There's also a wide range of discount vouchers giving reduced admission to attractions across the region when accompanied by a valid bus ticket on the day of entry.

The guides cover a range of popular destinations, for example *Chatsworth*, and the *Number 58 bus*, which links Macclesfield and Buxton via a spectacular journey over the A537 Cat and Fiddle road. On Sundays and Bank Holiday Mondays, the number 58 bus also connects to Bakewell and Chatsworth.

The Peak Connections *Days Out from Sheffield* guide highlights the wide range of destinations that can be visited by catching a bus or train in Sheffield to the Peak District. It provides a good mini-guide of places to visit and sights to see, together with relevant bus numbers and train stations for getting there easily using public transport, plus discount vouchers which can be used to visit Treak Cliff Cavern and Peveril Castle.

The Peak Connections Guide to *Castleton and Edale, Hope Valley (Bus 260)* passes through the stunning scenery between Edale Station and Castleton, via the Winnats Pass and the show caverns of Treak Cliff, Blue

John, Speedwell and Peak Cavern. Bus 260 operates all year on Sundays and bank holidays, and also on summer Saturdays.

The *Upper Derwent Valley–Park & Ride (Bus 222)* Peak Connections Guide operates on weekends and Bank Holiday Mondays, and offers a range of opportunities when visiting the area. You can enjoy a trip along the banks of the Ladybower, Derwent and Howden dams to see areas which are closed to traffic on summer weekends, or simply use the bus as a means of exploring different areas on foot by hopping on or off and walking the rest.

Ride and ramble

Peak Connections has also recently produced a book of 20 ride and ramble linear walks linked with public transport. It is available from tourist information centres in the area or from the National Park online shop (price £6.95).

Ride and Ramble features walks across the Greater Peak District, and you can plan your walk using the free bus timetable which accompanies the book. In addition, the family-focused leaflet *Hop On and Explore* features Bruce the Bus and Tess the Train to tempt the children.

Useful information
- **Traveline** (buses anywhere in the UK) – ☎ 0871 200 2233; www.traveline.org.uk.
- **Derbyshire County Council** – www.derby shire.gov.uk/buses; provides a comprehensive public transport website, which includes an interactive journey planner, timetable finder and route maps.

ACCOMMODATION

There's a wide range of accommodation on offer in the Peak District, and you'll find some of the most interesting and varied places to stay throughout this guide. For further inspiration, look up the **Visit Peak District and Derbyshire** website (www.visit peakdistrict.com).

Many places become fully booked at peak times, so it's a good idea to book as far in advance as possible, but last-minute deals are often available. When you've decided where you'd like to stay, making a booking is easy. You can contact the accommodation provider direct or visit www.visitpeakdistrict.com to check out the latest availability, ideas for short breaks and special offers, as well as to make a booking online.

You can also make a booking at any tourist information centre, where you will be charged a £3 booking fee and will be asked to pay a 10%, non-refundable deposit, which will be taken off your first night's stay at your chosen accommodation.

Self-catering

Some cottages are privately owned and managed, while others can be rented through agencies. Many have to be booked for a minimum of a week, but some are available for long weekends or midweek breaks – check when you book. Local contacts include:

- **Cottages4you** – ☎ 0845 268 9763; www.cottages4you.co.uk
- **Derbyshire Cottages** – ☎ 01228 406741; www.derbyshire-cottages.info
- **Derbyshire Country Cottages** – ☎ 01629 583545; www.derbyshirecountry cottages.co.uk
- **Peak Cottages** – ☎ 0114 262 0777; www.peakcottages.com
- **Peak Cottages Direct** – www.peak cottagesdirect.co.uk
- **Premier Cottages** – ☎ 0114 275 1477; www.PremierCottages.com
- **Visit Peak District and Derbyshire** – ☎ 0845 833 0970; www.visitpeakdistrict.com

National holiday letting companies include:

- **www.holiday-rentals.co.uk**
- **www.holidaylettings.co.uk**

· **The National Trust** – ☎ 0844 800 2070; www.nationaltrustcottages.co.uk

Both **The Landmark Trust** (☎ 01628 825925; www.landmarktrust.org.uk) and **The Vivat Trust** (☎ 0845 090 0194; www.vivat.org.uk) rescue and restore historic buildings and give them a new future as holiday lets. The Landmark Trust has two properties in the area: Edale Mill (see p. 264) and North Street, Cromford (part of the earliest planned industrial housing in the world, see p. 82), while Vivat Trust Holidays manages apartments at North Lees Hall, Hathersage (believed to have been the inspiration for Thornfield Hall in Charlotte Bronte's *Jane Eyre*, see p. 164).

Farm stay

Many Peak District farmers now offer either B&B or self-catering accommodation, and sometimes both. Staying on a working farm gives visitors an authentic taste of everyday farm life, as well as the pleasure of sampling local produce and experiencing the fruits of much of the good work that is being done to protect and enhance the environment. An excellent starting point for further information is **Peak District Farm Holidays** (www.peakdistrictfarmhols.co.uk). Other useful contacts are **Visit Peak District and Derbyshire** (www.visitpeakdistrict.com), **The National Trust** (www.nationaltrust.org.uk) and **Farm Stay UK** (www.farmstay.co.uk).

Camping

Camping offers a way to discover some of the Peak District's more remote areas. Many sites have a wide range of amenities in a variety of scenic locations, so the experience can be far from basic. Choices range from camping barns, also known as 'stone tents' to holiday parks with timber lodges and chalets. For further details, contact **Visit Peak District and Derbyshire** (www. visitpeakdistrict.com). Other useful contacts are **The National Trust** (www.nationaltrust. co.uk), www.find-a-campsite.co.uk, and www.campingandcaravanningclub.co.uk.

Youth hostels

Like camping and caravanning, youth hostels offer value for money accommodation in scenic and sometimes unusual settings. In the Peak District, you'll find particularly excellent examples in Eyam (see p. 128), Hartington (see p. 112) and Ilam (see p. 112). For full details visit www.yha.org.uk or call ☎ 01629 592700.

FOOD AND DRINK

Already prized for local delicacies such as Ashbourne Gingerbread and Bakewell Pudding, the Peak District is fast gaining even wider recognition and a well-deserved reputation for prime quality food and drink.

Visitors can literally trace the delicious transition from field to fork whether they buy premium produce direct from local producers at a farmers' market, farm shop, local shop or specialist fair, or stay or eat out at a variety of venues where local produce is the mainstay of the menu.

Local delicacies

Most people have heard of the famous **Bakewell Pudding** (see p. 93), created by accident in 1820 when the cook at the town's White Horse Inn (now the Rutland Arms Hotel) made a jam tart that went wrong. However, her mistake was hailed a mouth-watering success, and her puff pastry shell, layer of jam and filling of eggs, sugar, butter and almonds is still as popular today.

According to local legend, the recipe for **Ashbourne Gingerbread** (see p. 83) is believed to have been brought to the town by French prisoners during the Napoleonic Wars. Hearsay has it that the personal chef of a captured French general created it in 1805, and that his recipe was copied and has been made locally ever since.

Oatcakes are usually associated with Scotland, but Peak District versions are

The best... places to stay

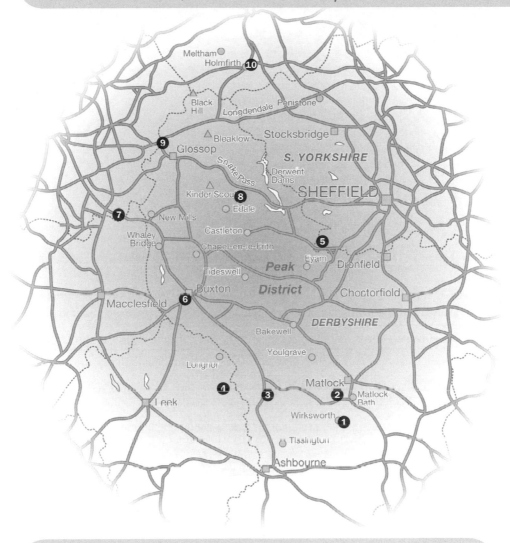

softer and freshly made with fine oatmeal, flour, yeast, sugar, salt and warm water to serve with both sweet and savoury fillings, traditionally cheese or jam, or to serve with a farmhouse breakfast. Similar to pancakes but more filling, the main difference between Derbyshire and Staffordshire Oatcakes is that Derbyshire ones are smaller and thicker, around 6–7 inches (15–18cm) in diameter, while Staffordshire's (see p. 225) are thinner and around 9 inches (22–23cm) wide.

Other sweet treats include Lumpytums; Tharf, or Thor, Cakes, and Wakes Cakes.

Lumpytums are balls made of oats, cooked in milk and served with butter or treacle. A cheeky local rhyme claims lumpytums give girls 'the rosiest cheeks and plumpest bums'! **Tharf**, or **Thor**, **Cakes**, made from oatmeal, black treacle, candied peel and spices were eaten on special occasions, especially on Bonfire Night, 5 November. **Wakes Cakes** are more like biscuits, made with butter, flour, sugar, currants, caraway seeds, lemon zest and egg, and traditionally eaten at local celebrations and festivals.

10... Peak District area specialities

1 Bakewell Pudding, created by accident in 1820, but still as popular today

2 Ashbourne Gingerbread, made according to a recipe brought to the town by French prisoners of war during the Napoleonic Wars

3 Derbyshire or Staffordshire Oatcakes, served with a range of sweet and savoury fillings

4 Wakes Cakes, traditionally eaten at local celebrations and festivals

5 Classic cheeses such as Stilton, Buxton Blue and Dovedale Blue (p. 83), and newer varieties such as Cheddleton & Chives and Moorland Oak Smoked, made in Staffordshire

6 Locally raised and slaughtered lamb, beef and other meats, much of it organic, available direct from suppliers, farmers' and country markets, local shops and specialist food fairs

7 Delectable dairy ice cream made from local milk at Bradwell's (p. 256), Frederick's (p. 102), Hilly Billy (p. 240), Our Cow Molly (p. 189), Hope Valley (p. 165) and Longley's (p. 305)

8 Choice chocolates from nationally known Thorntons, or hand-crafted confections made by Charlotte's Chocolates of Buxton (p. 210), Cocoadance of Castleton (p. 256) and Simon Dunn Chocolatier of Glossop (p. 286)

9 Locally brewed beers from a host of Peak-based microbreweries

10 Locally produced wine from The Vineyard at Renishaw Hall & Gardens, once the most northerly of its kind in the world

The best... places to buy fresh local produce

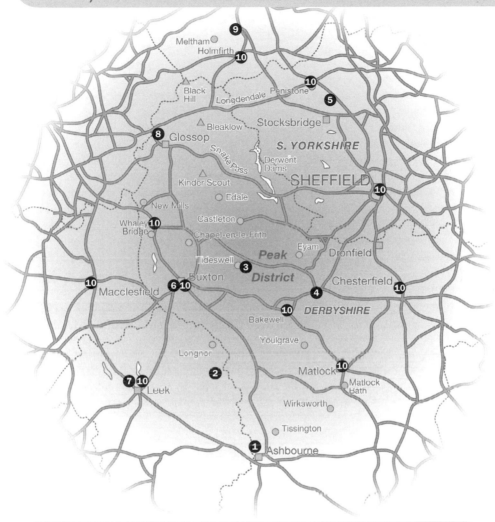

1. Patrick and Brooksbank, Ashbourne – one of the top 50 delicatessens in the country, p.83
2. Lower Hurst Farm, Hartington – award-winning, Soil Association-registered producers of quality organic beef and lamb, p.113
3. Tindalls Bakery & Delicatessen, Tideswell – bread, cakes, original pork pies, home-cooked local meats, delicious sandwiches and the area's famous Wakes Cakes, p.130
4. Award-winning Chatsworth Farm Shop, Pilsley – where first-class meat produced on the Chatsworth Estate is among the vast range of quality food and drink, p.152
5. Wortley Farm Shop, Wortley – for locally raised beef, pork, lamb and chicken, home-made sausages, burgers and pies, and a selection of Yorkshire cheeses, p.190
6. The Great Peak District Fair, Buxton – which showcases some of the area's finest food and drink, plus various arts and crafts, all under one roof, p.206
7. Festival of Fine Foods, Leek – offering everything from cheese and cakes to home-made pies and locally farmed meat on every third Saturday of the month, p.225
8. Multi award-winning J W Mettrick & Son Ltd, Glossop – for locally reared and slaughtered meat, plus traditional and more unusual sausages, p.286
9. Hinchliffe's Farm Shop, Netherton – award-winning butchers who make traditional pies, pasties and sausages from organically reared meat, p.305
10. Farmers' and country markets across the Peak District – you'll find everything from home-made cakes and local cheeses to organically reared meat and locally brewed ales

The area is also famous for its fresh local milk, butter, cream and cheese. Hartington has had a century-old association with making **Stilton**, known as the 'King of English cheeses' (see p. 107), and you'll also find local varieties of cheese such as **Buxton Blue** and creamy **Dovedale Blue**. Handmade cows' milk cheeses with local names are also made at the Staffordshire Cheese Company (see p. 225), and include Cheddleton & Chives, Moorland Oak Smoked and The Staffordshire.

Lamb has long been a traditional local speciality, for sheep have grazed the pastures of the Peak District for more than 6,000 years. Numerous farmers across the area supply home raised lamb, beef, other meats and associated products, much of it organic, either direct to the customer, through farm shops and local shops, at farmers' markets and specialist food fairs or to local accommodation providers and eateries, which serve it on their menus.

Anyone with a sweet tooth will appreciate locally sourced honeys, either with the gentle flavour of wild flowers from White Peak meadows or the more-ish, burnt sugar taste of the Dark Peak's moorland heather. And even though the land-locked Peak District is far from the salty tang of the seaside, ice cream is another delectable speciality, with award-winning varieties such as **Bradwell's** (see p. 256), **Frederick's** (see p. 102), **Hilly Billy** (see p. 240), **Our Cow Molly** (see p. 189), **Hope Valley** (p. 165) and **Longley's** (p. 305).

Chocoholics can choose from national brands such as Alfreton and Somercotes-based **Thorntons**, or hand-crafted confections made by **Charlotte's Chocolates** of Buxton (see p. 210), **Cocoadance** of Castleton (see p. 256) and **Simon Dunn Chocolatier** of Glossop (see p. 286).

And to wash it all down, real ale drinkers have a fine selection of locally brewed beers on tap thanks to a host of Peak-based micro-breweries, while wine lovers can sample the produce of locally grown grapes from **The Vineyard at Renishaw Hall & Gardens**, once the most northerly of its kind in the world (see p. 189).

Peak District food quality

Various groups and accreditation schemes have been set up to create a benchmark of quality for local food and drink. **Peak District Foods** and **Peak District Butchers** are groups of food producers whose fine fare is available direct, at farmer's markets, local shops and food events throughout the year, while the **Peak District Cuisine** logo indicates accommodation providers and eating places that serve local food and drink on their menus. Some offer the opportunity to buy online. For more information, visit www.peakdistrictfoods.co.uk, call ☎ 01332 594606, or pick up a *Savour the Flavour of the Peak District* booklet from a tourist information centre.

The **Peak District Environmental Quality Mark** is awarded to businesses such as farms, food producers, shops, eating places, craftspeople and accommodation providers that have made special efforts to conserve the natural environment of the Peak District National Park. For further details visit www.peakdistrict.gov.uk/eqm, call ☎ 01629 816321 or pick up *A Guide to Green Businesses in the Peak District* from a tourist information centre.

Foodie events

Throughout the year, farmers' and country markets are held at a number of venues across the Peak District, and in addition the Pavilion Gardens in Buxton regularly holds regional food fairs, as well as the Great Peak District Fair, a celebration of local food, drink, arts and crafts, every autumn (see p. 206). In Leek, there is a monthly Festival of Fine Foods in the Market Place (see p. 225), while Holmfirth stages a Food and Drink Festival (see p. 305) every September.

Other regular food and drink events include the Derbyshire Food and Drink Festival

The best... places to eat and drink

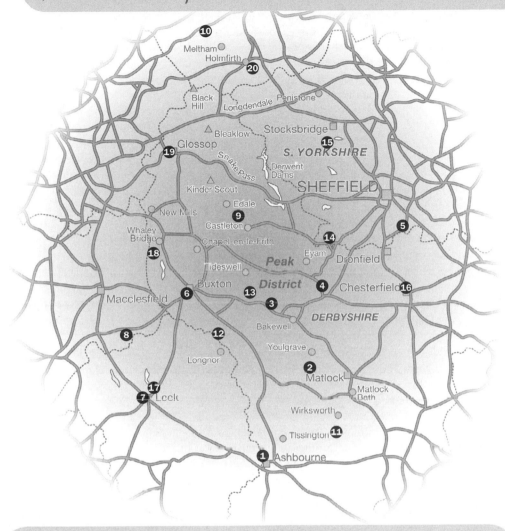

Restaurants and gastro pubs

1. The dining room, Ashbourne – award-winning cuisine with a conscience, p. 84
2. The Druid Inn, Birchover – popular gastro pub serves both traditional and contemporary food, p. 101
3. The Bull's Head, Ashford in the Water – cosy and welcoming village pub, p. 138
4. Fischer's Baslow Hall, Baslow – Michelin-starred restaurant in superb setting, p. 153
5. The Old Vicarage Restaurant, Ridgeway – quality food based on local seasonal produce in a picturesque setting, p. 191
6. The Dome Fine Dine Restaurant, Buxton – fine dining in the stunning setting of the University of Derby Buxton's showpiece campus, p. 211
7. Peak Weavers Rooms & Restaurant, Leek – award-winning restaurant in a 19th-century former convent, p. 226
8. The Ship Inn, Wincle – quintessential country pub with regularly updated menu, p. 242
9. Losehill House Hotel, Hope – chic restaurant with superb views, p. 254
10. The Olive Branch, Marsden – family-run restaurant, with a warren of snug rooms, open fire and decked outdoor area, p. 306

Real ale pubs

11. The Barley Mow, Kirk Ireton – local CAMRA Pub of the Year 2008 that oozes character, p.87
12. The Quiet Woman, Earl Sterndale – traditional pub packed with personality, p. 116
13. The Packhorse Inn, Little Longstone – cosy, unspoilt local with open fires serving real ales, p. 139
14. The Grouse Inn, Longshaw – recently won an award for its real ales, p. 168
15. The Strines Inn, Bradfield – in a traditional setting with open fires opposite Strines Reservoir, p. 174
16. Derby Tup, Chesterfield – serves the most extensive range of guest beers in the area, p. 194
17. The Wilkes Head, Leek – head to this cosy pub for locally brewed real ales, a real fire and regular live music, p. 228
18. The Swan, Kettleshulme – timber beams, stone fireplaces and a real fire create a traditional ambience, p. 242
19. The Globe, Glossop – real ale pub with its own brewery, p. 289
20. The Nook Real Ale Bar (Rose & Crown), Holmfirth – eight real ales feature in the well-stocked bar, p. 309

(May), the Great Kinder Beer Barrel Challenge & Beer Festival (September) and the Great Peak Food Fest (October), when a variety of venues ranging from accommodation providers to restaurants stage a range of events promoting local produce.

FESTIVALS AND ANNUAL EVENTS

Perhaps the best-known and most unique annual events celebrated in Peak District villages are the traditional **well dressings** during the summer months, when about 70 villages dress their wells and taps with intricate floral icons made out of petals, seeds, leaves and other natural materials, to give thanks for the gift of fresh water.

Other traditional events include **sheepdog trials** – the first one ever recorded was held at Longshaw in 1898 – country fairs and agricultural shows, and carol concerts around Christmas. **The Bakewell Agricultural Show**, also known as 'the Little Royal', has been held annually in August on the beautiful riverside showground since 1819, and is now thought to be the biggest two-day farming show in the country.

The major cultural event in the Peakland calendar is undoubtedly the two-week **Buxton Festival**, centred on Frank Matcham's elegant Opera House. This two-week event in July attracts artists and audiences from all over the world and now also features a Festival Fringe and a Literary Festival, which started in 2000.

Details of all events can be obtained from tourist information or visitor centres by picking up an events leaflet, or by visiting the website www.visitpeakdistrict.com.

Calendar of events

February

Ashbourne Shrovetide Football – believe it or not, this is how association football may have started. A day-long rough and tumble through the barricaded streets of Ashbourne, featuring the 'up'ards' versus the 'down'ards', the competing teams on either side of the Henmore Brook who attempt to score a goal at either end of the town. (See p 78.)

March

The annual **Flagg Races** are held on Easter Tuesday on Flagg Moor, off the A515 5 miles south of Buxton. It is one of the last traditional open country point-to-point races still taking place, and was first held in 1892. (See p 35.)

April

Peak District Walking Festival – the Peak District has always been a Mecca for walkers, and the Walking Festival, which is held in various locations throughout the area, features over 100 events from guided walks to evening talks and demonstrations.

May

Chatsworth International Horse Trials – competitors from all over the country and abroad attend this exciting two-day weekend event held in the Capability Brown landscaped parklands of Chatsworth by the River Derwent. (See p. 144.)

The **Castleton Garland Ceremony** held on Oak Apple Day (29 May) is another ancient custom whose origins are lost in the mists of time. A Garland 'King' parades through the village on horseback, completely encased in a framework pyramid of flowers, accompanied by his 'Queen' and local schoolchildren dancers, ending up at the parish church, where the garland is hoisted to the top of the tower. (See p. 28.)

The first of the season's **Well Dressings** is traditionally held on Ascension Day in the pretty estate village of Tissington, where the custom was first recorded in the 14th century. (See p. 123.)

June

The **Derbyshire County Show** is held in the grounds of Elvaston Country Park, near

10... special Peak District well dressings

1 Tissington – the earliest-recorded and traditionally the first of the season of Peakland well dressings, Tissington's six wells are unveiled on Ascension Day

2 Tideswell – the Shimwell family of Tideswell were responsible for the revival of the craft in many other villages. Tideswell's four well dressing designs often have an ecclesiastical theme

3 Youlgrave – Youlgrave dresses five wells, and is renowned for the originality of its designs, which are centred on The Fountain in the centre of the village

4 Ashford in the Water – about five wells are dressed on the Saturday before Trinity Sunday in the pretty Wye-side village of Ashford

5 Bakewell – the capital of the Peak usually has four well dressings, which are unveiled on the last Saturday in June, to coincide with the village carnival

6 Eyam – The tragic events of 1665–6 when the Plague struck the village often find their way into the themes of the three wells which are dressed in Eyam

7 Stoney Middleton – the setting of the three Stoney Middleton well dressings is superb, set in the secluded square known as The Nook, facing the parish church

8 Buxton – revived in 1840, Buxton's three well dressings are unveiled on the second Wednesday in July. But the one at the warm, healing waters of St Anne's Well however, has probably been celebrated for much longer

9 Wirksworth – adopted the well dressing custom in 1827, but now up to nine wells are dressed on the Saturday before the Spring bank holiday

10 Holymoorside – one of the villages which took up the custom most recently is Holymoorside, on the western edge of Chesterfield, which only started in 1979

Derby and is a traditional county show, featuring lifestyle and agri-business events with stallholders from all over the county. The **Buxton Fair** is also held in June on the Market Place behind the Town Hall, coinciding with the **Buxton Well Dressing** and **Carnival**. At the end of June, the **Peak District's Historic Border Country Walking Festival** takes place, featuring over 40 walks centred on Chesterfield and Bolsover.

July

This is the month of the **Buxton Festival**, **Buxton Fringe** and **Buxton Literary Festival**, all centred on the Opera House but extending to many other venues throughout the town (see p. 206). Artists attend the Buxton event from all over the world, and it has steadily grown in stature since its revival in 1979. The **Ashbourne Highland Gathering**, first held in 1985 and organised by the Ashbourne Pipe Band, also takes place this month and features pipe band and Highland dancing competitions and various other events. The **World Toe Wrestling Championships** are held at the Bentley Brook Hotel, on the A515 north of Ashbourne.

August

The well dressing season is in full swing by now, at the height of the Peak District's holiday season. Other major events include the two-day **Bakewell Show**, a major social event for the farming community of the Peak District, and the three-day **Chatsworth Country Fair**, which attracts huge crowds from all over the country. The **Ashover Agricultural Show** also takes place in August. The **International Gilbert & Sullivan Festival** is held in Buxton, the **English National Sheepdog Trials** take place at Ilam, in the shadow of Dovedale, and the **Longshaw Sheepdog Trials** take place at Longshaw, near Grindleford, on the weekend of the August Bank Holiday.

September

September marks the start of the **Matlock Bath Illuminations and Venetian Nights** when the Derwentside town is transformed into a fairyland of dancing lights. The two-week **Wirksworth Festival**, includes a range of visual and performing arts, but is perhaps best known for the weekend **Art Trails**, when about 100 local residents and businesses open their houses, shops, offices, churches and gardens for up to 250 artists to display their work. **The Amber Valley and Erewash Walking Festival** also takes place at various venues in the district over two weeks during September.

October

October is the month of the **Great Peak District Fair** held in the Pavilion Gardens at Buxton, when the varied flavours of locally produced food and drink from all over the Peak District can be sampled by visitors. There are nearly 100 exhibitors at the fair and top chefs show their skills. The fair also includes the **Great Peak Food Fest**, celebrating the best of local food and produce.

November

Running from the end of October through to the first of November is the **Chesterfield Market Festival** which includes music and drama, a huge Continental-style market, a Garden of Light and a beer festival, featuring some of Derbyshire's finest real ales. **Chesterfield Christmas Market** also takes place during November.

Chatsworth starts its annual **Dressed for Christmas** event in November, when beautiful traditional Christmas decorations cover the lower floors of the house, and daily special events and activities take place in the house and farmyard.

December

Castleton's famous **Christmas Lights** are switched on in mid November, and **Bakewell's Christmas Lights** follow soon afterwards. **Santa Specials** are run by **Peak Rail** at Matlock and the **Midland Railway** at Butterley and various villages hold carol concerts as Christmas approaches.

TRAVELLING WITH CHILDREN

It was the Victorian critic and artist John Ruskin who first described the Peak District as '*a lovely child's first alphabet; an alluring first lesson in all that is admirable*'. And there's certainly plenty of things to do with

10... Peak District festivals and shows

1 **Buxton Festival and Fringe** – the major cultural event in the Peak District

2 **International Gilbert & Sullivan Festival** – also in Buxton, this features the work of the Victorian light operatic composers

3 **Bakewell Show** – the farming shop window, showpiece and social event of the Peak District calendar

4 **Chatsworth Country Fair** – one of the biggest country lifestyle events in the calendar

5 **Chatsworth International Horse Trials** – features competitors from all over the world competing in the parklands of Chatsworth

6 **Wirksworth Festival** – has a range of visual and performing arts, including an Art Trail through the former lead-mining town

7 **Great Peak District Fair** – held in the Pavilion Gardens at Buxton, this features locally produced food and drink and includes the Great Peak Food Fest

8 **Ashbourne Shrovetide Football** – an day-long contest through the barricaded streets of Ashbourne, featuring the 'up'ards' versus the 'down'ards'

9 **Peak District Walking Festival** – over 100 events and guided walks held in various locations

10 **Castleton Garland Ceremony** – an ancient custom featuring a Garland 'King', who parades through the village completely encased in a framework pyramid of flowers

the kids when you are in the Peak, even when it rains.

Whether it's the **Children's Farmyard** at **Chatsworth**, where they can watch a cow being milked, or see otters and owls at the **Chestnut Centre**, near Chapel-en-le-frith, there's something for everyone. The more adventurous will enjoy **Gulliver's Theme Parks**, the **Cable Cars** at Matlock Bath, or **Go Ape!** at Poole's Cavern, Buxton.

SPORTS AND ACTIVITIES
Walking

It has been reckoned that more people go walking in the Peak District hills than anywhere else in Britain. Whether you are a hardened 'bog-trotter' who enjoys tramping across the peaty wastes of the Dark Peak moors, or you prefer the gentler walking provided by the glorious White Peak dales, there's something here to suit all tastes and experience.

With 1,600 miles of public rights of way, the Peak has plenty of opportunities for walkers. The 270 mile **Pennine Way** – Britain's first and toughest National Trail – starts from Edale on its way up the Pennine Chain to the Scottish Border. And the **Trans-Pennine Trail** through the Peak is part of the E8 European Walking Route, connecting the National Park to the far-off Turkish border – 2,500 miles away.

The Peak was the scene of some of the earliest and most celebrated battles for access to its high moorlands during the 1930s. Regular trespasses took place on land which had once been common, but which was enclosed by landowners during the 18th and 19th centuries. This culminated in the Mass Trespass on Kinder Scout in 1932, after which five ramblers were imprisoned for exercising their cherished 'right to roam'. This incident galvanised the rambling and outdoor movement, and eventually led to the National Parks and Access to the Countryside Act of 1949.

From 2005, the public's right to free and open access on foot in the National Park was increased from 240sq km/92sq miles to almost 500sq km/193sq miles, under the Countryside and Rights of Way Act 2000. Appropriately perhaps, in view of its long history of pressure for access, the Peak was the first National Park in England and Wales to benefit from the new legislation.

If the hills and dales are not to your taste, there's miles of easy, level walking suitable for wheelchairs or pushchairs on the converted railway lines of the Tissington and High Peak Trails, the Sett Valley and the Manifold Track.

One of the highlights of the Peak's walking year is the annual **Peak District Walking Festival**, which takes place in the Spring. Local experts guide participants through some of the finest Peak landscapes on walks designed for a range of abilities.

Useful websites which can tell you more about walking in the Peak District include www.visitpeakdistrict.com and www.peakwalk.org.uk or www.peakdistrictonline.co.uk. For details of local walking clubs, contact the Ramblers' Association on ☎ 020 7339 8500, or visit www.ramblers.org.uk. Local clubs always welcome visiting walkers: contact the Derbyshire Dales Group on ☎ 01773 783658; the Derbyshire Family Rambling on ☎ 01332 700184; the South Yorkshire and NE Derbyshire Group on ☎ 0114 266 5438; the Manchester and High Peak Group on www.manchester-ramblers.org.uk; the Staffordshire Group on ☎ 01782 642872; the Huddersfield Group on ☎ 01484 662866, or the East Cheshire Group at walk@eastcheshire.org.uk.

Climbing

It could be claimed that the sport of rock climbing was born in the Peak District. J W Puttrell, a Sheffield silversmith, made the first recorded steps onto the gritstone edge of **Wharncliffe Crag** in the Don Valley, northwest of Sheffield in 1885 – a year before the usually quoted birth date of the sport, William Haskett-Smith's ascent of Napes Needle in the Lake District. The so-called 'working class revolution' in the sport of rock climbing – previously it had been the preserve of middle and upper class climbers – also took place here in the 1950s. Mancunian tradesmen such as Joe Brown and Don Whillans took the sport to new, previously unheard of levels of difficulty on crags and edges like **Stanage Edge**, above Hathersage and **The Roaches**, in the Staffordshire Moorlands, sometimes using their mothers' clothes line for a rope.

Today, the Peak is still a Mecca for rock climbers, and many have gone on to conquer Himalayan giants after they cut their climbing teeth on Peakland rock. Any climbable rock face of grit or limestone is now covered by a network of routes of varying difficulty. There are, for example, over 650 climbing

The best... things to do with children

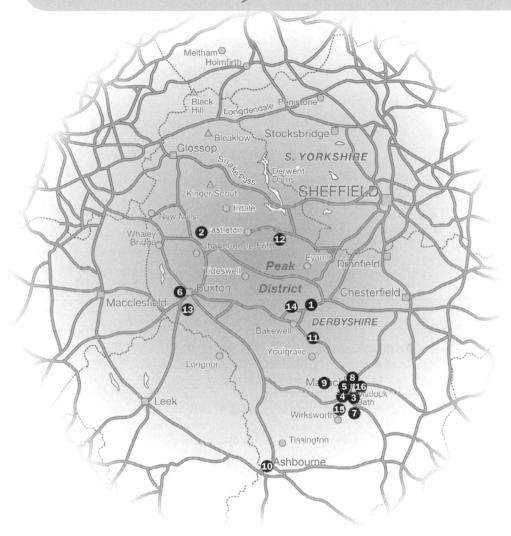

Fine weather

1. Chatsworth's Children's Farmyard and Playground – in the park at Chatsworth, p. 150
2. Chestnut Centre for otters, owls and other wildlife, p.31
3. Gulliver's Theme Parks – at Matlock Bath feature a Western World, a Fantasy Terrace, Lilliput Land and a Party House (see p. 79)
4. Cable Car Rides – at Matlock Bath take you high above the Derwent Gorge, with wonderful views, p. 69
5. Matlock Farm Park – at Two Dales, near Matlock, has adventure playgrounds and a go-kart track
6. Go Ape! – is a new high-wire forest adventure at Poole's Cavern, Buxton, p. 201
7. Crich Tramway Museum – take a ride on a vintage tram through reconstructed period streets, p. 89
8. Midland Railway, Butterley, and Peak Rail – offer the children a chance to ride on a real steam train, p. 73

Wet weather

9. Matlock Bath Aquarium – sited in the original Victorian Thermal Bath, p. 79
10. Museum of Childhood – at the National Trust's Sudbury Hall, near Ashbourne, p. 75
11. Toys of Yesteryear – is a new museum and toy shop, p. 98
12. The four show caves at Castleton – take an underground boat journey at Speedwell and enter the underground wonderland of Treak Cliff, p. 249
13. Poole's Cavern, Buxton – the most accessible of Peakland's underground wonders. Easy for pushchairs, p. 201
14. Old House Museum, Bakewell – award winning local museum, p. 91
15. National Stone Centre, Wirksworth – includes exciting and challenging exhibits for children, p. 73
16. Great Rutland and Masson Caverns, Matlock Bath – an awe-inspiring experience, p. 69

routes on Stanage Edge, including ones with challenging names such as the **Left and Right Unconquerable Cracks** – both of which were actually conquered by 1949.

Climbing can be a dangerous sport, so you should start by joining a recognised club. For more information on climbing and climbing clubs operating in the Peak District contact the British Mountaineering Council in Manchester on ☎ 0161 445 6111 or at www.thebmc.co.uk.

Caving

The earliest climbers, such as Puttrell, were also cavers, exploring the underground limestone wonders of the White Peak, especially around Castleton and Matlock Bath. Nowadays, however, the two esoteric sports are usually considered to be quite separate, and each have their own dedicated aficionados.

Apart from visiting the show caves at **Castleton, Matlock Bath** and **Buxton**, it is not advisable to venture underground without supervision. If you are interested in exploring the Peak's underground further, you should join a recognised club and receive proper training. New discoveries are still constantly being made under the Peak, and the recently discovered **Titan Cave** in Castleton has the deepest natural shaft in the UK – plummeting an awesome 464ft/141.5m.

The British Caving Association can be contacted for details about caving and caving clubs operating in the Peak District at The Old Methodist Chapel, Great Hucklow, Buxton, Derbyshire SK17 8RG or at www.british-caving.org.uk.

Cycling

There are nearly 60 miles of dedicated off-road cycle trails in the Peak District, including the traffic-free former railway trails such as the **Tissington and High Peak Trail**. In addition, there are other many opportunities for mountain biking on permitted bridleways and green tracks.

And you don't have to bring your own bike either. There are cycle hire centres at:

- Glossop
- Fairholmes in the Upper Derwent Valley
- Bakewell
- Parsley Hay on the Tissington Trail
- Middleton Top on the High Peak Trail
- Waterhouses in the Manifold Valley
- Ashbourne
- Carsington Water, near Wirksworth.

For more details, contact:

- Peak Cycle Hire – www.peakdistrict.gov.uk/cycle
- Derbyshire County Council Environmental Services Department – ☎ 0845 605 8058; www.derbyshire.gov.uk/countryside
- National Cyclists' Organisation – ☎ 0870 873 0060; www.ctc.org.uk
- International Mountain Bike Association – ☎ 01531 633500; www.IMBA-UK.com

Water sports

There are yachting clubs at the **Errwood Reservoir** in the Goyt Valley, at **Torside Reservoir** in the Longdendale Valley, and at **Carsington Water**, near Ashbourne. Carsington also offers facilities for windsurfing and powerboating.

The only place for real white-water canoeing is on the **River Derwent** at Matlock Bath. But there is also canoeing and rowing on Carsington Water, near Wirksworth and at **Rudyard Lake** in North Staffordshire.

Air sports

The **Derbyshire and Lancashire Gliding Club** at Camphill on Hucklow Edge has one of the most spectacular launch sites in the country, at over 1,360ft/415m above the sea and commanding great views across the Hope Valley. It is also one of the oldest gliding clubs in the country, founded in 1936, and you can take a trial flight for £65 to see if you like it. You can also enrol on a five-day residential course at Camphill where you can learn the skill of flying with the birds and enjoy the bar, dining room and lounge facilities on the site. Contact the club on ☎ 01298 871270, or visit www.dlgc.org.uk.

There are various sites throughout the Peak District where the thermals allow wonderful opportunities for **hang gliding** and **parascending**. These include Mam Tor, at the head of the Hope Valley; Stanage Edge, above Hathersage; The Roaches in the Staffordshire Moorlands; and from Shining Tor above the A537 and Goyt Valley.

The Peak District Hang Gliding Centre is based at Leek and operates from The Roaches and Shining Tor. It offers courses for beginners and has been described as one of the world's best. For more details, ring ☎ 07000 426445, or visit www.peakhanggliding.co.uk. The Derbyshire Flying Centre, based in Tideswell, offers both hang gliding and paragliding courses. Contact ☎ 01298 872313 or visit www.d-f-c.co.uk.

Traditional sports

The High Peak Hunt organises the annual **Flagg Races** point-to-point races on Easter Tuesday on Flagg Moor, off the A515, 5 miles south of Buxton. Until a few years ago there were several of these 'old-fashioned' point-to-point races around the country, but Flagg is now the only one left. The first Flagg Races were held in 1892 and apart from the war years and 2001 to 2003 (the foot-and-mouth years), the event has been held there ever since. For many spectators, the real attraction is the unique Hunt Members' race over natural hunting ground, starting in open country between the villages of Flagg and Pomeroy and finishing on the racecourse. See www. www.flaggraces.co.uk for more information.

Just how traditional the **World Toe-Wrestling Championships**, held annually in July at the Bentley Brook Inn, on the A515 north of Ashbourne, are cannot be said for sure. The event was invented in the Ye Olde Royal Oak Inn, Wetton, Staffordshire, by a group of walkers in the 1970s, who tried to devise a game in which Britain could be successful! Now it attracts entrants from all over the country. See p. 116 for more information.

ORGANISED HOLIDAYS AND COURSES

Walking

· **Drystone Walks** – ☎ 01332 781106; www.drystonewalks.co.uk; self-guided walking holidays in the Peak District, using less-popular upland and dale paths. The comprehensive walk pack includes full directions, maps and further information. Accommodation and luggage transfers arranged.

· **Peakland Walking Holidays** – info@walking holidays.org.uk; www.walkingholidays.org.uk; www.navigationcourses.co.uk; walking and navigation holiday courses run throughout the year, including short walking breaks and map and compass training courses led by navigation expert Pete Hawkins, who is based in Tideswell.

· **Simply Walking** – ☎ 01629 733269; www.simplywalk.co.uk. Self-guided walking holidays in the Peak District, featuring hand-picked bed-and-breakfast accommodation, luggage transfers, guidebooks and maps.

Walking and cycling

· **Peak Tours** – ☎ 07961 052590; www.peak-tours.com; offers a range of cycling and walking holidays and tours in the Peak District. Also offers cycle hire and delivery services to anywhere in the Peak.

Multi-activity

· **Peak Pursuits** – ☎ 01782 722226; www.peakpursuits.co.uk; walking, climbing and cycling holidays are offered by Peak Pursuits, which is based at Audley in North Staffordshire. Peak Pursuits even offers a mobile climbing wall for hire!

· **Blue Mountain Activities** – ☎ 01246 231767; www.bluemountainactivities.co.uk; based in Wingerworth, Chesterfield, Blue Mountain offers rock climbing, abseiling, canoeing, caving, mine exploration and other team-building activities.

- **Edale Youth Hostel Activity Centre** – Rowland Cote, Nether Booth, Edale; ☎ 0870 770 5808; www.yha.org.uk; in the shadow of Kinder Scout, Edale YHA offers courses in walking, navigation, climbing, caving and canoeing. There are also family multi-activity holidays all through the year.
- **Skylark Holidays** – ☎ 01283 701729; www.skylarkholidays.co.uk; includes guided walking tour holidays in the Peak District and Derbyshire and also craft-based holidays. Based at Sutton-on-the-Hill.

Riding and trekking

- **Northfield Farm Riding Centre** – ☎ 01298 22543; www.northfieldfarm.co.uk; Ride some of the ancient packhorse trails which are such a feature of the Peak District, featuring self-catering accommodation. British Horse Society approved, and based at the Northfield Farm Riding Centre in Flash, the highest village in England.

Special interest

- **Peak District Short Breaks** – ☎ 01298 23618; www.peakdistrictshortbreaks.co.uk; organises short breaks visiting local food producers for tastings and demonstrations. Transport and accommodation is included.
- **Peak District Photography Centre** – ☎ 01298 214438 or ☎ 01298 214415; www.peakphotocentre.com; based in Buxton, the Peak District Photography Centre offers residential courses in landscape photography and tutoring in the latest digital techniques from some of the finest Peak District photographers.

Residential centres

- **Losehill Hall Learning and Environmental Conference Centre** – ☎ 01433 620373; enquiries.losehill@peakdistrict.gov.uk; a Victorian country house set in 27 acres of beautiful parkland just outside Castleton, Losehill Hall is owned and managed by the Peak District National Park Authority. It offers a wide range of environmental learning services for people of all ages including school visits, teacher training, and training and development for environmental professionals. Losehill Hall also provides a setting for conferences, training courses and seminars.
- **Youth hostels** – there are Youth Hostels at Castleton, Edale, Crowden, Hartington, Hathersage, Ravenstor, Eyam, Gradbach Mill, Ilam and Youlgrave. For more details, contact www.yha.org.uk.

FURTHER INFORMATION

Visit Peak District & Derbyshire is the official mini tourist board for the area. Check its website (www.visitpeakdistrict.com) for more details of what to see and do and quality assured places to stay. With ideas for short breaks, walks and trails, and a comprehensive list of events throughout the season, there should be something there for everyone.

Local radio stations

- BBC Radio Derby – 104.5, 95.3, 96 FM and 1116 AM; www.bbc.co.uk/derby/local_radio
- BBC Radio Sheffield – 104.1, 88.6, 94.7 FM and DAB Digital; www.bbc.co.uk/southyorkshire/radio_sheffield
- BBC Radio Manchester – 95.1 FM and DAB Digital; www.bbc.co.uk/manchester/local_radio
- Peak FM – 107.4 and 102FM; www.peakfm.net

Weekly newspapers

- *Derbyshire Times* – www.derbyshiretimes.co.uk
- *Matlock Mercury* – www.matlockmercury.co.uk
- *Ashbourne News Telegraph* – www.ashbournenewstelegraph.co.uk
- *Buxton Advertiser* – www.buxtonadvertiser.co.uk

- *Glossop Chronicle* –
  www.glossopchronicle.com
- *Leek Post & Times* –
  www.thepostandtimes.co.uk
- *Macclesfield Express* –
  www.macclesfield-express.co.uk

Daily newspapers
- *Sheffield Star* – www.thestar.co.uk
- *Manchester Evening News* –
  www.manchestereveningnews.co.uk
- *Huddersfield Examiner* –
  www.examiner.co.uk
- *Derby Evening Telegraph* –
  www.thisisderbyshire.co.uk
- *Stockport Express* –
  www.stockportexpress.co.uk
- *Stoke Sentinel* –
  www.thisisstaffordshire.co.uk

Monthly magazines
- *Derbyshire Life and Countryside* –
  www.derbyshirelife.co.uk

- *Peak District Life* –
  www.peakdistrictlife.co.uk
- *Staffordshire Life* –
  www.staffordshirelife.co.uk
- *Reflections* –
  www.reflections-magazine.com

Useful websites
- Peak District National Park Authority
  – www.peakdistrict-npa.gov.uk
- National Trust – www.nationaltrust.org.uk
- Natural England –
  www.naturalengland.org.uk
- Friends of the Peak District –
  www.friendsofthepeak.org.uk
- Derbyshire Wildlife Trust –
  www.derbyshirewildlifetrust.org.uk
- Peak District Products –
  www.peakdistrictproducts.co.uk
- Visit Peak District and Derbyshire –
  www.visitpeakdistrict.com

THE BACKGROUND

HISTORY

The landscape of the Peak District is a manuscript on which, if you know how to read it, the story of man's occupation has been written over and over again. And the largely upland and uncultivated character of the Peak landscape has meant that some of the evidence left by the earliest settlers can still be seen, in addition to the surviving architecture of the villages and towns.

Prehistory

The earliest people in the area we now know as the Peak District date back to the Mesolithic, or Middle Stone Age, between 6,000 and 7,000 years ago. Animal skin-clad nomadic families visited the area in search of food, hunting game and gathering berries and fruits. They left behind little in the way of their physical presence because their camps were usually temporary, but we know they used the abundant rock shelters and caves found in the limestone areas of the White Peak, in places like the Dove and Manifold Valleys, where the awesome gaping void of **Thor's Cave** (see p. 105) seems to represent the archetypal cave man's dwelling.

Occasionally their flint tools can still be found, washed out from the enveloping peat on the high moors of the Dark Peak. These tiny slivers of stone, known as microliths, show that even the highest ground of the Peak District, which was at that time covered by a forest of oak and birch trees, was used by these earliest settlers in search of game. The only place where any definite traces of any permanent occupation have been found is at Lismore Fields west of Buxton, where the postholes of square buildings dating back to the Neolithic age, have been excavated.

But the most impressive monuments of the Stone Age are undoubtedly those constructed up to 6,000 years ago either to bury and honour their dead, or the impressive henge monuments and stone circles which were used for ritualistic purposes whose nature we can still only guess at.

Chief among these is the massive stone circle and henge of **Arbor Low**, south of Monyash (see p. 95), which is sometimes known as 'the Stonehenge of the North'. Unlike its over-interpreted and heavily visited Wiltshire contemporary, Arbor Low manages to retain its air of ancient mystery, situated at 1,230ft/375m on the limestone plateau with views extending in all directions.

It is easy to imagine Neolithic tribes and families gathering here around their campfires, perhaps for ritual ceremonies or the exchange of livestock, in the shadow of the massive henge embankment which enclosed the circle of massive limestone menhirs, all of which now lie broken and prostrate on the ground. A similar-sized Neolithic henge exists at the **Bull Ring** at Dove Holes, north of Buxton, although this is in a much more urban setting, and none of the stones have survived.

Veneration of the dead was an important part of Neolithic culture, and monumental mounds enclosing chambered tombs were raised at places like Five Wells, Taddington, and Minninglow, between Parwich and Elton, to honour them. Other large Neolithic barrows exist at Gib Hill, near to and probably predating Arbor Low, and at Long Low near Wetton.

It is obvious from a reading of the Peak District landscape that the climate in prehistoric times was much kinder and warmer than today. Vast field systems with clearance cairns, hut circles and burial mounds have been traced on the **Eastern Moors** above Baslow, indicating that a sizeable population must have lived here during the Bronze Age, between 4,000 and 3,000 years ago. Other signs of human activity during the Bronze Age again relate to the way that those first metal-workers honoured their dead. Under the heather of **Stanton Moor**, a gritstone outlier south of Bakewell, over 70 tumuli (burial mounds) date from the Bronze Age. Also, standing isolated in a birch grove, is the stone circle known as the **Nine Ladies**, who, legend has it were turned to stone for dancing on a Sunday.

The Bronze Age moved imperceptibly into the Iron Age some 3,000 to 2,000 years ago, and while we know about the Bronze Age occupants of the Peak from the remains left by for their dead, we know virtually nothing about how Iron Age people were buried. What they did leave behind are the magnificent hillforts which they constructed on the highest, most strategic, points in the landscape. These misnamed constructions were most probably used not as defensive structures at all, but as summer shielings, from where tribespeople could watch over their stock grazing on the upland pastures above their settlements in the valleys below.

The most striking of these hillforts is undoubtedly **Mam Tor**, which watches over Castleton (see p. 252) and the upper reaches of the Hope Valley like a mother hen over its chicks. It's an appropriate simile, because the name of this 16 acre/6 hectare enclosure is thought to mean 'mother mountain'. Mam Tor is one of the largest and most spectacularly-sited hillforts in the country, standing at 1,695ft/517m above the sea on the edge of the huge landslip on the east face of the hill – a superb natural defence if it was needed. Other notable hillforts in the Peak include **Castle Naze**, above Chapel-en-le-Frith, and **Fin Cop**, which overlooks the well-known viewpoint of

Monsal Head in the Wye Valley near Ashford in the Water.

Roman

The plentiful and easily obtained supplies of lead ore in the White Peak were probably what attracted the Romans to the Peak around AD80. Several pigs of lead have been found, bearing the inscription LVTVDARES, a reference to *Lutudarum*, which was either the name of the ore field or the lost Roman lead mining centre in the Peak.

The Roman lead mining interests were administered by the playing card square forts of **Navio**, near Bradwell in the Hope Valley (see p. 248), and **Ardotalia**, or Melandra, near Glossop (see p. 281). We also know there were an important urban centres based on the warm springs at **Buxton** (see p. 199) known as *Aquae Arnemetiae*, and at Chesterfield. An increasing number of Romano-British farmsteads, such as that excavated by Sheffield University at Roystone Grange, near Ballidon, and at Chee Tor above the Wye, have recently been discovered.

Roman roads knitted the Empire together, such as the route still followed by the ruler-straight A515 between Ashbourne and Buxton; the minor road linking Buxton to Navio, and Doctor's Gate, between Glossop (Melandra) over the Snake Pass to Navio.

The Dark Ages and Medieval Period

It was the first Dark Age settlers of the Peak – the *Pecsaetan* – who gave it its name. The Saxon word for any hill or knoll was *pec*, and the *Pecsaetan,* a word first used around AD700, were simply the hill-dwellers, to distinguish them from the Mercians of the surrounding lowlands.

These Saxon and Viking settlers also created many of the Peak's villages and towns, and names like **Bakewell, Tideswell, Hucklow** and **Glossop** all take their names from those earliest Peaklanders. They also

The best... churches, castles and country houses

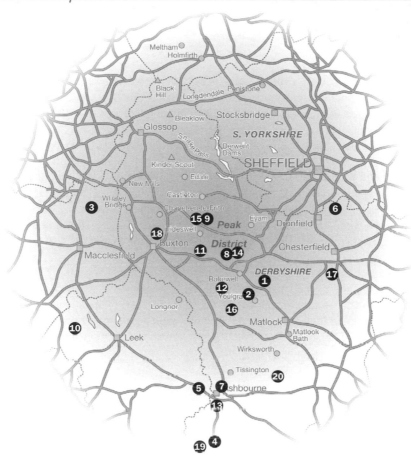

Castles and country houses

1. Chatsworth House – stately home of the Dukes of Devonshire, p. 144
2. Haddon Hall – medieval manor house, p. 90
3. Lyme Park near Stockport – the setting for BBC's *Pride and Prejudice*, p. 235
4. Sudbury Hall – grand, late 17th-century house with sumptuous interiors, p. 74
5. Ilam Park – outstanding views towards the hills of Dovedale, p. 108
6. Renishaw Hall – the stately home of the notorious Sitwell family, p. 189
7. Tissington Hall, – home of the Fitzherbert family for 400 years, p. 107
8. Eyam Hall – Home to the Wright family for over three centuries, p. 120
9. Peveril Castle, Castleton – William Peveril's 11th-century stronghold, p. 248
10. Little Moreton Hall – An iconic black-and-white, half-timbered manor house

Medieval churches

11. St John the Baptist – the so-called 'Cathedral of the Peak'. p. 124
12. All Saints – Bakewell's hilltop parish church commands fine views across the Wye valley, p. 96
13. St Oswald – this Early English-style church with its slender, spire is one of the most elegant in the Peak, p. 78
14. St Lawrence's – houses the register of the 259 names of those who died in the Plague, p. 124
15. St Edmund's – retains its 17th-century box pews, p. 253
16. All Saints – famed for its magnificent Perpendicular west tower, p. 96
17. St Mary and All Saints – The famous late 13th-century church of the Crooked Spire, p. 179
18. St Thomas à Becket – scene of the notorious imprisonment of 1,500 Scottish prisoners in the 17th century, p. 268
19. St Mary's – contains a wonderful collection of monuments to the Fitzherbert family, p. 108
20. St Mary's – with Saxon carved stones in the interior, p. 78

10... Peak District historical highlights

1 Millstones round their necks – the millstone is one of the classic images and marks the boundaries of the National Park. At Millstone Edge near Hathersage you can see the remains of old millstones abandoned after cheaper imports became available. The stones were used by the Sheffield cutlery industry, and also to sharpen steel wire into needles and pins

2 England expects – the Peak District had a memorial to the famous Battle of Trafalgar long before London's Nelson's Column. Local residents erected the impressive gritstone obelisk on Birchen Edge, near Baslow just five years after the battle, in 1810. Nearby are three rocky tors named after three of Nelson's ships: the Soverin [sic], the Reliance and the Victory

3 Derwent dams – the three largest reservoirs in the Peak District are the Derwent, Howden and Ladybower, in the Upper Derwent Valley. The Howden and Derwent dams were built between 1901 and 1916 of huge millstone grit blocks quarried from Grindleford and transported on a specially-built railway line. They are finished with Victorian gothic architectural embellishments including towers, crenulations, arched windows and buttresses. The Ladybower dam was built between 1935 and 1945

4 Tin town – the Derwent and Howden dams were built by hundreds of workers who were housed in a specially built village called 'Tin Town', because the walls were of corrugated iron

5 The Dambusters – for six weeks during the Second World War, the Derwent and Howden Dams were one of the sites used by the Royal Air Force's crack 617 Squadron to practise in their specially adapted Lancaster bombers for the famous 'Dambusters' raid on the Ruhr dams in 1943

6 Hung and drawn – on Gibbet Moor, east of Chatsworth, one of the last people to be gibbeted alive in England was punished for murdering a Baslow woman. He was sentenced to be hung in chains and left to die. But the man's agonized screams so haunted the Earl of Devonshire at nearby Chatsworth House, the punishment was abolished soon after

7 Bareleg Hill – there is an area of moorland just off the A53 Leek-Buxton road near the Royal Cottage Public House which goes by the strange name of Bareleg Hill. The story is that as Bonnie Prince Charlie and his men fled from staying at the Royal Cottage over the hill in 1745, their kilts blew up – hence Bareleg Hill

8 Looks like rain – Samuel Fox, born in 1815 in Bradwell in the Hope Valley, invented the 'Fox's Paragon' – the world's first collapsible umbrella frame – in 1851. It consisted of a 'U' section of string steel, and a similar product was used to make crinoline frames from 1855. Umbrellas with 'Fox Frames' were sold worldwide

9 Flash money – the village of Flash, standing at 1,518ft/462m on the Staffordshire moorlands, is reputably the highest in England, and gave its name to counterfeit money, sometimes called 'flash money'. Legend has it this was made or used in the village, because it was easy to evade the law by crossing the adjacent county boundaries into Derbyshire, Cheshire or Staffordshire

10 Trouble at t'mill – In the late 18th century, the Peak's rivers helped give birth to the Industrial Revolution by providing power for the world's first factories – including the cotton mills at Cromford, Calver, Cressbrook, Litton and Lumford, near Bakewell

left behind a rich legacy of intricately carved preaching crosses, like those now kept in the churchyards at Bakewell, Eyam, Hope and Ilam, which is unrivalled in Britain, south of Northumberland.

When the mailed fist of the Normans descended on England after the Battle of Hastings in 1066, it was important for them to impose their authority, and they did it first by the construction of simple castles designed to overawe the native population. These were simple earthen mounds or mottes, surrounded by an enclosing bailey, and good examples can still be seen at **Pilsbury**, in the Upper Dove, and overlooking the river crossing at **Bakewell**.

The greatest of the Peak's medieval castles was that built by the Conqueror's illegitimate son, William Peveril, at **Castleton** (see p. 248), which gave the planned township its name. The commanding keep and curtain wall dates from the 12th century, and were built to govern the 40sq mile Royal Forest of the Peak – a royal hunting ground and as a protected area, similar to today's National Park. Another medieval hunting forest, set up by the Earls of Chester, existed east of Macclesfield.

The medieval period has also left us with some magnificent churches, such as **Tideswell's** elegant decorated and perpendicular 'Cathedral of the Peak' (see p. 124), **Wirksworth's** 13th-century cruciform church of St Mary's (see p. 78), and **Chesterfield's** famous crooked spire of St Mary's and All Saints (see p. 179). This was also the age of the great landowning families, such as the Eyres, the Leghs, the Manners and the Cavendishes, who constructed their mansions in the valleys beneath the hills. Originally medieval houses such as **North Lees Hall**, above Hathersage, **Lyme Park** near Stockport, **Haddon Hall**, near Bakewell, and **Chatsworth** near Baslow, reflected the wealth and importance of their owners.

The industrial age

As already stated, lead has been mined in the Peak since Roman times, but the real lead boom took place in the 18th century, when at least 10,000 miners, who usually doubled as farmers, were employed in the

White Peak area. The most striking remains of the lead legacy are those of **Magpie Mine**, near Sheldon, which was worked off and on for two centuries, and the **Peak District Lead Mining Museum** at Matlock Bath (see p. 69), tells the fascinating story of 't'owd man', as the lead miners are known.

While the abundant quantities of underground water was a real problem for the lead miners, it was a valuable source of free power for the first industrialists of the Industrial Revolution. So pioneering engineers such as Richard Arkwright and Jedediah Strutt utilised the fast-flowing rivers of the Peak to power the first water-powered textile mills at **Cromford, Cressbrook, Macclesfield, Leek** and **Bakewell**.

Communications were also becoming important, and turnpike roads were constructed across the bleak moors of the Peak by men such as Thomas Telford, who built the road across the Snake Pass in 1821. Railways soon followed, such as the Cromford and High Peak across the limestone plateau in 1830, and the Midland Line linking London and Manchester through the Wye Valley in 1860.

The railways opened up the Peak to tourism, and places such as Buxton and Matlock and Matlock Bath were soon attracting well-to-do visitors, who admired the spectacular scenery and charming villages. The Seven Wonders of the Peak, first extolled by Thomas Hobbes, tutor to the Cavendish children at Chatsworth, became an accepted 'Grand Tour' for these visitors.

Pressure for access to the then-forbidden moors of the Dark Peak led to the Mass Trespass of 1932, and increased the demand to make the Peak District a National Park. But it would take another 19 years before the Peak District became Britain's first National Park, in 1951.

GEOGRAPHY AND GEOLOGY

The Peak District stands astride the border between Highland and Lowland Britain – with a foot in both camps. It is the first abrupt rampart of that more spectacular part of our islands – northern, or highland, Britain. And it is the last outpost of the softer, less austere features which make up the southern, lowland counties.

The change between these two, quite different landscapes can easily be seen as you approach the Peak from the Midlands and see the twin sentinels of **Thorpe Cloud** and **Buntser Hill** guarding the approaches to Dovedale; or from Leek in the west, when the serrated skyline created by **The Roaches** and **Hen Cloud** can leave you in no doubt that you are approaching hill country.

Many people come to the Peak District expecting to find sharply pointed summits, as in the modern dictionary definition of the word. But apart from the reef limestone shark's fins of Thorpe Cloud and Chrome and Parkhouse Hills in the Dove Valley; or the gritstone outliers of Hen Cloud when seen from The Roaches, or Shutlingsloe in the Staffordshire Moorlands, they will be disappointed. The overriding perspective of the Peak is horizontal, epitomised by the 1,000ft/300m tableland of the central and southern White Peak, balanced by the equally flat – although twice as high – Dark Peak plateaux of **Kinder Scout, Bleaklow** and **Black Hill** in the north.

While the White Peak is split by spectacular, steep-sided and narrow dales which are the real scenic highlights of the area – such as **Dovedale, Lathkill** and **Chee Dale** – the most obvious and significant landform of the Dark Peak is the line of precipitous gritstone edges, such as the diadem of tors, which ring the plateau of Kinder Scout, and the escarpments which frown down on the length of the Derwent Valley in the east and at The Roaches in the west.

Bedrock

The true bedrock, and oldest rock, in the Peak District is the limestone of the White Peak, which was laid down under a tropical sea during the Carboniferous period some

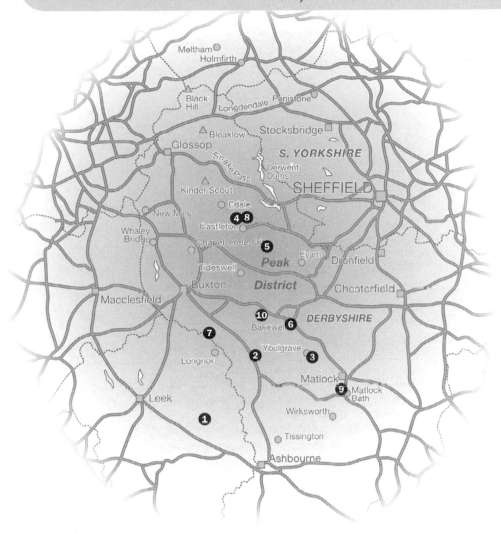

1. Thor's Cave, Manifold Valley – the archetypal caveman's dwelling, an awesome void in a sheer limestone crag high above the winding Manifold, p.105
2. Arbor Low stone circle, near Monyash – the stones are all prostrate now, but this remote Neolithic henge monument retains its air of mystery and ancient magic, p.95
3. Nine Ladies Stone Circle, Stanton Moor – not as impressive as Arbor Low, but the Nine Ladies still attract followers of the old religion, p.96
4. Mam Tor Iron Age hillfort – one of the largest and most impressive hillforts in the country, with outstanding views in all directions, p.248
5. Navio Roman fort, near Bradwell – all that remains of this once important 1st-century fort near Bradwell are the embankments which enclosed it, p.248
6. Saxon crosses in Bakewell churchyard – Bakewell has some of the finest Viking Age Celtic crosses and sculptures in the country, p.248
7. Pilsbury Castle – this is the finest motte and bailey castle in the Peak, p.105
8. Peveril Castle, Castleton – this 11th-century stronghold still lords it over the planned township which took its name, p.248
9. Peak District Lead Mining Museum, Matlock Bath – A fascinating insight into what was once of the most important industries in the White Peak, p.69
10. Magpie Mine, near Sheldon – the best-preserved lead mine remains in the Peak, full of ghosts and redolent of its long history, p.94

350 million years ago. What we now know as the Peak District was then considerably warmer and much nearer to the Equator, and submerged under a shallow, tropical sea.

Millions upon millions of tiny sea creatures, such as sea lilies and shellfish, lived and died in that warm, clear sea, and as they died, their tiny skeletons floated down to the bottom and gradually, over millions of years, built up the layers of pearly white limestone we see today. It has been reckoned that this limestone bedrock is around 6,000ft/2,000m thick, and it forms the bare bones of the Peak, outcropping in the startling white crags which line the sides of some of the dales. The fossils of those sea creatures, such as crinoids (a type of sea lily), or 'Derbyshire screws' as they are known locally, can still readily be seen in the stones of a drystone wall, or in the gateposts of fields where they have been polished by generations of passing cattle. At the edge of these tropical reefs, harder limestones formed, giving rise to those sharply pointed peaks in the Upper Dove. Injected into this layer cake of limestone were superheated gases from the Earth's molten interior, which cooled to form minerals such as lead, flourspar and the semi-precious Blue John stone, exclusively found around **Treak Cliff** at Castleton (see p. 250). It was the porous nature of the limestone which gave us the cave systems found around Matlock and Castleton (see p.67). Occasional volcanic eruptions shook the peacefulness of that tropical sea, giving rise to intrusions of lava and toadstone, as seen and once quarried in **Tideswell Dale** (see p. 122).

The next stage in the formation of the Peak District landscape was the blanketing of the underlying limestones by enormous, silt and sediment-filled rivers flowing down from the north, from what is now Scotland. These gritty layers of sediment created the sandstones now known as millstone grit, from the common use to which the stone was put. Indeed, it is a millstone which now forms the logo of the National Park, in recognition of the fact that is has always been a living, working landscape. The areas of millstone grit are usually badly drained because it is more impervious to water than limestone, and this gave rise to the formation of sphagnum moss and later blanket peat on the high moors of **Kinder Scout, Bleaklow, Black Hill** and the eastern and western moors. The hardness of the gritstone also gave rise to the abrupt Peakland edges – now the playground of rock climbers but once the source of mill and grindstones for much of Britain.

Finer and softer silt was responsible for the creation of the broad, shale valleys of the Derwent and Wye, which are now heavily wooded and the site of some of the Peak's finest landscaped parklands, such as those around **Chatsworth, Haddon** and **Lyme Park**.

The final polish was put on the Peak District landscape by the grinding power of Ice Age glaciers, which finished their landscaping work a mere 10,000 years ago. It was the action of the glaciers and their meltwater which carved out the dales and the broad shale valleys which punctuate and add so much to the overall character of the Peak District.

Geological wonders of the Peak

- **Watch your step** – Titan Cave in Castleton has the deepest natural shaft in the UK – it is an awesome 464ft/141.5m deep.
- **Home of Blue John** – Treak Cliff hillside outside Castleton is the only place in the world where Blue John, a banded purple and yellow semi-precious flourspar, is found, and still crafted into vases, bowls and jewellery. Only half a ton is allowed to be extracted every year.
- **Sticky stuff** – Elaterite – also known as elastic bitumen – is a soft, sticky, brown hydrocarbon. A secret location in the Peak District is the only place in the world where it can be found.

- **Traces of the Tropics** – millions of years ago the Peak District was a tropical lagoon. The fossils of tiny sea creatures can still be seen today, especially in the 26,000 miles of drystone walls – a length equivalent to a wall around the Earth at the Equator.

- **Adam's ale** – The Peak District has some of the purest natural mineral water in the world, and is famous for brands such as Buxton, Wildboarclough and Ashbourne. The water is naturally filtered during its long journey through hundreds of metres of porous rock. Some which

10... Peak District dales

1 **Lathkill Dale** – near Over Haddon. One of the quietest and loveliest of the dales, and part of the Derbyshire Dales National Nature Reserve

2 **Dovedale** – north of Ashbourne. Perhaps the most famous, and thus the busiest, of the dales, with spectacular rock formations and famous stepping stones

3 **Wolfscote Dale, northern extension of Dovedale** – Wolfscote Dale is much quieter than its southern neighbour, but just as beautiful

4 **Manifold Valley** – near Warslow. While neighbouring Dovedale is thronged with visitors, you can have the Manifold and places such as Thor's Cave to yourself

5 **Chee Dale** – on the Monsal Trail. Highlights include stepping stones and the magnificent 300ft bastion of Chee Tor, with the Wye winding beneath

6 **Monsal Dale** – near Great Longstone. Probably most famous for its much-photographed viaduct on the former Midland Line, as seen from Monsal Head

7 **Miller's Dale, also on the Monsal Trail** – Miller's Dale is part nature reserve, part industrial history, with its former station on the Midland Line now a ranger briefing base

8 **Edale** – in the heart of the highest country in the Peak, sylvan Edale lies in the shadow of Kinder Scout, with the Mam Tor-Lose Hill ridge opposite

9 **Alport Dale, off the Snake Pass** – only reached by a long walk off the Snake Pass, Alport Dale has been described as one of the Peak's secret treasures. Famous for its massive landslip known as Alport Castles

10 **Bradfield Dale** – On Sheffield's western fringe, Bradfield Dale is flooded by four reservoirs but retains its wild beauty

emerges today fell as rain up to 5,000 years ago.

- **Down by the riverside** – There are several rivers flowing through the Peak District, the longest being the River Derwent. Other rivers include the Bradford, Dove, Lathkill, Manifold, Wye, Don and Sett. The Peak District's rivers are renowned for their quality. The 17th-century author Charles Cotton described the River Lathkill as *'the purest and most transparent stream I ever yet saw, either home or abroad'*.
- **The Peak's Lake District** – The Peak District has more reservoirs (over 50) than the Lake District has lakes. From the Victorian period, the Peak District was seen as a source of a fresh, clean water for the growing surrounding urban conurbations. The high Peak District moorlands act like sponges, soaking up the high rainfall, and the water then flows into the valleys below. By damming these valleys, the water companies were able to collect, treat and distribute the water. Peak District reservoirs supply surrounding towns and cities with an amazing 450 million litres of water each day. That's equivalent to a shower a year for the entire world population.

WILDLIFE AND HABITATS

Standing as it does at the geographical crossroads of Britain, the Peak District supports an unrivalled range of wildlife species and habitats. The fact that it is the meeting place for so many northern and southern species makes it a naturalist's paradise – a fact which is reflected in the designation of more than half of the National Park as areas of special environmental protection, in addition to the many local or national nature reserves.

Among the southern species which reach their northernmost limit here are the nuthatch, the ivy-leaved bellflower and the stemless thistle, and equally, northern species such as the blue or mountain hare, the cloudberry and the globe flower, find their southernmost outposts here. More recently, the effects of global warming are constantly moving these boundaries northwards, and naturalists are noting that more southern species are gradually moving north as the average annual temperatures creep up.

The flagship nature reserve in the Peak District is undoubtedly the **Derbyshire Dales National Nature Reserve** (NNR), which covers 845 acres/342 hectares of Lathkill Dale, Monk's Dale, Cressbrook Dale, Long Dale and Hay Dale. The **Dovedale National Nature Reserve**, covering 1,687 acres/683 hectares of Dovedale, Wolfscote and Biggin Dale, was declared in 2006 – the first by Natural England, the Government watchdog which supervises nature and landscape conservation.

The White Peak dales

The best way to appreciate the wildlife riches of the Derbyshire Dales NNR is to take a walk in early summer through one of the limestone dales which make it up. Typical is **Lathkill Dale**, which runs for about 4 miles east of Monyash before it joins the Bradford at Alport. Other fascinating daleside nature reserves managed by the Derbyshire Wildlife Trust, apart from the **Dovedale NNR**, include **Miller's Dale Quarry** and **Chee Dale**, near Tideswell in the Wye Valley, and **Priestcliffe Lees**, near Taddington.

From the outskirts of Monyash, the upper reaches of Lathkill Dale are an open, dry valley where the scolding of wheatears, a summer visitor from Africa, will often greet you from the broken down drystone walls where they make their nests. The dale narrows as it enters the pinch-point of Ricklow Quarry, high up to your left, where the boulder scree slopes of fossil-rich, figured limestone show where the quarrymen once worked.

At a squeezer stile, the dale suddenly opens out, revealing huge crags of limestone on either side. In the dry stream bed to your left, dense stands of one of the Peak's real rarities, the rich purple-flowered Jacob's ladder, can be seen in early summer. The way is rocky now, but the sheep-grazed carpet of turf on either side of the path is rich in wildflowers, such as rockrose, bloody cranesbill, bird's foot trefoil, eyebright and thyme. Up to 50 species have been identified in a square metre of this velvety greensward, including in season, the gaudy spikes of early purple orchids.

In areas where lead was once mined, such as in Lathkill Dale and around **Magpie Mine**, near Sheldon (see p. 94), specialist lead-tolerant plants such as the mountain pansy and spring sandwort (locally and appropriately known as 'leadwort') thrive where normal plants would die in the poisoned soil. These flower-rich grasslands support a wide range of invertebrates, including the northern brown argus, green-veined white and orange tip butterflies. In some years there are colourful eruptions of beautiful clouded yellow and painted lady butterflies from the Continent.

As the dale narrows again between enclosing crags of limestone, a shallow cave on the right shows where the River Lathkill normally emerges in winter in a gushing torrent. The Lathkill is one of the few rivers in England which flows for its entire length on limestone – thus making it one of the purest and cleanest water courses in the country. In summer, however, it exhibits that strange habit of limestone rivers by disappearing into underground channels for much of its length. It is a curiosity the Lathkill shares with the Manifold and Hamps rivers in the southern Peak. The purity of the Lathkill and other limestone rivers means that they are the home of some aquatic rarities, such as the native freshwater crayfish – a kind of miniature lobster locally known as a 'crawkie' – and some fine brown and rainbow trout. Whizzing up and down the river as it enters the cool confines of Palmerston Wood you might be lucky enough to see the iridescent flash of a kingfisher, but more likely is the plump, bobbing shape of a dipper, seeming to curtsy to passers-by from a rock in the stream.

The native ashwoods on the northern bank of the Lathkill, like those found on the Staffordshire bank of Dovedale, are some of the finest in Britain, and provide the home to the rare, pink-flowered mezereon shrub, guelder rose, bird cherry and rock whitebeam. Other fine examples of semi-natural woodland can be seen at the Derbyshire Wildlife Trust's reserves at **Ladybower and Priddock Woods**, in the Upper Derwent Valley; **Brockholes Wood**, in Longdendale; the Staffordshire Wildlife Trust's woodland reserves at **Castern Wood** in the Manifold Valley; and in the **Coombes Valley** or the Royal Society for the Protection of Birds (RSPB) **Churnet Valley Woods** reserve, both south of Leek.

The Dark Peak moors

Often described as the wilderness of the Peak District, the extensive peat moorlands of **Kinder Scout**, **Bleaklow**, **Black Hill** and the **Eastern and Western moors** are actually, like every other landscape in Britain, the product of centuries of the work of humans.

The occasional emergence of the weathered bole of an ancient silver birch or oak from the side of a peat grough is evidence that these high moorland heights were once well wooded. Thousands of years of burning and grazing has created the open heather, purple moor and cotton grass covered moorland we see today. But centuries of industrial pollution and a long history of overstocking has resulted in large areas of bare peat, which is easily blown away in the wind or washed down into moorland streams by the frequent rain showers.

In fact, the Peak District contains some of the most degraded peat moorland in Britain. The National Trust has estimated that the 3,335 acres/1,350 hectares of exposed peat on its High Peak Estate alone is releasing 37,800 tonnes of previously locked-up carbon per year, equivalent to the carbon dioxide emissions of more than 18,000 cars. While healthy peatlands take in and store carbon, damaged peatlands like those of the Peak allow those harmful greenhouse gases to escape, and the Moors for the Future Project, based in Edale, is doing pioneering work in moorland restoration.

Although these moors have been described as 'land at the end of its tether', a surprisingly varied range of wildlife finds its home on these bleak uplands. Top of the food chain are the dashing birds of prey, and recent years has seen an encouraging increase in the numbers of birds such as the peregrine falcon, goshawk, hen harrier and hobby, all of which are unfortunately still subject to isolated incidents of illegal persecution. But the most characteristic bird of the heather moorland is undoubtedly the red grouse, and we have to thank this plump, furry-footed game bird for much of the glorious heather moorland which presents such a beautiful purple picture in late summer and early autumn. Most of these heather moors are managed exclusively for the grouse, which needs the hardy shrub for both its bread and board. The grouse are traditionally shot after the 'Glorious Twelfth' of August, although bags have been poor in recent years because of endemic disease. Other wading birds that may be encountered on the Dark Peak moors include the golden plover, the curlew and the dotterel. The 'chinking' call of the ring ouzel, or mountain blackbird, may also be heard in the steep-sided, rocky cloughs on the edge of the moors, along with bobbing dippers and grey wagtails.

To find out more about the Peak's wildlife, contact the **Derbyshire Wildlife Trust** (East Mill, Bridge Foot, Belper, Derbyshire DE56 1XH; ☎01773 881188; www.derbyshirewildlife trust.org.uk), the **Staffordshire Wildlife Trust** (The Wolseley Centre, Wolseley Bridge, Stafford ST17 0WT; ☎01889 880100; www. staffordshirewildlife.org.uk), or the **RSPB**'s regional office (Westleigh Mews, Wakefield Road, Denby Dale, Huddersfield HD8 8QD; ☎01484 861148).

Peakland wildlife wonders

- **Rarer than the tiger** – the entire world population of Derbyshire feather-moss (*Thamnobryum angustifolium*) comprises a single patch about a metre square under a secret waterfall in one of the White Peak dales.
- **Heather heaven** – three-quarters of the world's heather moorland is in the UK – and a large proportion of this is in the Peak District National Park. It is of global ecological and conservation importance, supporting rare and endangered plants and animals.
- **For peat's sake** – the Dark Peak's peat bogs are among the most important wildlife habitats in the world, home to many birds, thousands of rare insect species and a wealth of unusual plants. More than 94% of the UK's peat bogs have been damaged or destroyed – putting them at greater risk than the tropical rainforest. And they also act as an important 'carbon reservoir' which locks in carbon dioxide – almost as effective at combating global warming as the rainforests.
- **Beautiful bug** – the limestone dales of the Peak District are one of the world's strongholds for the tiny but attractive woodlouse *Armadillidium pulchellum*. The scientific name translates as 'beautiful little armadillo', reflecting the colourful, little chocolate-brown, orange-banded, armour-coated insect.
- **Beware triffids!** – two insect-eating plants live in the Peak District, the sundew and butterwort. Their sticky leaves trap unfortunate insects, curling up around their prey, and secreting digestive enzymes to digest the insect's juices.
- **Welcome back, Ratty** – Britain's fastest-declining mammal – the water vole, made famous as Ratty in *The Wind in the Willows* – is making a comeback in the

The best... wildlife sites

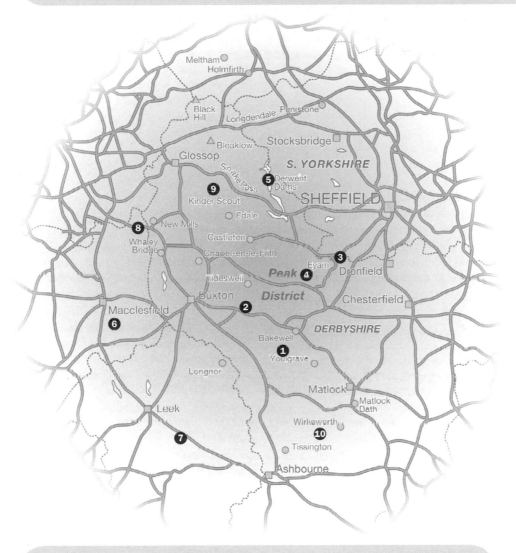

① **Lathkill Dale** – look out for dippers, kingfishers and, in the upper reaches in the summer, wheatears visiting from Africa, p.94

② **Wye Valley reserves** – Miller's Dale, Chee Dale and Cressbrook Dale are archetypical Derbyshire dale rivers and their banks are rich with wildflowers, p.134

③ **Eastern Moors** – you might be lucky enough to spot peregrine falcons, merlin and hen harriers, quartering the heather moorland above the Derwent, p.143

④ **River Derwent** – the Derwent itself is the haunt of dipper and other aquatic wildlife, with occasional rarities such as mergansers, p.68

⑤ **Derwent Dams** – home to a surprising variety of wildlife, including mergansers and grebes, p.169

⑥ **Macclesfield Forest** – Trentabank Reservoir is the home to a well-established heronry, p.234

⑦ **Coombes Valley RSPB reserve** – summer visitors include redstarts, wood warblers and pied flycatchers, and there are large flocks of fieldfares and redwings in winter, p.220

⑧ **Lyme Park** – Lyme Park is most famous for its large herd of red deer, the biggest in the Peak, and there is also a herd of fallow deer, p.235

⑨ **Kinder plateau** – the ubiquitous red grouse is the bird you are most likely to see – and hear – on the bleak Kinder plateau, p.259

⑩ **Carsington Water** – frequent visitors include kingfishers, teal, wigeon and great crested grebe, p.75

Peak District. Numbers had been reduced by up to 90%, caused by changes to habitats, pollution and competition from other animals. Thanks to conservation efforts since the 1990s, numbers have been increasing in the Peak District.

· **Hare today...** the Peak District has England's only population of mountain hares. The distinctive animals – which change their coats to white in winter and can reach speeds of 40mph – are not indigenous but descended from animals released for shooting in Victorian times.

· **Well protected** – the Peak District's dales and moorland have Europe's highest level of protection for wildlife sites. More than a third of the Peak District National Park is designated as a Site of Special Scientific Interest, due to its important plant and animal species and its geology.

CULTURE

From writers to artists and music to movies, the Peak District's unique character and varied landscape has proved a fertile seedbed for creative inspiration and imaginative ideas, both past and present. Whichever part of the area you visit, you'll find plenty of artistic and cultural activity to stimulate your mind and feed your soul.

Writers

Over the centuries, the Peak District has inspired a host of writers to wax lyrical about its manifold charms.

Philosopher **Thomas Hobbes** (1588–1679) described some of the Peak District's most celebrated attractions as early as 1636, in his famous poem *De Mirabilibus Pecci, or The Wonders of the Peak*. One section is dedicated to his pupil 'The Noble Lord' William Cavendish, of Chatsworth, who later became the second Earl of Devonshire. Hobbes's 'Wonders' included Chatsworth, Peak Cavern in Castleton, Eldon Hole, Mam Tor and St Anne's Well and Poole's Cavern in Buxton. Staffordshire-born poet **Charles Cotton** (1630–87) endorsed Hobbes' choice of 'Wonders' in a later work and eulogised fly-fishing on the River Dove in *The Compleat Angler* with his friend **Izaak Walton**. First published in 1653, it is one of the most re-printed books in English literature, having been re-issued more than 300 times. Cotton and Walton built a 'fishing temple' near Cotton's ancestral home, Beresford Hall, which can still be seen from the footpath to Beresford Dale. Cotton contributed '*instructions how to angle for a trout or grayling in a clear stream*', and Pike Pool, halfway down Beresford Dale, is where he landed a huge pike. Visitors to St Peter's Church in Alstonefield will see the Cotton family's imposing pew, which faces the congregation, rather than the pulpit.

Described as '*arguably the most distinguished man of letters in English history*', Lichfield-born **Dr Samuel Johnson** (1709–84) was a regular visitor to Ashbourne. Most famous as the collator of the first dictionary of the English language, Johnson was a great friend of the town's Reverend John Taylor, and was a frequent guest at his Mansion House on Church Street between 1740 and 1784. Johnson penned many sermons for his friend, and Taylor later presided at Johnson's burial service at Westminster Abbey. Johnson described his favourite Ashbourne pub, The Green Man and Black's Head Royal Hotel (see p. 87) as a 'very good inn' and visited so often he is said to have had his own chair there, with his name carved into it. Ashbourne also featured as the fictional Oakbourne in *Adam Bede,* the first novel written by **George Eliot** (1819–80). The book also features Snowfield, based on nearby Wirksworth, where Eliot stayed with relatives. Her uncle Samuel became manager at the town's Haraam Mill, which was among the first in the country to use water power, and his wife Elizabeth is believed to have been the basis for one of the book's characters, Dinah Morris.

Poet **William Wordsworth** (1770–1850) is known to have visited Matlock and Matlock Bath, and many claim that the River Dove features in his Lucy Gray cycle of poems: 'She dwelt among the untrodden ways beside the springs of Dove'. He also visited Chatsworth as he was riding from Bakewell to Matlock, and wrote a sonnet about the house and surrounding landscape. Castleton's Peveril Castle was the setting for the novel Peveril of the Peak by **Sir Walter Scott** (1771–1832), which recounts the tale of Derbyshire landowners on opposing sides during the English Civil War. Royalist ex-Cavalier Sir Geoffrey Peveril and Puritan Major Ralph Bridgenorth disagree over a plot to remove King James from the English throne, yet their children fall in love. The acrimony and intrigue is finally settled when the king intervenes on the young lovers' behalf.

Said to have stayed at the Rutland Arms in Bakewell while writing her much-loved novel, **Jane Austen** (1775–1817) is widely thought to have based Pemberley in Pride and Prejudice on Chatsworth House. Austen's description certainly gives credence to the theory: 'the eye was instantly caught by Pemberley House, situated on the opposite side of a valley, into which the road with some abruptness wound. It was a large, handsome, stone building, standing well on rising ground, and backed by a ridge of high woody hills; – and in front, a stream of some natural importance was swelled into greater, but without any artificial appearance. Its banks were neither formal, nor falsely adorned.' Austen is also thought to have based her fictional Lambton on Bakewell. North Lees Hall near Hathersage, now converted into self-catering apartments (see p. 164), is believed to have been the inspiration for Thornfield Hall, the home of Mr Rochester in Jane Eyre by **Charlotte Bronte** (1816–55). The Eyre family lived at the hall between 1750 and 1882. Charlotte visited them in 1845, two years before Jane Eyre was published, and based the book's fictitious

village, Morton, on Hathersage. Moorseats House is believed to be Moor House and Brookfield Manor thought to be Vale Hall.

Castleton's mysterious caves were the location for a spine-chilling short story entitled The Terror of Blue John Gap by the creator of Sherlock Holmes, **Sir Arthur Conan Doyle** (1859–1930). Meanwhile, The Jungle Book's creator, **Rudyard Kipling** (1865–1936), is named after Rudyard Lake, on the Staffordshire fringe of the Peak. When Kipling's parents were courting, they enjoyed walking by the lake, so when he was born they named him after the place where they first met. Born in India, Kipling also wrote the Just So Stories, Kim and the more political The Absent-minded Beggar, which helped to raise money for Boer War veterans. Nottinghamshire-born novelist and poet **D H Lawrence** (1885–1930), whose works included Lady's Chatterley's Lover, Sons and Lovers and Women in Love, returned to live in the village where his mother was born, Middleton-by-Wirksworth, in 1918. Lawrence and his German wife Frieda had been living in Cornwall, but they were hounded out as suspected spies and came to Middleton to live at Mountain Cottage.

The First World War also had a life-changing impact on the life of writer **Vera Brittain** (1893–1970), mother of politician **Shirley Williams**, who was born in Newcastle-under-Lyme but spent many of her formative years in Buxton. The family moved to the Peak District when she was 11, and she became a volunteer nurse with the Voluntary Aid Detachment (VAD) at the former Devonshire Royal Hospital, now the University of Derby Buxton, in 1915. Soon afterwards, she lost both her fiancé, Roland Leighton, and brother Edward, both of whom were killed in action, and she chronicled her shattering experiences in her best-selling Testament of Youth. The Lake District may have **Beatrix Potter**, but the Peak District also has a children's author of note in **Alison Uttley** (1884–1976), who was born in Cromford and was educated at Lea, near Matlock and Lady Manners School, Bakewell. Uttley read physics at Manchester University, where she became its second female honours graduate. Her great love for, and knowledge of, the countryside is reflected in her stories about such famous characters as Little Grey Rabbit and Sam Pig.

Another celebrated author, **Richmal Crompton** (1890–1969), was born in Bury, Lancashire, but was educated, and later taught at, the former St Elphin's boarding school for girls in Darley Dale, near Matlock, now a residential development. A keen supporter of the women's suffrage movement, ill health forced her to give up teaching and concentrate on writing. Perhaps best known for her hilarious *Just William* stories, featuring an mischievous 11-year-old schoolboy and his friends the 'Outlaws', she also wrote many novels and short stories aimed at an adult audience. Carnegie Medal winning author **Alan Garner** (b.1934) hails from Congleton and grew up in Alderley Edge, but has drawn inspiration for many of his famous fantasy fiction works from the Peak District. Garner, who attended Manchester Grammar School then studied classics at Oxford, is celebrated for such seminal children's books such as *The Weirdstone of Brisingamen, Elidor* and *The Owl Service*, though later works such as *Strandloper* and *Thursbitch* are more suited for adult readers. Another Carnegie Medal winning writer, **Berlie Doherty** (b.1943), was born in Liverpool and lived and worked for a while in Sheffield, but now lives in Edale, where many of her children's books, such as *Blue John* and *Jeannie of White Peak Farm* are set. Ladybower, Stanage Edge, Edale, Castleton and Eyam are just some of the locations which have inspired her. Other works include novels for adults, theatre and radio plays, television series and libretti for children's opera.

Various locations in the Peak District are immortalised in crime novels by ex-journalists Stephen Booth and **Val McDermid**. Multi-award winning novelist Booth sets his popular novels in both the Dark Peak and White Peak. *Dancing with the Virgins* features the Nine Ladies Stone Circle at Stanton Moor, *The Dead Place* is set at Ravensdale, near Monsal Head, while *Blood on the Tongue* includes the reservoirs in the Upper Derwent Valley. *One Last Breath* goes underground in Castleton's caverns, while *Blind to Bones* incorporates the traditional art of well dressing. Scottish-born McDermid lived in Buxton for 12 years, and books such as *A Place of Execution* reflect her fondness for the White Peak, which she has described as having '*amazing beauty in all seasons and which seems possessed of an almost unearthly quality of light*'. Pulitzer Prize winning author and journalist **Geraldine Brooks** based her novel *Year of Wonders* on the Plague Village of Eyam, ravaged by the disease in the 17th century. Brooks tells the story of the social, religious and romantic repercussions of the Plague year of 1666 on the quarantined community.

Artists and artisans

Curiously enough, the Peak's unique appeal hasn't fired the imagination of many prominent artists, though famous equine painter **George Stubbs** (1724–1806) did incorporate scenes from scenic Creswell Crags, on the fringe of the area, in some of his work. Nowadays the Peak boasts at least two well-known wildlife artists, **Pollyanna Pickering**, based at Oaker, near Matlock (see Local Knowledge, p. 97), and **Richard Whittlestone**, who works in a studio at Pilsley, on the Chatsworth Estate. In the north of the area, Holmfirth-based **Ashley Jackson** has become one of the country's most successful watercolour painters, thanks to his atmospheric paintings of brooding moorlands in the Dark Peak (see Local Knowledge, p. 301).

They may not be nationally or internationally renowned, but the Peak District plays host to a wide range of professional artists and craftspeople, ranging from furniture makers and potters to stained glass makers and textile designers. Many are members of organisations such as **Peak District Products**, whose president is the Duke of Devonshire's son, the **Earl of Burlington**, and whose members have a firm commitment to quality and service. They exhibit regularly at such venues as Cavendish Hall, Edensor and the Pavilion Gardens, Buxton, and in 2008 held the Great Dome Art Fair at the University of Derby Buxton's showpiece town centre campus, formerly the Devonshire Royal Hospital.

Art and craft fairs abound here if you're searching for a locally made souvenir to remind you of your visit, especially during the summer and in the run-up to Christmas: details can usually be found in local newspapers, on local radio or at tourist information centres. Each May, artists and craftspeople throughout the county throw open their studio doors during the **Derbyshire Open Arts** event (www.derbyshireopenarts.co.uk), welcoming visitors to watch them at work on everything from paintings to photography and ceramics to silverware.

You'll also find private art galleries in villages such as Grindleford and Rowsley, as well as work by local landscape photographers such as **Karen Frenkel** of Little Hucklow and nature photographers such as New Mills-based **Geoff Simpson**, whose images succinctly capture the spirit, scenery and wildlife of the area.

Music
Live music is a feature in many Peak District pubs, some of which stage regular folk and jazz nights, and singing is a popular spare time pursuit for choral singers and choirs across the area, including male voice choirs at Chapel-en-le-Frith and Tideswell. In the High Peak, several brass bands flourish in such places as Chapel-en-le-Frith, Buxton and Tintwistle.

WILLIAM MORRIS AND LEEK

'Have nothing in your houses that you do not know to be useful, or believe to be beautiful,' beseeched Victorian writer, artist and designer **William Morris** (1834–96), whose influence is much in evidence in the Staffordshire Moorlands market town of Leek. The prominent craftsman, poet and socialist came to Leek in the 1870s to study dyeing and printing techniques. His manager in London, George Wardle, put him in touch with his cousin, Thomas Wardle, who ran a silk dyeing works in the town. The Wardle family lived on St Edward Street, latterly at no. 62, where Morris stayed during his frequent visits to Staffordshire.

The impact of the Arts and Crafts movement on Leek's architecture can be spotted on the Leek Town Trail, outlined in a leaflet available from the town's tourist information centre, on the corner of Market Place and Church Street. Landmarks to look out for include the Parish Church of St Edward the Confessor, which features stained glass designed by pre-Raphaelite artist **Sir Edward Burne-Jones** (1833–98) and made by Morris & Co, plus Morris-inspired embroideries. Beloved Poet Laureate **John Betjeman** (1906–84) described the archetypal Arts and Crafts church of All Saints as 'one of the finest churches in Britain'. Designed by Norman Shaw, almost all the glass was designed by Burne-Jones and made by Morris & Co, while many of the embroideries are based on Morris's distinctive designs.

The elegant spa town of Buxton plays host to a number of high-profile music festivals throughout the year, including the **Buxton Opera House Festival of Live Music, Four Four Time**, in February; **Buxton Festival**, featuring everything from rarely performed operas to high-profile writers in July and the **International Gilbert and Sullivan**

Festival each August. On the national and international music scene, one of the Peak's most famous exports is **Lloyd Cole** (b.1961), lead singer of the mid-1980s pop group **The Commotions**. Born in Buxton, Cole grew up in Chapel-en-le-Frith and met the other members of the group when studying at Glasgow University. Another distinctive and respected voice is that of rock and blues singer **Joe Cocker** (b.1944), born John Robert Cocker in Crookes, Sheffield, who abandoned a career as an apprentice gas fitter to rise to international stardom in the 1970s, singing such classics as *Delta Lady* and *With a Little Help from my Friends*.

Over the years, Sheffield has also been the birthplace of such well-known bands as **ABC**, **Heaven 17**, **The Human League**, the **Longpigs**, **Pulp**, **Babybird**, **The Arctic Monkeys**, and heavy rock combo **Def Leppard**, mirroring changing music trends from the 1980s to the present day. **Jarvis Cocker** (b.1963, no relation to Joe) of Pulp and **Richard Hawley** (b.1967) of the Longpigs, have gone on to enjoy successful solo careers. A staunch Sheffield Wednesday FC supporter, Hawley in particular is famous for local references in his work, such as the city suburb *Lowedges* and local landmarks *Cole's Corner* and *Lady's Bridge*. Both Cocker and Hawley contributed to the album *Made in Sheffield* by another local singer, **Tony Christie** (b.1943), perhaps most famous for his 1970s hit *Is This the Way to Amarillo*, who hails from nearby Conisbrough, South Yorkshire.

Television and film

Over recent decades, the Peak District has become something of a star itself, as the stunning backdrop for countless films and television series, featuring actors from **Dame Judi Dench** and **Sir Anthony Hopkins** to **Keira Knightley** and **Matthew Macfadyen**. The Peak District and Derbyshire's movie map, *Great Films Great Locations*, available at tourist information centres or online at www.visitpeakdistrict.com/film, outlines the area's small screen and silver screen connections. Peak Experience's film and literature publication, *Front Row of the Peak*, is another informative guide to the area's movies, novels and television series (www.peak-experience.com).

Medieval **Haddon Hall** is one of the most popular locations, as the backcloth for productions such as *The Princess Bride* (1987), *Jane Eyre* (film in 1996, BBC television series in 2006), *Elizabeth* (1998) and *The Other Boleyn Girl* (2008). Another much sought-after setting is **Chatsworth**, featured in *Pride and Prejudice* (2005), *The Duchess* (2008) and Gothic horror movie *The Wolf Man* (2009).

Stunning **Stanage Edge** appeared in *Pride and Prejudice* (2005), *The Other Boleyn Girl* (2008) and *Wuthering Heights* (television series 2008/9), while the imposing façade of the National Trust's **Lyme Hall** near Disley achieved fame when actor **Colin Firth** fuelled many a woman's romantic fantasies when he emerged, in dripping wet white shirt, from the adjacent lake as moody Mr Darcy in the BBC 1995 drama *Pride and Prejudice*.

Horses and carriages from **Red House Working Carriage Museum** in Darley Dale (p. 73) are regularly seen in period productions such as *Emma* (1996), *Pride and Prejudice* (2005) and *The Duchess* (2008), while **Ilam Hall** and **Dovedale** have appeared in *Jane Eyre* (television series, 2006) and *The Other Boleyn Girl* (2008).

Crich, Fritchley and latterly the Staffordshire moorlands village of Longnor all starred as the fictional town of Cardale in the popular ITV medical drama *Peak Practice*. The series featured many famous Peak locations, such as Edensor Church, Idridgehay near Ashbourne, Hartington and The Roaches, which provided the dramatic backdrop for a medical emergency.

During the Second World War, Derwent and Howden reservoirs were training grounds for **Sir Barnes Wallis's** (1887–1979) bouncing bomb, used by the RAF's 617 Squadron to breach the Ruhr Valley dams in Germany in 1943. Top actors **Sir Michael Redgrave** (1908–85) and **Richard Todd** (b.1919) later joined the cast of the 1953 commemorative film *The Dam Busters*, which paid tribute to 617 Squadron's top secret mission.

10... Peak District film and television locations

1 Haddon Hall – authentic medieval setting for such films and period dramas as *Jane Eyre*, *Elizabeth* and *The Other Boleyn Girl*

2 Chatsworth – classic backcloth for recent films such as *Pride and Prejudice*, *The Duchess* and *The Wolf Man*

3 Stanage Edge – whose distinctive outline has appeared in such films and television series as *Pride and Prejudice*, *The Other Boleyn Girl* and *Wuthering Heights*

4 Ilam Hall and Dovedale – scenic backdrop for such films and television series as *Jane Eyre* and *The Other Boleyn Girl*

5 Crich, Fritchley and Longnor – and many other Peak District locations, which featured in the popular ITV drama *Peak Practice*, set in the fictional community of Cardale

6 The Derwent Valley – training ground for Sir Barnes Wallis's famous bouncing bomb used to breach German dams during the Second World War, which starred in the post-war film tribute *The Dam Busters*

7 Lyme Hall, Disley – served as the setting for BBC drama *Pride and Prejudice*

8 Hadfield, near Glossop – doubled as eccentric Royston Vasey in the darkly humorous BBC television series *The League of Gentlemen*

9 Holmfirth in West Yorkshire – setting for the evergreen BBC television comedy series *Last of the Summer Wine*, believed to be the longest-running sitcom in the world

10 Sheffield in South Yorkshire – which achieved worldwide fame in the Oscar and BAFTA winning film *The Full Monty*, the story of six unemployed men who bare all to earn money and regain their self-respect

The Dark Peak village of Hadfield, near Glossop, doubled as eccentric Royston Vasey, with its 'local shop for local people' in the darkly humorous *The League of Gentlemen* BBC television series (1999–2002) and film (2005). Long-standing local butcher's shop, award-winning J W Mettrick & Son (see p. 286) was transformed into Hilary Briss's dubious shop selling 'special sausages' and many other local landmarks, such as the War Memorial, achieved instant fame.

Further north, the evergreen BBC television comedy sitcom *Last of the Summer Wine,* which first took to the small screen in 1973, is set in and around the picturesque West Yorkshire town of Holmfirth. Written by Roy Clarke, it is believed to be the longest-running comedy programme in Britain and the longest-running sitcom in the world.

Many famous actors have appeared in the series, such as the late **Kathy Staff** (1928–2008) as belligerent battleaxe Nora Batty, the late **Bill Owen** (1914–99) as mischievous Compo and **Peter Sallis** as serious, unassuming Clegg. Other members of the cast have included the late, much-lamented **Dame Thora Hird**, **Sir Norman Wisdom**, **June Whitfield**, **Jean Alexander** (formerly Hilda Ogden in ITV soap opera *Coronation Street*), **Dora Bryan**, **Burt Kwouk** and the late comedian **Tony Capstick** (1944–2003), who grew up in Mexborough, South Yorkshire. You'll see reminders of the series wherever you go in Holmfirth, from Sid's Café to the Wrinkled Stocking Tea Room (see p. 299), and you can even stay in Nora Batty's Cottage (see p. 304).

Parts of Sheffield were used in the BAFTA award-winning 1997 film *The Full Monty*, starring **Robert Carlyle**, **Tom Wilkinson** and **Mark Addy**, about the after-effects of the Miners' Strike. The opening sequence of a promotional film about Sheffield from 1971 is taken from *City on the Move*, and among the locations used were the Shiregreen Workingmen's Club, Attercliffe, Fir Vale, Hillsborough and Ruskin Park, in Daniel Hill Street.

Famous actors who hail from the area include the late **Alan Bates** (1934–2003), who was born and brought up in Derby, later lived in Bradbourne, near Ashbourne and appeared in such films as *Whistle Down the Wind* and *Women in Love,* and **John Hurt** (b.1940), who was born in Shirebrook, east of Chesterfield, famous for roles in films such as *Midnight Cowboy* and *The Elephant Man.* Sheffield-born **Sean Bean** (b.1959) is perhaps best known for his roles as Richard Sharpe in the eponymous television series and as Boromir in the *Lord of the Rings* films.

Theatre

One of the country's finest examples of Frank Matcham design, Buxton Opera House is indisputably the Peak District's finest theatre. Built in 1903, the Edwardian architectural gem has hosted performances by legendary ballerina **Anna Pavlova** and actors such as **Dame Sybil Thorndike** and **Sir Alec Guinness**. In the mid-1970s, declining audiences saw it fall into disrepair, but thanks to the efforts of local and national supporters it reopened to host the first Buxton Festival in 1979. Extensive external and internal restoration work from 1999 to 2001 revitalised it in time for its 100th birthday celebrations and now it is a much-loved community asset, attracting audiences from far and wide and appealing to a range of tastes and age groups.

In recent years, Sheffield has become one of the leading live theatre venues outside London, and its three main theatres are all concentrated around Tudor Square in the city centre. Opened in 1971, the **Crucible Theatre** is the main producing repertory venue in the Sheffield Theatres complex, but also receives some touring shows in addition to hosting the annual World Snooker Championships. Originally opened in 1897, the **Lyceum Theatre** is a listed building and **WGR Sprague's** only surviving design outside London. Following its closure in 1968, the Lyceum endured spells as a bingo hall and a rock venue before undergoing a £12 million renovation and reopening as a major touring venue in 1991. The smaller **Studio Theatre** has a capacity of up to 400, and opened in 1971 and was refurbished in 1994.

In Chesterfield, the unusually named **Pomegranate Theatre** is Britain's oldest civic theatre, and celebrates its 60th anniversary in 2009. Along with Chesterfield Museum, it is housed in the Grade II listed Victorian building, formerly known as the Stephenson Memorial Hall, erected in 1879 as a tribute to railway pioneer **Sir George Stephenson** (1781–1848), who once lived in the town. Nowadays it hosts everything from drama to dance and music to ballet and aims to offer a balanced programme of entertainment and cultural activities throughout the year.

10... Peak District cultural sites

1 Chatsworth – veritable treasure house of works of art from all over the world, often used for filming, p. 144

2 Haddon Hall – described as the country's best preserved medieval manor house, and the backdrop for countless films, p. 90

3 Buxton Opera House – cultural centrepiece of the Peak, and the home of the Festival of Live Music, the Buxton Festival, and the International Gilbert and Sullivan Festival in August, p. 200

4 Derwent Valley Mills World Heritage Site – designated in 2001 for the outstanding importance of the area as the birthplace of the factory system, p. 68

5 Arts and Crafts Trail, Leek – famous for its former silk and cotton factories, supported by William Morris of the Arts and Crafts movement, p. 217

6 Buxton Museum and Art Gallery – featuring the award-winning Wonders of the Peak gallery, p. 203

7 Old House Museum, Bakewell – award-winning local museum housed in a cottage built by Richard Arkwright for his workers, p. 91

8 Peak District Mining Museum, Matlock Bath – tells the fascinating story of lead mining in the Peak through various interactive exhibits, p. 69

9 Brindley's Mill, Leek – where James Brindley – the Father of Britain's canals – began his extraordinary career by building his first water-powered corn mill in 1725, p. 217

10 Lyme Hall and Park – a Tudor house transformed into a huge Italianate palace in the 18th century, with a tranquil Victorian garden, surrounded by a vast medieval deer park, moorland and woodland estate, p 235

LOCAL HEROES
Bess of Hardwick

The original 'Material Girl', the redoubtable Bess of Hardwick, Countess of Shrewsbury and Lady Cavendish, married four times and amassed great wealth, including houses at **Chatsworth** (p. 144) and Hardwick, during her long lifetime. Born in 1527 at Hardwick Old Hall, near Chesterfield, she rose from humble beginnings to become the richest and most powerful woman in Elizabethan times, second only to Queen Elizabeth I herself. Her first, unconsummated, marriage was to Robert Barlow, heir to a neighbouring estate. She then married the twice-widowed Sir William Cavendish, Treasurer of the King's Chamber, who was more than twice her age, and became Lady Cavendish. Cavendish sold his land in Suffolk to buy the famous Chatsworth Estate in the Peak District in 1549. The couple began to build their new house in 1553, on the same site as the current house on the banks of the River Derwent.

Sir William died in 1557, but Bess completed the house in the 1560s. It became home to her and her fourth husband, George Talbot, the sixth Earl of Shrewsbury, who became custodian of the ill-fated Mary, Queen of Scots in 1568. Mary, also a frequent visitor to Buxton's historic **Old Hall Hotel** (p. 208), stayed at Chatsworth several times, lodging in an apartment now known as the Queen of Scots rooms. All that remains from Bess's time there is the Hunting Tower, on the hill overlooking the house.

In the 1590s, Bess built Hardwick Hall, '*more glass than wall*', as a statement of her wealth, with her initials emblazoned on every turret and rich embroideries and tapestries inside. Now owned by the National Trust, it remains much the same as it was when she died in 1608.

James Brindley

Born in the village of Tunstead, near Buxton in 1716, James Brindley had little formal education, but rose to become one of the foremost engineers of the 18th century. He is perhaps most famous as consulting engineer to the Duke of Bridgewater, when he commissioned the Bridgewater Canal to link Worsley and Manchester, widely believed to be the first British canal of modern times. Brindley's expertise resulted in innovative features such as the Barton aqueduct, which carried the canal over the river Irwell at a height of 42ft/13m. At 17 he was taken on as an apprentice by a millwright at Sutton, Macclesfield, then launched his own business as a wheelwright in Leek, Staffordshire, gaining a reputation for his expertise in repairing a variety of machinery, as well as designing a plant to drain a Lancashire coal mine and other machinery for a silk mill in Congleton.

After the Bridgewater project, Brindley, who became a lifelong friend of the Wedgwood family, was then much sought after as a master canal engineer, and extended the Bridgewater Canal to Runcorn, linking it with his next large-scale project, the Trent and Mersey Canal. He also deemed it possible to link England's four major rivers – the Mersey, Trent, Severn and Thames – but did not live to see his dream realised. Even so, he built 365 miles (587km) of canals during his lifetime, and many watermills – including one at Leek, now called **Brindley's Mill** (p. 217), which houses a small museum dedicated to his life and achievements. Brindley died in 1772, just days after finishing work on the Birmingham Canal.

Sir Richard Arkwright

Credited as one of the founders of the Industrial Revolution and inventor of the modern industrial factory system, Sir Richard Arkwright was born in Preston, Lancashire in 1792. He began his career as an apprentice barber, but became an entrepreneur after his second marriage, which provided him with an income that enabled him to expand his business into dyeing hair for wig making. When the fashion for wearing wigs fell out of favour, he turned his attention to textiles and developed a cotton spinning frame – later renamed the water frame after the switch to water power – in the late 1760s. He built the world's first **water-powered cotton mill at Cromford** (p. 71) in 1771. The mill complex and another of his mills, **Masson Mill** (p. 71), now form part of the UNESCO-designated Derwent Valley World Heritage Site.

Unlike many industrial entrepreneurs, Arkwright built terraced cottages for his workers near his mills at Cromford, and also built the Greyhound public house. He brought in workers from other places to live in the village and work in his mills, and established a highly disciplined factory system based on two 13-hour shifts per day. Anyone who arrived late couldn't work that day and also had an extra day's pay docked.

Arkwright originally lived at Rock House in Cromford, then bought an estate from Florence Nightingale's father, William, and began building Willersley Castle. During construction, fire broke out, causing severe damage, and Arkwright died in 1792, before work on the (Grade II) building was complete.

Florence Nightingale

Popularly known as the 'Lady of the Lamp', Florence Nightingale was born in Florence, Italy, in 1820 and named after her birthplace, though she is also associated with Lea Hurst, Holloway, near Matlock, inherited by her parents William and Frances along with the Nightingale name and arms. The family spent many summers there during her childhood, and it is said Nightingale was particularly fond of the (Grade II listed) building's balcony, with its view of the garden, a meadow, trees and river beyond. She also returned in later life to nurse her mother until her death.

Despite her parents' reservations, Nightingale devoted her life to nursing after, at the age of 16, she claimed: 'God spoke to me and called me to His service.' She is best remembered as a pioneer in the profession of nursing and for devising effective sanitation methods for hospitals. Her most famous contribution came during the Crimean War, when she and 38 volunteer nurses were sent to Selimiye Barracks in Scutari, Turkey, to care for wounded British soldiers. Nightingale's insistence on proper diet, hygiene, lighting and activity helped to lower death rates, along with improved sewerage systems and ventilation. When she returned home, the link she made between hospital deaths and poor living conditions led to improvements in sanitation in hospitals across the country. She was also instrumental in establishing formal training for nurses, setting up the Nightingale Training School and Women's Medical School. Awarded the Royal Red Cross by Queen Victoria in 1883, in 1907 she became the first woman to receive the Order of Merit. Nightingale died peacefully in her sleep at the age of 90.

The Cavendish family and the Dukes of Devonshire

The Cavendish family and the Dukes of Devonshire have enjoyed a long association with the Peak District since Sir William Cavendish and his famous wife Bess (see above) built the first house at **Chatsworth** (p. 144) in the 1500s. In 1618, William and Bess's son William was created Earl of Devonshire, and in 1694 the fourth Earl became first Duke of Devonshire, for his role in bringing William of Orange to the English throne. The first Duke built new family rooms and a suite of state apartments, in anticipation of a Royal visit from William and Mary. He also added the East Front, including the famous Painted Hall.

The fifth Duke (1748–1811) married the late Princess Diana's ancestor, Lady Georgiana Spencer, and is perhaps best known for his quest to create a northern spa town to rival Bath in nearby **Buxton** (p. 200).

He commissioned leading Yorkshire architect John Carr to redesign private drawing rooms at Chatsworth, then asked him to design the (Grade I listed) Crescent in Buxton, built between 1780 and 1789. Said to be Carr's own favourite work, the Crescent included two of the first purpose-built hotels in the country, lodging houses and an assembly room to accommodate visitors to the emerging spa resort. The fifth Duke also asked Carr to create lavish stables and an exercise area 'in the round' to cater for guests' horses. By the early 19th century, the building had become a hospital, giving people access to Buxton's healing waters.

The sixth Duke of Devonshire donated the building to the town, and in 1881 local builder Robert Rippon Duke crowned it with the UK's largest unsupported dome, larger than St Paul's Cathedral in London or St Peter's in Rome. Now the renovated Grade II* listed building is the showpiece town centre campus for the University of Derby Buxton, and the Cavendish link continues. The twelfth Duke, Peregrine Cavendish, is currently Chancellor of the University.

Ethel and Gerald Haythornthwaite

The Peak District's precious landscape attracts visitors from all over the world – and many parts of it have been preserved thanks to the efforts of the late Ethel Haythornthwaite, her second husband Lt Col Gerald Haythornthwaite and their supporters. Their foresight laid the foundations for Britain's first national park, established in 1951, plus tighter planning laws.

Daughter of Sheffield steel magnate T W Ward, Ethel was outraged when, in 1927, the **Longshaw Lodge Estate** (p. 160) on the fringe of Sheffield was on the market as suitable for a golf course with potential for building development. She and a dozen like-minded campaigners founded the Sheffield Association for the Protection of Local Scenery, the forerunner of the Council for the Protection of Rural England (CPRE).

Now known as the Campaign to Protect Rural England, the charity still has a thriving Peak District and South Yorkshire branch, now known as the Friends of the Peak District and is dedicated to protecting the area's beautiful landscape while preserving a living, working environment.

Thanks to Ethel and her colleagues, the Duke of Rutland's 747 acre Longshaw Estate was saved, along with high moorlands extending over a further 10,786 acres. Early triumphs also included blocking plans to blast away the unique geological formations of **Winnats Pass** (p. 251) above Castleton to build a dual carriageway. Ethel's campaigning scaled new heights when she met and married Gerald, a trained architect, in the 1930s. Her passion for protecting the landscape and his technical skills proved a formidable combination over the years. After the Second World War, Ethel became one of three members of the local branch of the CPRE to join the Hobhouse Committee, which was instrumental in establishing national parks in England and Wales. Other successes included preventing a Grand Prix racing circuit, modelled on Le Mans, from being built in Long Dale, near Hartington, and a long-standing battle against a 'motorway by stealth' across the National Park on the line of the A628 Woodhead Pass, which continues to this day. The couple devoted their lives to safeguarding the Peak District – Ethel for almost 60 years and Gerald for 59. Ethel died aged 92 in 1986, while Gerald died at 82 in 1995 and was buried on what would have been his wife's 100th birthday.

The Kinder Mass Trespassers

In the same way that the Haythornthwaites were dedicated to preserving the Peak landscape, the Kinder Mass Trespassers played a pivotal role in the long campaign to secure access to the English countryside. Their protest also contributed to legislation to establish Britain's national parks, and in

2000, to the Countryside and Rights of Way Act, which granted the right to roam over open country and common land.

Led by the late Benny Rothman (1911–2002), around 400 ramblers, most from Manchester and Sheffield, answered a call from the British Workers' Sports Federation to '*take action to open up the fine country at present denied us*'. On 24 April 1932, they gathered at Bowden Bridge quarry, Hayfield (now marked by a commemorative plaque) and marched on up William Clough to Kinder Scout, where they fought 'a brief but vigorous struggle' with keepers specially enrolled for the occasion. One keeper fell and damaged his ankle, and ramblers came to his aid.

Once on the Kinder Plateau, the Manchester ramblers met supporters from Sheffield, who had ascended the hill from Edale, and celebrated in a joint victory meeting at Ashop Head. When they returned to Hayfield, the Manchester contingent was met by police, and five men were arrested, joining a fellow rambler detained earlier in the day. Five of them, including Rothman, were subsequently sentenced to imprisonment ranging from two months to six months, mainly for riotous assembly, while the sixth was acquitted. Their protest sparked further rallies in the **Winnats Pass** (p. 251), attended by up to 10,000 ramblers opposed to restrictions on countryside access, followed by similar demonstrations of support in Surrey, Wales and Scotland.

Rothman, active in a wide variety of political and conservation campaigns and organisations throughout his long life, later said the Kinder protest had raised awareness of the need to secure access to Areas of Outstanding Natural Beauty, as well as influencing both landowners and legislators.

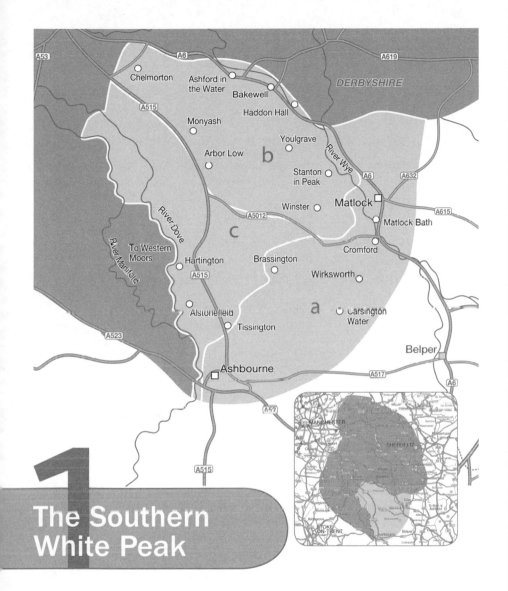

The Southern White Peak

a. Ashbourne, Wirksworth and the Matlocks
b. Bakewell and Youlgrave, including Haddon
c. Dovedale and the Manifold, including Hartington and Tissington

Unmissable highlights

01 Enjoy a Bakewell Pudding, **the famous sweet delicacy – incidentally, never known as a 'tart' here,** p. 93

02 Take a stroll through Dovedale, **and admire the spectacular rock scenery,** p. 105

03 Take to the skies in the Cable Cars, **Matlock Bath, for stunning views of High Tor and the Derwent,** p. 69

04 Go back in time at Haddon Hall, **in the country's finest medieval mansion,** p. 90

05 See the well dressings at Tissington, **where the ancient folk custom was first recorded,** p. 123

06 Visit the Stonehenge of the North, **Arbor Low, a remote and mysterious Neolithic monument,** p. 95

07 Go fossicking at the National Stone Centre, Wirksworth, and learn where the fossils came from, p. 73

08 Return to your childhood at the Museum of Childhood, **Sudbury Hall,** and play with the toys you were brought up on, p. 75

09 Tuck into a piece of Hartington Stilton, a tasty delicacy previously made in the village, p. 110

10 Pretend to be a caveman at Thor's Cave, Manifold Valley, surely the archetypal home of Fred Flintstone, p. 105

THE SOUTHERN WHITE PEAK

As you travel north on the A6 from Derby and cross the Derwent at
Whatstandwell, the wooded hills on either side of the road start to
close in. By the time you reach Cromford and Matlock Bath, towering
limestone crags, the most striking of which is the 300ft/90m bastion
of High Tor, frown down on the picturesque streets of Matlock Bath,
crowding in on the road and River Derwent.

Matlock and Matlock Bath have been a gateway to the Peak for centuries, and
became a minor inland spa during the 17th–19th centuries. Today Matlock Bath, with
its many attractions for young and old – ranging from the cable cars which take you
soaring through the air to the underground wonders of its show caves – is still one of
the major visitor destinations in the Peak.

Nearby Wirksworth was once a centre for lead mining and is still surrounded by
limestone quarries, some of which have been converted into the National Stone
Centre. But the town's cobbled, sloping Market Place, and the beautiful parish church
of St Mary, standing cathedral-like in its close, give Wirksworth its unique character.
To the west, typical stone-built White Peak villages such as Winster, Youlgrave and
Monyash, famous for their well-dressings, occupy sheltered spots on the limestone
plateau. The rolling plateau itself is criss-crossed by a network of drystone walls over
which the enigmatic stone circle of Arbor Low, west of Youlgrave, stands sentinel.

Continuing up the A6 from Matlock, past the gritstone plateau of Stanton Moor
with its Nine Ladies Stone Circle, you soon reach Bakewell the 'capital' of the
Peak District. Hidden in the trees by the side of the A6 as it approaches Bakewell
is Haddon Hall, the ancient home of the Dukes of Rutland and a popular film set,
often described as the most perfect medieval manor house in the country. Bakewell
itself is a pretty-near perfect little market town, spreading up from its medieval bridge
crossing the River Wye and crowned by the spire of the parish church of All Saints.
It is the focus for Peak District social life, and the Monday market, now held in the
ultra-modern Agricultural Business Centre, is still the biggest networking centre for
the Peak's rural population.

To the south, Ashbourne has long described itself as the Gateway to Dovedale, and
the pleasant, mainly Georgian, market town has some wonderful buildings, including
the gabled Tudor Grammar School and the stately parish church of St Oswald. The
nearby estate villages of Tissington and Hartington are a wonderful introduction to
the spectacular southernmost White Peak dales of the Dove and Manifold.

ASHBOURNE, WIRKSWORTH AND THE MATLOCKS

The Victorian novelist George Eliot described Ashbourne's elegant parish church of St Oswald as '*the finest mere parish church in the kingdom*'. Its slender, 215ft/65m spire is the tallest in the Peak, and Eliot used Ashbourne as 'Oakbourne' in her popular novel *Adam Bede*. Ashbourne has been a natural focus for the villages of the southern White Peak at least since 1257, when its market charter was granted. The street market is still held every Saturday on the cobbled, sloping market place at the top of the town, and every Shrove Tuesday, the town is still taken over by the playing of the Ashbourne football game, a boisterous reminder of how association football began (see Local Legends, p. 78). And Ashbourne is the southern terminus of the famous Tissington walking and riding trail.

Matlock Bath is the Blackpool of the Peak – a place of amusement arcades, fish and chip shops, and annual autumnal illuminations on the banks of the River Derwent. It is also a very popular resort of motorbikers at the weekend, and leather-clad biking enthusiasts love to inspect the ranks of gleaming machines parked along North and South Parade. Attractions include the Heights of Abraham and its fabulous show caves, Gulliver's Theme Park, the Cable Cars, and the Matlock Aquarium.

Just south of Matlock Bath on the A6, Cromford was a cradle of the Industrial Revolution, and is now the centrepiece of the Derwent Valley Mills World Heritage Site. In fact, Arkwright's Cromford Mill was the world's first successful water-powered cotton mill in the world, and his planned village across the A6 set new standards for worker accommodation and social care.

Wirksworth was built on stone, and six of its limestone quarries just outside the town have been converted to become the fascinating National Stone Centre. The Moot Hall in Chapel Lane is the home of the lead miners' Barmote Court, one of the most ancient in the country. The parish church of St Mary is one of the most interesting in the Peak, and stands in its close just off the sloping, cobbled Market Place. Nearby Carsington Water, opened in 1992 by the Queen, is a very popular visitor attraction. It is the ninth largest reservoir in England and at its highest level can hold 7,800 million gallons of water – enough to fill all the Derwent, Howden and Ladybower reservoirs in the Upper Derwent Valley, or to keep one person supplied with water for over 500,000 years! The 741 acre Carsington Water is owned and operated by Severn Trent Water and stores water pumped from the River Derwent at times of high rainfall, and is a popular place for birdwatchers and other nature lovers.

WHAT TO SEE AND DO

Heights of Abraham

Top of the kiss-me-quick attractions of Matlock Bath are the **Cable Cars**, which take you soaring high over the A6 and River Derwent from Matlock Station to the Heights of Abraham, named after General James Wolfe's famous victory at Quebec in 1759, and its caverns on the hills above. Once you get up to the Heights, with its castellated **Prospect Tower** affording outstanding views, there's plenty of other things to do. A guided tour through the **Great Masson Cavern** will take you from the flickering light of a lead miner's candle to the awe-inspiring sight of the whole cavern awash with colour. The **Great Rutland Cavern** was formerly the Nestus lead mine, and here you can experience the lives of the 17th-century lead miners who first discovered these caves.

The Cable Cars high above Matlock Bath

New attractions at the Heights include the **Fossil Factory**, where you are greeted by the fossilised remains of a giant, 3m long ichthyosaur from the days when dinosaurs ruled the earth. Fossils and geology are brought to life in this fascinating new visitor experience, while next door, the **Heath and Heaven**

HEIGHTS OF ABRAHAM AND CABLE CARS: Matlock Bath, Derbyshire DE4 3PD; ☎01629 582365; www.heightsofabraham.com. Entry: £10.50 adults, £7.50 concessions and children; open daily 10am–5pm, Feb to Nov.

photographic exhibition by renowned Peak photographer John Beatty shows panoramas of the Peak taken from the air on a single summer's day.

Local history and heritage

If industrial archaeology is your thing, then the **Peak District Mining Museum** at Matlock Bath is housed in The Pavilion between the A6 and the river. Here at the headquarters of the Peak District Mines Historical Society, the fascinating story of lead mining in the Peak is told through various interactive exhibits. These include a replica lead mine shaft, which children

PEAK DISTRICT MINING MUSEUM: The Pavilion, South Parade, Matlock Bath, Derbyshire DE4 3NR; ☎01629 583834; www.peakmines.co.uk. Entry: adults £3, concessions £2.50, children £2; open 10am–5pm (4pm winter), Sat, Sun and Bank Holidays; 11am–4pm weekdays except Mondays.

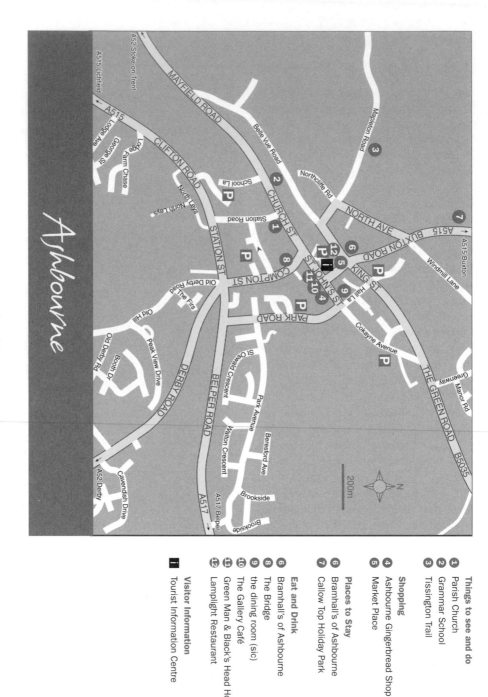

Ashbourne

Things to see and do
1. Parish Church
2. Grammar School
3. Tissington Trail

Shopping
4. Ashbourne Gingerbread Shop
5. Market Place

Places to Stay
6. Bramhall's of Ashbourne
7. Callow Top Holiday Park

Eat and Drink
6. Bramhall's of Ashbourne
8. The Bridge
9. the dining room (sic)
10. The Gallery Café
11. Green Man & Black's Head Hotel
12. Lamplight Restaurant

Visitor Information
i. Tourist Information Centre

can descend to get a feel of what it was actually like to be a lead miner.

Still on the industrial archaeology theme, just down the A6 is the **Sir Richard Arkwright's Masson Working Textile Mills Museum**, in the Masson Mills Megastore shopping complex at Matlock Bath. The mill was originally built by Arkwright in 1783 and was the showplace for his revolutionary use of water power. You can still see the mill machinery *in situ*, and be taken back two centuries to the days when cotton was king.

Cromford Mill, in Mill Lane off the A6, is the site of the first water-powered cotton mill in the country, and the centrepiece

The Peak District Mining Museum

SIR RICHARD ARKWRIGHT'S MASSON WORKING TEXTILE MILLS MUSEUM: Derby Road, Matlock Bath, Derbyshire DE4 3PY; ☎01629 581001; www.massonmills.co.uk. Entry: adults £2.50, concessions £2, children £1.50; open 10am–4pm Mon–Fri; 11am–5pm, Sat; 11am–4pm Sun.

of the Derwent Mills World Heritage Site, designated in 2001. It was here in 1771 that Richard Arkwright set up his original mill in the fortress-like buildings of Upper

Sir Richard Arkwright's Masson Mills

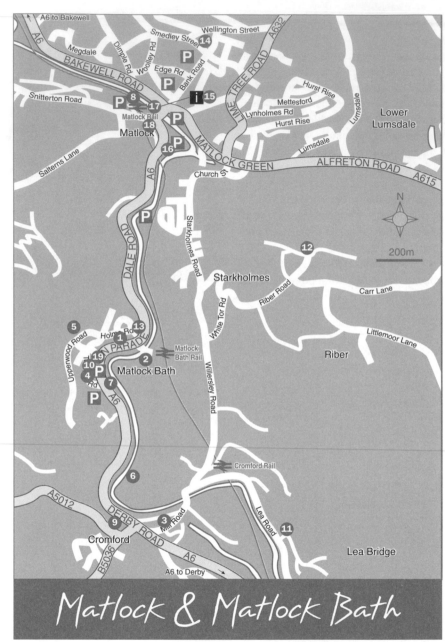

Matlock & Matlock Bath

Things to see and do
1. Aquarium
2. Cable Cars
3. Cromford Mill
4. Gulliver's Theme Parks
5. Heights of Abraham
6. Masson Mills Textile Museum
7. Peak District Mining Museum
8. Peak Rail

Shopping
6. Masson Mills Megastore
9. Scarthin Books

Places to Stay
10. Hodgkinson's Hotel
11. Pear Tree Farm
12. Riber Hall

Eat and Drink
13. The Balti

14. Café Central
15. Lemon Grass Restaurant
16. Monk & Monk Cellar
17. Peli-Deli
9. Scarthin Books
18. Regent House Tea Rooms
19. Temple Hotel

Visitor Information
i Tourist Information Centre

Mill, utilising the might of the River Derwent to power his machinery – and so ignite the first spark of the Industrial Revolution. Guided tours take you round the fascinating site, which is still in the course of restoration.

Steam buffs – and children – will love the experience of being pulled by a steam train on **Peak Rail's** restored section of the former Midland Line between Matlock and Rowsley. When the line closed in 1968, a group of enthusiasts resolved to restore it to its former glory – and there are long-term plans to restore the line and take it through the heart of the Peak District National Park. Various special events take place throughout the year, and especially popular are the Santa and Steam Specials at Christmas time. Trains – both steam and diesel-hauled – run at weekends and certain weekdays all year (call ☎ 01629 580381 for details).

The village of Darley Dale, on the A6 north of Matlock and a stop on the Peak Rail line, is also the home of the **Red House Stables Working Carriage Museum**, which has one of the finest collections of horse-drawn vehicles in the country. It has supplied carriages for many television and film period dramas set at Chatsworth or Haddon, and if you are feeling really grand, you can hire a coach-and-four seating 10 people for a three and a half hour sight-seeing tour of the Peak, including a drive through Chatsworth Park, (cost £750).

Stone is the foundation for the scenery of the White Peak, and you can learn all about its properties and fascinating history at the **National Stone Centre** just outside Wirksworth. The site covers 50 acres/20 hectares and no less than six former quarries, but about half is now designated as a Site of Special Scientific Interest (SSSI) for its geological features.

CROMFORD MILLS: Cromford Mill, Mill Lane, Cromford, Derbyshire DE4 3RQ; ☎01629 823256; www.arkwrightsociety.org.uk. Entry: adults £3, concessions and children £2.50; open 9am–5pm daily; guided tours.

Matlock Bath on the banks of the River Derwent

PEAK RAIL: Matlock Station, Matlock, Derbyshire DE4 3NA; ☎01629 580381; www.peakrail.co.uk. Entry: adults £6, concessions £4.60, children under 3 free, aged 3–5 £1, aged 6–15 £3; open all year, but call for details of opening times.

RED HOUSE STABLES WORKING CARRIAGE MUSEUM: Old Road, Darley Dale, Matlock, Derbyshire DE4 2ER; ☎01629 733583; www.workingcarriages.com. Entry: adults £5; concessions £3.50, children £2; open 10am daily.

CELEBRITY CONNECTIONS

Record-breaking round-the-world yachtswoman **Dame Ellen MacArthur** was born and grew up in the village of Whatstandwell, near Matlock, with her parents Ken and Avril, brothers Lewis and Fergus and beloved border collie cross, Mac. One of her favourite early haunts was the Midshires Way and network of tracks near the family home, where she and Mac spent many happy evenings and weekends. Her other childhood pursuits included family walks for hours in any weather, picking bilberries in summer on the moors, entering the annual village horticultural show, and trying her hand at well dressing, which she did at school in nearby Wirksworth.

However, Ellen's first love from an early age was sailing, an interest initially kindled by Arthur Ransome's famous *Swallows and Amazons* books, and she is patron of the Nancy Blackett Trust, which owns and operates Ransome's yacht of the same name. She loved the spirit of adventure in the books, and dreamed of sailing to a long-forgotten secret island. Her first experience of the thrills and challenges of the sport came at the age of four, when she sailed on *Cabaret,* her Auntie Thea's boat, on the East Coast. She soon became hooked, and saved her pocket money, boosted by a contribution from her Nan, to buy her first dinghy *Threep'ny Bit.* Much of her initial sailing was on home territory at Ogston Reservoir, but she soon ventured further afield to further her experience, both on inland lakes and reservoirs and at sea.

Aged just 19, Ellen sailed single-handed around Britain and won the Young Sailor of the Year award. The first major achievement that catapulted her into the public eye was achieving second place in the Vendee Globe solo round-the-world sailing race in her boat *Kingfisher* in 2001, after which she was awarded the MBE. However, her finest hour came in 2004/5, when she broke the solo record for sailing non-stop around the world. She achieved the feat in 71 days, 14 hours, 18 minutes and 33 seconds, on 7 February 2005.

There are many interactive exhibits for children to try, including drystone walling, and descriptions of how stone is used for everything from toothpaste to road-building.

Sudbury Hall
You might well recognise Sudbury Hall, the stately Jacobean pile close to Ashbourne

NATIONAL STONE CENTRE: Porter Lane, Middleton by Wirksworth, Derbyshire DE4 4LS; ☎01629 824833; www.nationalstonecentre.org.uk. Entry: adults £1.80, concessions £1.20, children 90p; open 10am–5pm summer, 10am–4pm winter; closed Christmas Day.

and now in the hands of the National Trust, as it featured in the BBC television costume dramas *Pride and Prejudice* and *Jane Eyre*. Among the memorable highlights inside the house are the richly decorated interiors, with intricate woodcarving by Grinling Gibbons.

Sudbury Hall also features the recently refurbished **National Trust Museum of Childhood** in the stable block. Here you can re-live your youth by seeing and playing with the toys of your childhood, while the children will enjoy the many interactive exhibits, which include a recreation of a Victorian chimney which they can actually scramble up, and a Victorian schoolroom which Dickens would surely have recognised.

SUDBURY HALL AND THE NATIONAL TRUST MUSEUM OF CHILDHOOD: Sudbury, Ashbourne, Derbyshire DE6 5HT; ☎01283 585305; www.nationaltrust.org.uk/eastmids. Entry: joint tickets for house and museum, adults £12.50, children, £7.50; open 1pm–5pm daily, 21 Mar to 2 Nov, except Mon and Tues; grounds 10.30am–5pm, 15 Mar–21 Dec.

Outdoor activities

There are very few lakes in limestone country, so the construction of the **Carsington Water** reservoir, west of Wirksworth, in 1992 gave recreational water-lovers a great opportunity. Today, the 741 acre/300 hectare reservoir has a thriving sailing club and facilities for windsurfing, canoeing and fishing, and there is a cycle hire centre

Sudbury Hall near Ashbourne

CARSINGTON WATER VISITOR CENTRE:
Ashbourne, Derbyshire DE6 1ST; ☎01629
540696; www.stwater.co.uk. Free entry but
£1 fee for car park; open 10am–6pm daily,
1 Mar–end Sept; 10am–5pm, 1 Oct–31 Dec;
10am–4pm, Jan–Feb.

if you want to cycle around the shores. There's also an adventure playground for the children, and for nature lovers the reservoir provides an important wetland habitat for many water-loving species of animals, birds and insects.

Carsington Sports and Leisure provides training courses for professionals and amateurs in many water-based activities, offering training in a wide variety of disciplines and using a diverse fleet of modern equipment. The centre is a Royal Yachting Association (RYA) recognised training centre, and also a British Canoe Union approved centre. In addition, RYA sailing, windsurfing and powerboat courses are regularly arranged, plus British Canoe Union kayaking courses.

CARSINGTON SPORTS AND LEISURE:
Carsington Water, Ashbourne, Derbyshire
DE6 1ST; ☎01629 540478;
www.carsingtonwater.com.

The courses run throughout the year to take advantage of the variety of conditions provided by Carsington Water.

If you are feeling energetic, you could hire a bike from the Cycle Hire Centre in Ashbourne (☎01335 343156; day's cycle hire £13), and go for a spin along the **Tissington Trail**, a converted former railway line which winds up over the limestone plateau, with spectacular, traffic-free views. The trail was created as a walking and riding route in 1968 after the former Ashbourne-Buxton line was closed. There are numerous picnic sites and parking places along the route between here and Parsley Hay, creating plenty of opportunities to stop and admire the stunning White Peak scenery.

Cycling on the Tissington Trail

LOCAL KNOWLEDGE

Former Blue Peter presenter **Simon Groom** and his wife Gilly live in an Elizabethan farmhouse at Dethick, near Matlock, where they run a bed and breakfast business and a working farm, managed to protect ancient woodland, maintain dry stone walls, preserve hedge laying and encourage habitat for wading birds.

The best thing about living in the Peak District: The pretty market towns and villages, where there's a new vibrancy. From Dethick, I can get to Derby in half an hour, then to London in under two hours. Living here I have the best of many worlds.

The Peak District's 'best kept secret': Edensor village, Chatsworth. Gilly and I got married there, and Kathleen Kennedy, sister of the US President John F Kennedy, is buried in the churchyard.

Favourite haunt/hangout: Peli Deli, Matlock and neighbouring Peli Beers, Matlock which offers superb real ales.

Best view: In Dethick churchyard, there's a seat with a breathtaking view across the Derwent Valley. It always inspires me, whatever the time of year.

Quirkiest attraction: Matlock Bath is the seaside without the sea. It's hugely popular with day trippers, a shrine for bikers and each autumn the town stages its own illuminations.

Best walk: It has to be the walk from Dethick up to Riber Castle and along Bilberry Knoll, looking down on the farm and fields where children's author Alison Uttley grew up. Then down to the Cromford Canal and back to Dethick.

Favourite restaurant: The Balti, Matlock Bath, one of the best Indian restaurants I have eaten in outside London. For special occasions, Hassop Hall.

Favourite takeaway: George's Tradition, Belper for fish and chips, or the Lemon Grass Café Restaurant, Matlock.

Favourite pub: The Jug and Glass, Lea, a former hospital run by Florence Nightingale. Good food and excellent Black Sheep bitter.

Secret tip for lunch: The Heathers Restaurant at Scotland Nursery, Tansley.

☂ Wet weather

A stroll round **Ashbourne**, which is well known for its antique shops and galleries, is well worthwhile, and don't miss a visit to the Early English-style **parish church of St Oswald**, one of the finest in the Peak. The white alabaster tomb depicting five-year-old Penelope Boothby by Thomas Banks is particularly moving.

Wirksworth's **Parish Church of St Mary**, standing in its close off the Market Place, is one of the most interesting churches in the Peak, and well worth a visit. Look out for the intricately carved 7th-century coffin lid, and the charming representation of a skirted, pickaxe-carrying lead miner, known locally as 'T'owd man'.

Wirksworth Church

Ashbourne football

Thankfully, football hooliganism is mainly a thing of the past now. But you can get an idea of the violent origins of the game if you visit the normally peaceful market town of Ashbourne on Shrove Tuesday and Ash Wednesday. Town centre shop fronts are boarded up and all traffic banned as Ashbourne's rumbustuous Shrovetide football game takes over the whole town. The two teams of local lads who are known as the 'Up'ards' and the 'Down'ards' – the Henmore Brook being the dividing line – fight in huge, swaying crowds to score in their opponents' 'goals', which are set 3 miles apart, originally at Sturston Mill and the former Clifton Mill, whose 'goal' is now marked by a commemorative stone.

A local or national celebrity usually starts the proceedings by throwing the decorated leather, cork-filled ball up into the air on the Shaw Croft and it is grabbed by one or other of the opposing teams. The ball then can be kicked, carried or generally transported through the streets, with steam rising off the bodies of the players in the general hectic scrummage. There are no boundaries and few rules to the Ashbourne football game, and at some stage, all the opposing players seem to end up in the Henmore Brook before the game is declared over, when either a 'goal' is scored or darkness falls.

Hope House Costume Museum at Alstonefield houses a huge collection of vintage costumes amassed by Notty Hornblower over 30 years. Some of the collection, which can only be seen by appointment, belonged to the landed gentry, other items to ordinary people.

HOPE HOUSE COSTUME MUSEUM: Hope House, Alstonefield, Ashbourne, Derbyshire DE6 2GE; ☎01335 310318; www.hopehousemuseum.co.uk. Entry: lectures £5 per head; by appointment only.

The outfits and costumes on show span over two centuries from the 1770s to the 1970s, and Notty gives a lecture on her collection to groups.

🏃 What to do with children

Children will love the rides in the various themed areas of the **Gulliver's Theme Parks,** just off the A6 at Matlock Bath. They can enter the world of the Wild West in the Western World, undertake a flight of fancy on the Fantasy Terrace, or enjoy the thrills and spills of the Switchback and log roller coaster in the Palais Royale area. And as if that wasn't enough to satisfy the younger thrill-seekers, there's the Party House and Lilliput Land areas, where various special events are held throughout the year.

GULLIVER'S THEME PARKS: Temple Walk, Matlock Bath, Derbyshire DE4 3PG; ☎01925 444888; www.gulliversfun.co.uk. Entry: adults £9.95, concessions £8.95, children free; open Mar to Oct.

The **Matlock Bath Aquarium** in the former Victorian Matlock Bath Hydro features a hologram gallery, petrifying well and gemstone and fossil collection, which are an ideal attraction for young visitors, especially on a wet day. Produced

MATLOCK BATH AQUARIUM: 110 North Parade, Matlock Bath, Derbyshire DE4 3NS; ☎01629 583624. Entry: adults £2.40, children under 5 free; open 10am–5.30pm daily, Easter to Oct 31, 10am–5pm, winter weekends and Christmas holidays.

by the latest laser technology, the hologram gallery is a mixture of three-dimensional photography and reality, while in the petrifying well, they can watch as objects are literally turned into stone. And then they can feed the fat carp in the Thermal Pool.

🛒 Shopping

Covering four floors of Sir Richard Arkwright's historic 18th-century Masson Mill, the **Masson Mills Megastore** at Matlock Bath is the place where you can pick up big brand named designer clothing at bargain prices.

MASSON MILLS MEGASTORE: Derby Road, Matlock Bath, Derbyshire DE4 3PY; ☎01629 760208; www.massonmills.co.uk. Open daily.

The **Wirksworth Factory Shop** at North End Mills (Cemetery Lane, Wirksworth DE4 4FG; ☎01629 824731; www.wirthsworthfactoryshop.co.uk) claims to be one of the

CELEBRITY CONNECTIONS

Cartoonist and writer **Bill Tidy**, famous for such popular strip cartoons such as 'The Cloggies' in *Private Eye* and 'The Fosdyke Saga' in the *Daily Mirror*, lives in Boylestone, south of Ashbourne. Born in Tranmere, Cheshire, in 1933, Bill left school at 15 and served in the Royal Engineers before returning to Liverpool to work as a layout artist for an advertising agency. He became a professional cartoonist in 1957 and met a young Italian girl, Rosa, on a flight to London two years later. He and Rosa married in 1960 and have three children and two grandchildren.

Over the years, Bill has worked for such publications as the *New Scientist*, *Daily Sketch*, *Mail on Sunday*, *Classic FM magazine* and *The Oldie*, and has written more than 20 books and illustrated more than 70. He has also appeared on numerous television and radio shows, has designed board games, ventriloquists' dummies, stage sets and trophies, and is in great demand as an after-dinner speaker.

Awarded the MBE in 2000, Bill's hobbies include supporting Everton FC, archaeology, enjoying real ale and good wines and growing vegetables.

largest factory shops in the country, and offers clothing for all the family, household linen, gifts and footwear at bargain prices. Previously a public house, saw mill, hosiery factory and one of five Wirksworth cotton mills which once produced a staggering 800 miles of 'red tape' a week, North End Mills also now features the Colours Restaurant and Coffee Shop. You should also taste some genuine Ashbourne gingerbread from the **Ashbourne Gingerbread Shop** in St John Street, just past the unique arch of the twin inn sign for the Green Man and Black's Head Hotel.

And if you like nothing better than browsing for books, the tiny **Scarthin Books** in the narrow Promenade behind the village dam in Cromford (DE4 3QF; ☎01629 823272; www.scarthinbooks.com) is a veritable treasure house of books old and new. Although it's crammed into a tiny space over three cramped floors, there's a café and you're almost bound to find something of interest.

The best... PLACES TO STAY

HOTEL

Riber Hall

Riber, Matlock DE4 5JU
☎ **01629 582795**
www.riber-hall.co.uk

Historic Elizabethan manor house set in a scenic location in pleasant grounds overlooking Matlock. Traditional bedrooms with a touch of opulence, including four poster beds and soft furnishings in keeping with the period atmosphere. Breakfast, lunch and evening meals available.

Price: B&B from £145 and DB&B from £210 for a double; B&B from £190 and DB&B from £255 for Deluxe Room 10.

Hodgkinson's Hotel

150 South Parade,
Matlock Bath DE4 3NR
☎ **01629 582170**
www.hodgkinsons-hotel.co.uk

Character, comfort and cuisine are the hallmarks of this Grade II listed hotel in the picturesque inland resort of Matlock Bath. Fully restored to reflect its Victorian past, it has eight individually designed and decorated en-suite rooms. Local produce on the menu in the candlelit restaurant.

Price: B&B from £38 for a single, per room per night; £120 for superior double, per room per night.

FARMSTAY

Pear Tree Farm

Lea Road, Lea Bridge,
Near Matlock DE4 5JN
☎ **01629 534215**
www.derbyshirearts.co.uk

Art courses and workshops run by professional and internationally renowned artists offer a farmhouse-based holiday with a difference in a picturesque location that has historical connections with Florence Nightingale. Rural retreat offering tuition in everything from creative writing to photography. Parties and special occasion groups welcome.

Price: B&B from £30 to £37.50 per person per night.

B&B

Henmore Grange

Hopton, Carsington,
Near Wirksworth DE4 4DF
☎ **01629 540420**
www.henmoregrange.co.uk

Recently refurbished farmhouse accommodation, full of charm and character, with exposed beams and stone walls, set in beautiful countryside next to Carsington Water. Ideal for small groups interested in fishing, walking, sailing and water sports, with sightseeing and shopping within easy reach. Peaceful setting, private parking.

Price: From £30 per person per night for an en-suite twin; £35 for an en-suite double.

The best... **PLACES TO STAY**

CAMPSITE

Callow Top Holiday Park

Buxton Road, Sandybrook, Ashbourne DE6 2AQ
☎ **01335 344020**
www.callowtop.co.uk

Caravan park and campsite just north of the market town of Ashbourne and close to Dovedale, the Manifold Valley and Tissington and High Peak Trails. Swimming pool, fishing lakes and inn serving real ale brewed on site. Heated swimming and paddling pool May to September.

Price: From £14.50 per night (low season, non-serviced pitch) to £21 per night (high season, part-serviced pitch).

SELF-CATERING

Hoe Grange Holidays

Brassington, Matlock DE4 4HP
☎ **01629 540262**
www.hoegrangeholidays.co.uk

Luxury self-catering log cabins next to the High Peak Trail. Ideal location for riders keen to holiday with their own horse just 500m from the Pennine Bridleway, offering miles of safe, off-road hacking. Well-equipped accommodation with whirlpool baths, full central heating and double glazing.

Price: From £300 to £750 per week.

10 North Street

Cromford DE4 3RG
☎**01628 825925**
www.thelandmarktrust.org.uk

Experience history in action by staying in part of the earliest planned industrial housing in the world, now part of a World Heritage Site. Built in 1771 by Sir Richard Arkwright to house mill workers. Sleeps up to four, has an open fire, small yard and croft, or paddock, at rear.

Price: From £297 per week.

UNUSUAL

The Old Lock Up and Chapel

North End, Wirksworth DE4 4FG
☎ **01629 826272**
www.theoldlockup.co.uk

Luxury and elegance in the old Magistrate's House, Coach House and Gothic Chapel, once visited by D H Lawrence and his wife Frieda. En-suite bedrooms, and your own pulpit and psalm board in the Grade II listed Chapel. Victorian-style guest lounge with open fire and extensive breakfast menu using local produce.

Price: B&B from £45 per person.

02 Well dressing

This unique folk custom attracts
thousands of visitors every year to the
50 or so villages that decorate their wells
or springs with these colourful floral icons,
originally a pagan custom designed to
give thanks for the gift of water, p. 123

03 Castleton caves

Castleton's four show caves each
give an entirely different view of the
Peak's usually unseen and secret
underground world of beautifully
lit caverns draped with colourful
stalactites and stalagmites and
veins of the Peak's unique semi-
precious stone, Blue John, p. 249

04 Chatsworth

You can't avoid the palatial pile of the Devonshires, which dominates the Derwent valley with its rolling landscaped parklands, beautiful manicured gardens and a veritable treasure house of works of art inside, p. 144

05 Haddon Hall

Smaller, older and much more intimate than Chatsworth, Haddon is instantly recognisable as the backdrop to many television and film period dramas, and has been described as the perfect English medieval manor house, p. 90

The best... FOOD AND DRINK

You'll find lots of fine fare to tickle your taste buds in Ashbourne, from top-class delicatessens and fresh food shops to organic meat producers. There's also plenty of choice if you want to eat out or visit a traditional country pub.

▶ Staying in

Described as one of the top 50 delicatessens in the country, **Patrick and Brooksbank** in Ashbourne (Market Place DE6 1ES; ☎01335 342631) boasts a huge selection of specialist cheeses and handmade chocolates. Many products are handmade on the premises using natural ingredients and cooked in small batches to retain their home-made character. Cheese is also a speciality at **The Cheddar Gorge** (Dig Street, Ashbourne DE6 1GF; ☎01335 344528), which sells around 70 varieties of English and Continental cheeses, including locally produced Stilton and Dovedale Blue. Freshly baked pies, quiches, scones, cakes, savouries, preserves, cooked hams, chocolates and Derbyshire honey are also available.

For fresh fish, game and poultry, head for **A L Hulme** (Church Street, Ashbourne DE6 1AE ☎01335 342141), believed to be the only family run shop of its type in Derbyshire. Fish is sourced daily from both Hull and more exotic waters, and both poultry and game (including venison and wild boar in season) are sourced locally. Ashbourne is also famous for its gingerbread, believed to have been created by a French prisoner of war who made his home in the town after the Napoleonic Wars. You can sample this mouth-watering local delicacy at the **Ashbourne Gingerbread Shop** (St John Street DE6 1GH; ☎01335 346753).

Local and organic produce are staples at **The Derbyshire Larder** in Matlock (Dale Road DE4 3LT; ☎01629 581189), which has a wide selection of cheeses, continental meats and olives. Takeaway food includes home-made soup and chilli, savouries, cobs to order, cakes, jacket potatoes and salad boxes. You can also source local, organic and Fairtrade foods at **Peli Deli** (Crown Square, Matlock DE4 3AT ☎07890 694841), where specialities include cheese, olives and olive oil. Centrally located **Hambridge Butchers** (Bank Road, Matlock DE4 3AQ; ☎01629 581558) sells a wide range of meats and cooked meats, while if you're in search of organic fruit and vegetables, visit **Scotts Garden** (Lumsdale Road, Matlock DE4 5NG; ☎07815 078228).

Local beef, lamb, pork and chicken, award-winning sausages and haslet and home-made black pudding are just some of the products on offer at **E W Coates Butchers** of Two Dales (Chesterfield Road DE4 2EZ; ☎01629 733504). Other specialities include home-cured and cooked hams, cooked meats, pork pies, pasties and oatcakes.

In Wirksworth, **The Real Food Company** (Market Place DE4 4ET; ☎01629 823123) offers home-made fare ranging from pasties hot from the oven to wholesome takeaway meals. Specialities include local lamb and minted vegetable pasties, Stilton, cheddar and cranberry lattice and triple chocolate shortbread.

For home-produced organic beef, pork and lamb, visit **Hearthstone Farm Shop** in Riber, near Matlock, which also sells organic vegetables, cheese, poultry and juices. Rare breed speciality pork sausages, joints and other products, plus home-cured bacon are the sizzling options at **Farmcraft Traditional & Rare Breed Meat Company**, Kniveton Wood, Ashbourne, while locally reared meat, seasonal vegetables, freshly baked bread and cakes and dairy products are among the fine fare on the menu at **The Farm Shop at Fairways**, Ashbourne.

Local suppliers who regularly attend farmers' markets in the area include organic meat, bacon and sausage producers **Derbyshire Dales Organics** of Bradley, near Ashbourne; the **Derbyshire Mushroom Company** of Atlow, near Ashbourne; meringue and curd makers **Jays Cottage** of Roston Cottage near Ashbourne, and specialist cake makers **www.babycakesdirect.co.uk** of Darley Dale. **Matlock Farmers' Market** is held at the Imperial Rooms on the third Saturday of the month from 9am to 2pm, while **Matlock Country Market** is held at the same venue on the first Friday of each month, from 9am to 11.55am.

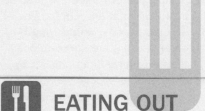

⊞ EATING OUT

FINE DINING

The Dining Room
33 St John Street Ashbourne DE6 1GP
☎ **01335 300666**
www.thediningroomashbourne.co.uk

Award-winning cuisine with a conscience is the hallmark of this Derbyshire Restaurant of the Year 2006, which prides itself on using as much fresh, organic and local produce as possible. Everything is produced on the premises, from cured and smoked salmon and bacon to ice cream and bread. Main courses around £20.

RESTAURANT

Bramhall's of Ashbourne
6 Buxton Road, Ashbourne DE6 1EX
☎ **01335 346158**
www.bramhalls.co.uk

Quality fresh ingredients are prepared and cooked with flair, creating timeless cuisine with a modern twist, served with a comprehensive wine list and real ales. Main courses around £16.50 to £19.95. Guests can also stay over in one of 10 individually designed rooms that combine a period feel with modern facilities.

EATING OUT

Lamplight Restaurant
4 Victoria Square, Ashbourne DE6 1GG
☎ 01335 342279/☎07891 456384
www.the-lamplight.co.uk

Originally a 16th-century hostelry called the Tiger Inn, this family run restaurant is full of original features and character, and specialises in traditional English and French cuisine. Midweek set menu (three courses, £15.95) from Tuesday to Friday, plus à la carte featuring meat, fish and vegetarian dishes (from £10.95) from Tuesday to Saturday.

The Bridge
Dig Street, Ashbourne DE6 1GF
☎ 01335 211888
www.thebridgeashbourne.com

Italian cuisine plus both traditional and contemporary British cooking in an inviting setting. Bar and restaurant options available. Bar mains include fillet steak (£15.50), fish and chips (£10.50) and ravioli di pesce (£9.50). Typical restaurant offerings are rack of lamb (£16), steak and ale pie (£12.50), and garganelli pasta with broccoli (£8.50).

The Lemon Grass Vietnamese Restaurant & Cafe
23 Firs Parade, Matlock DE4 3AS
☎ 01629 580730
www.lemongrassmatlock.co.uk

Extensive à la carte menu and takeaway service offering a taste of Vietnamese cuisine in the heart of the Derbyshire Dales. Buffet evenings every Friday and Saturday for £12.90 per person (booking recommended). Takeaway orders over £50 get £5 off. Start with home-made soups and appetizers, then choose from a wide selection of mains, including vegetarian, from £4.50.

The Balti
256 Dale Road, Matlock Bath DE4 3NT
☎ 01629 55069/☎01629 760069

A warm welcome, friendly service and freshly prepared food, whether you eat in or use the takeaway service, with free delivery within a 5-mile radius for orders over £15. House speciality is the 'Shabeena' with chicken, lamb, prawns, king prawn or vegetables. Main courses range from £8.95 to £13.95, takeaways around 20% cheaper.

Le Mistral
23 Market Place, Wirksworth DE4 4ET
☎ 01629 824840
www.lemistral.co.uk

Innovative, wholesome cuisine from bœuf bourguignon to moules frites, plus daily specials and vegetarian options, is served from 11am to 11pm, seven days a week. Much of the meat is sourced locally. Relaxed and sociable atmosphere, where guests can enjoy a full meal, light snack, glass of wine or bottled beer. Main courses range from £9 to £17.60.

GASTRO PUB

The Bear Inn & Hotel
Alderwasley DE56 2RD
☎ 01629 822585
www.bear-hotel.com

Locally sourced produce from meat and vegetables to ice cream and real ale are on the menu at this historic inn, where chefs fuse cooking traditions from across the globe to create classic dishes and imaginative specials, plus seafood and vegetarian options. Mains from £9.95 to £22.95. Live music, Sunday carvery and quality accommodation.

EATING OUT

CAFÉ

The Gallery Cafe
50 St John Street, Ashbourne DE6 1GH
☎ **01332 347425**
www.sjsg.org.uk

This multi award-winning gallery and café occupies a Grade II listed building which was once a magistrates' court. Most of the food, including cakes, is made on the premises and the family-run business caters for a variety of diets, including gluten free, lactose intolerance and vegetarians. Fairtrade, fine food and fine art.

Peli-Deli
1 Jubilee Buildings, Crown Square, Matlock DE4 3AT
☎ **07890 694841**
www.pelideli.com

Another café/delicatessen combining good food and drink with art in a variety of genres. Specialities include olive oil, cheese and olives, while all coffee served is roasted in the UK for freshness. Tuck into handmade cakes, bakes and bread made from fresh, organic and Fairtrade produce, much of it from local suppliers.

Café Central
76 Smedley Street, Matlock DE4 3JJ
☎ **01629 760460**
www.cafecentral.co.uk

Cheerful café and pizzeria two-thirds of the way up Matlock's famous 'steep hill', Dale Road, open most lunchtimes and Friday and Saturday evenings. Locally sourced food includes sandwiches, paninis, vegetable stew and cakes at lunchtime, pasta and pizza in the evenings. Unlicensed, but evening diners can bring their own wine.

Crown Yard Kitchen
(next to Heritage Centre, just off the Market Place)
Wirksworth DE4 4ET
☎ **01629 822020**
www.crownyardkitchen.com

Wide choice of freshly cooked local produce at reasonable prices, ranging from fresh breakfasts and an all-day menu featuring hot meals, sandwiches and paninis, plus Sunday roasts, accompanied by fresh ground coffee, wine or beer. Open late on Saturdays for evening dinner, closed Mondays.

Scarthin Books
The Promenade Scarthin, Cromford DE4 3QF
☎ **01629 823272**
www.scarthinbooks.com

Vegetarian café in what has been described as 'Britain's most enjoyable bookshop'. Organic produce used wherever possible, vegan and gluten-free options available. Home-cooked seasonal produce provides the basis for hearty meals, thick soups, salads and cakes, including eggs, fruit and vegetables from the owners' garden when in season.

TEA ROOM

Regent House Tea Rooms
35 Dale Road, Matlock DE4 3LT
☎ **01629 583660**

A traditional, comfortable tea room with table service in the heart of Matlock. Coffee is served in cafétieres, with a choice of 28 different beans from around the world. Around 36 leaf teas are brewed and served in china tea pots. Food, snacks and specials are served all day, including jacket potatoes at lunchtime.

🍺 Drinking

Microbreweries

Real ale connoisseurs have three microbreweries to choose from in this area – two in or near Ashbourne, and the other in Wirksworth. **Leatherbritches Brewery** is centrally located at the Green Man & Black's Head Royal Hotel, Ashbourne (DE6 1GH; ☎01335 864492), with Belt-n-Braces, Ginger Spice and Hairy Helmet among its intriguingly named offerings. Just up the road, on the way to Buxton, is the **Haywood Bad Ram Brewery** in a converted barn at Callow Top Holiday Park (DE6 2AQ; ☎07974 948247; www.callowtop.co.uk). Beers include Bad Ram, Dr Samuel Johnson (after the famous writer associated with Ashbourne) and Woggle Dance – but note that the brewery is closed during the winter. **Wirksworth Brewery** (DE4 4DR; ☎01629 824011; www. wirksworthbrewery.com) supplies Cruckbeam and T'owd Man to around 12 local pubs.

Real ale pubs

Famous for its association with Ashbourne's unique Shrovetide football game each February, the Green Man & Black's Head Royal Hotel (DE6 1GH; ☎01335 345783) is a 300-year-old coaching inn that stages a beer festival every August Bank Holiday and has cosy fires in winter. Further north, in the picturesque village of Fenny Bentley, low beams, flagged floors and coal and log-burning stoves create a cosy ambience in the **Coach and Horses** (DE6 1LB; ☎01335 350246). Home-cooked food features local produce, guest beers are served, and the garden offers a relaxed setting for drinking during the summer.

Said to be haunted, the Grade II listed 17th-century **Olde Gate Inne** at Brassington (DE4 4JH; ☎01629 540448) has a traditional country atmosphere, with oak beams, open fireplaces and a black-leaded range. Home-cooked food and guest beers are served, and boules are played in fine weather. Named local CAMRA Pub of the Year 2008, the gabled Jacobean **Barley Mow** at Kirk Ireton (DE6 3JP; ☎01335 370306) is full of character, with inter-connecting rooms, low beamed ceilings, mullioned windows and open fires in stone fireplaces. Six beers, including local ales and guest beers, are served straight from the cask from a small serving hatch.

For stunning views, seek out the **Thorn Tree** in Matlock (DE4 3JQ; ☎01629 580295), where the beer garden looks out over Bonsall Moor. Lunches and evening meals are available on certain days of the week, complemented by real ales and guest beers. If you're after a sophisticated drinking experience, try the stylish **Monk and Monk Cellar** in Matlock (79 Dale Road DE4 3LU; ☎01629 581751), which serves everything from healthy smoothies and coffee to alcoholic and non-alcoholic cocktails, fruit beers, Trappist brewed beers and other unusual bottled brews. Lord Byron was one of the famous visitors to the historic Georgian **Temple Hotel** (DE4 3PG; ☎01629 583911) above the bustling riverside promenade in Matlock Bath, which serves beer from several Derbyshire microbreweries.

Real ales are an ever-changing feature at the 18th-century **Boat Inn** in Cromford (DE4 3QF; ☎01629 823282), which holds three beer festivals a year, has a wine/ tapas bar in the basement and a garden. In Wirksworth, the Grade II listed **Hope and Anchor** (DE4 4ET; ☎01629 823340) boasts fascinating original features, outdoor courtyard seating for fine-weather drinking, bar meals and snacks and continually changing cask ales. Nearby is the **Royal Oak** (DE4 4FG; ☎01629 823000), a traditional, stone-terraced local serving a range of national, local and guest beers.

ⓘ Visitor Information

Tourist information centres: Matlock Tourist Information Centre, Crown Square, Matlock, Derbyshire DE4 3AT, ☎01629 583388, www.visitpeakdistrict.com, open daily; Carsington Water Visitor Centre, Ashbourne, Derbyshire DE6 1ST, ☎01629 540696, www.stwater.co.uk, open daily except Christmas Day.

Hospital: St Oswald's Hospital, Belle Vue Road, Ashbourne, ☎01335 342121.

Doctors: Lime Grove Medical Centre, Lime Grove Walk, Matlock DE4 3FD, ☎01629 581586; Hannage Brook Medical Centre, Hannage Way, Wirksworth DE4 4JG ☎01629 822434; Crich Medical Practice, Bulling Lane, Crich, Matlock DE4 5DX, ☎01773 852966; Dr PJP Holden & Partners, 8, Imperial Road, Matlock DE4 3NL, ☎01629 583465; Darley Dale Medical Centre, Columbell Way, Two Dales, Matlock DE4 2SA, ☎01629 733205; Brailsford & Hulland Medical Practice, Main Road, Hulland Ward, Ashbourne DE6 3EA, ☎01335 370482; Drs Tattersall, Ashworth, Gilchrist, Fulford, Mitchell & Mitchell, Gibb Lane, Sudbury, Ashbourne DE6 5HY, ☎01283 585215; The Brailsford & Hulland Medical Practice, Medical Centre, The Green, Church Lane, Brailsford, Ashbourne DE6 3BX, ☎01335 360328; The Surgery, Clifton Road, Ashbourne DE6 1RR, ☎01335 342666; The Health Centre, Compton, Ashbourne DE6 1DA, ☎01335 343784.

Supermarkets: Ken's Supermarket, St John's Street, Wirksworth, ☎01629 825564; Kwik Save Stores, Firs Parade, Matlock, ☎01629 580242; Midlands Co-operative Society, Shawcroft Centre, Dig Street, Ashbourne, ☎01335 346274; Sainsbury's Supermarket, Cawdor Quarry, Cawdor Way, Matlock, ☎01629 583521; Somerfield Stores, Dig Street, Ashbourne, ☎01335 342645; Somerfield Stores, Bakewell Road, Matlock, ☎01629 57463.

Taxis: Ashbourne Taxis, Calwich, Ashbourne, ☎01335 324414; Cross Dales Taxi Service, Edward Street, Wirksworth, ☎01629 820028; Deejay Taxis, Cromford, ☎01629 822072; Fox Cars, Matlock Green, Matlock, ☎01629 583333; Greenway Cars, Church Lane, Ashbourne, ☎01335 342964; J B Taxis, Tansley, Matlock, ☎01629 583535; Martin's Taxis, Ian Avenue, Wirksworth, ☎01629 826787; Matlock Taxis, Causeway Lane, Matlock, ☎01629 584195; M J's Taxis, Porter Lane, Wirksworth, ☎01620 826060.

FURTHER AFIELD

Crich Tramway Village

A whole Edwardian cobbled street, complete with clanking trams and municipal buildings, has been re-created in a former limestone quarry at the **Crich Tramway Village** at Crich, near Matlock. The village lies in the shadow of the Sherwood Foresters memorial tower on Crich Stand – a landmark for miles around with views as far as Lincoln Cathedral away to the east. You can enjoy a ride on many of the trams, which have been collected from all over Europe.

CRICH TRAMWAY VILLAGE: Crich, Matlock, Derbyshire DE4 5DP; ☎01773 854321; www.tramway.co.uk. Entry: adults £10, concessions £9, children £5; open 10.30am–4pm, 9 Feb to 24 and weekends in Mar, daily 10am–5.30pm, 21 Mar to 2 Nov.

One of the trams in the Crich Tramway Village

BAKEWELL AND YOULGRAVE
INCLUDING HADDON

Bakewell is justly known as the capital of the Peak District, and with a population of just under 4,000, it is the largest settlement and headquarters of the National Park authority.

There has probably been a market here for at least 1,000 years, and the weekly livestock market, now held in the modern Agricultural Business Centre on the outskirts of the town centre, still attracts farmers and livestock dealers from all over the Peak every Monday. There is also a lively street market on Mondays, held in the square behind the Visitor Centre, which itself is housed in the ancient Old Market Hall, just up from the venerable 14th-century bridge over the River Wye. The Old House Museum in Cunningham Place behind the dominating spire of All Saints Parish Church, tells the story of Bakewell through the ages, and is a perfect, award-winning example of what a local museum should be.

Just off the A6 is romantic Haddon Hall, a seat of the Dukes of Rutland for 800 years, and often described as the perfect medieval manor house. Its mellow gritstone walls and untouched interior have made Haddon a popular film set for many movies, recently including *Jane Eyre*, *Pride and Prejudice* and *The Other Boleyn Girl*. The near by village of **Youlgrave**, standing on a ridge between the valleys of Lathkill and Bradford Dales, is also dominated by the tower of its parish church, and is a lively, one-street village whose residents have wholeheartedly adopted a pioneering sustainable living project. And also close by is **Winster**, which was famous as a lead mining centre, with many remains scattered among its green fields. It is also the home of the Peak's only Morris Dancing team, which regularly performs its own tunes and dances outside the Old Market Hall (National Trust) and around the Peak villages in summer.

The southern White Peak was obviously attractive to early humans, as the enigmatic remains of the Arbor Low stone circle, near Monyash, and the Nine Ladies Stone Circle on Stanton Moor, illustrate. Both these ancient monuments retain their secrets, which stretch back an unimaginable 4,000 years.

WHAT TO SEE AND DO

Haddon Hall
Romantic **Haddon Hall** has been a seat of the Dukes of Rutland for eight centuries and is now the home of Lord and Lady Edward Manners. This perfect medieval manor house stands high on a limestone bluff overlooking the River Wye, making its

battlemented towers and walls an ever-popular backdrop as the setting of many films and television costume dramas. Haddon has a much more ancient, lived-in feel than its more illustrious neighbour over the hill, Chatsworth. It is perhaps best-known for the fictional Victorian romance of the elopement of Dorothy Vernon – you can see her rather stern-faced effigy in Bakewell parish church. But Haddon is also famous for its oak-panelled Long Gallery, time-worn stepped courtyard and beautiful hanging gardens overlooking the Wye and Dorothy's fabled bridge, which is actually a packhorse bridge of much later date.

Local history and heritage

The **Old House Museum** in Bakewell has won many awards as an outstanding example of a local history museum. It is quite difficult to find, tucked away in Cunningham Place and reached by a steep ginnel behind the parish church, but it is well worth the effort. In a house originally built by Richard Arkwright for his workers at Bakewell Mill, and then rescued from dereliction by the local history society, It tells the story of five centuries of Bakewell's history through a series of fascinating exhibits and displays.

Just down the A6 at Rowsley is **Caudwell's Mill**, the only complete Victorian water turbine powered roller flour mill in the country. A mill has stood on this site for 400 years, but the present mill, which still grinds wholemeal flour which you can buy in the mill shop, was built by John Caudwell on the River Wye in 1874. It now forms the centrepiece of a crafts complex in the buildings of the mill yard, and there is an excellent café/restaurant.

Tudor **Winster Market Hall** was the first property the National Trust acquired in the Peak District, as long ago as 1906, and is a reminder of the time when a weekly market of locally produced goods was an important feature of local village life. The arcaded ground floor echoes Bakewell's Old Market Hall, although in that case, they

HADDON HALL: Bakewell, Derbyshire DE45 1LA; ☎01629 812855; www.haddonhall.co.uk. Entry: adults £8.50, concessions £7.50, children £4.50; open 12 noon–5pm, Sat, Sun and Mon, 29 Mar to 28 Apr; May to Sept; Sat Sun and Mon, Oct, 10.30am–3.30pm, 6 Dec to 14.

Haddon Hall has appeared in *Jane Eyre* and *Pride and Prejudice*

OLD HOUSE MUSEUM: Cunningham Place, off North Church Street, Bakewell, Derbyshire DE45 1DD; ☎01629 813642; www.oldhousemuseum.org.uk. Entry: adults £3, children £1.50, children under 5 free; open daily 11am–4pm, Apr to Oct.

CAUDWELL'S MILL: Rowsley, Derbyshire DE4 2EB; ☎01629 734374. Entry: adults £3.50, concessions £2.50, children £1.25; open daily 10am–5.30pm except Christmas.

Bakewell

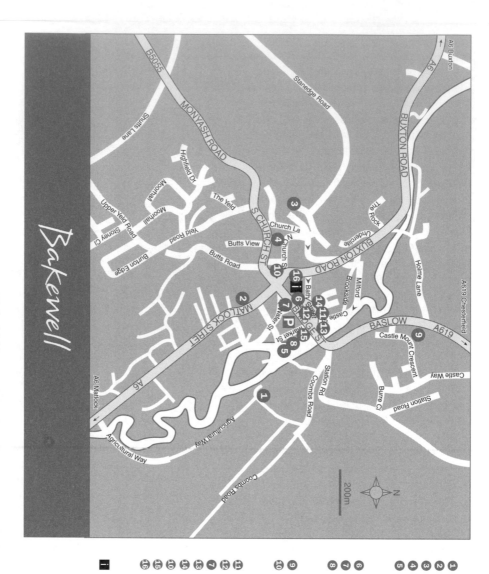

Things to see and do

1. Agricultural Business Centre & Market
2. M&C Motorcycle Collection
3. Old House Museum
4. Parish Church
5. River Wye

Shopping

6. Armstrong Butchers
7. Old Original Bakewell Pudding Shop
8. Original Farmers' Market Shop

Places to Stay

9. Castle Hill Farm House
10. Rutland Arms Hotel

Eat and Drink

11. Albert's Resturant & Bar
12. Frederick's Ice Cream Parlour
13. Old Original Bakewell Pudding Shop
14. The Peacock
15. Piedaniel's
16. Rutland Arms Hotel
17. Upstairs Café & Gift Shop
18. The Wheatsheaf

Visitor Information

i. Tourist Information Centre

Bakewell Pudding

Mention Peak District food to most people and they'll probably come up with the name of the Bakewell tart. But don't make the mistake of calling the delicious, almond paste and puff pastry delicacy a 'tart' in Bakewell. Here, it is known by its proper title of Bakewell Pudding – and a pudding is exactly what it is. Made to a recipe which is a still closely guarded secret in three shops in the ancient market town, it is now exported all over the world – and it bears no relation to the Mr Kipling variety.

But the original Bakewell Pudding came about as a complete mistake. A flustered cook in the Rutland Arms Hotel in the centre of town was charged by the owner, Mrs Ann Greaves, to make a strawberry tart for some expected important visitors. Mrs Greaves explained that the egg mixture was to be stirred into the pastry, and the strawberry jam spread on top of the pastry. But the panicking cook either forgot or misunderstood the instructions and didn't stir the egg mix into the pastry but poured it over the strawberry jam. So what was meant to be a tart turned out to be a pudding. The accidental delicacy was so well received by Mrs Greaves' guests that she instructed her cook to continue making them in that way – and the Bakewell Pudding was born.

Among the shops which claims to have the original recipe is the Olde Original Pudding Shop in the Square (see p. 100). The original owner, Mrs Annie Wilson, actually claimed to have been one of the guests at the hotel when the cook made her famous mistake and wrote down the recipe in pencil in a shaky hand in a small notebook, which is now kept in a fireproof safe.

The Olde Original Pudding Shop claims to be the home of the original recipe for the Bakewell pudding

The Old Market Hall, Bakewell

have been filled in and the building now serves as the tourist information centre.

Lathkill Dale, part of Natural England's Derbyshire Dales National Nature Reserve, is many people's favourite Derbyshire dale, and a stroll through the narrow, wooded dale either from Monyash or Over Haddon, is a delight, especially in early summer. Hidden in the trees of Palmerston Wood are the substantial ivy-covered remains of the **Mandale Lead Mine**, showing that this now sylvan spot was once a hive of industry.

The humps and bumps in many White Peak fields show evidence of the work of lead miners, who delved below the ground to reach the precious veins of galena, or lead ore, for centuries. The most impressive remains of a complete lead mine can be seen at **Magpie Mine**, near Sheldon, which is now a field study centre for the Peak District Mines Historical Society, but always open to the public via adjacent footpaths. Lead was mined at Magpie for over 200 years, and you can still see the circular Cornish-built pumping house chimney alongside the square Derbyshire one, the Agent's House, and the circular powder house. Even the corrugated iron-clad remains of the engine house of the last unsuccessful attempt to win the precious galena from the limestone in the 1950s are now protected.

CELEBRITY CONNECTIONS

Former West Derbyshire MP, now journalist and broadcaster, much-travelled **Matthew Parris** retains his links with the Peak District and has a house near Bakewell. He is particularly fond of the scenery among the hills on the Staffordshire side of the River Dove, with their steep grassy slopes, sharp limestone peaks and views towards the mountains of North Wales, and he is an enthusiastic supporter of the annual Buxton Festival.

After working at the Foreign Office and Conservative Research Department, Matthew was on the staff at Margaret Thatcher's office until her first election victory in 1979, when he became an MP. He gave up his seat in 1986 to become presenter of London Weekend Television's political programme, *Weekend World*. A prolific writer, Matthew has written numerous books on politics and travel, and has made various expeditions abroad, including trips to Mount Kilimanjaro, Zaire, the Sahara, Peru and Bolivia. More recently, he wrote a book about his family's quest to renovate a derelict 16th-century mansion in Catalunya, Spain.

Prehistoric Peak District

You can still get a real feeling for the mystery and former importance to the earliest settlers of the ritual prehistoric stone circles of Arbor Low, just off the A515 near Monyash and the Nine Ladies, on Stanton Moor, just south of Rowsley.

ARBOR LOW STONE CIRCLE: www.english-heritage.org.uk. Entry: voluntary admission charge at Upper Oldhams Farm; open daily; parking at farm.

Arbor Low is often described as the Stonehenge of the North, and it dates from approximately the same Neolithic period as its more famous Wiltshire counterpart,

The prehistoric stone circle of Arbor Low

The Nine Stones Close, near Harthill

although its circle of stones now lie prostrate in the emerald turf. But whereas Stonehenge is fenced off and grossly over-interpreted, Arbor Low, standing high (at 1,230ft/375m) on the limestone plateau, manages to retain its enigmatic secrets.

It's an easy walk across the heather-clad moor from the Stanton-in-Peak to Birchover road to reach the **Nine Ladies Stone Circle**, in its grove of silver birches on Stanton Moor. Legend has it that these small irregular stones are the remains of a group of women who dared to dance on the Sabbath, and were turned to stone by the Devil, and the nearby King Stone was said to be their fiddler. Actually, they form part of a ritual monument dating from the Bronze Age, about 4,000 years ago. There are numerous other barrows and tumuli hidden in the heather of Stanton Moor, proving this analogous gritstone incursion in the heart of limestone country served as a necropolis for the Bronze Age community.

NINE LADIES STONE CIRCLE: www.english-heritage.org.uk. Entry: free; open daily; parking on road.

Local churches

Bakewell's hilltop **Parish Church of All Saints** is one of the most interesting in the Peak. It commands fine views across the Wye valley, and its sloping churchyard contains two of the finest 10th-century Celtic preaching crosses in the area. The scroll and vine carving on the crosses owes much to the Hiberno-Norse style, and may indicate the possibility of a school of carvers in the area at the time. Inside the south porch is another fine collection of Saxon and medieval stonework, and there are plans to interpret these important remains inside the church, which was heavily restored in the 19th century.

All Saints Parish Church, Youlgrave, is famed for its magnificent west tower, a fine example of Perpendicular architecture, and don't miss the quarter-size effigy tomb of

LOCAL KNOWLEDGE

One of Europe's foremost wildlife artists, **Pollyanna Pickering** lives at Oaker near Matlock, and her original paintings hang in corporate and private collections across the globe. Winner of numerous art, business and conservation awards and an honorary graduate of the University of Derby, her Pollyanna Pickering Foundation raises funds for worldwide conservation, animal welfare and disaster relief.

The best thing(s) about living in the Peak District: I feel very lucky to live here. Although I have travelled the world to study and paint endangered species in their natural habitats, I could find enough inspiration within 30 miles of my front door to keep me painting for the rest of my life.

Favourite haunts: Carsington and Tittesworth reservoirs are great for bird watching and relaxing.

Best thing to do on a rainy day: Shop! The Cavendish Arcade in Buxton has a vibrant mix of independent retailers.

Favourite activity in the Peak: I love to walk – you see areas and views that can't be reached by road, and I am constantly finding new places. I always carry a sketchpad and pencils – a good excuse to keep pausing on some of the more strenuous uphill pathways!

Favourite place to paint: Chatsworth. Wonderful views from the Hunting Tower, and I often sketch the deer. I must have painted the house in every season!

Best view: The classic view across Monsal Dale from Monsal Head is hard to beat.

Quirkiest attraction: The well dressings. This ancient custom is thriving, and I always love to see new and original designs each year.

Favourite restaurant/pub: The Druid Inn at Birchover, which serves everything from classic/hot sandwiches through to two or three course meals.

Favourite takeaway: The Lemon Grass Restaurant and Cafe, Matlock – fresh and light, authentic Vietnamese food.

Secret tip for lunch: The Dome Restaurant in the former Devonshire Royal Hospital, now the University of Derby Buxton. Excellent food at a reasonable price, prepared and served by hospitality and catering students.

Thomas Cockayne, who was killed in a teenage brawl in 1488, in the chancel. The Youth Hostel in Youlgrave is housed in the village's former Co-op shop, and close to the circular fountain, which once supplied the village with its water, is Thimble Hall (private), according to the *Guinness Book of Records*, the world's smallest detached house.

Horse riding

Haddon House Stables breeds its own Hanoverian horses, and provides a variety of hacking out opportunities for adults who are competent and capable riders through the hills and dales of the area around Bakewell, Lathkil Dale and Over Haddon. You'll get a warm welcome with the quality horses and a friendly atmosphere at Haddon House.

> HADDON HOUSE STABLES: Over Haddon, Bakewell, Derbyshire DE45 1HZ; ☎01629 813723; www.haddonhousestables.co.uk.

Wet weather

The wonderful world of motorcycles has been created by Peter Mather and Phil Crosby at the **M&C Collection of Historic Motorcycles** in Tannery Yard, Bakewell, down an alley off the Matlock Street, in premises which were once an original Bakewell Pudding bakery. This hidden gem displays touring and sporting machines, in addition to many other more exotic types, surrounded by a fascinating array of associated memorabilia.

> THE M&C COLLECTION OF HISTORIC MOTORCYCLES: Tannery House, Matlock Street, Bakewell, Derbyshire DE45 1EE; ☎01629 815011; www.mccollection.net. Entry: adults £2, children free; open bank holidays and summer weekends; phone for details.

What to do with children

The **River Wye**, which flows through Bakewell, is always a popular spot for children, as they love to feed the ducks, Canada geese and swans which congregate in large numbers on the banks near the ancient town bridge. Even more fascinating are the antics of the trout which often steal the crumbs thrown in the water from under the birds' beaks!

And while you are enjoying some retail therapy at the **Peak Village** shopping outlet at Rowsley (☎01629 735326; www.peakvillage.co.uk), the children can have their photographs taken with a life-sized model of the famous *Chitty Chitty Bang Bang* car in the fascinating **Toys of Yesteryear** exhibition. There is also a Hornby 'OO' railway layout and a military vehicle panorama displaying Dinky toys, plus exhibits featuring other toys dating from the last century.

> TOYS OF YESTERYEAR MUSEUMS & TOY SHOPS: Peak Village Shopping Centre, Chatsworth Road, Rowsley, Derbyshire DE4 2JE; ☎01629 732111; www.toysofyesteryear.co.uk. Entry: adults £3, concessions £2.50, children over 4 £2; open daily from 10am.

The best... **PLACES TO STAY**

HOTEL

Rutland Arms, Bakewell

The Square Bakewell, Derbyshire DE45 1BT
☎ **01629 812812**
www.rutlandarmsbakewell.com

Early 19th-century hotel in the heart of Bakewell, where author Jane Austen is reputed to have stayed. Individually styled rooms ranging from standard to four poster, with recently upgraded bathrooms and wireless internet connections. Varied menus featuring local produce in the Four Seasons Restaurant and the Brasserie.

Price: from £47 (single) to £194 (four poster, Jane Austen) per night.

INN

The Kings at Ivy House

Biggin-by-Hartington Newhaven, Buxton SK17 0DT; ☎ 01298 84709
www.thekingsativyhouse.co.uk

Award-winning country guest house with huge log fire, flagstone floors and old glazed bar area in a converted Grade II listed coaching inn dating back to the 18th century. Quality accommodation offering a host of extras, including fresh flowers, bathrobes and toiletries. Locally sourced food for breakfast and dinner, special diets catered for.

Price: DB&B £65 per night, single occupancy supplement £20 per night.

FARMSTAY

Knotlow Farm

Flagg, Buxton SK17 9QP
☎ **01298 85313**
www.knotlowfarm.co.uk

Welcoming, family-run B&B in a traditional farmyard setting, with an indoor horse riding arena and caravan and campsite. The farmhouse accommodation was completely renovated in 2008 to create a homely and comfortable atmosphere. Walking enthusiasts will appreciate the Limestone Way, which runs through part of the farm.

Price: B&B £35 per person per night (double), £45 for a single; caravans £12 per night; tents £5.

B&B

Poppy Cottage

Main Street, Birchover, Matlock DE4 2BN
☎ **01629 650847**
www.poppycottagebandb.co.uk

Small, family run accommodation providing a high standard of hospitality for up to four guests. Only one booking is taken at a time to ensure complete privacy. Beautifully decorated and cosy, with open fire and extras such as freshly laundered bathrobes and complimentary toiletries. Hearty breakfasts feature local produce.

Price: from £65 for a single; from £75 for a double.

Castle Hill Farm House

Baslow Road, Bakewell DE45 1AA
☎ **01629 813168**
www.castlehillfarmhouse.co.uk

Grade II listed, 17th-century farmhouse, minutes from the centre of Bakewell with beamed ceilings, restored to preserve traditional features while offering modern day comforts. Idyllic setting with beautiful views of the river Wye. Traditional English breakfasts and vegetarian and gluten-free diets catered for, using local produce.

Price: B&B from £60.

SELF-CATERING

Blakelow Farm Cottages

Bonsall Lane, Winster, DE4 2PD
☎ **01629 650814**
www.blakelowcottages.co.uk

Three tastefully appointed cottages, each accommodating between two and four guests. Candle Cottage, for two people, oozes romance with its vaulted ceiling, crystal chandelier and sumptuous décor, while Cranberry Cottage offers contemporary luxury living for four. Christmas Cottage, for four, boasts open plan living with log-burning stove.

Price: From £385 to £675 per week (inclusive).

The best... FOOD AND DRINK

Bakewell is best known for its mouth-watering Bakewell Pudding, delicious served with local cream, ice cream or custard, and if you visit Frederick's Gelateria, you'll even find Bakewell Pudding flavoured ice cream. Look out too for quality meat, preserves and smoked foods. Eating out is easy thanks to a variety of restaurants, gastro pubs, cafés and tea rooms, plus a clutch of charming pubs.

▷ Staying in

For quality local and British produce, much of it sourced within a 30-mile radius, visit **The Original Farmers' Market Shop** (Market Street, Bakewell DE45 1HG; ☎01629 815814). Gourmets can choose from a wide range of breads, meats, cheeses and other tasty treats, including food from farms and producers in the Peak District National Park. Anyone interested in sampling Bakewell's world-famous pudding should head for **The Old Original Bakewell Pudding Shop** (The Square DE45 1BT; ☎01629 812260), where customers can enjoy it 'in-house', warm with cream and custard, in the first-floor café, or buy it to take away. Bakehouse tours are also available for parties of 20 or more, when you can watch pudding makers in action and even have a go at making the celebrated delicacy. The ground-floor shop also sells a variety of local and British foods, from biscuits to wine.

For quality beef, lamb, corn-fed pork, poultry, award-winning home-made sausage and oven-ready meals, visit **Andrew Armstrong (Farmers & Butchers)** (The Square DE45 1BT; ☎01629 812165). Home-cured ham, dry-cured bacon, pies, sausages and cooked meats are available from **New Close Farm Shop** at Over Haddon (DE45 1JE; ☎01629 814280). Home-grown and local vegetables are incorporated in home-made chutneys and pickles from **Golden Meadow Preserves** of Middleton-by-Youlgrave, while home-made jams and marmalades, using local spring water, are available from **Irene's Marmalade** of Youlgrave.

Fragrant home-smoked meat, poultry and fish, both cooked and cold, can be sourced from the **Derbyshire Smokery** of Flagg (Ashbourne Road SK17 9QQ; ☎01298 83595), where the range includes duck, locally sourced chicken, turkey, trout, salmon, mackerel and other fish. **Bakewell Farmers' Market** is held at the Agricultural Business Centre, usually on the last Saturday of the month, from 9am to 2pm, whereas the **Bakewell Country Market** is held in the Town Hall (The Square DE45 1BT) on Saturday mornings between 9.30am and 12.30pm (☎01433 631243).

EATING OUT

FINE DINING

The Rutland Hotel
The Square, Bakewell DE45 1BT
☎ 01629 812812
www.rutlandarmsbakewell.com

Award-winning menus featuring locally sourced produce in both The Four Seasons Restaurant and Brasserie. Options in the restaurant range from fillet of beef and pan fried sea bass to vegetable pasta bake and vegetable moussaka, while desserts include the famous Bakewell Pudding, produced in the place where it was invented. Two courses cost £23.95, three courses £27.95.

RESTAURANT

Piedaniel's
Bath Street, Bakewell DE45 1BX
☎ 01629 812687
www.piedaniels-restaurant.com

Locally sourced food cooked fresh on the premises and served in an elegant setting. Choices range from meat and fish to vegetarian options, including starters such as black pudding, smoked bacon and potato salad and mains such as braised lamb steak and matelote of mixed fish. Lunch costs £12, evening starters £5, mains £12.

Albert Restaurant and Bar
Theme Court, Bridge Street, Bakewell DE45 1DS
☎ 01629 810077
www.albertrestaurant.co.uk

Quality English food using locally sourced ingredients. Carnivores can tuck into Derbyshire reared beef from a local farm, saddle of lamb or Barnsley chop, while fish-eaters and vegetarians can savour sea bass, tuna, pea and leek tart and field mushrooms duxelle. Starters cost from £4.50, mains from £8.95.

GASTRO PUB

The Druid Inn
Main Street, Birchover DE4 2BL
☎ 01629 650302
www.thedruidinn.co.uk

Drinkers and diners can sample the best of both worlds at this 17th-century establishment, which has four dining areas. Traditional and contemporary food is prepared using local produce and served in the bar and snug, upper and lower restaurants or outside terrace with scenic views. The set menu costs from £14 (two courses) to £17 (three courses).

CAFÉ

The Old Original Bakewell Pudding Shop
The Square, Bakewell, Derbyshire DE45 1BT
☎ 01629 812193
www.bakewellpuddingshop.co.uk

Tuck into Bakewell's famous speciality, its almond-flavoured pudding, in the first-floor, beamed café, where you can also watch pudding makers at work or even have a go at making one yourself. Puddings, biscuits, sweets, fudge, jams, chutneys, honeys, wines and other specialist products are also on sale in the shop downstairs or online.

EATING OUT

Upstairs Cafe and Gift Store
2-3 Market Street, Bakewell DE45 1HG
☎ 01629 815567

Busy, modern coffee shop in the heart of Bakewell, above the Original Farmers Market Shop. Fresh, quality food and friendly, efficient service. Wide variety of snacks and daily specials. House wine, cold continental and smooth beers are also available.

Fredericks Ice Cream Parlour
1 Bridge Street, Bakewell DE45 1DS
www.bakewellicecreamparlour.co.uk

If you don't fancy Bakewell Pudding itself, you can sample Bakewell Pudding flavoured ice cream in this stylish venue, which has won awards for the dramatic use of steel, glass and natural light in its chic interior. Other flavours in Fredericks' award-winning selection range from pistachio to pomegranate and raspberry. Also available are sandwiches, cakes, coffee, tea, wine and champagne.

TEA ROOMS

The Old Smithy
The Green, Monyash,
Near Bakewell DE45 1JH
☎ 01629 810190
www.oldsmithymonyash.piczo.com

Small, family-run business using local produce in its large range of main meals, including the famous all-day 'Smithy's Breakfast'. Other treats include Derbyshire's award-winning Smith's Creamland ices and a wide range of beers, wines and spirits, including Peak Ales from the Chatsworth Estate. Restaurant-style menu for bistro nights and pre-booked parties.

Edge Close Farm Tea Rooms
Flagg, Buxton SK17 9QT
☎ 01298 85144
www.edgeclosefarmtearooms.co.uk

Fully licensed family-run tea room serving home-made and freshly cooked food based on local produce, including all-day breakfasts, sandwiches, soup, jacket potatoes and cakes. Wines, spirits, beers, tea, coffee and soft drinks are also served. Booked parties, meetings and conferences catered for outside tea room hours.

🍺 Drinking

One of Bakewell's most historic pubs is **The Peacock** on Bridge Street (DE45 1DS; ☎01629 813635), built in the early 19th century as a hotel and coaching inn to accommodate the large number of visitors to the town. Original owner Francis Machin, of nearby Birchover, his wife Hannah and four daughters are said to haunt the inn, which boasts a traditional bar with cosy fireplace and garden, and serves home-cooked bar and restaurant meals made from locally sourced produce at both lunch and dinner. Another welcoming hostelry is **The Wheatsheaf**, also on Bridge Street (DE45 1DS; ☎01629 812985), which offers home-cooked food based on local produce, including steaks, home-made pies, trifles and crumbles, in its large dining room.

Local brews from Whim Ales Ltd and Peak Ales are among the attractions at **The Lathkil Hotel** in Over Haddon (DE45 1JE; ☎01629 812501), which enjoys sweeping views over Lathkill Dale and serves lunch and dinner in its bar and restaurant. Visitors can sit out in the garden in fine weather, and dogs are welcome. The unspoilt **Flying Childers** pub in Stanton in Peak (DE4 2LW; ☎01629 636333) is named after a famous racehorse once owned by the Duke of Devonshire, and boasts real fires and a beer garden. Popular with locals and visitors alike, real ale fans will find a range of guest ales that change regularly. Home-made soups and snacks are served at lunchtimes and dogs are welcome.

In Youlgrave, visitors and locals alike head for **The Farmyard Inn** on Main Street (DE45 1UW; ☎01629 636221), a former farm which boasts many original features and became an inn in 1829. As well as its range of beers, it offers a good selection of red, white, rose, sparkling and dessert wines and champagne. Another homely village pub is **The Bull's Head** in Fountain Square, Youlgrave (DE45 1UR; ☎01629 636307), a family-run establishment which dates back to the 17th century. Beers include occasional guest beers, plus a good range of wines, complemented by bar snacks, an à la carte menu and traditional Sunday lunch. Another cosy haunt with traditional snug, wood burning stove and games room is **The Miners' Standard** at Banktop, Winster (DE4 2DR; ☎01629 650279), where fine, cask-conditioned ales and home-cooked bar food are served at lunch and dinner time. Down in the centre of the village itself, near the historic market hall, is the **Old Bowling Green** (DE4 2DS; ☎01629 650219), where up to four constantly changing beers from local microbreweries are served, and good food is served in the evenings and on Sundays.

Good food, real ales and a warm welcome are on offer at the **Bull's Head** at Monyash (DE45 1JH; ☎01629 812372), where children and dogs are welcome. Home-made food using local produce is served both lunchtime and evening, along with a selection of real ales, including examples from Whim Ales. There are cosy log fires, a games room and a large beer garden next to a children's play area. Visitors to the **Cock and Pullet** in Sheldon's Main Street (DE45 1QS; ☎01629 814292) may be forgiven for thinking that it's one of the oldest pubs in the Peak District, thanks to its coal fire, wooden beams and antique furniture, but in fact it's one of the newest. Opened in 1995, it was once a derelict barn, but is now popular haunt for people who appreciate both real ales and home-cooked food at lunchtime and in the evenings.

Situated on the main A515 road between Buxton and Ashbourne is the unusually named **Bull i'th'Thorn** (SK17 9QR; ☎01298 83886). One of Derbyshire's oldest pubs, it became an inn in 1472, and has a carved oak sign over the door, depicting a bull caught in a thorn bush. A selection of ales and other drinks, snacks and meals are available, plus camping facilities and a rare breed animal visitor centre for families.

Just off the A515 in the charming village of Chelmorton is the **Church Inn** (SK17 9SL; ☎01298 85319), a traditional pub catering for both locals and walkers, with a convivial atmosphere, real fire, quality ales and home-cooked food, plus outdoor seating on a front patio.

ⓘ Visitor Information

Tourist information centre: Bakewell Visitor Centre, The Old Market Hall, Bridge Street, Bakewell, Derbyshire DE45 1DS, ☎01629 816558, www.peakdistrict.gov.uk, open daily.

Hospitals: Minor injuries A&E, Whitworth Hospital, Darley Dale, ☎01629 580211; Main A&E, Chesterfield Royal Hospital, Calow, Chesterfield, ☎01246 277271.

Doctors: Bakewell Medical Centre, Butts Road, Bakewell, ☎0844 477 3408, www.bakewellmedicalcentre.net;

Youlgrave Medical Centre, Alport Lane DE45 1WN, ☎01629 636207; Winster Surgery, Leacroft Road, Winster DE4 2DI, ☎01629 650207.

Supermarket: Co-op Supermarket, Market Street, Bakewell, ☎01629 816900.

Taxis: John Thorp Private Hire, Bakewell, ☎01246 583219; Neil Chapman Private Hire, Wyedale Drive, Bakewell, ☎01629 812454; Peak Premier Travel, Over Haddon, ☎01629 636877.

DOVEDALE AND THE MANIFOLD
INCLUDING HARTINGTON AND TISSINGTON

Dovedale is perhaps the most famous of the White Peak dales, but a place to be avoided on bank holiday weekends when the large car park soon fills up, and a crocodile of walkers files through its narrow confines. But the startling rock formations rising clear out of the ash woodlands, such as the Tissington Spires, Ilam Rock and Pickering Tor, are worth the effort at other times on the easy, three-mile path through the dale. This was where Izaak Walton and Charles Cotton, of nearby Beresford Hall, conceived and wrote the fisherman's bible, *The Compleat Angler*, in 1653. If you prefer serenity, then the parallel dale of the Manifold, easily reached from Ilam or Grindon, might be preferable, and its rock features such as Beeston Tor and the awesome gaping void of Thor's Cave – an archetypal caveman's dwelling if ever there was one – are just as impressive. Further up the dale on the Manifold Track, the bulk of Ecton Hill contains the Peak's only copper mine, the profits from which enabled the sixth Duke of Devonshire to construct the famous Crescent at Buxton.

WHAT TO SEE AND DO

Walking and pony trekking

A stroll through **Dovedale** is a must, but try to avoid summer weekends or bank holidays, when you may have to queue to cross the famous Stepping Stones at the entrance to the dale. The 3 mile walk as far as **Milldale** passes some of the finest rock architecture in the Peak, including Tissington Spires, Ilam Rock, the great rock fang of Pickering Tor, and the hidden cave and natural rock bridge of Reynard's Cave.

Much less busy but just as beautiful is the nearby **Manifold Valley**, threaded by the former railway line of the Leek and Manifold Light Railway, and now an easy, wheel-and-pushchair-friendly metalled track. You pass the awesome void of **Thor's Cave**, high on a cliff above the valley, and Beeston Tor, where other evidence of early humans has also been uncovered.

Other easy walking is available on the **Tissington and High Peak Trails**, both former railway lines which cross the White Peak plateau and command fine views. It is also an easy 3 mile walk from Hartington to visit **Pilsbury Castle**, the finest Norman

Inside Thor's Cave

motte and bailey remains in the Peak, commanding a strategic position at the head of the Dove valley.

TISSINGTON TREKKING CENTRE: Tissington Wood Farm, Tissington, Ashbourne, Derbyshire DE6 1RD; ☎01335 350276.

The **Tissington Trekking Centre** at Tissington Wood Farm, Tissington is ideally situated for pony trekking adventures in the Dovedale and Ashbourne areas. Riders of all abilities are welcomed.

Hartington

Hartington is centred on the square with its restored mere (pond), and is a convenient centre for exploring the Dove Valley. Tudor **Hartington Hall**, just outside the village, is allegedly the place where Bonnie Prince Charles stayed on his ill-fated march on London in 1645, and is now a beautifully restored youth hostel. You can actually stay in the bedroom where, allegedly, the prince slept.

The Mere, Hartington

According to tradition, the tasty, blue-veined Stilton cheese can only be made in Derbyshire, Leicestershire or Nottinghamshire. The former Nuttalls Cheese Factory, off the village square at Hartington, just qualified, because it was a quarter of a mile inside the Derbyshire boundary, and was where the famous Hartington Stilton was made for many years. It is still sold in the village's specialist cheese shop in Stonewell Lane (see p. 110).

Tissington Hall

Tissington Hall has been the home of the Fitzherbert family for 400 years. It was built by Francis Fitzherbert in 1609 to replace a moated manor house to the north of the church and is now open to the public, with an adjoining award-winning tea room. The present incumbent, Sir Richard Fitzherbert, plans to introduce a new scheme in 2009 which will allow guests to stay in the house. The £2,000 price tag for four days will include accommodation and dinner at the hall, along with visits to 10 other properties, including Chatsworth and the National Trust's Calke Abbey.

TISSINGTON HALL: Tissington, Ashbourne, Derbyshire DE6 1RA; ☎01335 352200; www.tissington-hall.com. Entry: £7.50 entrance to hall and gardens; open daily 10am–5pm, Easter week, summer half-term and certain dates in Jul–Aug. Call for details.

Tissington Hall

CELEBRITY CONNECTIONS

Actor **Tom Chambers**, famous for his role as lady-killer medic Sam Strachan in BBC television's *Holby City* and his fleet feet and supple hips on *Strictly Come Dancing*, was born in Darley Dale, near Matlock. An ex-pupil at Matlock Pre Prep School and member of Matlock Golf Club, Tom hails from Parwich, north of Ashbourne, and his parents Stuart and Rosemary still live in the village.

Tom honed his performance skills at the National Youth Music Theatre and the Guildford School of Acting. After some theatre work and several minor roles on television, his career took off when he landed a part in the British-made film *Fakers*.

A life-long dancing fan, he was thrilled to win the 2008 *Strictly Come Dancing* competition, partnering Danish Latin-American professional Camilla, and hopes the experience will help him fulfil his ambition to make and appear in a *Singing in the Rain*-style British movie.

Ilam Park

Ilam Park (National Trust), near Ashbourne, is set beside the River Manifold, and enjoys outstanding views towards the hills of Dovedale and walks into the Manifold Valley, where the river, like other limestone rivers in the Peak, disappears underground during the summer months. There is a well-appointed information centre and tea room.

> ILAM PARK: Ilam, near Ashbourne, Derbyshire DE6 2AZ; ☎01335 350503; www.nationaltrust.org.uk. Open daily 11am–4pm all year.

Wet weather

Just across the road from Tissington Hall is the squat Norman tower of the **parish church of St Mary**, one of the oldest and most interesting in the area. Many of the Fitzherberts from Tissington Hall are buried here, in a variety of impressive tombs.

LOCAL KNOWLEDGE

Artist and book illustrator **Sue Prince OBE** moved to the White Peak in 1984, when she and her husband Terry took the helm at Beechenhill Farm, Ilam, overlooking the breathtaking Manifold Valley. While Terry runs the 37 hectare organic dairy farm, Sue runs a busy bed and breakfast and self-catering business, which includes a romantic hideaway for two and a restored hay barn. Now a member of the Peak District National Park Authority, Sue is also a food and eco-tourism campaigner.

Favourite restaurant: The George, Alstonefield, offers a simple but superb menu, excellent chef and lovely atmosphere.

Best walk: From Beechenhill Farm up to Ilam Moor Lane and down Jacob's Ladder, into Dovedale. I particularly love it in winter, when the trees are bare and you can see through them. It's like a secret view, because we have so few visitors at that time of year. Turning left, Hall Dale is filled with wild flowers and orchids in the spring. Coming back to Ilam Moor Lane, you pass the 'walled walk' then suddenly discover a secret, warm 'bowl' surrounded by mature trees. This is the Old Lime Kiln, the perfect place for quiet contemplation, encircled by nature.

Favourite pub: The Coach and Horses, Fenny Bentley is warm and 'buzzy' with good food and drink.

Favourite takeaway: Longnor Fish and Chip Shop. Proper fish and chips, cooked while you wait. Mouthwateringly delicious!

Best thing to do on a rainy day: Exploring the antique and second-hand bookshops in Ashbourne, then visiting Tissington Nursery, where you can buy rare plants that you won't generally find elsewhere. Finally, enjoying leisurely afternoon tea at the Old Coach House Tearooms. Bliss!

Secret tip for lunch: The Gallery Cafe, Ashbourne. Light, beautifully prepared lunches, surrounded by paintings and sculptures.

🏃 What to do with children

It's a little further afield, but bored children will love the **Alton Towers**, Britain's premier theme park, which is situated between Ashbourne and Uttoxeter. White knuckle rides such as Nemesis, Oblivion, Ripsaw, Submission and The Blade, should satisfy even the most laidback youngsters. More gentle, year-round activities at Alton Towers include the Cariba Creek Waterpark, which also caters especially for children.

ALTON TOWERS: Alton, Staffordshire Moorlands ST10 4DB; ☎0870 520 4060; www.altontowers.com. Entry: adults £29, children £22, family of four £81, family of five £98; open 10am–4pm, 28 Mar to 1 Nov.

One of the many rides at Alton Towers theme park

🛒 Shopping

Don't leave **Hartington** without buying a delicious, blue-veined Stilton cheese from the **Cheese Shop**, in the broad village square, where markets were held from the early 13th century. Hartington Cheese Factory, which is just a quarter of a mile inside the Derbyshire boundary, is able to make true Stilton, as it can only originate from Derbyshire, Leicestershire or Nottinghamshire.

The Old Cheese Shop in Hartington

The best... PLACES TO STAY

HOTEL

Izaak Walton Hotel

Dovedale DE6 2AY
☎ 01335 350555
www.izaakwaltonhotel.com

Peacefully situated hotel with sweeping views over Dovedale to Thorpe Cloud. Many of the bedrooms also enjoy excellent views and have Wi-Fi facilities. Fishing on the River Dove, immortalised in Izaak Walton's *The Compleat Angler*, can be booked.

Price: B&B from £110 single/£145 double.

INN

Bentley Brook Inn

Fenny Bentley, Ashbourne DE6 1LF
☎ 01335 350278
www.bentleybrookinn.co.uk

A busy country inn offering a range of well-equipped accommodation, including free Wi-Fi in the bar. Meals served in the restaurant feature many organic and GM free ingredients from local suppliers. Outside is a safe children's play area and patio.

Price: B&B from £60–£80 for double to £110 for a family room.

FARMSTAY/ORGANIC

Beechenhill Farm

Ilam, Ashbourne DE6 2BD
☎ 01335 310274
www.beechenhill.co.uk

Comfortable bed and organic, locally sourced breakfast, stylish cottages and converted hay barn for special events on an organic farm with dairy cows and sheep. Garden with Swedish hot tub and cave, table tennis, garden chess and draughts. Explore the farm trail or 'meet the bees' kept by a local honey producer.

Price: B&B from £38 per person per night; self-catering from £270 per week.

Throwley Hall Farm

Ilam, Ashbourne DE6 2BB
☎ 01538 308202
www.throwleyhallfarm.co.uk

A Georgian farmhouse and self-catering holiday cottages on a working beef farm specialising in pedigree Charolais cattle overlook the scenic Manifold Valley. Full English breakfast served. Large garden with climbing frame, swings and slides.

Price: B&B from £30 pppn; self-catering from £200 to £1,100.

B&B

The Hayloft

Church Street, Hartington SK17 0AW
☎ 01298 84368
www.hartingtonhayloft.co.uk

Restored to a high standard to retain its original character and charm, this late 19th-century Hayloft has solid oak floors, hand-made, local furniture and full en-suite facilities. Breakfasts include produce from members of Peak District Cuisine.

Price: B&B £30 per person per night.

CAMPSITE

Rivendale Caravan and Leisure Park

Buxton Road, Alsop-on-le-Dale, nr Ashbourne DE6 1QU
☎ 01335 310311
www.rivendalecaravanpark.co.uk

A camping meadow and B&B accommodation managed in an eco-friendly way, including wild camping area. Enjoy the snug simplicity of a 'yurt'. Traditional Scandinavian hot tubs for hire.

Price: tent, caravan and motor home pitches from £9.50 to £17.

The best... PLACES TO STAY

SELF-CATERING

Tom's Barn and Douglas's Barn

**Parwich, Orchard Farm, Parwich,
Ashbourne DE6 1QB
☎ 01335 390519
www.tomsbarn.co.uk**

Two ex-cowsheds imaginatively converted
to romantic retreats for couples, offering
luxury in a tranquil village setting. Tom's
Barn has a galleried bedroom, while
Douglas's barn has an extra-long king size
bed. Welcoming 'goodie bag' of local foods
and herbs on arrival.

Price: from £275 to £510 per week.

Church Farm Holiday Cottages

**Alsop-en-le-Dale, Ashbourne DE6 1QP
☎ 01335 390216
www.churchfarmholidaycottages.co.uk**

Freshly baked cakes await visitors on
arrival at Pinster or Winnets Cottages,
converted from a stone barn at Grade II
listed Church Farm, which specialises in
rare breed Gloucester cattle and pigs.

Price: from £240 per week.

Dovedale Cottages

**Church Farm Stanshope,
Ashbourne DE6 2AD
☎ 01335 310243
www.dovedalecottages.co.uk**

A selection of four luxury cottages, some
on the owners' organic farm in Dovedale.
The Ancestral Barn has beamed ceilings,
while 16th-century Church Farm Cottage
once formed part of the main farmhouse.
Dale Bottom Cottage is in Dovedale, while
Lilac Cottage is near Hartington.

Price: from £392 per week.

Rushley Farm

**Ilam, Ashbourne DE6 2BA
☎ 01538 398205
www.cottageguide.co.uk/theorchards**

Live life in the slow lane in this self-
catering cottage that sleeps six, has a
dining room, cosy log fire and boasts
panoramic views of Dovedale. Ideal base
for walking. Visitors can buy local foods
and the owners' own produce from the
farm.

Price: from £375 per week.

HOSTEL

YHA Ilam Hall

**Ilam, Ashbourne DE6 2AZ
☎ 0845 371 9023
www.yha.org.uk**

Ilam Hall Youth Hostel is a Victorian gothic
manor house owned by the National Trust,
boasting 84 acres of country park on the
banks of the River Manifold.

Price: from £7.50 to £9.95 pppn.

YHA Hartington Hall

**Hall Bank, Hartington,
Near Buxton SK17 0AT
☎ 0845 371 9740
www.yha.org.uk**

Magnificent manor house dating back
to 1611, with oak panelling, stove fires,
squishy sofas and a warm welcome.
Refurbished to a high standard, with
single, two-bedded rooms, en-suite family
bunk rooms and 'The Roost' for couples,
with galleried bedroom, lounge and diner.
Fully licensed bar and the award-winning
Eliza's restaurant.

Price: from £10.50 to £13.95 pppn.

The best of... THE WHITE PEAK

THE SOFTER, MORE FEMININE FACE OF THE PEAK IS REPRESENTED BY THE LIMESTONE WHITE PEAK, WHERE GLORIOUS DALES SUCH AS DOVEDALE, WYE DALE AND CHEE DALE DISSECT THE PLATEAU, WHICH IS COVERED IN A NETWORK OF DRYSTONE WALLS SEPARATING LOVELY VILLAGES LIKE TISSINGTON AND LITTON. THIS IS ALSO WHERE THE ANCIENT FOLK CUSTOM OF WELL DRESSING TAKES PLACE.

A weir in the River Wye in Water cum Jolly Dale, with the popular climbing crag of Rubicon Wall in the background.

Top: The winding Wye in Chee Dale.
Middle: Buxton's 2008 well dressing celebrating Poole's Cavern – the first Wonder of the Peak. Bottom: Daffodils decorate the village pond at Tissington in the spring.

Top: St Lawrence's Church, Eyam, has many reminders of the Plague. (The Saxon Cross can be seen between the two dipper yews in the centre.) Middle: The Cable Cars at Matlock Bath, with the ruins of Riber Castle in the background. Bottom: Patterns of drystone walls near Litton.

Top: A family Wye a boating trip on the River Derwent at Matlock Bath.
Middle: The famous Stepping Stones in Dovedale. Bottom: Looking down on the Wye in Cressbrook Dale, with Cressbrook Hall in the background.

The best... FOOD AND DRINK

Hartington's name is synonymous with Stilton, but in this area you'll also find flavoursome organic meat and multi-award winning sausages and bacon. Dine in everything from restaurants and gastro pubs, or an excellent selection of tea rooms serving local produce, and don't overlook the traditional pubs offering locally brewed ales.

⏩ Staying in

The scenic Dovedale and Manifold Valleys are among the richest local landscapes when it comes to locally produced food, particularly meat and cheese. In Hartington, you'll find the award-winning, Soil Association registered **Lower Hurst Farm** (SK17 0HJ; ☎01298 84900), producers of quality organic beef and lamb. Fresh and frozen meat is available from the farm shop, or delivered direct to your door. For speciality cheese, head for the **Old Cheese Shop** at Hartington (Stonewell Lane SK17 0AH; ☎01298 84935), which stocks more than 30 British cheeses, including regional favourites such as Buxton Blue, Dovedale and Stilton.

Rare breed, traditionally reared meat is used to make multi award winning sausages and bacon at the **Peak District Farm Shop** at Stanshope (DE4 2AD; ☎01335 310436), where high welfare and husbandry standards for both animals and the environment are a top priority. Meat can be bought fresh or blast-frozen. Another quality outlet for top class, locally reared meat is **White Peak Farm Butchery** in Tissington (The Old Slaughterhouse, Chapel Lane DE6 1RA; ☎01335 390300), where sausages in various flavours, including red onion and sage and venison, and bacon are specialities, along with beef, lamb, pork and poultry.

EATING OUT

RESTAURANT

The Izaak Walton Hotel
**Dovedale, Ashbourne,
Derbyshire DE6 2AY
☎ 01335 350555
www.izaakwaltonhotel.com**

Enjoying breathtaking views across Dovedale, the Haddon Restaurant offers creative takes on classic dishes, complemented by fine wines. Starters range from roast wild mushroom soup to ham hock terrine, while mains include pan-roasted White Peak chicken and fillet of Derbyshire beef. Lunch costs £23.95, dinner from £35.

Eliza's Restaurant and Eliza's Cafe Bar
**YHA Hartington, Hall Bank, Hartington, Near Buxton SK17 0AT
☎ 0845 371 9740
www.yha.org.uk**

An award-winning restaurant and café bar idyllically situated in a magnificent 17th-century manor house standing in extensive grounds. The emphasis is on locally sourced produce and recipes, freshly prepared in-house to create wholesome and hearty meals.

GASTRO PUB

The George
**Alstonefield, Ashbourne DE6 2FX
☎ 01335 310205
www.thegeorgeatalstonefield.com**

Unspoilt, family-run pub serving home-made, locally sourced food on a menu which changes according to what is in season. Lunchtime options include sandwiches, pie of the day, beer-battered haddock and chips and specials. A typical evening menu might include Ashbourne mushroom and Stilton wellington, or a trio of White Peak sausages. Main course averages £8.50.

The Bluebell Inn and Restaurant
**Buxton Road, Tissington DE6 1NH
☎ 01335 350317
www.bluebelltissington.co.uk**

Home-made dishes using locally sourced produce such as beef, pork, lamb, eggs, milk and ice cream feature on this multi-award-winning pub's wide-ranging menu. Diners can choose from around 40 main courses, which include options for those on gluten-free, wheat-free, dairy-free and vegetarian diets.

TEA ROOMS

Ilam Hall Tea Room
**Ilam Park, Ilam, Ashbourne DE6 2AZ
☎01335 350245**

A welcoming atmosphere, and value-for-money, traditional home-cooking can be enjoyed at this unlicensed, self-service tea room in the Manifold Valley, part of the National Trust's South Peak Estate. Open weekends during the winter, seven days a week during July and August.

The Hayloft Tea Room
**Sennilow Farm, Church Street, Hartington, near Buxton SK17 0AW
☎ 01298 84358
www.hartingtonhayloft.co.uk**

Tasty, value-for-money fare served with a warm welcome in a restored limestone barn with many original features. Options include filled rolls, ploughman's lunches, toasted sandwiches, local oatcakes, home-made cakes, scones and cream teas. Daily specials and particular stress on using local produce where possible.

EATING OUT

Beresford Tea Rooms
Market Place, Hartington SK17 0AL
☎ 01298 84235

Sit down for a sandwich, bowl of soup or scone with clotted cream when you buy your stamps, for this tea rooms shares its space with Hartington's award-winning Post Office. Other specialities include filled Derbyshire oatcakes, home-made cakes and warming hot pot in winter. Open every day in the summer, closed Wednesdays in winter.

The Old Coach House Tea Rooms
Tissington, Ashbourne DE6 1RA
☎ 01335 350501
www.tissington-hall.com

Morning coffee, hot and cold lunches and afternoon tea served in this award-winning tea room, part of the picturesque estate village of Tissington. Outdoor tables and seating is available, and large parties welcome. Open every day from March to October, Thursday to Sunday in winter.

Drinking

Arbor Light and Hartington Bitter are among the ales brewed at **Whim Ales** of Hartington (SK17 0AX; ☎01298 84991), situated in outbuildings at Whim Farm. Whim's beers can be found in up to 70 outlets, including the brewery's tied house, the **Wilkes Head** at Leek. Look out also for one-off, occasional and seasonal brews. Whim Ales are also served in the **Charles Cotton Hotel**, Market Place, Hartington (SK17 0AL; ☎01298 84229), which has an annual beer festival in October and serves an ever-changing selection of real ales in its cosy bar. Meals, prepared using local produce where possible, are available all day in the bar and tea room and in the restaurant in the evenings and at Sunday lunchtime. Also in the Market Place at Hartington is the **Devonshire Arms** (SK17 0AL; ☎01298 84232), a historic 17th-century coaching inn which has real fires and serves a range of real ales, including guest beers. Snacks and meals are available at lunchtime, with the emphasis on à la carte dining in the evening.

In Parwich, the village pub, **The Sycamore Inn** (DE6 1QL; ☎01335 390212), is much more than a place to enjoy a drink and a meal, because it also houses the village shop, where locals and tourists can buy everything from free range eggs to toiletries. Everything from light bites to full meals are served at both lunchtime and in the evening, and the shop's opening hours dovetail neatly with those of the pub. The Sycamore was recently a regular haunt for fans of Parwich actor Tom Chambers of BBC television's *Holby City*, who wowed audiences by winning the 2008 series of the BBC's *Strictly Come Dancing*. Locals flocked there to watch him strut his stuff on the dance floor.

Home-cooked food made from local produce plus real ales and guest beers keep customers content at the **Coach & Horses** at Fenny Bentley (DE6 1LB; ☎01335 350246), a traditional 16th-century coaching inn with flagged floors, very low beams and coal and log-burning fires. Outside drinking areas are a boon in summer, when even more guest beers are served. Sunday lunch featuring prime local produce, including Derbyshire beef, is a particular speciality at the **Dog & Partridge** at Thorpe (DE6 2AT; ☎01335 350235). Food is served throughout the week, both at lunchtime and the evening, plus a selection of real ales, wines, lagers and spirits. Former home to the 'Official World Toe Wrestling Championships', **Ye Olde Royal Oak** at Wetton (DE6 2AF; ☎01335 310336) is also known for its real ales, malt whiskies and meals incorporating local food.

Both real ales and guest beers are on the menu with home-cooked food using locally sourced food where possible at **The Watts Russell Arms** in the hamlet of Hopedale, near Alstonefield (DE6 2GD; ☎01335 310126). Good food and beers are also staples at the 16th-century, limestone-built **Packhorse Inn**, Crowdecote (SK17 0DB; ☎01298 83618). For a traditional pub packed with personality, head for **The Quiet Woman** at Earl Sterndale (SK17 0BU; ☎01298 83211), where you'll discover an unspoilt local hostelry with a real fire, low beams, real ales (including examples from Leek Brewery) and old-fashioned pub games, including dominoes. (The name, incidentally, refers to the pub sign which depicts a headless woman.)

ⓘ Visitor Information

Tourist information centres: Ashbourne Tourist Information Centre, 13 Market Place, Ashbourne, Derbyshire DE6 1EU, ☎01335 343666, www.visitpeakdistrict.com; Manifold Valley Visitor Centre, Hulme End, near Buxton, Derbyshire SK17 0EZ, ☎01298 846679, www.enjoystaffordshire.com, open Easter to Oct.

Hospital: St Oswald's Hospital, Belle Vue Road, Ashbourne, ☎01335 342121.

Doctor: The Surgery, Waterfall Lane, Waterhouses ST10 3HT, ☎01538 308207, or as Ashbourne.

Supermarkets: Sainsbury's, Coopers Mill, Compton, Ashbourne, ☎01335 347601; Midlands Co-op, Dig Street, Ashbourne, ☎01335 346274; Somerfield, Shawcroft Centre, Dig Street, Ashbourne, ☎01335 342645.

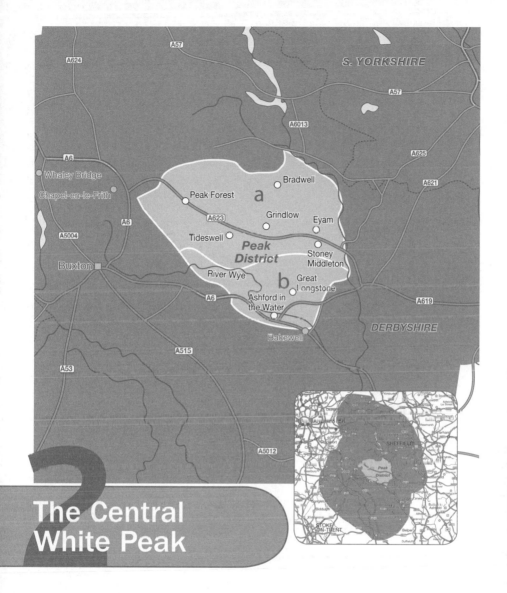

2 The Central White Peak

a. Tideswell and Eyam

b. Wye Dale, Ashford in the Water and the Longstones

Unmissable highlights

01 Enjoy the view from Monsal Head, and get a bird's eye view of the Monsal Viaduct and the Wye, p. 133

02 Follow the Plague Trail in Eyam, scene of the heroic quarantine during the terrible 17th-century 'visitation' of the Plague, p. 121

03 Go back in time at Eyam Hall, home of the Wright family for 300 years, p. 120

04 Stroll along the Monsal Trail, through some of the most stunning riverside scenery in Britain, p. 134

05 Soar with the birds from the Gliding Club on Hucklow Edge with the Derbyshire and Lancashire Gliding Club, p. 124

06 Tuck into some fish 'n' chips made in the former tollhouse at Stoney Middleton, p. 135

07 Have a pint and enjoy the view at the Barrel, Bretton, one of the highest and oldest pubs in the Peak, p. 131

08 Get to know the donkeys at the Freshfields Donkey Village, near Peak Forest, p. 126

09 Admire the well dressings at Tideswell, Eyam, Litton, Stoney Middleton and Foolow, p. 123

10 Enjoy the serenity of 'the Cathedral of the Peak', by visiting the wonderfully light and airy Tideswell parish church, p. 124

THE CENTRAL WHITE PEAK

The central White Peak is that great cracked uplift of limestone lying between the Hope and Wye valleys. It is centred on the ancient villages of Tideswell, Eyam, Ashford in the Water and Hucklow, and includes the prominent, landmark ridges of Longstone and Hucklow Edges, which run west to east across the landscape.

The plateau is split by several beautiful and steep-sided dales, which echo the ridges by generally running west to east, as the rivers which cut them at the end of the last Ice Age run off the Pennine watershed over to the west. These dales, followed faithfully by footpaths such as the Monsal Trail, include the series threaded by the River Wye, which from Ashford is named successively as Monsal Dale, the delightfully named Water-cum-Jolly Dale, Cressbrook Dale, Miller's Dale, Chee Dale and finally Ashwood and Wye Dale as it approaches Buxton. Further north lies the mini-Cheddar gorge of Middleton Dale, and Abney Clough, which borders on the gritstone country below heather-covered Eyam Moor.

On the plateau above the dales, the abiding feature which most visitors coming from the south remark on is the mile after mile of painstakingly constructed drystone walls which separate the emerald green fields. Most of these were constructed during the 18th and 19th centuries as a result of the Enclosure Movement, and they are an iconic feature of the Central White Peak landscape.

TIDESWELL AND EYAM

Tideswell and Eyam are two of the most popular villages in the Peak District for visitors, both redolent of history and famous for their annual summer well dressings. **Tideswell's** stately parish church of St John the Baptist is known as 'the Cathedral of the Peak' and was described by no less an authority than Sir John Betjeman as '*a grand and inspiring church of the 14th* century'. The Perpendicular tower with its turrets and pinnacles watches over most views of the bustling village, and inside, the flowing tracery in the clear windows of the chancel give it a wonderfully light and airy feel – just like a cathedral, in fact. Tideswell's well dressings are among the finest in the Peak, usually taking place at the end of June. The themes are usually ecclesiastical, and a series depicting English cathedrals is particularly well remembered for its intricate detail and artistic excellence. The Shimwell family of Tideswell were acknowledged experts, and reintroduced the ancient skills to many other Peakland villages. Other villages in the area which have well dressings include Litton and Foolow, which has a charming village green, complete with medieval cross and duck pond.

It was the tragic 'visitation' of the Plague in 1665–6 which really put **Eyam** (pronounced 'Eem') on the map, and thousands of visitors still come to marvel at the unselfish sacrifice made by the villagers, as they quarantined themselves in an attempt to halt the spread of the dread disease to neighbouring villages (see Local Legends). There are touching memorials on cottages throughout the village and in the parish church to those who died, and the excellent Eyam Museum tells the story of the terrible events of three centuries ago.

Great and Little Hucklow are twin villages tucked beneath the escarpment of Hucklow Edge, where on days when there are good thermals, the gliders of the Derbyshire and Lancashire Gliding Club soar from one of the most spectacular launch sites in the country.

WHAT TO SEE AND DO

A wander around the 'Plague village' of **Eyam** is a humbling experience, as you pass so many cottages which carry a plaque showing just how many villagers died there during the terrible Plague years. Opposite the tiny village green in the centre of Eyam, with its restored wooden stocks for former wrongdoers, stands the Jacobean **Eyam Hall**, the home of the Wright family for over three centuries. Guided tours are available throughout the summer months, and don't miss the recently restored knot garden and the tapestries in the upstairs rooms.

EYAM HALL: Eyam, Hope Valley, Derbyshire S32 5QW; ☎01433 631976; www.eyam hall.co.uk. Entry: adult £6.25, concessions £5.75, children £4; open 12 noon–4pm, Weds, Thurs, Sun and Bank Holiday Mondays, 25 Mar to 4 May; group bookings only in Apr, May and Oct.

Eyam Hall

Eyam Plague

The self-imposed quarantine by the villagers of Eyam after the Plague struck in the mid-17th century has been called '*the greatest epic in the annals of rural life*'. In a 14-month period between September 1665 and November 1666, 259 Eyam villagers died from the dread disease, and some whole families were wiped out. Many cottages in the village are marked with plaques recording the names of the victims. This appalling death rate was made even higher than it might have been because the residents unselfishly decided to quarantine themselves inside the village boundaries in order that the disease would not spread. Neighbouring parishes and the Earl of Devonshire left supplies for them at special points on the village boundary, which can still be seen.

This astonishing act of selfless heroism was led by the rector, the Reverend William Mompesson, and his non-Conformist predecessor, Thomas Stanley. They saw what could happen if the disease was allowed to spread, and in another effort to try to contain it within the village, they held all their church services out-of-doors in a little rocky hollow beneath the village known as Cucklett Delph. A commemorative service is still held there every year, coinciding with the well dressings.

There were many tragic stories from the Plague years in Eyam, but perhaps none as touching as that of the Hancock family from Riley House Farm on the eastern outskirts of the village. Within the space of a week, Mrs Hancock buried her husband, three sons and three daughters as they each in turn succumbed to the disease. Their poignantly simple graves can still be seen at Riley Graves (National Trust) on the Grindleford road.

Cottages in Eyam

The award-winning **Eyam Museum**, just out of the village centre on Hawkhill Road, graphically tells the story of the Plague years, through vivid descriptions and displays. Set up by the villagers themselves, it's the perfect place to start your visit to Eyam, and hear the tragic story of the 'Plague village'.

EYAM MUSEUM: Hawkhill Road, Eyam, Hope Valley, Derbyshire S32 5QP; ☎01433 631371; www.cressbrook. co.uk/eyam/museum. Entry: adults £1.75, concessions and children £1.25; open daily 10am–4.30pm, Mar to Nov; closed Mon except Bank Holidays.

You can also descend from the village centre into **Cucklett Delph**, in the dale below the village, to see where the villagers worshipped in the open air in another bid to halt the spread of the Plague. A short walk outside the village off the minor road leading east towards Grindleford are the evocative **Riley Graves** grouped inside a walled enclosure (see above).

Fit and competent walkers may want to try to find the Bronze Age **Wet Withins Stone Circle**, on Eyam Moor, reached from the minor Sir William Hill road, but it is notoriously difficult to locate in the often waist-deep heather. There are numerous other burial mounds and clearance cairns nearby, and the heather when in bloom in the late summer is some of the finest in the Peak.

It is an easy walk downhill from the village of **Tideswell** to enter **Tideswell Dale**, once the site of ugly basalt extraction works, but now a nature reserve, thanks to an early effort at restoration by the National Park authority.

Well dressings

Perhaps the most famous and enduring of the Peak District's customs is that of well dressing, which was probably originally a pagan ritual, when gifts and oblations were strewn around springs or wells to give thanks to the gods for the life-giving gift of water. This would have been especially important to villagers on the fast-draining limestone White Peak plateau. The custom was later adopted by Christianity, and the first recorded examples took place at Tissington in 1758. Every summer, each village takes it in turn to decorate their wells or springs with intricate floral icons, which nowadays often have a Christian or biblical theme and coincide with the village Wakes Week. Some villages, such as Tideswell, have adopted an ecclesiastical theme such as cathedrals, while others, such as Youlgrave and Ashford in the Water, adopt modern themes or anniversaries.

More village well dressings take place in the Peak today than ever before, as incomers are caught up with and intrigued by this unique example of folk art. It is a real community effort, as many villagers are involved in the process of creating the beautiful dressings.

The design of the dressing is first traced onto paper. Then the wooden frame is soaked for several days in the local river or stream, to ensure it retains moisture. Next, the wet clay is 'puddled', usually by trampling by foot, to make it pliable, and pressed firmly into place in the boards and smoothed over to create a good, even surface. Now the paper template of the design is 'pricked out' onto the wet clay, using a pin wheel or other sharp instrument,

A detailed view of a well dressing in Tissington

and the design is outlined in the clay, using black alder cones, seeds or wool. Then villagers scour the surrounding countryside for the seeds, flower petals, lichens and other natural materials for colouring-in the dressing. But the real art of well dressing is in the 'petalling', as villagers carefully press down overlapping flower petals, mosses, lichens, grass and rushes to colour in and shade the design. Finally, the boards are erected near the village well, spring or pump, roped off and decorated, to stand for about a week and be admired by thousands of visitors.

The hamlet of **Wheston**, north west of Tideswell, contains many fine 16th and 17th-century houses, but is most famous for its almost complete 15th-century village cross, which depicts the crucifixion. Another glorious walk is along wooded **Abney Clough**, beneath Eyam Moor, or along quarry-scarred **Longstone Edge**, which has commanding views across the White Peak.

DERBYSHIRE AND LANCASHIRE GLIDING CLUB: Camphill, Great Hucklow, Buxton, Derbyshire SK17 8RQ; ☎01298 871270; www.dlgc.org.uk. Entry: visits and flights by appointment only.

The really adventurous might like to try a trial flight at the **Derbyshire and Lancashire Gliding Club**, which is based at Camphill, on the western end of the 416m/1,360ft escarpment of Hucklow Edge. This spectacular launch site overlooks Bradwell and the Hope Valley, and must be one of the most spectacular in the country. You get an awe-inspiring, birds-eye view of the Peak from the cockpit one of the club's winch-launched gliders. The club has been operating from Camphill since 1936.

DERBYSHIRE FLYING CENTRE: Cliffside, Church Street, Tideswell, Debyshire SK17 8PE; ☎0845 108 1577; www.d-f-c.co.uk.

Alternatively, try the **Derbyshire Flying Centre**, established in 1987 by Stephen Hudson, a member of the British Hang Gliding team. It has negotiated access to training hills for hang gliding, paragliding and paramotoring throughout the National Park, and has access to free-flying hill sites covering all wind directions and all pilot abilities. Participants usually use a classroom opposite the Shoulder of Mutton Pub, next to Lyndal House in Church Street, Bradwell.

☂ Wet weather

Both village churches at **Eyam** and **Tideswell** are worth a visit at any time, but perhaps particularly on a wet day. In Tideswell's parish church of **St John the Baptist** – which has been dubbed 'the Cathedral of the Peak' – look out for the fine carved woodwork executed by the local Hunstone family, and the fine brass in the chancel floor of Robert Purseglove, who was born in Tideswell and founded the local grammar school, and went on to become a Protestant bishop under Edward VI and a Roman Catholic one under Mary Tudor.

A register of the 259 names of those who died in the Plague years is kept in the **Parish Church of St Lawrence** at Eyam. You can also see the chair allegedly belonging to William Mompesson, the rector who, in partnership with his non-conformist predecessor William Stanley, suggested that the villagers should quarantine themselves to stop the disease from spreading. The truncated Saxon cross in Eyam

St Lawrence, Eyam

LOCAL KNOWLEDGE

David James is chief executive of Visit Peak District & Derbyshire. A keen sportsman, he coaches the Tideswell under-10s football team and is a qualified FA Coach. Married to Melanie, who runs two self-catering cottages in Tideswell, the couple have two children.

Best thing about living in the Peak District: Breathtaking views, dramatic landscapes, historic buildings, great places to eat and a variety of events, such as Buxton Festival.

Best kept secret: Arbor Low. No one knows what the stones are for, but someone made a massive effort to put them there.

Favourite haunt: Chatsworth House and grounds. No matter how many times you go, they take your breath away.

Things to do on a rainy day: A visit to one of the many sports centres for a swim or game of badminton, or to National Trust properties such as Calke Abbey, Kedleston Hall and Hardwick Hall.

Favourite activity: Cycling, essentially off road. Hire a bike from Parsley Hay, Derwent Reservoir or Middleton Top and enjoy stunning countryside without seeing a car.

Quirkiest attraction: Crich Tramway Village and its vintage trams. Visiting the Heights of Abraham via cable car, then enjoying the caves and other family activities at the summit.

Favourite restaurant: The Devonshire Arms, Beeley for pub/bistro meals. For more formal dining, the East Lodge Hotel, Rowsley, the dining room, Ashbourne, or Buckingham's, Chesterfield.

Favourite takeaway: Little India, Stoney Middleton. Excellent food and the friendliest staff on the planet.

Favourite pub: The Chequers Inn at Froggatt Edge. Award-winning bistro meals, cosy log fire and an exceptionally warm welcome.

Secret tip for lunch: The award-winning Walnut Club, Hathersage. Fabulous organic food, limited menu but exceptional value.

David James
Chief Executive

churchyard, one of the finest in the Peak, is close to the tabletop grave of Elizabeth Mompesson, wife of the rector at the time of the Plague, who tragically died at the height of the outbreak. The **Eyam Museum** in Hawkhill Road is another good wet weather alternative.

What to do with children

The children will love the **Freshfields Donkey Village**, near the village of Peak Forest, founded by a large group of well-known actors and actresses, including Dame Judi Dench, Lord Richard Attenborough and June Brown (Dot Cotton in television's *EastEnders*) who wanted to build a sanctuary for abused and neglected donkeys. Run by the Michael Elliot Trust, the sanctuary welcomes visitors, and you can wander through the fields and meet the donkeys personally.

FRESHFIELDS DONKEY VILLAGE: Michael Elliot Trust, Peak Forest, Derbyshire SK17 8EE; ☎01298 79775; www.donkey-village.org.uk. Entry: donations welcome; open daily 12pm–4.30pm, 21 Mar to 1 Nov, weekends 1 Nov to 26 Dec.

CELEBRITY CONNECTIONS

Veteran actress **June Brown**, most famous for her role as Dot Cotton in the BBC television soap opera *EastEnders*, lives in Surrey, but has a long-standing link with the Peak District. The Old Vic-trained actress has been both president and patron of Freshfields Donkey Sanctuary in Peak Forest for more than a decade, and frequently spends weekends with its four-legged residents and the special needs children who benefit from the charity's work.

Freshfields was set up by former actor, writer and producer John Stirling and his wife Annie, an ex-dancer, costume designer and dressmaker, as a refuge for abused and neglected donkeys. At the time, the couple lived in a Victorian flat in Buxton, and their first two equine friends took up residence in their garage. Since then, the charity has grown from strength to strength and over the years has developed as a therapy centre where both children and donkeys benefit.

Actress **Jane Lapotaire** was its first president, closely followed by June, who has remained involved ever since. Other high-profile patrons include **Edward Fox** (vice president), **Dame Judi Dench**, **Sir Bobby Charlton**, **Sir Richard Attenborough**, **Lord David Puttnam**, **Mark Knopfler**, **Chris de Burgh**, **Lesley Garrett**, **Martin Shaw**, **Jenny Seagrove** and **Hayley Mills**.

The best... PLACES TO STAY

INN

The Queen Anne Inn

Great Hucklow, Buxton SK17 8RF
☎ 01298 871246

Traditional country free-house dating from 1621, reputed to be haunted by a previous landlord. Roaring log fires and comprehensive range of cask ales. Comfortable en-suite bedrooms and bar food based on local produce.

Price: B&B £45 single/£65 double.

FARMSTAY

Hall Farm House

Litton, Buxton SK17 8QP
☎ 01298 872172
www.users.waitrose.com/~jfscott

Spacious Victorian house offering bed and breakfast accommodation and a self-catering cottage in its grounds. Tasty breakfasts, made largely with local produce, and spacious garden which guests are welcome to use.

Price: From £25 to £28 pppn. Self-catering from £275 to £500 per week.

B&B

Bretton Cottage

Bretton, Eyam S32 5QD
☎ 01433 631076
www.peakholidayhomes.com

Former 17th-century farmhouse with spacious en-suite rooms furnished and equipped to a high standard, and panoramic views across excellent walking country. Predominantly organic breakfast menu using local produce.

Price: from £60 for a single; from £80 to £92 for a double.

Cressbrook Hall

Cressbrook, Buxton SK17 8SY
☎ 01298 871289
www.cressbrookhall.co.uk

Designed by Thomas Johnson of Lichfield in 1835, Cressbrook Hall stands in a magnificent setting, overlooking a limestone gorge created by the River Wye. Set in 23 acres, both bed and breakfast and self-catering accommodation in limestone cottages are available.

Price: B&B from £52.50 for a double/twin; from £70 for a family.

SELF-CATERING

Croft View Cottage

Foolow, near Eyam S32 5QA
☎ 01433 630711
www.croftviewcottage.co.uk

Cosy, well-furnished and well-equipped 'home from home', with log burning stove, sitting room with beams and large cottage garden. Cot, high chair, bed rail and steam steriliser for young families.

Price: from £300 to £500 per week.

The best... PLACES TO STAY

Candlelight Cottage

**c/o Lower Barn, Foolow,
Eyam S32 5QR; ☎ 01433 631528
www.candlelightcottage.co.uk**

Romantic, oak-beamed cottage offering a tranquil retreat in the traditional Peak village of Litton, near Tideswell. Recently renovated and tastefully furnished, with leather sofas, luxury bathroom and Aga.

Price: from £347 to £560 per week.

Markeygate Cottages and Barn

**Markeygate House, Bank Square,
Tideswell SK17 8NT
☎ 01298 871260
www.markeygatecottages.co.uk**

Grade II listed and individually designed, Markeygate Cottages boast modern amenities, original oak beams, log fires, private courtyard and plenty of garage space for storage. Markeygate Barn has two bedrooms.

Price: from £210 to £400 per week.

HOSTEL

YHA Eyam

**Hawkhill Road, Eyam S32 5QP
☎ 0845 3719738
www.yha.org.uk**

Victorian folly which resembles a tiny, turreted castle, situated on a hillside overlooking the famous Plague village of Eyam.

Price: from £13.50 to £17.95 pppn.

The best... FOOD AND DRINK

Quality dairy produce and meat, scrumptious pork pies, traditional Wakes Cakes and handmade biscuits are just some of the treats in store in this mainly agricultural area of the White Peak. You can also dine out in a variety of local eating places, and enjoy local brews in welcoming pubs.

CELEBRITY CONNECTIONS

Television presenter **Julia Bradbury's** schoolgirl passion for the Peak District, nurtured by her Tideswell-born father, has matured into an abiding love which is reflected in her role as president of the Peak District & South Yorkshire branch of the Campaign to Protect Rural England (CPRE). Julia, now host of BBC 1's prime-time consumer show *Watchdog* and presenter of BBC Four's *Wainwright's Walks* and *Railway Walks*, learned to love the area as a teenager while attending King Edward VII School in Sheffield.

Julia's father Michael took her on regular outings to the Peak District, especially to the White Peak. She fondly recalls walks along the Monsal Trail and its striking former railway viaduct to Monsal Dale, tickling her first trout at Shatton, and she lists Cressbrook and Monks Dale among her favourite places. Julia describes the Peak District and South Yorkshire landscape as very close to her heart, and as president of the local CPRE branch is working to encourage more people to get out and enjoy it, experience its beauty and support efforts to safeguard it in the future.

Julia's love of the limelight first came to the fore as a child, when she went to acting classes, and appeared in the stage production *Peter Pan* at Sheffield's Crucible Theatre, starring Joanne Whalley and Paula Wilcox. After leaving school at 16, she moved to London, and after a short spell working in the family fashion business, she realised her ambition to work in television. She has since worked on programmes such as the BBC's *Top Gear*, *Royal Ascot* and *Kill It, Cook It, Eat It* and ITV's *Wish You Were Here*, as well as co-presenting the launch of Channel Five.

▶ Staying in

For a cornucopia of locally produced and home-made food, call at **Tindall's Bakery & Delicatessen** in Tideswell (Commercial Road SK17 8NU; ☎01298 871351). Everything from bread and cakes to original pork pies and home-cooked local meats, plus delicious sandwiches made to order and the area's famous Wakes Cakes, is on offer here. Quality dairy produce, including milk, cream, free range eggs, butter, ice cream and farmhouse yoghurts, plus English and continental cheeses, spring water, fruit juices and bread, are available from **Peak District Dairy** in Tideswell. As well as running a business from Heathy Grange Farm (Sherwood Road SK17 8PJ; ☎01298 871786), the dairy has a farm shop/café in the centre of Tideswell village (Queen Street SK17 8JT; ☎01298 873100), where customers can sample snacks, drinks and award-winning ice cream.

Family butchers **G B Siddall** of Eyam (The Square S32 5RV; ☎01433 631611) supply a range of quality meat including beef, pork, lamb and chicken, plus home-made pork pies and cooked meats. Handmade biscuits, baked to mainly traditional recipes using locally sourced and organic ingredients where possible, are made by award-winning **Just Biscuits** (Eyam Hall Craft Centre, Eyam S32 5QW; ☎01433 621319; www.justbiscuits.co.uk) and are sold at farmers' markets, in local shops and their own shop, and online.

 EATING OUT

RESTAURANT

The Stables at Eyam
Eyam Hall, Eyam S32 5QW
☎ **01433 630505**
www.stablesateyam.co.uk

First floor restaurant overlooking the gardens of Eyam Hall towards the village's St Lawrence's church and world famous Plague Cottages. Relaxed, friendly atmosphere created with candles, wooden beams and stone walls. Lunch (mains cost from £4.75) and dinner (mains cost from £8.50) served with wines from around the world.

GASTRO PUB

The Devonshire Arms
Peak Forest, near Buxton SK17 8EJ
☎ **01298 23875**
www.devarms.com

Revamped coaching inn offering fresh, locally produced food on menus that change regularly, plus a choice of traditional Sunday roasts. Sample starters (from £3.50) include stir-fried tiger prawns and sautéed mushrooms, while mains (from £8.50) range from prime fillet steak and rump of lamb to halibut and tuna steak. Accommodation available.

EATING OUT

CAFÉ

Vanilla Kitchen
Queen Street, Tideswell SK17 8PF
☎ **01298 871519**
www.vanillakitchen.co.uk

Multi-award winning, licensed café serving organic, Fairtrade coffee, breakfasts, lunches and home-baked cakes. Emphasis on local, seasonal ingredients. Families welcome: there is a children's table and baby changing facilities. Special events include a supper club and children's singing mornings. Woodhouse Cottage self-catering accommodation also available, from £220 per week.

TEA ROOM

Eyam Tea Rooms & Bistro
The Square, Eyam, Derbyshire S32 5RB
☎ **01433 631274**

These long-established tea rooms specialise in home-made cakes, gateaux, scones and savoury snacks, plus a cooked lunch menu, including vegetarian options. It will open by request for private parties and also holds regular gourmet and theme nights.

Drinking

Real ales, including constantly changing guest beers, plus good food, ranging from sandwiches to meals, are all on offer at the historic **Queen Anne Inn** in Great Hucklow (SK17 8RF; ☎01298 871246). Another traditional pub featuring a range of cask ales, fine malt whiskies and freshly cooked food based on locally sourced, seasonal produce is **The Barrel Inn** at Bretton (S32 5QD; ☎01433 630856), claimed to be the highest and one of the oldest pubs in Derbyshire. Believed to be the fifth oldest pub and in England, **Ye Olde Bulls Head** in Little Hucklow (SK17 8RT; ☎01298 871097) claims to date back to the 12th century. It is well worth a visit to enjoy the ambience of its small downstairs rooms with open fires, collections of trinkets, tankards and mining equipment and 'the cave' up in the roof. This unspoilt pub is also known for its good selection of beers and home-cooked food.

Ghosts, including two young girls and an ex-landlady, are said to haunt the **Miners Arms**, a 17th-century inn and restaurant in the famous Plague village of Eyam (S32 5RG; ☎01433 630853). Both pub and restaurant meals are available at lunchtime and in the evening. Another 'ghostly' hostelry is **The Moon Inn** at nearby Stoney Middleton (S32 4TL; ☎01433 630203), where a Scottish pedlar was murdered 250 years ago by rival local pedlars, while the landlord turned a blind eye. Today's pub is far more hospitable! Family-owned and with a welcoming atmosphere, the **Bulls Head Inn** (S32 5QR; ☎01433 630873) lies in the centre of the picturesque village of Foolow and has flagged floors, roaring open fires and an inglenook fireplace in its oak-panelled restaurant. Fresh home-cooked food from local suppliers is complemented by traditional cask beers, malt whiskies and wines from around the world.

Home-prepared food and quality beers are also features at the 17th-century **George Hotel** in Tideswell (SK17 8NU; ☎01298 871382), where there is a garden and children and dogs are welcome. Good food and well-kept cask ales are served in a historic, cosy, traditional setting at the **Red Lion** in Litton (SK17 8QU; ☎01298 871458). For substantial meals in a comfortable, family-run pub, visit the **Anglers Rest** at Millers Dale (SK17 8SN; ☎01298 871323), which has welcoming coal fires and a good range of cask ales and draught lagers, plus a pool table and dart board. Much of the home-prepared food is locally sourced, and visitors with hearty appetites will appreciate 'Pie Night' each Thursday.

Situated in the small community of Sparrowpit on the main A623 Chesterfield to Manchester road, is the **Wanted Inn and Toll Bar House** (SK17 8ET; ☎01298 812862), which boasts a long, eventful, and sometimes bloody, history. When two runaway lovers were murdered at the nearby Winnats Pass on the approach to Castleton in the 18th century, their riderless horses are said to have galloped to Sparrowpit, stopping outside the inn. Almost a century later, a nearby field was the venue for a bloody prize fight that drew spectators from all over the country. These days life is far more civilised, thanks to the inn's selection of real ales, lagers, spirits and wines and home-cooked food at lunch and dinner.

ⓘ Visitor Information

Tourist information centre: Bakewell Visitor Centre, The Old Market Hall, Bridge Street, Bakewell, Derbyshire DE45 1DS, ☎01629 816558, www.peakdistrict.gov.uk, open daily.

Doctors: Eyam Surgery, Church Street, Eyam, Hope Valley S32 5QH, ☎01433 630836; Tideswell Surgery, Parke Road, Tideswell SK17 8NS, ☎01298 871292.

Supermarkets: See Bakewell, p. 104.

Taxis: See Bakewell, p. 104.

WYE DALE, ASHFORD IN THE WATER AND THE LONGSTONES

The valley of the River Wye is, after the Derwent, the major rivercourse of the Peak, and it passes through some of its most spectacular limestone landscapes. West from Ashford and the famous viewpoint of Monsal Head, 150m/500ft above the river, this was the route chosen by the Midland Railway when it engineered its way through the very heart of the peak in the 1860s. The line, notoriously expensive to maintain with its series of tunnels and viaducts, closed under the Beeching axe in 1968 and was eventually bought and converted to the popular Monsal walking and riding trail by the National Park.

The power provided by the Wye was in great demand during the early years of the Industrial Revolution, and early industrialists such as Richard Arkwright constructed a series of cotton mills along its length. Cressbrook Mill, just up the river from Monsal Head, was originally built by Arkwright in 1783, and is still an imposing, Georgian structure, complete with its bell cupola, and is now restored and converted to residential use. The same use is now put to Litton Mill just upstream from Cressbrook, built by Ellis Needham a year earlier. But unlike at Cressbrook, where mill-owner William Newton treated his child apprentices well, Needham was notorious for the inhumane treatment of his. It became the subject of a polemical pamphlet, *The Memoirs of Robert Blincoe*, which eventually helped to change the law on the use of child labour.

The isolated, butte-like rock of Peter's Stone, near Wardlow Mires, just off the A623 west of Stoney Middleton, has a grisly history. It was the scene of the last gibbeting in Derbyshire in 1815, when the body of 21-year-old Anthony Lingard was hung in chains following his execution for the murder of toll-keeper Hannah Oliver at Wardlow Mires. The twin villages of Great and Little Longstone lie at the foot of Longstone Edge, a limestone ridge which is riddled, like so much of the White Peak, with the remains of old lead mines, but which is currently scarred by limestone and fluorspar quarries.

WHAT TO SEE AND DO

The village of **Ashford in the Water**, consisting mainly of 18th-century cottages and a fine parish church, is a candidate for one of the prettiest in the Peak, and is renowned for its summer well dressings. The picturesque stone-built 17th-century **Sheepwash Bridge**, which spans the River Wye at Ashford in the Water, has been the subject of countless paintings and photographs, and gets its name from the fact that sheep were once washed in the river here before shearing.

The Sheepwash Bridge in Ashford

The best time to visit Ashford in the Water is undoubtedly in mid-May, around Trinity Sunday, when five wells are dressed in the village according to the ancient custom. It was the Sheepwash Well, under the canopy of the shelter near the famous Sheepwash Bridge, which started the revival of the custom in 1930 after a break of many years. Ashford well-dressers are among the most traditional and inventive of all groups in the Peak District, adhering to the strict rule of using only purely natural, locally found materials. But the Ashford dressers often show a fair degree of ingenuity in their choice of themes. For example in the Chinese Year of the Dog, they used a traditional Willow Pattern theme, and they also paid tribute to the work of the Land Army in the Second World War.

But the dressing which often gets the most attention, as in many other villages, is the Children's' Well, situated in Greaves Lane, which is decorated by the village children. **Great** and **Little Longstone's** well dressings are held in mid-July.

Easy, family-style walking is provided by the popular **Monsal Trail**, which follows the former line of the Midland Railway as it threaded through some of the most challenging terrain and most beautiful scenery along the valley of the Wye. The many tunnels needed on the line are now closed off for safety reasons, and some of the viaducts are also out of bounds, but the trail dips in and out of the dale by the rushing river in a most delightful manner. There are plenty of car parks and picnic sites along the trail, the highlights of which include **Miller's Dale** (once the terminus for visitors to Buxton); the Site of Special Scientific Interest (SSSI) and nature reserve at **Miller's Dale Quarry**, and the tremendous limestone buttresses of **Chee Tor**.

The so-called **Roman Baths** in The Nook at **Stoney Middleton** are certainly not Roman, but were built on the site of warm springs by one of the village's most distinguished residents, Victorian Lord Chief Justice, Lord Denman. Stoney Middleton is squeezed comfortably between the high limestone crags of Middleton Dale, another popular venue for modern rock climbers.

Cottages in Monsal Dale

CELEBRITY CONNECTIONS

Former deputy leader of the Labour Party, now a prolific author and journalist, **Roy Hattersley** was born and spent much of his early life and political career in Sheffield but now lives in Great Longstone. The life-long socialist and life peer began electioneering for his local MP and city councillors at the age of 13, was educated at the City Grammar School and studied Economics at Hull University. His mother Enid was also a well-known city councillor, serving as Lord Mayor of Sheffield in the early 1980s.

While Labour was in power in the 1960s, Roy was deputy to the then Minister of Defence, Denis Healey, and in the Wilson Government of 1974, he became Minister of State for Foreign and Commonwealth Affairs. A supporter of Britain's entry into the EEC, he then had the job of re-negotiating its terms of membership. When Margaret Thatcher came to power in 1979, Roy spent the rest of his political career in Opposition and served as deputy to Neil Kinnock.

A long-standing supporter of Sheffield Wednesday FC, Roy has written numerous books, both fiction and non-fiction, newspaper articles and the humorous diaries of his doggy friend 'Buster', his constant companion on walks in the Peak District. He is also a former chairman of Buxton Festival, responsible for launching its highly successful literary series, and a former president of the Peak District & South Yorkshire branch of the CPRE.

St Martin's Parish Church, Stoney Middleton

☔ Wet weather

There's not an awful lot to do in the Wye Valley when its wet, but there are fine churches at **Ashford**, **Great Longstone** and **Stoney Middleton** which would richly repay visits. **Holy Trinity Church** at Ashford, preserves, hanging high in the chancel roof, ancient virgin crants, or crowns, which were white paper garlands carried at the funerals of unmarried girls from the village. The vigorously carved tympanum, over the Norman doorway, shows a boar and wolf standing either side of the Tree of Life, and is one of the finest in the Peak. On the north wall is a tablet in Ashford black marble commemorating Henry Watson of Bakewell, who opened Ashford's 'marble' quarry in 1748. The medieval (mainly 13th–15th-century) church of **St Giles** at Great Longstone is particularly noted for its Perpendicular-style woodwork and fine 15th-century roof. But it suffered, along with many others, from a 19th-century restoration by Norman Shaw.

St Martin's Parish Church, tucked away in its close by the Dale Brook at Stoney Middleton, is one of the most unusual in the Peak. Tacked onto its medieval, 15th-century, Perpendicular tower is a small, octagonal nave with a lantern storey, built in the mid-18th century. Like Great Longstone, Stoney Middleton was once a boot and shoe making centre. And while you are in Stoney Middleton, you might like to take a snack at the **Lover's Leap café**, which shelters under an overhanging crag where jilted lover Hannah Badderley unsuccessfully tried to commit suicide in 1762, only to be saved by her voluminous skirt, which acted as a parachute. Or you could try some tasty fish and chips, served in the octagonal former tollhouse, a listed building dating from 1840.

The best... **PLACES TO STAY**

HOTEL

Riverside House Hotel

Fennel Street, Ashford in the Water, Bakewell DE45 1QF
☎ **01629 814275**
www.riversidehousehotel.co.uk

Tastefully appointed, ivy-clad Georgian country house in a tranquil setting beside the River Wye. Beautifully decorated bedrooms, each individual in style, with traditional features. Garden rooms have their own private patios. Fine dining in the Riverside Room Restaurant.

Price: B&B from £135, DB&B from £220.

INN

The Ashford Arms

Church Street, Ashford in the Water DE45 1QB; ☎ **01629 812725**
www.ashford-arms.co.uk

Village inn full of distinctive nooks and crannies, offering good quality bed and breakfast accommodation with en-suite facilities. Many rooms have exposed beams and stonework. Bar meals and restaurant serving creative meals using local, fresh produce.

Price: B&B from £65 to £85.

B&B

River Cottage

The Duke's Drive, Ashford in the Water DE45 1QP
☎ **01629 813327**
www.rivercottageashford.co.uk

Award-winning B&B on the banks of the River Wye. Stylish accommodation with en-suite or private bathrooms and antique furniture. Range of breakfast options based on the best of local produce and fishing available.

Price: B&B from £88 for a double.

Forge House

Main Street, Great Longstone DE45 1TF
☎ **01629 640735**

Period home situated in large gardens, with private parking. Elegantly appointed rooms with en-suite bathrooms featuring spa baths and showers.

Price: B&B from £40 per person per night.

Willow Croft

Station Road, Great Longstone DE45 1TS
☎ **01629 640576**
www.willowcroftbandb.com

Refurbished en-suite rooms in rural setting with private gardens. English breakfasts including dishes such as eggs Benedict and kippers.

Price: B&B £40 to £50 for a double/twin.

SELF-CATERING

The Lodge & Dove Cottage

Chestnut House, Little Longstone DE45 1NN
☎ **01629 640542**
www.longstoneholidaycottage.co.uk

Limestone-built Dove Cottage, which sleeps two to four people, and The Lodge, which accommodates two to six, are situated just five minutes walk from Monsal Head. Welcome tea tray with local produce on arrival.

Price: from £220 to £528 per week.

The best... FOOD AND DRINK

Gourmet delights on offer here include locally produced beef and lamb, prize-winning black pudding, fresh dairy produce and, more unusually, pickled onions. Eat out at a fine dining restaurant or gastro pub, or sample locally brewed ales in traditional pubs with flagged floors and open fires.

▶ Staying in

Locally produced beef and lamb, plus cooked meats, pies, sausage and prize-winning black puddings are among the sumptuous fare on sale at **Castlegate Farm Shop** in Stoney Middleton (Main Road S32 4TN; ☎01433 630400). Buy fresh milk from the farm gate at **Church Lane Farm**, Great Longstone (Church Lane DE45 1TB; ☎01629 640673), a dairy and beef farm with wildflowers and hay meadows and a prize-winning herd of Charolais cattle. And if you have a penchant for pickles, you should make a beeline for **Ibbotsons of Ashford** (Church Street, Ashford in the Water DE45 1QB; ☎01629 812528), one of the most endearing and individual food shops in the Peak District. Ken Ibbotson's special pickled onions are renowned far and wide. You can also buy made-to-order sandwiches, cooked meats, delicatessen products, chutneys, preserves, coffees, ice cream and fresh fruit and vegetables.

EATING OUT

FINE DINING

The Riverside House Hotel
**Riverside House,
Ashford in the Water DE45 1QF
☎ 01629 814275
www.riversidehousehotel.co.uk**

With tastefully designed décor and creative, imaginative menus to match, the Riverside House Hotel is the perfect choice for celebrating a special occasion. Diners can opt for the Riverside Rooms with their inglenook fireplace and formal dining, or enjoy a relaxed three-course lunch or dinner, quick snack or deli-sandwich in the Conservatory Room. A seven-course dinner costs £44.95.

GASTRO PUB

The Bull's Head
**Church Street,
Ashford in the Water DE45 1QB
☎ 01629 812931**

Cosy and welcoming village pub with dark wooden beams, open fires, brasses around the bar and a well-deserved reputation for excellent, home-made food. Each day's menu is chalked up on a blackboard, changes frequently and features local and seasonal produce. Normally at least two real ales on tap, pleasant garden and outdoor seating area. Main courses average £10.

⚜ Drinking

Innovation, passion and knowledge are the buzzwords at multi-award winning **Thornbridge Brewery** at Ashford Hall, Ashford in the Water (DE45 1NZ; ☎01629 641000; www.thornbridgebrewery.co.uk), which supplies around 120 outlets with interestingly named brews such as Jaipur, Jaywick, Kipling, Lord Marples and Saint Petersburg, an imperial Russian stout. The brewery also sells bottle-conditioned beers. **The Crispin Inn** at Great Longstone (DE45 1TZ; ☎01629 640237) is a traditional, family-owned village pub whose unusual name comes from the patron saint of cobblers (a former village industry) and serves a choice of beers. Home-cooked food is served at both lunchtime and in the evening, with an extensive specials board and Sunday lunch menu. Children and dogs are welcome.

Nearby, Little Longstone is home to the unspoilt **Packhorse Inn** (DE45 1NN; ☎01629 640471), which serves real ales from Thornbridge Brewery and serves home prepared food such as pies, lasagne, fish and chips, plus Sunday lunch. Open fires give it a cosy feel, and walkers and dogs are welcome. Originally built as the Bull's Head in the 19th century, **The Monsal Head Hotel** (DE45 1NL; ☎01629 640250) was rebuilt as a railway hotel, due to its proximity to a long-departed railway route that once provided many small Derbyshire communities with a direct link to London. The railway is now the Monsal leisure trail for walkers and cyclists, and this free house has unrivalled views across Monsal Dale and its former railway viaduct. A range of cask ales, lagers, wheat beers and wines complements a comprehensive bar and restaurant menu.

Flagged floors and warm, welcoming fire set the scene at the **Three Stags Heads** at Wardlow Mires (SK17 8RW; ☎01298 872268), where real ales and seasonal food, including game, are served. Opposite the pub is Peter's Stone, or Gibbet Rock, where in 1816, Anthony Lingard was the last man to be publicly gibbeted in Derbyshire after murdering a woman.

ℹ Visitor Information

Tourist information centre: Bakewell Visitor Centre, The Old Market Hall, Bridge Street, Bakewell, Derbyshire DE45 1DS, ☎01629 816558, www.peakdistrict.gov.uk.

Hospitals: Minor A&E injuries, Whitworth Hospital, Darley Dale, ☎01629 580211; Main A&E, Chesterfield Royal Hospital, Calow, Chesterfield, ☎01246 277271.

Doctors: Bakewell Medical Centre, Butts Road, Bakewell, ☎0844 477 3408, www.bakewellmedicalcentre.net;

Youlgrave Medical Centre, Alport Lane DE45 1WN, ☎01629 636207; Winster Surgery, Leacroft Road, Winster DE4 2DI, ☎01629 650207.

Supermarket: Co-op Supermarket, Market Street, Bakewell, ☎01629 816900.

Taxis: John Thorp Private Hire, Bakewell, ☎01246 583219; Neil Chapman Private Hire, Wyedale Drive, Bakewell, ☎01629 812454; Peak Premier Travel, Over Haddon, ☎01629 636877.

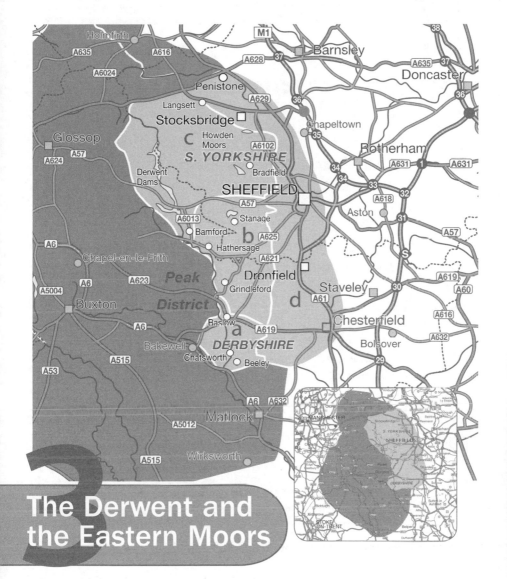

The Derwent and the Eastern Moors

a. Chatsworth, Beeley and Baslow

b. Hathersage, Grindleford and Stanage

c. The Upper Derwent and Bamford

d. Chesterfield, Sheffield and Bradfield

Unmissable highlights

01 See what it's like to live like a lord, at Chatsworth House, one of the premier stately homes of England, p. 144

02 Experience the transformation of Sheffield at the Peace Gardens, Millennium Galleries and Winter Gardens, p. 176

03 See the last resting place of Robin Hood's lieutenant, at Little John's Grave, in Hathersage churchyard, p. 160

04 Relive the heroics of the Dambusters and see where the navvies lived at Tintown, in the Upper Derwent Valley, p. 170

05 Wonder at the prehistoric earthworks of Carl Wark, above Hathersage, p. 159

06 Enjoy the splendid view from Bradfield Parish Church, the finest in the Peak, p. 175

07 Marvel at the rock gymnasts on Stanage Edge, near Hathersage, p. 159

08 Twist your neck by taking a tour to admire Chesterfield's famous crooked spire, p. 179

09 Pick up a bargain at Chesterfield's bustling street market, p. 184

10 Pay homage to the Padley martyrs at Padley Chapel, near Hathersage, p. 162

THE DERWENT AND THE EASTERN MOORS

The River Derwent is the major physical feature of the eastern moors region of the Peak District as it carves its way south from the bleak moorland heights of Howden Moor above the Upper Derwent Valley, where it has been dammed to create what has been dubbed the 'Peak's Lake District' – the triple reservoirs of Howden, Derwent and Ladybower.

From Bamford its course runs through pleasant, tree-lined banks beneath the famous eastern gritstone edges of Stanage, Burbage, Froggatt, Curbar, Baslow, Birchen and Gardom's – a 12 mile escarpment which frowns down on the river. In the south of the area, the Derwent forms an attractive foreground to the glorious parklands of Chatsworth, landscaped by Lancelot 'Capability' Brown three centuries ago, and now the setting of one of Britain's premier stately homes and the home of the Duke of Devonshire. The neat estate villages of Edensor, Pilsley, Beeley and Baslow also form part of the vast Chatsworth estate.

Further east, Sheffield has a unique distinction among European cities in that it has large parts of a national park within its boundaries. Known to Sheffielders as their city's 'Golden Frame', the eastern moorlands of the Peak abut the western suburbs of the city and have been long valued by its residents as both their backyard and playground. The same proximity to the moors is enjoyed by the residents of Chesterfield, Derbyshire's second most populous town, and the home of the famous Twisted Spire of the parish church. The Sheffield city boundary extends out to the gritstone ramparts of Stanage Edge – a Mecca for rock climbers all over the world – and to the pretty twin villages of High and Low Bradfield and the valley of the River Loxley, which eventually joins the Sheaf in Sheffield.

CHATSWORTH, BEELEY AND BASLOW

Although it's in the heart of Derbyshire, this is Devonshire country. The area is dominated by the Duke of Devonshire's magnificent mansion at Chatsworth – which has long carried the epithet 'the Palace of the Peak' – and its attendant estate villages.

It was Daniel Defoe in his *Tour thro' the Whole Island of Great Britain*, published in 1742, who first described Chatsworth as '*a palace for a prince*'. He marvelled that '*any man who had a genius suitable to so magnificent a design… would build it in such a place where the mountains insult the clouds…*'

WHAT TO SEE AND DO

Chatsworth – the house and gardens

The present house, a veritable treasure trove of works of art, is largely the creation of the fourth Earl of Devonshire (later to become the first Duke), the Dutch architect William Talman and later Thomas Archer, built between 1678 and 1707. It replaced Bess of Hardwick's original Tudor mansion, of which the Hunting Tower in the woods above the house is the only remainder. Today it is in the top five privately owned stately homes in the

Chatsworth House

country, attracting over 600,000 visitors annually to its house, gardens, children's farmyard and adventure playground. The current (12th) Duke and Duchess have made the grounds an ever-changing gallery of modern outdoor sculpture.

The house itself certainly repays a full day's visit, especially if the weather is wet outside. Among the highlights are the magnificent **Painted Hall** by Louis Lageurre, the sumptuous State Rooms, the Sculpture Gallery and the Library.

CHATSWORTH: Bakewell, Derbyshire DE45 1PP; www.chatsworth.org. Entry: Discovery Pass (one visit to house and two to either garden or farmyard), adults £16, concessions £12.50, children £10; house and garden only, adults £11.50, concessions £9.50, children £6.25; open daily 11am–4.30pm, 12 Mar to 31 Oct (lower floors only open for Christmas decorations, 1 Nov to 23 Dec).

There is also a well-appointed shop in The Orangery. The upper part and ceiling of the Painted Hall has not been changed since it was first painted by Louis Lageurre (1663–1721), and the exuberant allegorical paintings, recently restored to their former colourful magnificence, leave a lasting impression. The marble floor and sweeping staircase were not part of the original design, but were added later. Most of Chatsworth's main social functions, including the Christmas party for estate children, are held in the opulent surroundings of the Painted Hall.

Chatsworth's State Rooms have recently been renovated and re-presented to evoke a clearer sense of how they might have looked in the 18th and 19th centuries. They include the **Great Chamber**, with its wonderful ceiling painted by Antonio Verrio (1639–1707), which includes a rather unflattering portrait of Mrs Hackett, the first Duke's housekeeper, whom Verrio apparently disliked, as Atropos, one of the three

The Great Dining Room at Chatsworth House

Chatsworth and Mary Queen of Scots

When you approach Chatsworth House, you may notice a raised, roofless block to the left of the entrance road, with a set of grand steps leading up to it. This was a lodge in one of the fishponds which provided much-needed fresh fish for the house, and part of the original house built by Bess of Hardwick. It's known as Queen Mary's Bower, and may have been built specially for Mary Queen of Scots, who was held at Chatsworth five times between 1570 and 1581, because her coat of arms is placed over the gateway at the top of the steps. You can imagine the tragic queen-in-waiting, apparently in almost constant pain, looking at Bess's fine house across the water, and wondering day after day what her fate might be. Her sister, Queen Elizabeth I, had charged Bess's fourth husband, George Talbot, Earl of Shrewsbury, to: 'use her honourably but do not allow her to escape'.

Mary arrived at Chatsworth with her extensive retinue in 1570, after Plague had struck her former place of imprisonment at Tutbury Castle, in south Derbyshire. While at Chatsworth, her health improved and she was to be seen out riding most days. Modern visitors are still shown the suite of nine 'Queen of Scots' rooms where she lodged in that part of the Tudor house which was later completely rebuilt by the sixth Duke. Later she was transferred to more secure quarters at Sheffield Castle, 15 miles away. She begged unceasingly to be allowed to take the waters at Buxton to ease her condition, and at length, after she had been taken back to Chatsworth, the Queen consented, in spite of the Earl claiming that she made 'over much use of physic and baths'. While taking the waters at Buxton, Mary stayed at the Old Hall (now the Old Hall Hotel, see p. 208), where in 1584 she inscribed on a window:

> Buxton, whose fame thy milk-warm waters tell,
> Whom I, perchance, no more shall see, farewell.

The words were prophetic, because Mary was eventually beheaded at Fotheringhay Castle in Northamptonshire three years later in February 1587.

Fates, cutting the thread of life. The ceiling of the **State Drawing Room** was also painted by Lageurre. This magnificent, Mortlake tapestry-walled room must have made an out-of-this-world bedroom for the 20 girls who slept here during the Second World War, when Chatsworth was commandeered for use as a girls' school. The **State Music Room** is probably best known for its wonderful *trompe l'oeil* painting of a violin and bow, which can be seen in the inner door of the central doorcase. It is so real that you really feel, if were to you believe your eyes, that you could reach out and touch it. It was painted by the Dutch artist Jan van der Vaardt (c1653–1727), and although just a detail, is often one of the best remembered sights of a visit to Chatsworth.

Continuing the tour, you visit the **Chapel**, built between 1688 and 1693, and featuring yet another ceiling painted by Laguerre, featuring scenes from the life of Christ. Verrio painted the *Doubting Thomas* scene over the altar. The Chatsworth **Library** was the first Duke's Long Gallery, but it is now filled with over 17,000 books including, among other rarities, one of the most famous bird books ever published, John James Audubon's handsomely illustrated *Birds of America.*

The **Great Dining Room** was finished in 1832, and made a real impression on the 13-year-old Princess (later Queen) Victoria, when she attended her first-ever dinner with grown-ups on a visit with her mother shortly after it was completed. The sixth Duke, who had it built, is said to have commented: '*it is like dining in a great trunk and you expect the lid to open*'. The 'lid' is a great domed and gilded ceiling. Finally, the **Sculpture Gallery** was built by the sixth Duke to display his beloved collection of marble statues, including his personal favourite, *The Sleeping Endymion with his Dog* by Antonio Canova (1757–1822). More modern sculptures include heads of the Prince of Wales, John Betjeman, Harold Macmillan and Andrew, the late eleventh Duke.

In addition to the glorious **Chatsworth gardens**, which include the beautiful **Cascade** and **Emperor Fountain**, there are many glorious and easy walks through the parklands. These can range from a stroll by the mighty Derwent, which Defoe described as '*a fury of a river*', perhaps

GARDENS AT CHATSWORTH: Chatsworth, Bakewell, Derbyshire DE45 1PP; www.chatsworth.org. Entry: adults £7.50, concessions £6, children £4.50; open daily 11am–4.30pm 12 Mar to 23 Dec.

enjoying a picnic and watching the herds of red and fallow deer on the other bank, or through the magnificent woodlands of Stand Wood behind the house. An easy walk with steps provided will take you up to the Tudor **Hunting Tower** (private), part of Bess of Hardwick's original design, with wonderful views across Chatsworth's rolling parklands.

On the other side of the river from the House, on the path which leads through New Piece Wood and across Calton Pastures down into Bakewell, stands the gabled, black-

The grounds at Chatsworth

CELEBRITY CONNECTIONS

Star-struck visitors to this part of the Peak District shouldn't be too surprised if they think they recognise actress **Keira Knightley** around these parts. For the seasoned screen goddess has filmed in the area at least twice: first as Elizabeth Bennet in *Pride and Prejudice*, released in 2005, and more recently as Lady Georgiana Spencer in *The Duchess*, released in 2008. During *Pride and Prejudice*, Keira and the cast were filmed at such famous locations as Chatsworth and Haddon Hall, and in one memorable scene, the cape-clad star stood on iconic Stanage Edge, gazing wistfully out on to the valley below. She and co-star **Matthew Macfadyen** stayed at the Peacock at Rowsley during the filming, which later played host to the stars of *The Other Boleyn Girl*, released in spring 2008, including **Natalie Portman, Scarlett Johanssen, Eric Bana, Kristin Scott Thomas** and director **Justin Chadwick**.

When Keira returned to film *The Duchess,* she and actor boyfriend **Rupert Friend** got away from it all in a self-catering cottage in the Staffordshire Moorlands area of the Peak District. Fellow members of the cast, such as **Ralph Fiennes, Hayley Atwell, Dominic Cooper** and **Charlotte Rampling** stayed at Breadsall Priory Hotel on the outskirts of Derby.

and-white **Russian Cottage** (also private). This was built, along with the 88m/290ft **Emperor Fountain** in the gardens, by the sixth Duke to commemorate a forthcoming visit by Tsar Nicholas I of Russia in 1844. Unfortunately, the Tsar did not turn up. High on the moors to the east of the house, a signed footpath leads from Hell Bank Plantation on the minor road which runs from Beeley to Holymoorside to the remote and enigmatic Bronze Age round barrow known as **Hob Hurst's House**, below Harland Edge. The moors above Chatsworth are some of the best-managed in the Peak, and in late summer are ablaze with purple heather.

Estate villages

The pretty, neat estate villages of **Beeley**, **Pilsley** and **Edensor** all have charming cottages, mostly laid out by the sixth Duke of Devonshire's brilliant architect and gardener, Joseph Paxton, and John Robertson. **Beeley**, at the southern end of Chatsworth Park, lies just off the main road, but the 17th-century Devonshire Arms (one of many around here) is worth a visit, and the parish church usually has a fine display of daffodils in the spring.

A story which is often repeated is that the 19th-century model village of **Edensor** (pronounced 'Ensor'), was 'transplanted' by the fourth Duke because it spoiled his view from the house. In fact, only half the village was removed because it obstructed the approach through the park. The other half, still occupied, is where it has always

The George Gilbert Scott Church in Edensor

been, although it was transformed by the sixth Duke with new and refaced houses of varying eclectic designs ranging from Italianate to Gothic rustic by John Robertson.

The elegant **George Gilbert Scott Church** and churchyard is the last resting place of generations of Cavendishes, including Kathleen Kennedy, sister of US president John F Kennedy, who was married to William Hartington, elder brother of the 11th Duke. The duke was killed in the Second World War, when many of the Edensor's former residents were evacuated to the neighbouring village of Pilsley. Today, Pilsley is home to Chatsworth's popular farm shop, which attracts large numbers of shoppers, keen to purchase locally sourced meat and vegetables.

At the northern end of the Park is the village of **Baslow**, standing at the confluence of the Bar Brook and the Derwent. The broach-spired parish church is notable for its clockface, and nearby is a 17th-century, three-arched bridge over the Derwent, which features a tiny toll house with an entrance just 1m/3½ft tall.

🌂 Wet weather

The house at **Chatsworth** is always a good wet weather alternative, and you could easily spend a whole day just exploring its hundreds of sumptuous rooms and works of art. The broach-spired parish church at **Baslow** is famed for its clockface in the tower which commemorates Queen Victoria's Diamond Jubilee, the letters of her name and the date (VICTORIA 1897) taking the place of the usual numbers. Inside the church, a whip used to drive stray dogs out of the church before services began is an unusual preserved ecclesiastical artefact.

What to do with children

Children of all ages will love the **Chatsworth Children's Farmyard**, where they can feed and touch the animals, and watch a cow being milked, or the adjacent **Adventure Playground**, with its colourful slides, roundabouts and swings.

CHILDREN'S FARMYARD & ADVENTURE PLAYGROUND: Chatsworth, Bakewell, Derbyshire DE45 1PP; www.chatsworth.org. Entry: children £5.25, adults £5, concessions £4; open daily, 10.30am–4.30pm 12 Mar to 23 Dec (closed 29–31 Aug).

The best... PLACES TO STAY

HOTEL

The Cavendish Hotel

Baslow, Bakewell DE45 1SP
☎ **01246 582311**
www.cavendish-hotel.com

Both standard and superior accommodation is available at this stone-built hotel, which overlooks the adjacent Chatsworth Estate. Superior rooms feature four poster, brass or king size beds, luxury bathrooms, fine art and antique furniture. Many locally sourced ingredients are on the menu in the Gallery Restaurant, along with around 70 different wines.

Price: from £121 for a single; from £155 for a twin/double.

Hassop Hall Hotel

Hassop, near Bakewell DE45 1NS
☎ **01629 640488**
www.hassophallhotel.co.uk

Elegantly appointed, family-run hotel in picturesque gardens and rolling parkland. En-suite rooms range from standard to superior, decorated to a high standard, yet maintaining their country house charm. Extensive menu of classic dishes served in the restaurant, overlooking the park and gardens, available for lunch, dinner, Sunday lunch and for special celebrations.

Price: from £95 for a standard room; from £225 for a superior room.

The best... PLACES TO STAY

The Peacock at Rowsley

Rowsley, Matlock DE4 2EB
☎ 01629 733518
www.thepeacockatrowsley.com

Luxury en-suite accommodation styled by award-winning international designer India Mahdavi, which has played host to film stars such as Keira Knightley, Matthew Macfadyen and Kristin Scott Thomas. Comfortable yet contemporary, one room has a four-poster bed, another an antique bed from Belvoir Castle, while all boast antique furniture and paintings.

Price: B&B from £145 for a double.

INN

The Devonshire Arms

Devonshire Square, Beeley, near Matlock DE4 2NR
☎ 01629 733259
www.devonshirebeeley.co.uk

Country charm blends with contemporary chic at the Devonshire Arms. Eight individually styled cottage bedrooms are named after local dales and thoughtfully furnished, with large beds and sumptuous fabrics. Downstairs guests can eat and drink in the bar, featuring original oak beams, original fireplaces and copper-topped counter, or the colourful, modern brasserie.

Price: B&B from £145 for a double.

FARMSTAY

Bubnell Cliff Farm

Wheatlands Lane, Baslow DE45 1RF
☎ 01246 582454
www.bubnellcliff.co.uk

Traditional farmhouse on working dairy farm in peaceful setting on the Chatsworth Estate. Spacious rooms, roaring log fires and magnificent views of Chatsworth Park and Baslow and Curbar Edges. Hearty farmhouse breakfasts using locally sourced produce where possible, including black pudding and Derbyshire oatcakes when available.

Price: B&B £55 for a double.

B&B

Holly Cottage

Pilsley DE45 1UH
☎ 01246 582245

Quality en-suite B&B accommodation on the Chatsworth Estate. Cosy, well-furnished rooms boast a range of features, including Wi-Fi internet access. Hearty breakfasts feature locally sourced produce, including sausages, bacon and black pudding from nearby Chatsworth Farm Shop, free range eggs and fresh bread. Special dietary requirements catered for.

Price: B&B from £55 for a twin; from £60 for a double.

The best... FOOD AND DRINK

Particular emphasis is placed on local produce in this area, especially home-raised, traditionally reared beef and lamb at places such as the Chatsworth Farm Shop. You'll also find a huge choice of places to eat out, from a Michelin-starred restaurant and sister gastro pub to cosy cafés and tea rooms. Real ales, wooden beams and roaring fires welcome visitors in local pubs.

Local heroes – Max Fischer

Master chef Max Fischer, acclaimed as one of the highest-rated members of his profession in the UK, and his wife Susan run Michelin-starred Fischer's Baslow Hall, where fine food and first-class accommodation attract discerning guests from far and wide. German-born Max left school at 16 to train in his home town of Luneburg, and in 1977 was appointed head chef of the Schlosshotel Kronberg, where he prepared banquets for the likes of Prince Charles, Margaret Thatcher and Richard Nixon. He met Susan, from Leicestershire, while working at the Bell Inn at Aston Clinton, one of the first British Relais et Chateau members.

The couple realised their long-cherished ambition to run their own business when they opened Fischer's Restaurant in nearby Bakewell in the 1980s. Fischer's Baslow Hall – once home to engineer and designer Sebastian Ziani de Ferranti and local motor car dealers George Kenning and T C Harrison – earned its coveted Michelin star in 1994. Max, Susan and their head chef, Sheffield-born Rupert Rowley, have since opened a sister venture, Rowley's Restaurant and Bar, also in Baslow, a stylish, all-day dining and drinking venue. Like Fischer's Baslow Hall, Rowley's is committed to using quality local produce and suppliers, and also has a cookery club and stages regular live jazz.

In recent years, Max has left more of the cooking to Rupert so that he can indulge his passion for gardening by growing herbs, vegetables and fruit for the restaurant in his beloved kitchen plot. Rupert is relishing the challenge, having previously worked with such legendary names as Raymond Blanc, John Burton Race and Gordon Ramsay. Max particularly enjoys the fresh air and beautiful scenery of the Peak District, especially the Dark Peak moors, when the heather is in flower. One of his favourite walks is from Baslow Hall through the neighbouring village of Bubnell, past the river Derwent.

▶ Staying in

There are nearly always queues at the popular **Chatsworth Farm Shop** in the estate village of Pilsley, which specialises in the best of local and regional food, and offers quality produce fresh from the estate, tenant farms, Derbyshire suppliers and small food producers. Traditional butchers supply a vast array of meat, poultry and game, and delicious home-cooked meats and pies are available from the delicatessen counter while the in-shop bakery provides wonderful fresh bread and cakes. Launched by the then Duchess of Devonshire more than 30 years ago, the farm shop now plays a key role in the local agricultural community by supporting local farmers, market gardeners and small producers.

> CHATSWORTH FARM SHOP: Pilsley, Bakewell, Derbyshire DE45 1UF;
> ☎01246 583392;
> www.chatsworth.org/shopping/farmshop.htm.
> Open daily except Christmas.

You can also have traditionally reared beef and lamb delivered to your door through an internet-based initiative launched by local farmers and backed by the Prince of Wales, called **Peak Choice Ltd** (☎01629 735303 or ☎07814 252945; www.peakchoice.co.uk).

🍴 EATING OUT

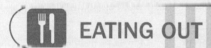

FINE DINING

Fischer's Baslow Hall
Calver Road, Baslow,
Derbyshire DE45 1RR
☎ 01246 583259
www.fischers-baslowhall.co.uk

Michelin-starred restaurant in superb setting amid landscaped gardens fringing the Chatsworth Estate. Painstaking attention to detail, emphasis on local produce, some of which is grown in Max Fischer's kitchen garden. Luncheon, dinner and menu *du jour*. Specialities include marinated Derbyshire venison and caramelised Derbyshire pork belly. Two-course luncheon £23; dinner £68. Individually styled accommodation also available.

The Peacock at Rowsley
Rowsley, Matlock DE4 2EB
☎ 01629 733518
www.thepeacockatrowsley.com

Relaxed dining at lunch or dinner in the main restaurant or more intimate Wye Room, complemented by wines from around the world. Sample choices at lunch (mains from £14.75) include scampi in lemonade batter, rib-eye steak and smoked haddock fish cake, while among options for dinner (mains from £25.50) are pork fillet, duck breast and brill.

EATING OUT

East Lodge Hotel & Restaurant
Rowsley, Matlock DE4 2EF
☎ 01629 734474
www.eastlodge.com

Friendly, unstuffy service in a beautifully situated, award-winning venue. Modern British cooking using the best of seasonal ingredients, locally sourced where possible. Extensive vegetarian selection and special diets catered for, plus champagne breakfasts and teas. A two-course luncheon costs £17.50, three-course luncheon £23, two-course dinner £29.50 and three-course dinner £36. En-suite accommodation is also available.

Hassop Hall Hotel
Hassop, Near Bakewell DE45 1NS
☎ 01629 640488
www.hassophall.co.uk

Classic luncheons, dinners, Sunday lunches and celebration luncheons and dinners in a historic and unique setting with panoramic views of the surrounding park and gardens. A two-course luncheon costs £19.45, three-course luncheon £21.95, Sunday lunch £30.95, two-course dinner £24.95 and four-course dinner £33.50.

RESTAURANTS

Carriage House Restaurant
Chatsworth, Bakewell DE45 1PP
☎ 01246 565300
www.chatsworth.org

Award-winning restaurant offering freshly made local and seasonal food prepared by Chatsworth's team of chefs and bakers. Located in the elegant 18th-century stable block designed by James Paine, the Carriage House is fully licensed and self-service.

Chatsworth Farm Shop Restaurant
Pilsley
Bakewell DE45 1UF
☎ 01246 583392
www.chatsworth.org

Fresh home-cooked food based on locally sourced produce prepared by the shop's award-winning chefs and bakers in an informal setting with stunning views over the Chatsworth Estate. Breakfast, lunch and afternoon tea served. Typical dishes include hot Derbyshire oatcakes filed with Chatsworth ham and farmhouse Cheddar and roast of the day. Main courses cost from around £4.95 to £8.50.

EATING OUT

The Cavendish Hotel
Baslow DE45 1SP
☎ **01246 582311**
www.cavendish-hotel.net

Imaginative food based on fresh ingredients, many locally sourced, with the emphasis on flavour and presentation, served in the relaxed, informal atmosphere of the Gallery Restaurant with views of Chatsworth. Wine list offering more than 70 choices from around the world. Two courses cost £29.50, three courses £38.50, four courses £43.50 and five courses £51.50.

Il Lupo
Eaton Hill, Baslow DE45 1SB
☎ **01246 583164**
www.illupo.co.uk

Keep the wolf from the door at this authentic Italian restaurant upholding the Latin traditions of good food, friendship and hospitality. It offers a wide selection of starters, pizza, pasta, steaks, pork, poultry, fish, lamb and vegetarian options, plus a complementary wine list. A three-course lunch costs £7.95 and four-course Sunday lunch £8.95, while mains cost from £8.50.

GASTRO PUB

The Devonshire Arms
Devonshire Square, Beeley, Matlock DE4 2NR
☎ **01629 733259**
www.devonshirebeeley.co.uk

Fascinating mix of traditional bar area and ultra-modern, colourful restaurant serving a mix of culinary classics and more contemporary fare, much of it featuring Chatsworth Estate produce such as Old Spot pork, lamb and gammon. Cask ales include choices from local breweries such as Peak Ales and Thornbridge Hall. Mains cost from £10.95.

Rowley's
Church Lane, Baslow DE45 1RY
☎ **01246 583880**
www.rowleysrestaurant.co.uk

Enticing selection of modern and traditional British food served in a chic venue. Options range from light bites such as soup, salads and sandwiches to fresh fish and steaks, many from local suppliers. Beers include cask ales from Thornbridge brewery at Ashford in the Water. Lunch mains cost from around £9.50, dinner mains from £13.

EATING OUT

CAFÉ

Cafe on the Green
Nether End, Baslow DE45 1SR
☎ **01246 583000**

Service with a smile, good selection of hot and cold snacks, including paninis, and hot and cold drinks in a friendly, bustling atmosphere.

Charlie's Cafe and Bistro
Church Street, Baslow DE45 1RY
☎ **01246 582619**

Good quality, locally sourced food served in a relaxed atmosphere, ranging from full English breakfast at £5.75 to lunch plates at around £6.95, plus daily specials and afternoon tea. Bistro open Thursday to Saturday evenings: booking essential.

The Old Smithy Cafe
Chapel Hill, Beeley DE4 2NR
☎ **01629 734666**

Local produce is home-cooked on the premises to create everything from sandwiches to specials such as quiche, lamb, rarebit and sausage casserole, plus some vegetarian choices. Wine and beer is served, including local brews from Peak Ales and Thornbridge Brewery. Shares premises with the village shop and has indoor and outdoor seating.

Farmyard Café
Chatsworth, Bakewell DE45 1PP
☎ **01246 565300**

Family-friendly food in a brightly decorated, bustling setting at Chatsworth's popular farmyard and adventure playground. Options include hot dogs, mini Cornish pasties, children's picnic boxes and ice cream, as well as sandwiches and cakes. Cakes and a party hut can be pre-booked for birthday celebrations.

TEA ROOM

Cavendish Rooms
Chatsworth, Bakewell DE45 1PP
☎ **01246 565300**

Full waitress service focusing on the art of serving afternoon tea in Chatsworth's imposing 18th-century stable block. Quintessentially English experience with a licensed bar, where you can enjoy tea and fancies or sip a glass of champagne.

Edensor Tea Rooms
Edensor, Chatsworth DE45 1PH
☎ **01246 582283**
www.chatsworth.org

Freshly baked scones and cakes, home-made Bakewell Pudding, light lunches and soups using seasonal vegetables, plus a selection of teas and coffees are available at this picturesque tea room on the Chatsworth Estate. Takeaway soup and sandwiches, and picnic baskets from £5 per person. Jams, marmalades, jellies and chutneys also on sale.

🍺 Drinking

Locally named beers ranging from Bakewell Bitter to Chatsworth Gold are brewed at **Peak Ales** on the Chatsworth Estate (Barn Brewery DE45 1EX; ☎01246 583737; www.peakales.co.uk). The brewery was launched in 2005 in previously derelict farm buildings, and now supplies around 30 outlets. Cheery log fires and charming oak beamed rooms welcome visitors at the Virginia creeper-clad 17th-century **Eyre Arms** at Hassop (DE45 1NS; ☎01629 640390), where a range of hand-drawn real ales are available and can be enjoyed in an attractive beer garden in fine weather. The Grade II former coaching inn takes its name from the Eyre family, which owned most of the surrounding land, and its coat of arms can be seen above the carved stone fireplace. Home-made food, ranging from sandwiches to three-course meals and specials, is served at lunchtime and in the evening.

Another traditional stone-built pub with good beers and home-cooked food, including a popular carvery, is **The Devonshire Arms** at Pilsley (High Street DE45 1UL), one of the Chatsworth Estate villages, which welcomes walkers and children. It's a convenient place to stop for refreshment if you're planning a trip to the nearby Chatsworth Farm Shop. In Baslow, the **Wheatsheaf** (Nether Road DE45 1SR; ☎01246 582240) serves well-kept beers and traditional food, while the **Robin Hood Inn** (on the A619 Chesterfield Road DE45 1PQ; ☎01246 583186) is a popular haunt for walkers pausing for real ales and home-cooked bar food.

To enjoy real ales in an unusual setting surrounded by hundreds of foreign bank notes, antique fire-fighting equipment, oak beams and log burning fires, visit **The Bridge Inn** at Calver (S32 3XA; ☎01433 630415). Traditional bar meals, snacks and sandwiches, including vegetarian options, are served at lunchtime and in the evening, and the large riverside garden seats up to 200 people.

ⓘ Visitor Information

Tourist information centre: Bakewell Visitor Centre, The Old Market Hall, Bridge Street, Bakewell, Derbyshire DE45 1DS, ☎01629 816558, www.peakdistrict.gov.uk.

Hospitals: A&E, Chesterfield Royal Hospital, Calow, Chesterfield, ☎01246 277271; Northern General Hospital, Herries Road, Sheffield, ☎0114 243 4343.

Doctors: Ashenfell Surgery, Church Lane, Baslow, ☎01246 582216; or see Bakewell (p. 104).

Taxis: Sickleholme Private Hire, Bamford, ☎0777 376 3445.

HATHERSAGE, GRINDLEFORD AND STANAGE

The modern villages of the Derwent Valley are almost all on the river and each have their ancient stone bridges providing safe crossings of Defoe's 'furious' Derwent. The many mills which once harnessed its power are now, in many cases, converted into luxurious living accommodation, such as that at Calver (which once doubled as Colditz Castle, in the television series of the same name) and Bamford.

The village of Hathersage, situated below the long gritstone escarpment of Stanage Edge (where there is a Robin Hood's Cave), is forever associated with Robin Hood's faithful lieutenant, Little John, who was allegedly born and was buried in the village. You can still see his considerable grave, maintained by the Ancient Order of Foresters, in the village churchyard, between two clipped yews just outside the church door. Also sheltering below Stanage Edge stands the Tudor tower house of North Lees Hall (private see p.164), the home of the Eyre family for many generations, and said to have been the model for Thornfield Hall in Charlotte Brontë's smouldering Victorian classic, *Jane Eyre*. There could well be a nub of truth in the story, because it is documented that Charlotte stayed with her close friend, Ellen Nussey, in Hathersage while she was writing the book.

The manor house at Upper Padley, in the woods on the north bank of the Derwent near Grindleford, was originally built in the late 13th and early 14th centuries by the De Bernacs, who came from Normandy with William the Conqueror. The manor eventually passed to the Roman Catholic Fitzherbert family by marriage in the 16th century and became a missionary haven for priests for almost 30 years. On 12 July 1588, Padley Manor House was raided by the Lord Lieutenant of Sheffield, the Earl of Shrewsbury, and two priests were found. Nicholas Garlick and Robert Ludlam were arrested and taken to Derby Gaol, where they were charged together as having come into England as Catholic priests. They were both convicted of high treason and sentenced to death and hung, drawn and quartered on St Mary's Bridge, Derby on 24 July. The remaining gatehouse of the manor, now converted to a chapel, has become a place of pilgrimage for Catholic visitors.

WHAT TO SEE AND DO

The airy promenades along any of the gritstone edges of **Baslow**, **Curbar**, **Gardom's**, **Birchen**, **Froggatt** or **Stanage** provide wonderful views across the Derwent Valley, and north towards Eyam Moor, Win Hill and Kinder Scout. You can also admire the gymnastics of the rock climbers as they defy gravity on the sheer faces of the gritstone edges below your feet. There are, for example, over 650 rock climbing routes on **Stanage Edge** alone, and many of the routes are given descriptive names to match their severity, such as the Left and Right Unconquerables on Stanage or the nautical flavoured climbs on Birchen Edge, where names like The Crow's Nest, Kiss me Hardy and Emma's Dilemma echo the historic Nelson Monument on the moor above.

Fitter walkers with a knowledge of navigation might like to trace the prehistoric remains on **Gardom's Edge** or **Big Moor**. For example, an easy footpath leads up from the **Robin Hood Inn** on the A619 Baslow–Chesterfield road to some well-documented sites. Extensive remains of Bronze Age occupation have been discovered here, showing that this now bleak moorland was quite heavily populated up to 4,000 years ago, when the climate was kinder and the soils richer. These remains include the settlement site at **Swine Sty** and numerous clearance cairns, field systems and stone circles. It is worth visiting the huge, flat replica boulder which is covered with enigmatic 'cup and ring' carvings, collectively known as rock art, which still baffles archaeologists trying to fathom their meaning.

Hiking above Stanage Edge

Local legends – Robin Hood and Little John

The romantic image of Robin Hood, the hooded figure in Lincoln green, dispossessed by the Normans and forced to hide in the leafy depths of Sherwood Forest from where he and his Merrie Men ambushed the gentry and shared the spoils with the peasants, is an abiding British icon. Likewise his faithful companion, the towering figure of Little John, whom it is claimed was born in the Derwentside village of Hathersage, is a constant and popular figure in the folklore of England. And in the churchyard of St Michael and All Angels at Hathersage, situated below the long gritstone escarpment of Stanage Edge (where there is, incidentally, a Robin Hood's Cave), you can still see his considerable, 10ft/3m long grave which is maintained by the Ancient Order of Foresters, between two clipped yews just outside the church door.

Hathersage is forever associated with Robin Hood's faithful lieutenant, who was allegedly born John Little and was a nailmaker in the village before he was called up to join the Merrie Men. The dilapidated cottage where he apparently lived was still there in the late 19th century, and it is claimed that his bow of spliced yew, some arrows, chain mail armour and green cap were formally displayed inside the church, and bought out annually for the village's May Day celebrations.

And when the grave in the churchyard was opened in 1780, a thigh bone was found which measured $28^{1}/_{2}$ in long – surely the sign of a giant. His legend lives on, because a pub in the village still carries his name, and on the moors above Longshaw there is a Little John's Well.

There are also many pleasant riverside walks through the woods from Grindleford or Hathersage, or through the National Trust's **Longshaw Estate**, one of the trust's first landscape acquisitions in the Peak, from **Longshaw Lodge** above Hathersage. Longshaw Lodge was built as a shooting lodge for the Duke of Rutland in 1830 and was acquired by the forerunner of the Sheffield branch of the Campaign for the Protection of Rural England in 1927 and passed to the National Trust in 1931. Today it is run as a country park where the newest facility in the grounds is a

> LONGSHAW ESTATE: Hathersage, Sheffield S11 7TZ; ☎01433 637904; www.nationaltrust.org.uk/eastmids. Entry: free, estate open daily all year; visitor centre 10.30am–4pm daily, 1 Feb to 6 Apr and 27 Oct to 31 Jan; 10.30am–5pm, daily 7 Apr to 26 Oct (closed Mon and Tues except 28 Jul to 7 Sept).

Moorland Discovery Centre for educational groups. There is also a café and shop in the Lodge itself. Longshaw is also the home of one of the oldest **sheepdog trials** in the country, which take place in front of the lodge every August bank holiday.

The **David Mellor Design Museum and Country Shop** in the award-winning Round Building just outside Hathersage, is a great place to visit. David Mellor is recognised as

North Lees Hall, supposedly the inspiration for Thornfield Hall in *Jane Eyre* (see p. 158)

(see p. 158)

DAVID MELLOR DESIGN MUSEUM AND COUNTRY SHOP: The Round Building, Hathersage, Sheffield S32 1BA; ☎01433 650220; www.davidmellordesign.co.uk. Entry: free, open daily.

one of the best-known British designers of the 20th century, responsible, among other things, for the modern traffic light, the square pillar box and a range of tastefully designed street furniture and cutlery. You can see cutlery being made in the circular Round Building, which was designed by Sir Michael Hopkins on the foundations of the village's former gas holder. And you enjoy your lunch or coffee in the café under the constantly changing red, red and amber, and green lights of a working traffic light.

Outdoor activities

Peak Activities is based at Rock Lea in Hathersage and claims to be the most accessible activity centre by public transport in the UK. It provides safe and reliable outdoor sports activities with specialists and chartered development

PEAK ACTIVITIES LTD: Rock Lea Activity Centre, Station Road, Hathersage, Hope Valley, Derbyshire S32 1DD; ☎01433 650345; www.iain.co.uk.

training and team building experts. Among the activities provided at Rock Lea are abseiling, rock climbing, caving, mine exploration, orienteering and hillwalking, in addition to specialist multi-sports courses for families and team building and management training for business people.

Wet weather

A visit to the atmospheric **Padley Chapel** near Grindleford, is a must. This is where on 12 July 1588, the year of the Armada, Nicholas Garlick and Robert Ludlam, two Roman Catholic priests were arrested and taken to Derby where they were hung, drawn and quartered in Derby a few days later. The gatehouse of the manor, now converted to a chapel, is a place of pilgrimage for Catholic visitors.

PADLEY CHAPEL: Padley, Grindleford, Hope Valley, Derbyshire; ☎01433 650352; www.padley.catholicweb.com. Open Sun/Wed 2pm–4pm from Easter to 9 Sept.

Padley Chapel

What to do with children…

If you fancy a dip and the weather is fine, then the **Open Air Swimming Pool** in **Hathersage** is worth a visit. An open air swimming pool is an unusual feature these days, but the full-length pool is very popular when it is open during the summer season.

HATHERSAGE OPEN AIR SWIMMING POOL: Oddfellows Road, Hathersage, Hope Valley S32 1DU; ☎01433 650843. Entry: adults £4.20; children £2.10; concessions £2.70; open daily 7.30am–6pm, 29 Mar to 23 May and 8 Sept to 20 Sept; 7.30am–7pm 24 May to 7 Sept.

… and how to avoid children

One of the best art and photographic galleries in the Peak is **The Derwent Gallery**, situated in the Derwentside village of Grindleford. The Gallery's reputation is based on the high proportion of original British art work, especially by local artists

THE DERWENT GALLERY: Main Road, Grindleford, Hope Valley, Derbyshire S32 2JN; ☎01433 630458; www.derwentgallery.com. Open Tues–Sun.

and photographers, on show, and for the quality of its presentation. All the pictures are framed on site by the owner, Robin Ashmore.

The best... **PLACES TO STAY**

BOUTIQUE

The Maynard

Main Road, Grindleford S32 2HE
☎ **01433 630321**
www.themaynard.co.uk

Traditional meets modern in this stylish hotel. Bedrooms have been revamped by a local interior designer in contemporary style and feature king-sized beds, plasma screen satellite TV and Wi-Fi internet connections. Meals are served in the bar and restaurant, and an alfresco dining area overlooks landscaped gardens and the Derwent Valley.

Price: B&B from £65 for a double.

HOTEL

The George Hotel

Hathersage S32 1BB
☎ **01433 650436**
www.george-hotel.net

Sister hotel to the Cavendish Hotel, this 500-year-old former inn retains its original character while ministering to modern needs, with contemporary decor and award-winning cuisine. Accommodation includes standard, superior and room with a four-poster bed. Informal, contemporary dining focusing on fresh food and flavour in George's restaurant.

Price: B&B from £121 for a double.

INN

The Chequers Inn

Froggatt Edge, Hope Valley S32 3ZJ
☎ **01433 630231**
www.chequers-froggatt.com

Traditional 16th-century inn combining country charm with modern comfort. En-suite bedrooms are cosy, comfortable and full of character. Innovative cuisine based on locally sourced produce. A wide-ranging menu of British and European dishes is complemented by an imaginative wine list and traditional ales. Garden for dining alfresco, panoramic views.

Price: B&B from £75 for a double/twin; from £80 for a four poster.

B&B

Cannon Croft

Cannonfields, Hathersage S32 1AG
☎ **01433 650005**
www.cannoncroftbedandbreakfast.co.uk

Multi-award-winning en-suite accommodation with warm welcome, stunning views and extensive breakfast menu. Individually designed rooms have flat screen television, well-stocked hospitality trays and other extras. Full English/Derbyshire and vegetarian breakfasts available, plus specials such as mumbled eggs, kipper on the bone and smoked haddock, featuring the best local produce.

Price: B&B from £32 per person per night.

The best... PLACES TO STAY

Hillfoot Farm

Castleton Road, Hathersage S32 1EG
☎ 01433 651673
www.hillfootfarm.com

Extended farm house offering comfortable accommodation in the heart of the Hope Valley. En-suite rooms and conservatory where guests can relax. Full English or vegetarian breakfast using locally sourced produce served in oak-beamed dining room. Large car park and secure bike shed.

Price: B&B £26 to £30 pppn.

SELF-CATERING

North Lees Hall

Hathersage, c/o Vivat Trust Holidays, 70 Cowcross Street, London EC1M 6EJ
☎ 0845 090 0194; www.vivat.org.uk

If you have literary leanings and yearn for a romantic getaway in breathtaking scenery, North Lees Hall is the perfect destination. Designed by Robert Smythson in 1590, it is believed to have been the inspiration for Thornfield Hall in Charlotte Bronte's *Jane Eyre*. Facilities include four poster beds, open fires and roof terrace.

Price: Apartment 1, £515 to £710 per week; Apartment 2, £705 to £920 per week.

Morley Cottage

Main Road, Hathersage S32 1BB
☎ 01433 650807
www.morley-cottage.co.uk

South-facing cottage that accommodates two people, overlooking gardens, farmland and woodland. Sympathetically converted with well equipped kitchen, cosy lounge with oak beams, bedroom with en-suite shower facilities and cot suitable for a small child. Double doors from the lounge open on to a private patio garden area.

Price: from £220 to £325 for a week.

Bridgefoot Cottage

Froggatt S32 3ZN
☎ 01433 630120

Grade II, 16th-century farmhouse which sleeps four in an idyllic setting on the banks of the River Derwent. Flagged floors, oak-beamed ceilings, fireplaces and kitchen with Aga create a cosy atmosphere. Large sitting room with multi fuel stove, downstairs bathroom with Victorian bath and two double bedrooms, one with four-poster bed and en-suite shower room.

Price: from £495 to £875 for a week; from £275 for short breaks.

The best... FOOD AND DRINK

Take your pick of delis offering a range of delicious produce and delectable ice cream made from local milk in this scenic area of the Hope Valley. Eating out is also a pleasure, from fine dining to down-to-earth cafés, and there's a good selection of traditional pubs.

▶ Staying in

Locally produced food and drink can be found in abundance at **Country Choice** in Grindleford (Main Road S32 2JN; ☎01433 639333). You can buy locally baked cakes and bread, locally grown vegetables, meat from Stoney Middleton and dairy products from Tideswell, then wash it all down with real ales from Thornbridge Brewery and Peak Ales. Other attractions are a well-stocked deli counter, specialist chutneys, pickles, mayonnaise, sauces, biscuits and coffees, plus wines and spirits. If you need a rest after all that shopping, or are taking a break while out walking or sightseeing, you can enjoy a latte or cappuccino at the breakfast bar inside or at tables and chairs outside. Another local food shop and café worth a visit is **Coleman's Deli** in Hathersage (The Square, Main Road S32 1DD; ☎01433 650505), where you'll find a wide range of delicacies to eat in or take away. Takeaway options include a wide variety of sandwiches, paninis and wraps, and you can even order your own personalised picnic or hamper to complement a special day out. Picnics start at £4.95 per person, while bespoke hampers start at £15.

While in the area, you can't miss **Hope Valley Ice Cream** (Thorpe Farm, Hathersage S32 1BQ; ☎01433 650659), home-made by the Marsden family, using their own milk. Choose from deliciously named flavours such as Camilla's Vanilla, award-winning Gertrude's Whisky and Ginger, Rusty Buttercups Rum and Raisin or Simply Stanage. You can buy the ice creams at a number of local shops, including Country Choice and Coleman's Deli, or you can visit the farm's ice cream parlour, open every Saturday and Sunday afternoon from 2pm to 5pm.

Hope Valley Country Market takes place at the Methodist Church Hall, Main Road, Hathersage (S32 1AA; ☎01433 620297) on Fridays from 9.30am to 11.15am (closed from mid-December to end of January).

EATING OUT

FINE DINING

The Walnut Club
The Square, Main Road,
Hathersage S32 1BB
☎ 01433 651155
www.thewalnutclub.com

Michelin Bib Gourmand rated restaurant specialising in traceable organic, free-range and wild produce cuisine, based on largely local and Fairtrade food. Typical dishes include local game, rabbit and The Walnut Club's Bakewell Tart (*sic*) for dessert. All dietary and allergy requirements catered for. Live jazz. Main courses cost from £14.95.

RESTAURANT

The Maynard
Main Road, Grindleford S32 2HE
☎ 01433 630321
www.themaynard.co.uk

Wide range of meals, including several vegan and vegetarian options, complemented by a good selection of wines, are served in both the contemporary bar and restaurant, which has views over the garden and scenic Derwent Valley beyond. A three-course dinner costs £30 per person.

The George Hotel
Hathersage S32 1BB
☎ 01433 650436
www.george-hotel.net

The emphasis is on flavour here and fresh ingredients, sourced locally where possible, are presented simply and served informally in relaxed surroundings. Sample starters include smoked haddock and Gruyère fish cake and pigeon, red onion and pancetta pasty, while among typical mains are confit of local free range pork shoulder and spiced pumpkin ravioli. Mains cost £26.50 for two courses to £39.50 for four courses.

GASTRO PUB

The Chequers Inn
Froggatt Edge, Hope Valley S32 3ZJ
☎ 01433 630231
www.chequers-froggatt.com

Recent winners of the Pub of the Year award in the Derbyshire Food & Drink Awards, this AA Rosette pub has innovative cuisine using locally sourced, fresh produce. Both British and Continental dishes are complemented by a good wine list and traditional ales. Meals can be served indoors or out in the garden in good weather. Start with grilled sardines or garlic prawns, followed by pot-roasted lamb shank or home-made homity pie. Starters cost from £4.75, mains from £8.

CAFÉ

David Mellor Design Museum Café
The Round Building,
Hathersage S32 1BA
☎ 01433 650220
www.davidmellordesign.co.uk

Stylish venue in which to relax and enjoy a light lunch, sandwich, home-made cake or pudding made using local produce. Designed by Corin Mellor, the café is a fine example of informal modern dining style, equipped with his father, David Mellor's tableware, with sliding doors to provide extra seating on the terrace in the summer.

EATING OUT

Coleman's Deli
The Square, Main Road, Hathersage S32 1BB
☎ **01433 650505**
www.colemansdeli.co.uk

Lively and friendly family-run business offering an eat-in, takeaway, picnic, hamper and catering service using Fairtrade, local and organic produce. Eat-in and takeaway options include sandwiches, paninis, wraps, salad boxes and home-made cakes and soups. Deli counter and shop serving everything from pork pies to pâté and coffee to chocolates.

Grindleford Station Cafe
Upper Padley, Grindleford
☎ **01433 001020**

You'll either love it or hate it, but most people agree that visiting this café, near the mouth of the Totley Tunnel (when it was built, the longest railway tunnel in the UK) is an experience. Hikers and bikers tend to love its large plates of fried food and numerous signs that leave visitors in no doubt of the house rules.

TEA ROOM

Cintra's Tea Room
Main Road, Hathersage S32 1BB
☎ **01433 651825**

Wide selection of home-made breakfasts, meals and cakes served in this quaint tea room, which has a large secluded garden that seats up to 80 people. Local produce used where possible to make such dishes as pies, quiches and lasagne on the premises.

Longshaw Estate Tea Room
Longshaw, Grindleford, Derbyshire S11 7TZ
☎ **01433 637904**
www.nationaltrust.org.uk

National Trust tea room and shop serving a variety of fare, overlooking panoramic views of the scenic Longshaw Estate. Outdoor seating where visitors can relax in fine weather with a cup of tea, cake or ice cream. Opening times vary according to the season: check before you visit.

🍺 Drinking

In Grindleford you can sample real ales, including at least one guest ale, bottle conditioned beers and wines from around the world in the bar of the **Sir William Hotel** (Sir William Hill S32 2HS; ☎01433 630303). The lounge and bar offer a choice of traditional bar meals, cakes and sandwiches, and walkers, hikers, cyclists and dogs are welcome in the Walkers Retreat and Snug. Guest beers from local breweries, regular pub quizzes and live music are popular features at the **Millstone Inn** in Hathersage (Sheffield Road S32 1DA; ☎01433 650258), which once served the nearby millstone quarries but is now a favourite haunt for climbers and walkers.

Situated on 9 acres of land on the banks of the River Derwent, **The Plough Inn** at Hathersage (Leadmill Bridge S32 1BA; ☎01433 650319) has a cosy bar with real log fires and serves a range of hand-pulled ales from around the world, plus modern European and traditional food. Named after Robin Hood's famous right hand man (who is reputed to be buried in the village's St Michael and All Angels churchyard), the **Little John Inn** at Hathersage (Station Road S32 1DD; ☎01433 650225) serves a variety of locally brewed, traditional hand-pulled brews, including its own Little John Ale. An extensive menu of home-cooked food is also available. At least five real ales are always on offer at **The Scotsman's Pack Inn** in Hathersage (School Lane S32 1BZ; ☎01433 650253), named after the packhorse men who used to ply their goods (including tartans) and bring news. Food ranges from baguettes and sandwiches to daily specials. An outside patio area looks out on a trout stream.

Once a popular stop for livestock drivers and stagecoaches, the **Fox House Vintage Inn** at Longshaw (S11 7TY; ☎01433 630374) now caters mainly for walkers, visitors and business people and serves a selection of real ales and bar meals. Also in Longshaw, the **Grouse Inn** (S11 7TZ; ☎01433 630423) recently won an award for its real ales, including guest beers and serves everything from home-made sandwiches to full meals at lunchtime and in the evening.

ℹ️ Visitor Information

Tourist information centres: Bakewell Visitor Centre, The Old Market Hall, Bridge Street, Bakewell, Derbyshire DE45 1DS, ☎01629 816558, www.peakdistrict.gov.uk, open daily; Castleton Visitor Centre, Buxton Road, Castleton, Hope Valley S33 8WN, ☎ 01629 816558, www.peakdistrict.gov.uk.

Hospitals: A&E, Chesterfield Royal Hospital, Calow, Chesterfield, ☎01246 277271; Northern General Hospital, Herries Road, Sheffield, ☎0114 243 4343.

Doctors: Ashenfell Surgery, Church Lane, Baslow, ☎01246 582216; Eyam Surgery, Church Street, Eyam, Hope Valley S32 5QH, ☎01433 630836; Tideswell Surgery, Parke Road, Tideswell SK17 8NS, ☎01298 871292; Evelyn Medical Centre, Marsh Avenue, Hope S33 6RJ, ☎01433 621557.

Taxis: Sickleholme Private Hire, Bamford, ☎0777 376 3445.

THE UPPER DERWENT AND BAMFORD

This is the Peak District's own Lake District. Dominated by the triple reservoirs of Howden, Derwent and Ladybower, which flooded the Upper Derwent Valley to slake the insatiable thirsts of the booming industrial populations of Sheffield, Derby, Nottingham and Leicester, this is the biggest expanse of open water in the Peak. And that subtle mixture of water, trees and high, enclosing moorland is extremely popular with visitors. Over a million and a quarter people throng the Upper Derwent annually, necessitating an award-winning traffic and visitor management scheme which was a unique example of cooperation between the water company (Severn Trent), the National Park authority, and local landowners and agencies.

The upper end of the valley, from Fairholmes northwards to King's Tree, is closed to traffic on summer weekends and Bank Holidays, and a well-patronised minibus and cycle-hire service swings smoothly into operation. There is a well-maintained National Park visitor centre at Fairholmes, in the shadow of the Derwent Dam.

WHAT TO SEE AND DO

The upper two dams in the Derwent were built between 1901 and 1916, employing an army of over 1,000 navvies and their families who were housed in a temporary village at Birchinlee while the work took place. This self-contained community had its own shops, recreational hall, hospital, police station and school, housed in nearly 100 corrugated iron structures, which gave the settlement its local nickname of **Tin Town**. A specially built railway brought the stone for the dams up from Bamford and carried the people out to the cities for shopping. Nothing now remains of Tin Town, but its story is told at the **Fairholmes Visitor Centre** (see below). The third, and largest reservoir and dam was the Ladybower, constructed between 1935 and 1943, which necessitated the demolition of two ancient villages which once stood in the

The Derwent Dam

valley bottom. The populations of both Derwent and Ashtopton were re-housed at Yorkshire Bridge, Bamford, and 100 bodies from the churchyard reburied at Bamford. The foundations of their homes, the church and the Victorian pile of Derwent Hall can still be seen in times of drought when the water is drawn down.

The other famous story of the Derwent Dams is that of the **Dambusters**, because it was here that the brave crews of 617 Squadron trained for their epic raid on the Ruhr dams in May 1943. The twin towers of the Howden and Derwent dams were thought to be a fair match for those which provided hydro-electric power for Hitler's Germany, so low level practice flights were undertaken here in Derbyshire in rehearsal for that fateful raid. New pilots of the modern 617 Squadron still undertake their first flights over the Derwent reservoirs, and there is a memorial in the gateway to the Derwent Dam.

The Derwent Dams during a 'Dambuster'

Other reservoirs created to supply Sheffield and Stocksbridge fill the narrow valleys which drain the Bradfield Moors off the Strines road between Moscar and Langsett. These include the **Dale Dyke Reservoir**, scene of a fateful collapse in 1864, when 244 people died and 20,000 more lost their homes in Bradfield, Loxley and Sheffield as a veritable tsunami of flood waters surged through, taking everything in

Tin Town and the Dambusters

During the construction of the mighty masonry walls of the Derwent and Howden Dams in the Upper Derwent Valley between 1901 and 1916, a thriving little temporary township accommodated the navvies and their families at Birchinlee, between the two dams. Known locally as 'Tin Town' because most of the 100 buildings had corrugated iron walls, Birchinlee was home to up to 1,000 people at the time. The bustling community boasted a range of shops, a recreation hall, school, hospital, 'canteen' (as the pub was known), and a police station. It had its own football and cricket teams who competed in local leagues, and the railway which brought the stone for the dams also served to bring supplies to the shops, and to take the residents out of the valley to the surrounding towns.

The site of Tin Town is now lost in the forestry planted after the dams were built, but a plaque records its existence in a layby just below the Howden Dam. The third and lowest dam on the Derwent at Ladybower was constructed between 1935 and 1943, and involved the de-population, demolition and eventually flooding of the twin villages of Derwent and Ashopton, at the foot of the Snake Pass.

The Derwent and Howden Reservoirs were also used by the legendary Dambusters of 617 Squadron as they trained in their Lancaster bombers for their daring raid on the similarly situated dams of the Ruhr Valley in Germany in 1943, during the Second World War. And even today, one of the first sorties for new pilots of 617 Squadron is to fly over the Derwent Dams in their supersonic jets.

Derwent Reservoir

its wake. The reservoir-dominated village of **Langsett** has some pleasant cottages and a fine, cathedral-like tithe barn, now used as a village community centre and ranger base.

One of the most famous roads in the Peak threads through the south of the area, just to the north of the pleasant gritstone village of Bamford. This is the A57 **Snake Road**, engineered by Thomas Telford in 1821 as a turnpike link between Sheffield and Glossop and reaching a height of 1,679ft/512m at its summit between Kinder Scout and Bleaklow. It follows the line of the Roman Doctor's Gate road for much of its length. This is excellent walking country with a range of options from a gentle stroll and perhaps a picnic with the family around the placid waters of the **Ladybower or Derwent reservoirs**, to the more serious 'bog-trotting' across the bleak moorlands of **Derwent Edge**, or the **Cut Gate track**, which runs down to Langsett. Similarly easy 'round the reservoir' walks can be enjoyed around the **Langsett Reservoir** in the north of the area. The turreted tower on Langsett's dam wall is said to have been modelled on Lancaster Castle.

Snake Pass in the snow

The 3 mile walk to **Derwent Edge** is a more serious proposition, demanding good footwear and waterproofs, as the weather on the moors is notoriously changeable. You can extend your walk along the edge to the distinctive rocky outcrops of **The Salt Cellar** and the **Wheel Stones**, also known as the Coach and Horses from their resemblance to that early form of inter-city transport. Further north is **Margery Hill**, at 546m/1,791ft, the highest point in South Yorkshire. The Cut Gate track, as mentioned above, is a tough moorland route which runs up from the northernmost extremity of the Howden Reservoir at the reconstructed **Slippery Stones** packhorse bridge (which formerly stood in Derwent village) to Langsett.

☂ Wet weather

The **Upper Derwent Visitor Centre** at Fairholmes, in the shadow of the Derwent Dam, has informative displays on the story of Tintown, the Dambusters, what happens to the water stored in the reservoirs, and the catchment areas of the surrounding moorland.

> UPPER DERWENT VISITOR CENTRE: Fairholmes, Derwent, Bamford, Hope Valley S33 0AQ; ☎01433 650953; www.peakdistrict.gov.uk. Entry: free, open Easter to end Sept and weekends.

Then there's the **Parish Church of St John the Baptist** at Bamford, which was built by local landowner William Cameron Moore in 1860 and contains some touching reminders and memorials to the 'lost villages' of Derwent and Ashopton.

🚴 What to do with children

You can hire a range of cycles from the **Derwent Cycle Hire Centre**. which is located near the visitor centre to cycle through peaceful woodlands and traffic-free roads around the Derwent, Howden and Ladybower Reservoirs. The centre can also provide tandems, trikes, hand-cranked tricycles and powered mobility scooters for the less able, but you will need to contact the centre for details.

> DERWENT CENTRE: Fairholmes Car Park, Derwent, Bamford, Hope Valley S33 0AQ; ☎01433 651261; www. peakdistrict.gov. uk/cycle. Open every day Mar to Oct, Nov to Feb, see website for details.

Cycling below the Howden Dam

The best... **PLACES TO STAY**

HOTEL

The Rising Sun

Castleton Road, Bamford S33 0AL
☎ 01433 651323
www.the-rising-sun.org

Privately owned, 18th-century country inn with traditional décor, welcoming lounge, pleasant gardens and period-furnished bedrooms. Executive suites have super king-size beds. Lunch and dinner offers British fare with modern European and Oriental influences, complemented by real ales and fine wines.

Price: B&B from £70 for a double.

INN

Yorkshire Bridge Inn

Ashopton Road, Bamford S33 0AZ
☎ 01433 651361
www.yorkshire-bridge.co.uk

Bars with wooden beams, stone-built conservatory, courtyard and spacious beer garden are all features of this 19th century inn. Fresh local produce is served. En-suite rooms, one with four poster bed.

Price: B&B from £38 per person per night.

SELF-CATERING

Ladybower Apartments

c/o The Yorkshire Bridge Inn, Ashopton Road, Bamford S33 0AZ
www.ladybowerapartments.co.uk

Luxury holiday apartments in the former pump house for nearby Ladybower Reservoir, each sleeping four to six people. Stunning setting next to the reservoir. Quality, contemporary furnishings add style to well-equipped accommodation. Most bedrooms are en-suite with television.

Price: From £375 for a week.

Derwent View

12 Ashopton Drive, Bamford S33 0BU
☎ 01433 651637
www.derwentview.co.uk

Modern, detached, ground level accommodation for up to six people, situated in attractive, lawned gardens with outdoor furniture and barbecue, and encircled by the beautiful countryside of the Hope Valley. Well-equipped, with two bedrooms with en-suite bathroom facilities, twin-bedded room, DVD player and library, dishwasher, washing facilities and parking.

Price: From £375 for a week.

Stanley House

c/o the Waggon and Horses, Langsett, Sheffield S36 4GY
☎ 01226 763167
www.langsettinn.com/stanley

Recently redecorated and re-furnished 100-year-old cottage on the old village green, sleeping up to six people. Fully equipped kitchen, comfortable living room with cosy coal effect pot-belly stove, conservatory and sweeping views.

Price: From £350 for a week.

The best... FOOD AND DRINK

Cask conditioned and guest ales and a good selection of wines complement lunchtime and evening meals at **The Angler's Rest** in Bamford (Main Road S33 0DY; ☎01433 659415), where children and dogs are welcome and there are regular quiz nights. Real ales, including local brews, are on tap at the **Strines Inn** above Bradfield Dale (S6 6JE; ☎0114 285 1247), set amid scenic countryside opposite the Strines Reservoir. Originally the 13th-century home of the Worrall family, the bulk of the current building was added three centuries later. Visitors warm themselves in front of open fires and tuck into bar meals ranging from sandwiches and salads to hearty, filled Yorkshire puddings.

Attractively situated in the Loxley Valley, the **Plough Inn** at Low Bradfield (New Road S6 6HW; ☎0114 285 1280) is a former 18th-century farm and now a free house, selling a variety of guest beers and food made from local produce. Folk nights are also a regular feature of the calendar. Guest ales and hearty food, including home-cooked pies, are served at the hospitable **Royal Hotel** at Dungworth (Main Road S6 6HF; ☎0114 285 1213), where children, walkers and well-behaved pets are welcome.

Freshly prepared food, real ale and a real fire welcome visitors at the **Waggon & Horses** in Langsett (S36 1GY; ☎01226 763147), family-run for more than 30 years. The Grade I, early 19th-century inn overlooks Langsett Reservoir and the Pennine moors and favours conversation and dominoes over fruit machines and piped music.

ⓘ Visitor Information

Tourist information centre: Upper Derwent Visitor Centre, Fairholmes, Derwent, Bamford, Hope Valley S33 0AQ, ☎01433 650953, www.peakdistrict.gov.uk, open Easter to end Sept and weekends.

Hospitals: A&E, Northern General Hospital, Herries Road, Sheffield, ☎0114 243 4343.

Doctors: Ashenfell Surgery, Church Lane, Baslow, ☎01246 582216; Eyam Surgery, Church Street, Eyam S32 5QH, ☎01433 630836; Evelyn Medical Centre, Marsh Avenue, Hope S33 6RJ, ☎01433 621557.

Taxis: Sickleholme Private Hire, Bamford, ☎0777 376 3445.

CHESTERFIELD, SHEFFIELD AND BRADFIELD

Sheffield has long been proud of its so-called 'Golden Frame'. It's the only sizeable city in Europe to have large parts of a national park within its boundaries, which extend west from the suburbs of the city across the moors as far as Stanage Edge, above Hathersage. And Sheffielders have always been strong supporters and keen users of the attractions of the glorious Peak District on their doorsteps. To them, 'going to Derbyshire' is an essential feature of every weekend or day off, and they come out into the Peak in huge numbers by car, bus, train or even on foot. Easily accessible on foot are the twin villages of High and Low Bradfield, and the reservoirs of the Loxley valley.

Chesterfield, probably most famous for the twisted spire of its parish church, is equally lucky, with the pretty villages of Holymoorside, Brampton and Barlow on its western doorstep, and the peaceful, tree-lined reservoirs at Linacre are also very convenient. Further north, the industrial town of Stocksbridge is close to the wooded escarpment of Wharncliffe Crags, where some of the earliest pioneers of rock climbing, notably J W Puttrell, first tested their skills on the abrasive gritstone in the last years of the 19th century. Langsett Reservoir, in the upper reaches of Sheffield's river, the Porter or Little Don, is another popular destination, with pleasant waterside walks around its wooded shores.

The hilltop market town of Penistone, the highest market town in Yorkshire, was once one of the most important agricultural centres in the northern Peak, and still holds an annual agricultural show in September at which the local Roman-nosed Penistone sheep are shown. Penistone dates back to the Norman Conquest, and the oldest bulding is the medieval parish church of Saint John the Baptist Church. The nearby hamlet of Thurlstone is famous for its hand bell ringers.

WHAT TO SEE AND DO

High and Low Bradfield

A walk around the twin villages of High and Low Bradfield, on the western fringe of Sheffield, is always enjoyable, especially if you visit the lofty 15th-century **parish church of St Nicholas** at High Bradfield, which enjoys one of the finest views from any churchyard in the Peak. As you enter the sloping churchyard, you will pass the 18th-century octagonal **Watchhouse**, which was built to deter and frustrate body-snatchers from the graveyard. Bradfield also features no less than two motte and bailey castle

175

sites, one known as Bailey Hill and the other, behind the church, Castle Hill.

The shores of the string of reservoirs, which have been formed as the streams and rivers which run off the Bradfield Moors were dammed, also make for pleasant walking. Most interesting, perhaps is the **Dale Dyke Reservoir**, which burst through its newly built dam on a fateful night in March 1864 and flooded through the Loxley Valley as far as Sheffield, killing

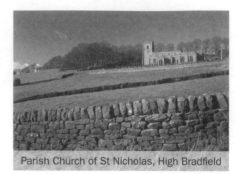
Parish Church of St Nicholas, High Bradfield

244 people and making 20,000 homeless. The site of the former dam wall is now marked by a plaque in the trees.

There are pleasant walks round the **Linacre Reservoirs**, west of Chesterfield, and through the trees of **Wharncliffe Wood**, beneath the rocks of Wharncliffe Crags, and through the council-managed trees of **Eccleshall Wood**, on the western edge of the city.

Sheffield and around

There are many things to see and do in **Sheffield** itself, especially in the transformed city centre. A good way to see it all is to take part in a free (donations requested) walking tour, which are led by volunteers and take in all the major sites of interest in the city. The tours take place at 10.15am every Tuesday and Thursday, starting at the tourist information centre on Norfolk Row, where you can book your place or also by ringing Sheffield Tourism on ☎0114 221 1900.

The oldest building in the city centre is the **Cathedral Church of St Peter and St Paul**, in Cathedral Square. The oldest parts of the building are the medieval chancel and sanctuary which were built in 1430, but there are stones from an earlier, Norman church in the east wall. The ultra-modern lantern-topped porch and Chapel of St George were added in 1966. Perhaps the most famous monuments inside the cathedral are in the Shrewsbury Chapel, which was added in 1520 by local landowners, the Earls of Shrewsbury, to house their family tombs. The grandest of these is that of the sixth Earl, the last husband of Bess of Hardwick (see p. 60), who was the unwilling chaperone of Mary Queen of Scots at Chatsworth in the late 16th century (see p. 146).

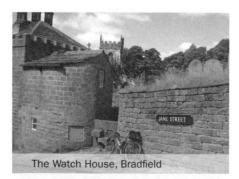
The Watch House, Bradfield

The magnificent Victorian Gothic **Town Hall**, designed by E W Mountford and opened in 1897, is appropriately topped by the bronze figure of Vulcan, the mythical god of fire. The unloved and much-derided 'Egg Box' former offices of the city council have now been demolished and replaced by the wonderful **Peace Gardens**, with their accessible fountains, much loved by children (and some adults) on hot summer days, colourful gardens and gentle cascades.

One of Sheffield's architectural and cultural treasures, the **Millennium Galleries** on Arundel Gate is an outstanding venue for art and design, in the heart of the city and linked to the stunning **Winter Gardens** (see Wet weather below). Alongside innovative contemporary and historical design, and home to Sheffield's metalwork and John Ruskin galleries, the Millennium Galleries is famous for bringing masterpieces from national galleries and museums to the city in prestigious touring exhibitions. The Cafe Azure offers a wide range of refreshments.

MILLENNIUM GALLERIES: Arundel Gate, Sheffield S1 2PP; ☎0114 272 2106. Entry: free; open 8am–5pm, Mon to Sat; 11am–5pm Sun.

GRAVES ART GALLERY: Surrey Street, Sheffield S1 1XZ; ☎0114 278 2600. Entry: free; open 10am–5pm Mon–Sat.

Opposite the Millennium Galleries and above the Central Library, the **Graves Art Gallery** is home to an outstanding collection of 19th and 20th-century modern art, including works by Picasso, Cezanne and Stanley Spencer.

The recently restored 19 acre/7.6 hectare **Sheffield Botanical Gardens** are on the western side of the city, about a mile from the city centre. They were originally designed by Robert Marnock in the Gardenesque style and opened in 1836. The site now has 15 different garden areas featuring collections of plants from all over the world, including Mediterranean, Asian, American prairie-style, woodland and rock and water plantings. The National Collections of *Weigela* and *Diervilla* are kept here. The Gardens also contain several listed buildings including the restored Grade II* listed curvilinear **Glass Pavilions**, some of the earliest ever built,

SHEFFIELD BOTANICAL GARDENS: Clarkehouse Road, Sheffield S10 2LN; ☎0114 268 6001. Entry: free; open 8am–dusk, Mon to Fri, 10am–dusk, Sat/Sun (summer); 8am–4pm Mon to Fri, 10am–4pm Sat/Sun (winter).

which were officially re-opened by Prince Charles in 2003. The recent renovations, which cost about £7 million, were the first and most complete by a botanical garden in the country, in which the voluntary sector, notably the Friends of the Botanical Gardens, raised more than £1 million of the funding.

The **Kelham Island Museum** is a living and working museum which celebrates the famous 'Made in Sheffield' mark of quality by preserving Sheffield's industrial heritage. The main attraction is the mighty 12,000 HP River Don Engine, particularly when it is 'in steam'. Younger visitors can enjoy the interactive experience of being 'processed' like the steel which made the city famous. There is also a transport collection, including the Sheffield *Simplex* car built in 1920, and a Rolls Royce jet engine.

KELHAM ISLAND MUSEUM: Alma Street (off Corporation Street), Sheffield S3 8RY; ☎0114 272 2106; www.Kelham Island Museum.com. Entry: adult £4, concessions £3, children free; open daily 10am–4pm Mon to Thurs; 11am–4.45pm, Sun; year round.

Another great day out is provided by the **Abbeydale Industrial Hamlet**, a unique preserved industrial works dating from the 18th century, on Abbeydale Road South, on

In the Abbeydale Industrial Hamlet

ABBEYDALE INDUSTRIAL HAMLET:
Abbeydale Road South, Sheffield S7 2QW;
☎0114 2367731; www.simt.co.uk. Entry:
adults £3, concessions £2; open 23 Mar
to 5 Oct, Mon–Thurs 10am–4pm, Sun
11am–4.45pm.

the western edge of Sheffield. Originally known as the Abbeydale Works, it was one of the largest water-powered sites on the River Sheaf. The main products were agricultural scythes, but other edge tools were made too, such as grass hooks and hay knives. In the hamlet, you can see waterwheels, tilt hammers, a grinding hull and the only intact crucible steel furnace surviving in the world today. The site is a listed building and a Scheduled Ancient Monument.

The recently refurbished, award-winning **Weston Park Museum**, in the leafy surrounds of Weston Park, close to the university and opposite Sheffield Children's Hospital, is just a mile from Sheffield city centre. The city's collection of beautiful, varied and unusual treasures are brought to life by incredible facts and hands-on interactive displays. **Weston Park** also contains the best collection of archaeological remains from the Peak

WESTON PARK MUSEUM: Western Bank,
Sheffield S10 2PT; ☎0114 278 2600;
www.museums-sheffield.org.uk. Entry:
free, open 10am–5pm, Mon–Sat;
11am-5pm, Sun.

District. You can see here much of the collection of Thomas Bateman, the famed 19th-century pioneer archaeologist, who thoroughly explored most of the Peak's barrows and monuments. The famous Benty Grange helmet, one of only a handful of Anglo Saxon helmets ever found in Britain, is also here, alongside a meticulous reconstruction of what it might have looked like when it was buried 1,000 years ago near Parsley Hay with its unknown owner.

Chesterfield

St Mary and All Saints, the famous **Crooked Spire** church, was built in the late 13th century and finished around 1360. It is the largest church in Derbyshire, and contains the alabaster tombs of the Foljambe family. That famous spire (which gives its name to the local football club, who are known as the 'Spireites') stands 228 ft/69m high and leans 9ft 5in/3m from its true centre. It is thought that the spire became twisted because unseasoned wood was used during its construction. After 32 tons of lead tiles were placed on top, the timber dried out and it was the weight of the lead which twisted the spire. Tours of the tower to the base of the Crooked Spire take place from Monday to Saturday (weather permitting) between Easter and Christmas. Times of the tours are advertised on a notice inside the south-west doors of the church, and the dizzying climb, not recommended for those who suffer from vertigo, takes about 40–45 minutes.

CHURCH OF ST MARY AND ALL SAINTS CHURCH: Church Way, Chesterfield, Derbyshire S40 1XJ; ☎01246 206506; www.chesterfieldparishchurch.org.uk. Entry: adults £3.40, children £1.50; open daily; see text for details of tours up to spire.

The Crooked Spire church, St Mary and All Saints, Chesterfield

The **Chesterfield Museum and Art Gallery**, in St Mary's Gate, Chesterfield, tells the story of Chesterfield from its Roman origins to the present day. An ever-changing programme of temporary exhibitions and events explain the town's growth from its original role as a market and later as an important industrial and coal mining centre on the North Derbyshire coalfield. Local artists also exhibit in the art gallery.

CHESTERFIELD MUSEUM AND ART GALLERY: St Mary's Gate, Chesterfield S41 7TD; ☎01246 345727; www.chesterfield.gov.uk. Entry: free; open daily 10am–4pm except Wed/Sun.

For those who fancy seeing this area on horseback, the BHS-approved **Alton Riding School** at Alton, near Ashover, south of Chesterfield (Alton, Chesterfield S42 6AW; ☎Tel:01246 590267; www.go-chesterfield.co.uk/alton-riding-school) offers a range of hacking and trekking opportunities for riders of all ages and experience on the eastern side of the Peak District.

Wet weather

The Revolution House (S41 9JZ) in the village of Old Whittington, 3 miles north of Chesterfield, is a good place to go on a wet day. It takes its name from the 'Glorious' Revolution of 1688. Formerly an alehouse known as the Cock and Pynot ('pynot' is the local dialect word for a magpie), it was in this thatched building that three local noblemen – the Earl of Devonshire (from nearby Chatsworth), the Earl of Danby and John D'Arcy – met to plan their part in the momentous events which led to the overthrow of King James II

THE REVOLUTION HOUSE: High Street, Old Whittington, Chesterfield, ☎01246 345727; www.chesterfield.gov.uk. Entry: free; open daily 11am–4pm, Good Friday to end Sept; closed Tues.

 ## CELEBRITY CONNECTIONS

Comedian, actor, writer and television presenter **Michael Palin** first acquired the taste for globe-trotting on his doorstep, here in the Peak District. Born in Broomhill, Sheffield, young Michael perceived the Peak as 'exotic, faraway lands that I could reach without spending a lot of money' during his cash-strapped youth. He travelled here by bus or on his bike, and Ladybower and Derwent Dams, Hathersage and Grindleford were popular destinations. Other regular haunts included the caves in Castleton, such as Speedwell, Blue John and Treak Cliff. He fondly recalls his first visit to Speedwell, 'with its glistening, dripping, shiny, cold, wet walls, the shaft underneath and the great pit at the end. It really stimulated my imagination and fascination for strange places'.

As a child, Michael visited many of the area's historic churches with his father, whose favourite place was Monsal Dale. His own personal preference is for the gritstone edges near Sheffield, such as Stanage, with its 'lonely scenery, fantastic views and sense of wide open spaces'. He cherishes the Peak District for its wealth and variety of landscapes: 'It has villages, beautiful houses, elaborate stone-work on churches and pubs, valleys, hills, rivers and so on in quite a confined space. You see things that, when you're on your travels, you might have to go many hundreds of miles to see, especially in places like Russia or Canada. That's what makes the area so special'.

Although he lives in London and now travels all over the world, Michael is an honorary Friend of the Peak District, as part of a scheme launched by the Peak District & South Yorkshire branch of the CPRE. As well as supporting the charity's commitment to the life of the Peak District and its efforts to preserve its unique landscape, the role transports him back to 'the first 15 to 20 years of my life, when I found it a wonderful place in which to be let loose, providing me early on with the inspiration to travel and go to places that were different from where I lived'.

LOCAL KNOWLEDGE

Carol Robinson grew up in Beeley on the Chatsworth Estate, where her family were tenant farmers and have links going back to the 17th century. After studying and working away, she returned as Chief Executive of the CPRE/Friends of the Peak District, the independent charity which works to protect and enhance the landscapes of the National Park.

The best thing about living in the Peak District: The peace and quiet at the end of the day. Now I'm in Sheffield, I really appreciate how important the Peak District is as a national resource. It's loved by so many people as a place of tranquility, beauty and wildness.

The Peak District's 'best kept secret': 'Sites of Meaning' – a series of boundary marker stones around Middleton and Smerrill.

Best thing to do on a rainy day: The Peak District Mining Museum at Matlock Bath, which explains the history and importance of lead mining. You can also visit a real mine.

Best view: From Beeley Moor. On a clear day you can see into Stoney Middleton dale and beyond.

Best walk: Take the bus or train to Hope, then cross the fields up on to the ridge from Lose Hill to Mam Tor for great views of the Dark Peak, Kinder Scout and the Hope Valley. If you carry on down Cave Dale into Castleton you see the best of the White Peak too, and can walk back to Hope along the river.

Quirkiest attraction: The Archimedes screw at Torr Weir on the River Goyt in New Mills, the first community funded hydro-electric scheme in the UK.

Favourite restaurant: East Lodge Hotel at Rowsley. Elegant, relaxed atmosphere and excellent food, with lots of local ingredients.

Favourite takeaway: Stoney Middleton fish and chip shop.

Favourite pubs: The Flying Childers at Stanton, the Lathkill Hotel in Over Haddon or the Millstone Inn in Hathersage.

in favour of William and Mary of Orange. The ground floor of the cottage has a display of 17th-century furniture, and upstairs there is a changing programme of exhibitions on local themes.

If the weather in Sheffield is not so kind, you can enjoy more than 2,500 plants from around the world in one of the largest temperate glasshouses to be built in the UK during the last century at the award-winning **Winter Gardens**, adjacent to the Peace Gardens and the Millennium Galleries. This unexpected green world of tropical and sub-tropical plants in the heart of the city is housed in a soaring timber-and-glass arched structure that is 230ft/70m long and 72ft/22m high – which apparently makes it large enough to house 5,000 domestic greenhouses. Refreshments are available.

What to do with children

The children will love the new, regularly changing exhibitions and displays, from Egyptian mummies to a traditional butcher's shop, and from 'Snowy', the ever-popular, life-sized polar bear, to living ants and bees at the **Weston Park Museum** in Sheffield (see above). It won the *Guardian* Family Friendly Museum Award in 2008. Creative activities are available daily for families and school groups, and an attractive new café serves fresh and tasty refreshments.

HEELEY CITY FARM: Richards Road, Heeley, Sheffield S2 3DT; ☎0114 258 0482; www.heeleyfarm.org.uk. Entry: free; open daily.

Children are always welcome at the **Heeley City Farm**, a friendly farm and environmental visitor centre in Heeley, Sheffield. Here they can meet friendly animals, play in the under-8s playground and enjoy the farm café, which serves healthy, farm-cooked meals, while parents browse in the peat-free Garden Centre and Gift Shop.

Entertainment

Theatre

In recent years, **Sheffield** has become one of the leading live theatre venues outside London, and its three main theatres are all concentrated around Tudor Square in the city centre (☎0114 249 6000; www.sheffieldtheatres.co.uk). Opened in 1971, the 980-seat **Crucible Theatre** is the main producing repertory venue in the Sheffield Theatres complex, but also receives some touring shows in addition to famously hosting the annual World Snooker Championships. Originally opened in 1897, the **Lyceum Theatre** is a 1,068-seat listed building and W G R Sprague's only surviving design outside London. Following its closure in 1968, the Lyceum endured spells as a bingo hall and a rock venue before undergoing a £12 million renovation and reopening as a major touring venue in 1991. The smaller **Studio Theatre** has a capacity of up to 400, and opened in 1971 and was refurbished in 1994. Winner of the 2002 Peter

The Crucible Theatre (left) and Lyceum Theatre (behind) in Tudor Square, Sheffield

Brook Empty Space Award, the Studio hosts a mix of small-scale in-house and touring productions, and is also home to the acclaimed Ensemble 360's triannual Music in the Round Festival.

Chesterfield's **Pomegranate Theatre** (☎01246 345222; www.pomegranatetheatre. co.uk) claims to be Britain's oldest civic theatre, and is preparing for its 60th anniversary in 2009. The building is a Victorian, Grade II listed, 546-seat proscenium arch theatre, offering a wide range of professional touring and local amateur productions.

Cinema

The four-screen **Showroom Cinema** (7 Paternoster Row, Sheffield S1 2BX; ☎0114 275 7727; www. showroom.org.uk) in the heart of the Cultural Industries Quarter is claimed to be one of the largest independent cinemas in the country, and was recently voted the best independent cinema in the country by *Guardian* readers. There is also an **Odeon Cinema** in Sheffield (Arundel Gate, Sheffield S1 1DL; ☎0871 2244007; www.odeon.co.uk).

Chesterfield also has a 10-screen cinema at **Cineworld**, in the Alma Leisure Park off the Derby Road, showing all the latest releases (☎0871 200 2000; www. cineworld.co.uk).

Events

The award-winning **Hallam FM Arena** (☎0114 256 5656; www.sheffieldarena.co.uk) is one of the country's largest indoor entertainment venues, with a capacity of 12,000. It attracts almost one million people each year, and has established an excellent reputation for hosting world-class events. With its ice floor facility, the Hallam FM Arena is also home to Sheffield's Superleague ice hockey team, The Steelers, who play around 30 home games every year.

🛒 Shopping

Reinvented Sheffield is now one of the top shopping cities in Britain, and there is a vast range of shopping opportunities in streets such as **The Moor** and **Fargate** in the city centre. Probably most famous, however, is the **Meadowhall Shopping Centre** (☎0114 256 8800; www.meadowhall.co.uk) to the east of the city centre but easily reached via the Meadowhall Passenger Transport Interchange, by train, supertram, or bus. But be warned, more than 400,000 customers visit the 270 stores every week, so you need to get there early. Seasonal events are often held in the enormous malls of the shopping centre.

You'll be surprised at the bargains you'll find among the more than 200 stalls at **Chesterfield Market**, held in the cobbled Market Place every Monday, Friday and Saturday all year round. This traditional open air market has been held since at least 1165, and the town was granted a Market Charter in 1204. It outgrew its original site near the church and was moved to its present site early in the 13th century. There's also a flea market every Thursday, a farmers' market on second Thursday of every month, and a car boot sale in Holywell Cross Car Park every Sunday. The refurbished traditional **Market Hall**, originally built in 1857 'for the shelter and safeguard of market people' offers meat and fish, fabrics and designer clothes, footwear and perfumes, and many speciality shops all under cover.

CELEBRITY CONNECTIONS

Latin American dance specialist **Darren Bennett**, who won series two of BBC television's *Strictly Come Dancing* with his celebrity partner, actress **Jill Halfpenny**, was born and grew up in Deepcar, north of Sheffield. Darren, who has a twin brother, Dale, also a dancer, began dancing at the age of just six and his favourite styles are the samba and foxtrot. Before meeting his Russian professional dance partner and wife **Lilia Kopylova**, who won *Strictly* in 2005 with cricket star **Darren Gough**, Darren worked as a shoe company sales manager.

Within five months of meeting, Darren and Lilia had forged a prize-winning partnership, achieving top honours in both the International and British Youth Dance Championships. A great fan of science fiction, Darren is now a professional dancer, coach and choreographer, working closely with Lilia. His parents, Tony and Judith, both former professional dancers, run the City Limits Dance School in Walkley, Sheffield.

The best... **PLACES TO STAY**

BOUTIQUE

Buckingham's Hotel and The Restaurant With One Table

Newbold Road, Chesterfield S41 7PU
☎ **01246 201041**
www.buckinghams-table.com

Originally a pair of Victorian semi-detached houses, sympathetically converted to create a comfortable, relaxed hotel. Run by master chef Nick Buckingham and his wife Tina, offering warm, friendly service and bedrooms that are a 'home from home' with modern facilities. Meals prepared to personal requirements using the very best market produce.

Price: B&B from £95 for a double.

HOTEL

Norfolk Arms Hotel

2 Ringinglow Village, Sheffield S11 7TS
☎ **0114 230 2197**
www.norfolkarms.com

Built as a coaching inn in 1805, this Grade II listed hotel has modern en-suite bedrooms and other facilities, yet retains its original charm and character. Situated on the fringe of the Peak District National Park, yet only 5 miles from Sheffield city centre. Locally sourced food served in the bar and restaurant.

Price: B&B £95 for a double.

Ringwood Hall Hotel

Brimington, Chesterfield S43 1DQ
☎ **01246 280077**
www.ringwoodhallhotel.com

Grade II listed former Georgian manor house set in 30 acres, 6½ acres of which are formal gardens. Combines period charm and character and traditional hospitality with modern facilities, including Wi-Fi broadband access in some rooms, conference facilities and health and fitness club. Also three luxury apartments in hotel grounds.

Price: B&B from £115 for a superior double/twin.

The Rutland Hotel

452 Glossop Road, Sheffield S10 2PY
☎ **0114 266 4411**
www.rutlandhotel-sheffield.com

Traditional Victorian style and contemporary design fuse seamlessly at this city hotel, just a short drive from the boundary of the Peak District National Park. Chic, modern bedrooms with stylish design features, warm and relaxed atmosphere and attentive service. Breakfast options include the 'Great Yorkshire' and vegetarian, and all menus promote local food and produce.

Price: B&B £115 for a double.

The best... PLACES TO STAY

INN

Robin Hood Inn

Little Matlock, Stannington, Sheffield S6 6BG
☎ 0114 234 4565
www.robin-hood-loxley.co.uk

Let your imagination run riot at this stylish inn on the north-western fringe of Sheffield, where rooms are named after key figures in the Robin Hood legend. En-suite, individually styled accommodation with a contemporary edge and modern facilities, including Wi-Fi internet access. Home-cooked meals featuring local produce, cask ales.

Price: B&B from £80 for a double.

FARMSTAY

Temperance House Farm

Bradshaw Lane, Wadshelf, Chesterfield S42 7BT
☎ 01246 566416
www.temperancehousefarm.co.uk

Family-run, Grade II listed farmhouse surrounded by $6^1/_2$ acres of grassland, on which the owners keep a small flock of pedigree Suffolk sheep. Traditional country-style accommodation with beamed ceilings and period-style furniture. Full English breakfast or lighter options served. Self-catering accommodation also available.

Price: B&B from £50 for a double.

B&B

Nesfield Cottage

Nesfield, Barlow, Dronfield S18 7TB
☎ 01246 559786
www.nesfieldcottage.co.uk

Super-king-size beds and crisp white cotton sheets set the tone for a comfortable stay in well-appointed rooms, charmingly named after birds. Pleasant views over open countryside, close to good walking and cycling. Freshly cooked breakfasts locally sourced where possible, include options for vegetarians and those requiring special diets.

Price: From £27 to £36 per person per night.

Loadbrook Cottages

Game Lane, Loadbrook, Near Stannington, Sheffield S6 6GT
☎ 0114 233 1619
www.loadbrook.co.uk

Traditional 18th-century Yorkshire farmhouse offering both B&B and self-catering accommodation on the fringe of the Peak District National Park, yet only 20 minutes from Sheffield city centre. Both en-suite and family B&B rooms available, all diets catered for. Attractive garden and scenic views over open countryside.

Price: B&B £55 to £65 for a double.

The best... PLACES TO STAY

The Royal Hotel

Dungworth, near Bradfield, Sheffield S6 6HF
☎ 0114 285 1213

Early 19th-century, family-run public house with en-suite rooms, north west of Sheffield. Three public rooms, all with open fires, including the 'dungeon' for families, complete with child's safety gate, toys and games. Locally sourced meat used to make the pub's famous pies, plus fish and vegetarian options.

Price: B&B £55 for a twin/double.

SELF-CATERING

Foxholes Farm

c/o Parkside, High Bradfield, Sheffield S6 6LJ
☎ 0114 285 1383/1710
www.foxholesfarm.co.uk

Five cottages, three within a Grade II listed building and the other two in a converted barn, each sleeping between three and five people. Available for short breaks or longer stays, ideal base for walking, pony trekking, climbing, fishing and other activities. Central heating, fully equipped fitted kitchens, stereo and TV with DVD or VCR.

Price: from £35 to £70 for a cottage.

Pear Tree Farm Barn

Rowthorne Village, Glapwell, Chesterfield S44 5QQ
☎ 01623 811694
www.peartreefarmbarn.co.uk

Tastefully converted stone barn overlooking open countryside, close to historic Hardwick Hall. Two en-suite bedrooms, one twin (loft suite) and one double, sleeps four. Impressive 30ft long lounge/diner with vaulted ceiling, exposed stonework and wood/solid fuel burning stove. Well-equipped kitchen, comfortably furnished, internet access, landing library and garden.

Price: From £245 to £555 for a week.

UNUSUAL

Wortley Hall Ltd

Wortley Village, Sheffield S35 7DB
☎ 0114 288 2100
www.wortleyhall.org.uk

Enjoy B&B or self-catering accommodation in the ancestral home of the Earls of Wharncliffe, established as an education and recreation centre in 1951 and operating on co-operative principles. Quality service and affordable prices, en-suite accommodation, restaurant, games room and bar lounges. Pleasant walks in 26 acres of formal gardens and woodland.

Price: B&B £40 for a double.

The best... FOOD AND DRINK

There's a mind-boggling selection of fine food and drink on the fringes of Chesterfield and Sheffield, ranging from English and Continental cheeses and locally produced honey to a famous relish and water buffalo steaks, burgers and sausages. Wash it down with wine from what was once the most northerly vineyard in the world, quality teas and coffees or real ales from one of several microbreweries, which you can also enjoy in a variety of city and country pubs.

▶ Staying in

If you're in search of English and Continental cheeses, you'll find a huge range at **R P Davidson Cheese Factor** in Chesterfield (31 The Market Hall S40 1AR; ☎01246 201203 or ☎07970 281717). Options include cheeses from Chesterfield's twin town, Troyes, such as Chaource. You can have a free nibble before you decide what to choose, and you can also buy accompaniments such as Lincolnshire Plum Bread and Red Pepper Jelly. Those planning a wedding can even order a cake made entirely of whole cheeses!

For a wide variety of quality teas and coffees from around the world, **Northern Tea Merchants** in Chesterfield (Crown House, 193 Chatsworth Road S40 2BA; ☎01246 232600) is the place to contact. Registered organic processors of tea and coffee with both the Soil Association and the Organic Food Federation, the company imports some of the finest teas and coffees from around the world. Teas come from Africa, China, India, Japan and Sri Lanka, while coffees are sourced from Africa, India, Indonesia, Latin America and New Guinea. You can even buy green coffee beans and roast them yourself. For a full range of delicatessen foods, **Koo Delicatessen** in Chesterfield (470 Chatsworth Road S40 3AD; ☎01246 297848) is a popular choice. Hampers and picnic baskets (including rugs) are also available, to suit any price range or occasion. Another excellent food shop and small café, this time in the town centre, is **Deli-Ethics** (69–71 Low Pavement S40 1PB; ☎01246 200050).

For organic food, try **Organic Heaven** (4 Theatre Yard, Low Pavement, Chesterfield S40 1PF; ☎0845 223 5453). As well as an extensive vegetarian takeaway service offering both savoury and sweet items, you can buy organic juice, fresh, chilled and frozen produce and ecological detergents and toiletries. Bio-active, locally produced honey and natural beehive products made from hives kept on ancient wild flower meadows can be sourced from **Medibee** at Troway (Troway Hall S21 5RU; ☎01246 292425). If you have an inkling for the unusual, head for **The Farmhouse Pantry**, a specialist butcher and delicatessen in Dronfield Woodhouse (Barnes Lane S18 8YE; ☎01246 298123), where exotic cuts such as water buffalo and crocodile are on the menu. The water buffalo is raised at the family farm at Eastmoor, near Chesterfield and is made into as steaks, burgers and sausages. Award-winning black pudding, dry-cured bacon and old-fashioned products such as brawn, tripe and tongue are also on sale.

Award-winning ice creams with flavours ranging from Bakewell Pudding to pomegranate and raspberry are available from **Frederick's of Chesterfield** (76–88 Old Hall Road, Brampton S40 1HF; ☎01246 206957), which also runs gelaterias in both Queen's Park, Chesterfield and Bakewell. Family-owned for four generations, the company was launched in Sheffield in 1898 and moved to Chesterfield in 1925.

The Vineyard at Renishaw Hall & Gardens (Renishaw, Sheffield S21 3WB; ☎01246 432310, www.sitwell.co.uk) was once the most northerly in the world, though thanks to global warming, there are now others in Leeds, the Lake District and even Norway! It was created in 1972, enjoyed a record year in 2003, when it produced 2,000 bottles, and won a bronze medal in the Mercian Vineyards Association wine competition in 2007.

In Sheffield, you can buy speciality foods sourced from within an 80 mile radius of **Urban Dell** (The Chimes, Campo Lane S1 2EG), which also has a sister café, while for locally sourced, quality meat, award winning pies and sausages contact **John Crawshaw Butchers** of Stocksbridge (518–520 Manchester Road S36 2DW; ☎0114 288 3548). But for a true taste of Sheffield, try locally made Hendersons Relish from **Hendersons Ltd** (41 Leavygreave Road S3 7RA; ☎0114 272 5909), one of Yorkshire's best-kept secrets. Made to a secret recipe and suitable for vegetarians, this spicy sauce provides a unique accompaniment to meat dishes, pies and fish and chips and can be added to casseroles, pasta dishes, soups and marinades.

If you long to sample the warmth of sunnier climes, **Yabba's Caribbean Food & Deli** (158–160 Abbeydale Road S7 1FH; ☎0114 258 1111) will wake up your taste buds. All Yabba's preserves and condiments are handmade in small batches using local ingredients. Fresh sandwiches, chilled foods, specialist teas and coffees, handmade chocolates, gift wrapping service and hampers are also available. In a similar vein, family-run **Sheff's Special** (372 Ecclesall Road South, Sheffield S11 9PY; ☎0114 235 6362) specialises in mojo, a green chilli sauce with fresh lime and coriander, and mixed bean chilli and cheese pie. All food is free from artificial additives and available from local farmers' markets.

North-west of Sheffield, **The Postcard Café and Stores** at Low Bradfield (Woodfall House, Woodfall Lane S6 6LA; ☎0114 285 1235) stocks a range of deli, organic, vegetarian and Fairtrade items, including cheeses, cooked meats, savoury mousses and terrines, soya and rice milk, canned foods, dried beans, pulses, fruit and rice, baby foods, coffees, teas, chocolate and cleaning materials. The shop also stocks home-made ice cream from **Our Cow Molly** of Dungworth (Cliffe House Cottage S6 6GW; ☎0114 233 2683).

Farm shops abound in this area. Around Chesterfield, try:

· **Dunston Park Farm Shop** – Dunston Road S41 9RW; ☎01246 237186
· **Hardwick Park Farm** – Hardwick Estate, Doe Lea S44 5QJ; ☎01246 859091
· **Redwood Smokehouse and Factory Shop** – Bolsover Business Park, Bolsover S44 6BD; ☎01246 827972
· **Unstone Hill Farm Shop** – Chesterfield Road, Unstone S18 4AF; ☎07776 085331

In and around Sheffield, take your pick from:

- **Bradfield Meats** at Ughill – Crawshaw Farm S6 6HU; ☎0114 285 1315; also has a mobile shop
- **Coppice House Farm Shop** – Rivelin Valley Road S6 5SG; ☎0114 230 8389
- **Hazlehead Hall Farm Shop** at Penistone – Lee Lane, Mill House Green S36 9NN; ☎01226 764800
- **Whirlow Hall Farm** – Whirlow Lane S11 9QF; ☎0114 235 2678; offers home-grown fruit and potatoes as well as home-reared pork, bacon, gammon and sausages.

Locally raised beef, pork, lamb and chicken, plus home-made sausages, burgers and pies, a selection of Yorkshire cheeses and a range of other delicacies are available from **Wortley Farm Shop** (Park Avenue S35 7DR; ☎0114 288 2232).

Farmers' markets are held regularly in:

- **Chesterfield** – Market Place S40 1AH; ☎01246 345999; on the second Thursday of the month 9am–4pm and the second and last Sunday of every month 10am–2pm
- **Penistone** – S36 6BZ; ☎07880 554 986; second Saturday of the month 9am–1pm
- **Sheffield** – Barkers Pool S1 2JA; ☎0114 273 5281; fourth Sunday of the month 10am–4pm

A Country Market is also held in Chesterfield (Market Place S40 1AH; ☎01246 866429; every Saturday 7.30am–4pm), and slightly further afield, the **Derbyshire Food and Drink Festival** is held at Bolsover Castle every May

EATING OUT

FINE DINING

Buckingham's Hotel and The Restaurant With One Table
Newbold Road, Chesterfield S41 7PU
☎ **01246 201041**
www.buckinghams-table.com

Excellence comes as standard at this cosy restaurant, where award-winning chef Nick Buckingham strives to ensure the best quality. It has just one table, which seats 10 and can be booked exclusively or as an open table to dine with fellow guests. Open Table costs from £38 per person.

The Old Post Restaurant
Holywell Street, Chesterfield S41 7SH
☎ **01246 279479**
www.theoldpostrestaurant.co.uk

Simple, elegant cooking using quality, locally sourced produce is the key to success here, where dishes are prepared and cooked to order. Lunch, dinner and 'early bird' evening menus available. A la carte starters cost from £5.50, mains from £15.95.

The Old Vicarage Restaurant
Ridgeway Moor, Ridgeway Village, Near Sheffield S12 3XW; ☎ **0114 247 5814**
www.theoldvicarage.co.uk

Quality food and a warm welcome in the only Michelin-starred restaurant in the city. Dishes change frequently to reflect the availability of local seasonal produce. Typical options include Chatsworth lamb, saddle of Ridgeway lamb, fish and vegetarian choices. A four-course meal costs £60.

RESTAURANT

La Bistro Chameleon
370 Chatsworth Road, Chesterfield S40 2DQ
☎ **01246 277344**
www.la-bistro-chameleon.co.uk

Retro and modern cuisine influenced by traditional French farmhouse cooking, based on traditionally reared meat, fresh fish, fruit, vegetables, herbs and spices with an innovative twist. Mains include fillet of beef, rack of English lamb and fish and cost from £15.95.

Bateman's Mill Hotel and Restaurant
Mill Lane, Old Tupton, Chesterfield S42 6AF
☎ **01246 862200**
www.batemansmill.co.uk

Light snacks to full meals available in the traditional bar/restaurant, with its exposed beams and stonework. Focus on modern European dishes with an emphasis on local produce, including meat, fish and vegetarian choices. Bar mains cost from £7.50, three course dinner £26.95.

O-Tokuda
37 Knifesmithgate, Chesterfield S40 1RL
☎ **01246 556996**

Japanese fusion food prepared on the premises: a choice of sushi, sashimi and nigiri, plus hot dishes prepared before your very eyes on a sizzling hot plate (teppanyaki), with great style and flair by resident chefs. Book in advance. Takeaway service is also available.

EATING OUT

Artisan and Catch
32–34 Sandygate Road, Crosspool, Sheffield S10 5RY
www.artisancatch.co.uk

Diners have a choice of rustic bistro menu at Artisan, or seafood in a lively café atmosphere at Catch. Traditional fare at Artisan includes bangers and mash and duck shepherd's pie. Catch specialities include chowder, fruits de mer and mini fish tapas. Artisan fixed-price menu costs from £25 for three courses, Catch options cost £3 to around £30.

Moran's Winebar and Restaurant
289 Abbeydale Road South, Dore, Sheffield S17 3LB
☎ 0114 235 0101
www.moranssheffield.co.uk

Modern European cuisine in a welcoming and relaxed setting. Fresh food from quality and local suppliers and producers, plus carefully selected wine list. Lunch, dinner and traditional Sunday lunch served. Sample dinner menu includes pan-fried fillet of English beef and home-made wild mushroom and goats cheese ravioli. Lunch options cost from £3.50, dinner mains from £12.95.

Cubley Hall
Mortimer Road, Cubley, Penistone S36 9DF
☎ 01226 766086
www.cubleyhall.co.uk

Dine in a converted hewn-stone barn at this former gentleman's home, now a hotel and free house. Both restaurant and bar meals, many of them based on local produce, are served, and a children's menu is available. Three-course à la carte meals cost on average £16.

GASTRO PUB

The Trout Inn
33 Valley Road, Barlow, Dronfield S18 7SL
☎ 0114 289 0893
www.barlowvillage.co.uk/trout_inn

Tickle your tastebuds in this country restaurant decorated with fishing baskets and other marine memorabilia. Modern British food served in a relaxed, welcoming setting at lunch and dinner, complemented by wines and beers including weekly guest ales. Options include lamb shank, selection of home-made pies, sea bass and locally caught trout; mains start from around £9.25.

The Red Lion Pub and Bistro
Darley Road, Stonedge, Ashover, Chesterfield S45 0LW
☎ 01246 566142
www.thefamousredlion.com

Locally sourced meat and specialist fish from all over the UK are staples at this attractively appointed pub and bistro, which enjoys sweeping views of the surrounding countryside. Main courses range from grills to roasts, with salads, platters and sandwiches available at lunchtimes. Lunchtime mains cost from £10, evening mains from £11.

EATING OUT

The Robin Hood Inn
**Greaves Lane, Little Matlock,
Stannington, Sheffield S6 6BG
☎ 0114 234 4581
www.robin-hood-loxley.co.uk**

Home-cooked food, much of it locally sourced, freshly prepared on the premises to traditional family recipes. Starters, mains, desserts, specials and sandwiches served, plus a Sunday lunchtime carvery. Classics range from gammon steak and shoulder of lamb to fresh fish in beer batter and vegetable fritter. Main courses cost from £8.25.

Montagu's (at The Wortley Arms)
**Halifax Road, Wortley,
Sheffield S35 7DB
☎ 0114 288 8749
www.wortley-arms.co.uk**

Seasonal dishes incorporating quality regional produce, many sourced from within 20 miles, served in contemporary, relaxed setting. Choices range from modern avant-garde to traditional. Sample starters include pan fried foie gras and Bresaola Round Green Farm venison, while typical main courses range from half roast lobster to fillet of beef. Mains cost from £14.50 to £17.

CAFÉ

Queen's Park Gelateria and Café
Queen's Park, Chesterfield, Derbyshire

Located in Queen's Park, next to Chesterfield's county cricket ground, this café sells all 19 flavours of Frederick's award winning ice cream, plus breakfasts, soups, jacket potatoes, baguettes, wraps, salads, pasta, main courses, high tea and children's meals. Home-cooked and freshly prepared using both local and Italian produce. Takeaway service.

Koo Coffee & Bistro
**475a Chatsworth Road,
Chesterfield S40 3AD
☎ 01246 205604
www.koocoffeeanddeli.co.uk**

Simple yet sophisticated menu and speciality coffees and teas based on quality produce sourced locally and internationally. Options include breakfasts, bagels, small and large plates, open sandwiches, salads, cakes and desserts, complemented by hot and cold drinks, wine and beers. Regular wine tasting and other special events.

TEA ROOM

Hackney House Tea Rooms
**Hackney Lane, Barlow,
Dronfield S18 7TD
☎ 0114 289 0248**

Home-made fare made on the premises ranges from sandwiches and paninis to savoury pies and puddings in this traditional tea room on the fringe of the Peak District. Speciality teas and coffee served, open seven days a week.

🍷 Drinking

No fewer than nine independent breweries flourish in and around this area. In **Chesterfield**, you'll find **Brampton Brewery** (Chatsworth Business Park, Chatsworth Road S40 2AR; ☎01246 221680; www.bramptonbrewery.co.uk), which brews Best, Golden Bud, Impy Dark and Wasp Nest. In Staveley, the **Spire Brewery** (Gisborne Close, Ireland Business Park S43 3JT; ☎01246 476005; www.spirebrewery.co.uk) produces such lines as Chesterfield Best Bitter and Land of Hop and Glory, as well as seasonal and bottle conditioned beers.

Based at the Speedwell Inn in Staveley, **Townes Brewery** (Lowgates S43 3TT; ☎01246 472252) brews such ales as Speedwell Bitter, Lowgate Light and Staveley Cross, and its bottle-conditioned beers can be drunk by vegetarians and vegans. Family-run **Bradfield Brewery** in High Bradfield (Watt House Farm S6 6LG; ☎0114 285 1118; www.bradfieldbrewery.co.uk) is situated on a working farm in the Peak District and brews a range of 'Farmers' ales using pure spring water. Its products, including bottle-conditioned beers, supply more than 200 outlets.

In the Sheffield area, **Abbeydale Brewery** (Unit 8, Aizlewood Road S8 0YX; ☎0114 281 2712; www.abbeydalebrewery.co.uk) boasts both regular and seasonal beers, while the **Crown Brewery** is based at the city's Hillsborough Hotel (54–58 Langsett Road S6 2UB; ☎0114 232 2100) and produces regulars such as Middlewood Mild, Hillsborough Pale Ale, Loxley Gold and Stannington Stout. In the city centre, you'll find the **Kelham Island Brewery** (Alma Street S3 8SA ☎0114 249 4804; www.kelhambrewery.co.uk), which brews five regular lines and monthly seasonal specials, while the **Little Cart Brewery** operates in the Wellington (1 Henry Street S3 7EQ; ☎0114 240 2295). Crucible Best and Seven Hills are among the locally inspired names available from the **Sheffield Brewing Co** (Unit 111, J C Albyn Complex, Burton Road S3 8BT; ☎0114 272 7256; www.sheffieldbrewery.com).

In the centre of Chesterfield, the **Rutland Arms** (Stephenson Place S40 1XL; ☎01246 205857) serves up to 12 real ales and good food, including filled Yorkshire puddings; while the **Portland Hotel** (West Bars S40 1AY; ☎01246 245410) is near the town's famous market and sells local brew, plus up to four guest ales. North of the town centre, the award-winning **Derby Tup** (Sheffield Road, Whittington Moor S41 8LS; ☎01246 454316) serves the most extensive range of guest beers in the area, continental beers and traditional cider and prides itself on being a drinkers' pub. In Brampton, head for **Brampton Manor** (107 Old Road S40 3QR; ☎01246 277760), which serves a range of local ales and has regular live music, or the multi-award-winning **Peacock** (Chatsworth Road, Brampton S40 3BQ; ☎01246 275115), which offers good beer, a beer garden, dominoes and weekly folk singing.

Around Sheffield, try **The Cricket Inn** at Totley Bents (Penny Lane S17 3AZ; ☎0114 236 5256), which overlooks a village cricket green and has a cosy bar with open fire plus an open-plan restaurant. Live jazz and rock and original features such as small rooms and stained-glass windows make the **White Lion** at Heeley (615 London Road S2 4HT; ☎0114 255 1500), one of the city's most interesting pubs, serving regular and guest real ales. Also in Heeley is the award-winning **Sheaf View** (Gleadless Road

S2 3AA; ☎0114 249 6455), a freehouse brimming with brewery memorabilia, real ales and malt whiskies.

On the fringe of the Peak District, you'll find real ales, food and open fires at the **Dore Moor Inn** (Hathersage Road, Dore S17 3AB; ☎0114 262 1031), and an old-fashioned feel at the renovated Victorian **Ranmoor Inn** (Fulwood Road S10 3GD; ☎0114 230 1325), which has regular and guest beers and serves food, as well as hosting impromptu singing sessions around the piano. At Stannington, cask ales brewed both locally and further afield can be enjoyed in a traditional tap room or stylish lounge at **The Robin Hood Inn** (Greaves Lane, Little Matlock S6 6BG; ☎0114 234 4565). To the north of the city centre is the family-run **Hillsborough Hotel** and Crown Brewery (54–58 Langsett Road S6 2UB; ☎0114 232 2100), which holds seasonal beer festivals, themed events, folk music and regular quiz nights. Another popular haunt, renowned for local and continental beers, single malt whiskies and real cider, is the **New Barrack Tavern** (601 Penistone Road S6 2GA; ☎0114 234 9148).

Local cask ales and ice cold lagers are served in the traditional setting of 18th-century **The Wortley Arms** at Wortley, between Sheffield and Barnsley (Halifax Road S35 7DB; ☎0114 288 8749), originally built as a coach house, with solid oak beams and real fire. Substantial meals include the Wortley Wedge (roast sandwich of the day), Wortley Burger and Wortley Ploughman's. Further north at Penistone, the **Wentworth Arms** (Sheffield Road S36 6HG; ☎01226 762494) is conveniently near the Trans-Pennine Trail, serving real ales (including mild) and hosting pool, darts and an old-fashioned jukebox.

ⓘ Visitor Information

Tourist information centres:
Chesterfield Tourist Information Centre, Rykneld Street, Chesterfield S40 1SB, ☎01246 345777/8, www.tourism. chesterfield.gov.uk, open daily; Sheffield Tourist Information Centre, 1 Tudor Square, Sheffield, South Yorkshire S1 2LA, ☎0114 221 1900, www.tourism. sheffield.gov.uk, open daily; in addition, there are tourist information points in St John's Church, Penistone, open on Thurs and Sat, and at St Saviour's Church, Thurlstone, open on Tues.

Hospitals: A&E, Chesterfield Royal Hospital, Calow, Chesterfield, ☎01246 277271; Northern General Hospital, Herries Road, Sheffield, ☎0114 243 4343; Barnsley General Hospital, Gawber Road, Barnsley, ☎01226 730000.

Doctors: Lodge Moor Medical Centre, 68, Rochester Road, Sheffield S10 4JQ, ☎0845 123 6736; Medical Centre, Station Road, Barrow Hill, Chesterfield S43 2PG, ☎01246 280185; Home

Hall Medical Centre, Wardgate Way, Chesterfield S40 4SL, ☎01246 211435; Chatsworth Road Medical Centre, Storrs Road, Chesterfield S40 3PY, ☎01246 568065; Staffa Health, 19a, Heath Road, Holmewood, Chesterfield S42 5RB, ☎0844 4772433; The Whittington Medical Centre, High St, Old Whittington, Chesterfield S41 9JZ, ☎01246 455440.

Supermarkets: Tesco, Meltham Lane, Chesterfield, ☎0845 677 9156; Sainsbury's, Rother Way, Chesterfield, ☎01246 202379; Lidl, Chatsworth Road, Chesterfield, ☎0870 444 1234; Chesterfield & Dist, Co-op, High Street, Chesterfield, ☎01246 277836; Sainsbury's, Archer Road, Sheffield, ☎0114 267 8440; Somerfield, 849 Eccleshall Road, Sheffield, ☎0114 266 1800; Morrisons, Ecclesfield, Sheffield, ☎0114 245 6545; Tesco, Herries Road, Sheffield, ☎0845 677 9622.

Taxis: Sheffield City Taxis, City Road, Sheffield, ☎0114 239 3939; Chesterfield Taxis ☎01246 660007.

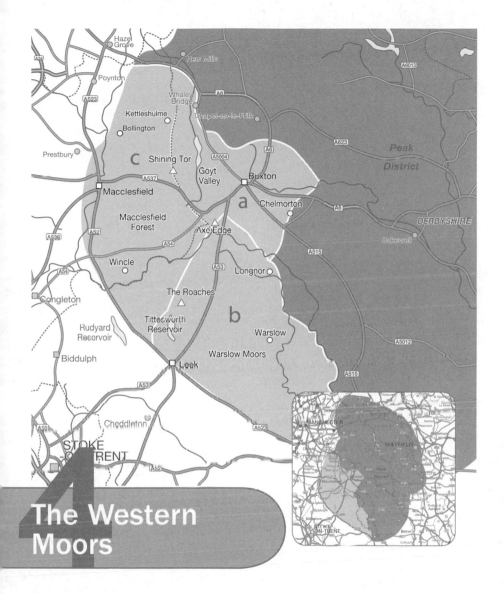

4 The Western Moors

a. Buxton and the Goyt Valley

b. Leek, Longnor and the Roaches

c. Macclesfield and Macclesfield Forest

Unmissable highlights

01 Marvel at the Georgian splendour of The Crescent in Buxton, p. 200

02 Wonder at the enormous space under Buxton's echoing Dome, p. 199

03 Enjoy a night out at Buxton Opera House and bask in its rococo glory, p. 200

04 Imagine past glories in the ruins of Errwood Hall, in the Goyt Valley, p. 214

05 Watch the yachts on Errwood Reservoir, also in the Goyt Valley, p. 214

06 Be the monarch of all you survey on the airy crest of The Roaches or Ramshaw Rocks, p. 217

07 Follow in the footsteps of the Green Knight to Lud's Church, in Back Forest, near the Roaches, p. 223

08 Take the Silk Road to Macclesfield and its Silk Industry Museum and Paradise Mill, p. 232

09 Pick up a bargain among the bustling stalls on Leek Market, p. 222

10 Watch the herons at Trentabank Reservoir, Macclesfield Forest, p. 232

THE WESTERN MOORS

The Western Moors are truly the 'Wild West' of the Peak District. This is a land of mists and legend, where myths haunt strange and spectacular rock formations like those at Shutlingsloe, The Roaches, Ramshaw Rocks and Lud's Church near Leek, and where secluded valleys like Wildboarclough, the Goyt and the Dane lie under the bleak, brooding moors.

Some of these valleys have been flooded by reservoirs, such as the Errwood and Fernilee in the Goyt, which necessitated the depopulation of the valley in the interests of water purity. The evocative ruins of Errwood Hall, hidden deep in the rhododendrons and azaleas of the Goyt Forest, tell of the valley's former glory, when the wealthy Grimshaw family ruled the roost.

The conifers of Macclesfield Forest now also cloak a wild moorland area which was the hunting ground of the Earls of Chester in medieval times, and which are now a popular recreational area for the people of the former silk town, and many others from further afield. At the heart of the western moors is the lovely little Georgian market town of Buxton, the cultural capital of the Peak and, at over 1,000ft/300m above the sea, one of the highest market towns in England. The Romans were the first to be attracted by Buxton's warm springs, and they named the town *Aqua Arnemetiae* – which translates as '*the spa of the goddess of the grove*'. During the late 18th century, the wealthy fifth Duke of Devonshire used the profits won from his copper mines in the Manifold Valley in an attempt to make Buxton a spa town to rival Bath or Cheltenham. By the time the sixth Duke had ascended to the title, Buxton was a thriving health resort, boosted by the coming of the railway in 1863.

The architectural legacy of those days is still very evident in Buxton, and is epitomised by sweeping Crescent, modelled on John Wood's in Bath; the imposing Dome, originally the Duke's Stables and Riding School latterly the Royal Hospital and now part of the Buxton campus of the University of Derby; the Pavilion and Pavilion Gardens; the imposing Palace Hotel, the largest and grandest in the Peak; and Frank Matcham's exuberant gold and gilt rococo masterpiece, the Opera House, now home to the internationally respected Buxton Festival of Music and the Arts.

BUXTON AND THE GOYT VALLEY

You can still taste the tepid, slightly effervescent mineral water which first attracted the Romans to **Buxton**, the elegant market town at the heart of the Peak, in the public tap opposite The Crescent, where there is usually a queue of people collecting it in containers. Buxton was only excluded from the Peak District National Park because of the huge limestone quarries which border it to the south. But in many ways, it is still the cultural capital of the district, with its stunning Georgian architecture and Opera House, which is known as 'the theatre in the hills' and the venue of the annual Buxton Festival.

Among the many other attractions of Buxton is the excellent Museum and Art Gallery in Terrace Road, and Poole's Cavern, one of the original Wonders of the Peak, on Green Lane. Poole's Cavern fringes Buxton's Country Park, with its popular viewpoint of Solomon's Temple on Grin Low and the more modern attraction of the Go Ape! adventure course.

WHAT TO SEE AND DO

Buxton discovery trail

Start your walking tour of Buxton's architectural highlights at John Carr's grand and sweeping **Crescent**, built for the fifth Duke of Devonshire in 1784 as a kind of Georgian 'leisure centre' to provide accommodation for visitors to his spa. This Grade I listed building is currently under restoration. **The Pump Room** opposite was built in 1894 by Henry Currey as an additional water treatment and remained in use until 1981. Closed at the moment, it will reopen as part of the Crescent and Thermal Spa redevelopments. **St Ann's Well** by the Pump Room was presented to the town and its residents in 1940, and allows the general public to sample the precious Buxton spa water, which gushes out at a constant temperature of 28°C. **The Natural Baths** nearby are on the site of the original Roman baths, and again were designed by Henry Currey, opening in 1854. When reopened, they will form the centrepiece of the new Spa Pool and Treatment Rooms of the refurbished hotel.

To the right of the Crescent is the **Cavendish Arcade**, originally built as part of Currey's plans as a thermal bath in 1854. It was rebuilt as a speciality shopping arcade in 1987 which retained the original plunge pool with its Minton tiling, and a strikingly modern stained glass barrel ceiling by Brian Clarke, said to be the biggest in Britain. Passing the **Old Hall Hotel** (see p. 208) and turning right you climb up to the **Opera House**, Frank Matcham's ornate masterpiece which opened in 1903 and is now the home of the Buxton Festival and a varied programme of other events throughout the year. Guided tours of the beautiful little theatre, including backstage, take place every Saturday morning, starting at 11am and costing £2.50 per head.

The **Pavilion Gardens**, to the left of the Opera House, were designed by Edward Milner, a pupil of Joseph Paxton from Chatsworth, and opened in 1871 on 23 acres/9 hectares of land by the River Wye given to the town by the seventh Duke of Devonshire. This peaceful and relaxing area in the centre of town

The Crescent, Buxton

includes the ornate Victorian bandstand, a 20ft/6m fountain, a 'Snail Back' garden, and a miniature railway. Overlooking the Gardens is the **Pavilion** itself, which was originally known as the Winter Gardens when it opened in 1875. The **Conservatory** retains the slightly steamy atmosphere of the Winter Gardens, and the **Octagon**, designed by Robert Rippon Duke and opened in 1876 as a concert hall, now plays host to a variety of concerts, craft and antique fairs, book and toy fairs, auctions, exhibitions and farmers' markets.

The Opera House, Buxton

Buxton Country Park and Poole's Cavern

Poole's Cavern is one of the great caverns of the Peak District and also claims to have been named as the first Wonder of the Peak in the 17th century. Named after a former outlaw, it is a natural limestone cave situated in the beautiful woodland of **Buxton Country Park**, and has welcomed visitors for over 5,000 years, ever since Neolithic tribes first used its spacious chambers as a temporary shelter. Modern visitors can enjoy the latest facilities in a new visitor centre, restaurant and exhibition. Guided tours through Poole's Cavern begin every 20 minutes, and expert guides lead you on a one-hour journey deep into the hidden landscape underneath the Peak. The cavern is well lit with good pathways and – useful to know for these with young children or the infirm – there are only 26 steps throughout the tour. Among the amazing formations you will see on

POOLE'S CAVERN AND BUXTON COUNTRY PARK (INCLUDING GO APE! HIGH WIRE ADVENTURE): Green Lane, Buxton, Derbyshire SK17 9DH; ☎01298 26978, **Go Ape!** ☎0845 643 9215; www.poolescavern.co.uk. Entry: £7 adults, £4 children, £5.50 concessions (non-refundable £1 charge for telephone bookings); open daily 9.30am–5pm, Mar to Nov, 10am–4pm, weekends, Dec to Feb. Go Ape! open mid-Mar to Oct, weekends in Nov.

the tour are Mary Queen of Scots' Pillar (she was imprisoned in at the Old Hall, now a hotel in the middle of Buxton, and allegedly visited the cave), the Frozen Waterfall, the Poached Egg Chamber, and the Flitch of Bacon.

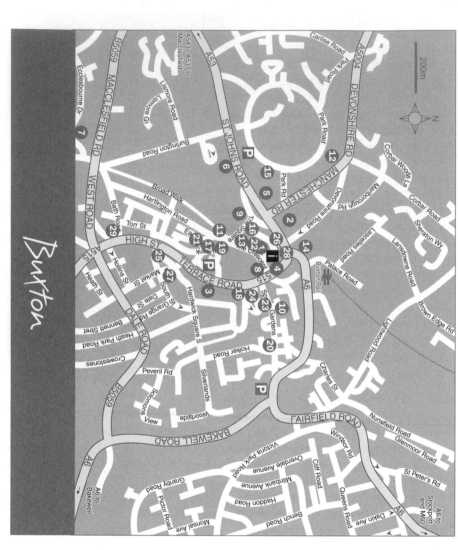

Buxton

Things to see and do
1. The Crescent
2. The Dome
3. Museum & Art Gallery
4. Parish Church
5. Pavilion Gardens
6. Poole's Cavern
7. Pump Room

Entertainment
9. Opera House

Shopping
10. Spring Gardens

Places to Stay
11. Buxton's Victorian Guest House
12. Lee Wood Hotel
13. Old Hall Hotel
14. Palace Hotel
15. Stoneridge Guest House

Eat and Drink
16. No 6 The Square Tea Room
17. Beltane
18. Café@The Green Pavilion
19. Columbine Restaurant
20. The Devonshire Bakery
2. The Dome Fine Dine Restaurant
21. The Eagle Hotel
22. Project X
23. Hargreaves
24. Kwei Lin Chinese Restaurant
25. Michelangelo's Ristorante
26. Monk at Buxton
13. Old Hall Hotel
6. Pavilion Gardens
27. The Place
28. Simply Thai
29. The Swan

Visitor Information
i. Tourist Information Centre

Buxton Country Park also incorporates a **Go Ape!** adventure course (see *What to do with children*). It is an easy walk from here to reach the stunning viewpoint of **Solomon's Temple** on Grin Low, which stands at 1,445ft/440m above the sea, and commands extensive views over Buxton and the rolling countryside of the White Peak to the east, and the brooding western moors to the south and west. The circular battlemented folly of Solomon's Temple was built by local landowner Solomon Mycock in 1896.

Poole's Cavern

Buxton Museum and Art Gallery

The award-winning Wonders of the Peak gallery is a must-see highlight of the **Buxton Museum and Art Gallery**, in Terrace Road just below the Market Place. This takes you through on a journey through time from the Big Bang at the very beginnings of the universe, to the

Solomon's Temple

trophy-hunting Victorians, who were the first archaeologists to investigate past civilisations in the Peak. Several vastly different environments are re-created in this fascinating gallery, complete with the sounds and smells of each period, which the children will love. You can see the sights and smells of the prehistoric forest, see and hear a bear in its Ice Age cave, crawl inside a Neolithic burial chamber, salute a Roman soldier... and even meet a mermaid many miles from the sea. Other permanent exhibits in the museum include a comprehensive

BUXTON MUSEUM AND ART GALLERY: Terrace Road, Buxton, Derbyshire SK17 6DA; ☎01298 24658; www.derbyshire. gov.uk/leisure/buxton_museum. Entry: free; open 9.30am–5.30pm, Tues to Fri; 9.30am–5pm, Sat; 10.30am–5pm, Sun, Bank Holidays, Easter to end of September.

fossil record of the Peak District, evidence of Pliocene mammals from caves, and a photographic archive of images of the town. The minerals collection includes good examples of Blue John and the unique Tomlinson Collection of Ashford Black Marble ornaments.

The Art Gallery's collection is predominately 19th and 20th-century works in watercolours, oils and prints, including paintings by Brangwyn, Chagall, Chahine and their contemporaries, and there are also constantly changing non-permanent art exhibitions.

Horse riding

The British Horse Society approved **Buxton Riding School** (Fern Farm, Fern Road, Buxton SK17 9NP; ☎01298 72319; www.fernfarmcottages.co.uk) has about 60 horses and ponies of every shape and size, most of which are available for hire. Lessons are provided by fully-experienced staff for would-be riders of all ages.

The **Northfield Farm Riding and Trekking Centre** must be one of the highest in the country, situated on the edge of Flash, England's highest village, five miles south of Buxton off the A53. The rides are mostly two hours in length and follow old packhorse trails to such beauty spots as Three Shires Head, where the three counties of Cheshire, Staffordshire and Derbyshire meet. A variety of over 30 mostly home-bred horses and ponies are used, suiting all ages and standards.

> NORTHFIELD FARM RIDING AND TREKKING CENTRE: Northfield Farm, Flash, Buxton, Derbyshire SK17 0SW; ☎01298 22543; www.northfieldfarm.co.uk.

Wet weather

In addition to the wonderful Museum and Art Gallery as a rainy day destination in Buxton, the town's elegant **Parish Church of St Mary the Virgin** in West Road is of interest. Relatively modern, it was built in 1915 in the Arts and Crafts Gothic style. **St Anne's Church** was designed by Sir Jeffry Wyatville in the Italianate style for the sixth Duke of Devonshire as part of his spa plans, and sports a large portico and tower rising to a dome.

The Dome, Buxton

What to do with children

The **Wonders of the Peak gallery** in the Buxton Museum and Art Gallery is a must for the children, and they will love the sights, sounds and smells of their journey back in time through the history and prehistory of the Peak. Tell them to watch out for the bear in the cave!

Older children will enjoy the **Go Ape!** adventure playground at Poole's Cavern in Buxton Country Park (see above). Go Ape! is an award-winning high-wire forest adventure course of rope bridges, Tarzan swings and zip slides up to 40ft high among the trees of the Buxton Country Park. Appealing to a wide age range, visitors are fitted with a climbing harness, given instructions, and then trek from tree to tree high above the woodland floor.

LOCAL KNOWLEDGE

Award-winning Buxton businesswoman **Louise Potter** owned and managed the town's historic Old Hall Hotel for 25 years. Still living 'over the shop', she is now at the helm of the award-winning No. 6 Tea Rooms, and is on the board of Buxton Festival, Buxton Opera House and Visit Peak District and Derbyshire.

Best thing about living in the Peak District: The wonderful open spaces, the hills, the air and the people.

Best kept secret: Tissington Hall and its surroundings are wonderful.

Favourite haunt: The Wine Bar at the Old Hall Hotel, Buxton. Very convenient, especially when visiting the Opera House for a pre-theatre supper. Friendly staff and good food.

Best thing to do on a rainy day: Visit Chatsworth House and Garden, then lunch in the Carriage House restaurant. I love the garden as much in the rain as in the sunshine. It's also much quieter, and I can pretend it's mine!

Favourite activity: A visit to Buxton Opera House. The diversity of the programme is wonderful. One minute you're transported to the opera, the next night you're dancing to The Drifters.

Best view: The Pavilion Gardens from No. 6 The Square. I am so lucky to live overlooking this historic and wonderful park, originally laid out by Chatsworth gardener Sir Joseph Paxton and developed by his protégé Edward Milner in the 1870s.

Best walk: The Goyt Valley. I love walking my dogs there. There are so many options, and it's right on my doorstep.

Favourite restaurant: Fischers at Baslow Hall. This is a very special night out and the ideal venue for a family celebration.

Favourite takeaway: Simply Thai in Buxton. Excellent food, and it's just round the corner!

Favourite pub: The Druid Inn, Birchover. Brilliant, imaginative food and a good spot to enjoy a drink.

CELEBRITY CONNECTIONS

Comic actor **Tim Brooke-Taylor** was born in Buxton in 1940. Educated at Winchester College and Pembroke College at Cambridge University, he read law and met contemporaries such as John Cleese, Graham Chapman and Bill Oddie. A leading light in the Footlights Club, of which he became president, he was also a member of his college drama society, the Pembroke Players. After university, he co-wrote and performed in the BBC radio comedy show *I'm Sorry I'll Read That Again* alongside Cleese, Oddie and Graeme Garden.

After appearing in the television series *On the Braden Beat* with Canadian broadcaster Bernard Braden, Tim joined Cleese, Chapman and comedian Marty Feldman as co-writer and performer in the television comedy series *At Last the 1948 Show*. The talented foursome co-wrote the famous 'Four Yorkshiremen' sketch, subsequently performed by members of Monty Python's Flying Circus. In 1970, Tim joined Garden and Oddie to form The Goodies for a television comedy series that ran for more than a decade on the BBC and latterly London Weekend Television. The Goodies even appeared on BBC's *Top of the Pops*, performing their hit single *Funky Gibbon*.

Tim has appeared in various television sitcoms, stage productions and radio programmes over the years, including BBC Radio 4's popular 'antidote to panel games', *I'm Sorry I Haven't a Clue*.

🎭 Entertainment

Apart from the famous international **Buxton Festival** and its associated **Fringe, Puppet** and **Literary Festivals** in July, the Opera House in Water Street (booking office ☎0845 127 2190; www.buxtonoperahouse.org.uk) plays host to several other festival-type events during the year. The annual **International Gilbert & Sullivan** Festival takes place in August, and there is a **Shakespeare Festival** in September. The **Four-Four Time Festival** of contemporary music takes place in February, and the traditional **Pantomime** in December. An on-going programme of refurbishment has been aided by a lively Friends organisation, ensuring that this little gem of a theatre is loved by artists and audiences alike.

The Pavilion Gardens is host to the **International Fiddlers' Convention, Brass Band Festival** and **Annual Antiques Fair** in May and the **Great Peak District Fair** and **Great Peak Food Fest** in October and November, respectively.

🛒 Shopping

The Bookstore, Brierlow Bar on the A515 Ashbourne Road just outside Buxton is claimed to be the largest bargain bookshop in the country, with over 20,000 titles in its 5,000sq ft premises. In this bibliophiles' paradise you can browse at your leisure in the four large rooms, and enjoy self-service drinks at the same time. Owner David McPhie is renowned for his shrewd choice of good-quality, new books in more than 50 different categories, 95% of which are sold at half price or less. And when you've bought your books, you can watch the goldfinches on the feeders in the car park.

THE BOOKSTORE BRIERLOW BAR: Ashbourne Road, near Buxton, Derbyshire SK17 9PY; ☎01298 71017; www. bookstore-derbyshire.co.uk. Open daily.

The best... PLACES TO STAY

HOTEL

The Old Hall Hotel

The Square, Buxton SK17 6BD
☎ 01298 22841
www.oldhallhotelbuxton.co.uk

Reputed to be the oldest residential hotel in England, and host to the ill-fated Mary Queen of Scots on several occasions, the Old Hall Hotel has an unrivalled setting overlooking Buxton's showpiece Pavilion Gardens and Edwardian Opera House. Individually appointed bedrooms, choice of dining in the intimate wine bar or elegant restaurant.

Price: £50 per person per night for a standard double.

Barcelo Buxton Palace Hotel

Palace Road, Buxton SK17 6AG
☎ 01298 220011
www.Barcelo-Hotels.co.uk/Buxton

With an imposing exterior designed by Henry Currey in 1868, the Palace Hotel is conveniently situated in the heart of Buxton, just 300m from the railway station. Its 122 bedrooms range from standard singles to four spacious suites, some with wheelchair access. Guests can dine in the Dovedale Restaurant and use the Health & Leisure Club and beauty facilities. There is a daily parking charge.

Price: DB&B from £135 for a standard double; £75 for room only.

Lee Wood Hotel

The Park, Buxton SK17 6TQ
☎ 01298 23002
www.leewoodhotel.co.uk

Overlooking elegant Devonshire Park and with beautiful scenery beyond, the Lee Wood offers an ideal base for touring the Peak District. Each of the 40 en-suite bedrooms are comfortably furnished and individually decorated. Breakfast, lunch and dinner are prepared to order using fresh ingredients. Traditional Sunday lunch is also served.

Price: B&B from £90 for double.

B&B

Grendon Guest House

Bishop's Lane, Buxton SK17 6UN
☎ 01298 78831
www.grendonguesthouse.co.uk

Award-winning B&B offering space, luxury and a warm welcome overlooking pleasant garden and countryside, yet within walking distance of Buxton town centre. Lots of extra touches to make it feel like home from home. Full English, vegetarian and lighter breakfast options based on locally sourced ingredients where available. Dinner available some evenings.

Price: B&B from £30 per person per night.

The best of... THE DARK PEAK

THE GRITSTONE-DOMINATED DARK PEAK, WHERE BROODING
MOORLANDS ARE PUNCTUATED BY VERTICAL ROCKY EDGES AND
WEIRDLY-SHAPED TORS SCULPTED BY AEONS OF WIND AND FROST,
REPRESENTS THE MORE RUGGED, MASCULINE SIDE OF THE PEAK.
THE HIGHEST POINTS ARE KINDER SCOUT AND BLEAKLOW, WHICH
TOWER ABOVE THE SURROUNDING SHALE VALLEYS.

Conical Lose Hill dominates the Hope Valley, with Mam Tor to the far left.

Top: The southern escarpment of Kinder Scout, near Kinder Low;
Middle: Mountain biking under Stanage Edge, in the background; Bottom: A snowy view from
Mam Tor's summit down the Great Ridge towards snow-capped Derwent Edge.

Top: A moorland pool on Kinder's peaty summit; Middle: Looking up Golden Clough towards the peak of Ringing Roger on Kinder; Bottom: Looking down the Great Ridge towards Black Tor and Lose Hill, with the pimple of Win Hill Showing on the right

Top: A climber enjoys a glorious sunset on Stanage Edge;
Middle: Sunset over Little John's village of Hathersage;
Bottom: The Boxing Glove Stones on Kinder's northern edge

The best... PLACES TO STAY

Stoneridge Guest House

Park Road, Buxton SK17 6SG
☎ **01298 26120**
www.stoneridge.co.uk

Elegant late Victorian house overlooking Buxton's cricket ground, within strolling distance of the town centre. En-suite bedrooms with modern facilities including Wi-Fi internet connection and chic, modern décor, including tartan and white bed linen. Full 'Stoneridge', vegetarian and vegan breakfasts based on locally sourced and Fairtrade products. Packed lunches and dinner available.

Price: B&B from £62.50 to £70 for a double.

Buxton's Victorian Guest House

3A Broad Walk, Buxton SK17 6JE
☎ **01298 78759**
www.buxtonvictorian.co.uk

Refurbished Victorian house which once belonged to the Duke of Devonshire, overlooking the award-winning Pavilion Gardens. En-suite, individually decorated rooms include a family suite and room with four poster bed. Comfortable guest drawing room and selection of buffet and hot breakfast options, including kippers, vegetarian and Derbyshire oatcakes.

Price: B&B from £36 per person per night for a standard double.

SELF-CATERING

The Old Stables at Fern Farm

Fern Farm, Fern Road, Buxton SK17 9NP
☎ **01298 72319**
www.fernfarmcottages.co.uk

There are two well-appointed holiday cottages on the 95 acre Fern Farm in sympathetically converted farm buildings. Each sleeps four people and has central heating, modern kitchen and bathroom and polished wooden floors. Small patio with outdoor furniture. Within walking distance of Buxton town centre, and with British Horse Society approved riding and walking on the doorstep.

Price: From £255 for a week.

The best... FOOD AND DRINK

▶ Staying in

Environmentally aware shoppers can satisfy their palates as well as their principles at the award-winning workers' co-operative **Wild Carrot** in Buxton (5 Bridge Street SK17 6BS; ☎01298 22843). Everything from traditionally made bread and home-baked goods to organic fruit and vegetables and eco-friendly cleaning products to natural beauty care is available. Locally sourced products include quiches from Buxton, cakes and savouries from Youlgrave and honey from Longnor. Organic fruit and vegetables come mainly from Lancashire and Lincolnshire, and are a popular draw when delivered to the shop on Tuesdays and Thursdays.

For locally raised and slaughtered pork, beef and lamb, head for **Arnold Mycock & Sons** in Buxton (1 Scarsdale Place SK17 6EF; ☎01298 23330), where the majority of meat is sourced from nearby farms, including two belonging to the Mycock family. Other quality products available are home-made sausages and cooked products such as hams, meat pies and brawn. **Waitrose** in Buxton (Spring Gardens Centre SK17 6DP; ☎01298 767469) also stocks locally sourced and organic foods (including fruit and vegetables, deli), foods catering for special diets and real ales. You'll also find a well-stocked deli counter at **Bon Appetit** (15 Terrace Road SK17 6DU; ☎01298 212414), with a variety of cheeses, cooked meats, olives and salads, as well as a comprehensive takeaway food service including sandwiches, breakfast buns, soups and salads.

Freshly baked bread, pastries and cakes can be bought at the **Devonshire Craft Bakery**, (34 Spring Gardens SK17 6BZ; ☎01298 22923), while further sustenance for the sweet-toothed can be found in chocolates and cakes, handmade on the premises, at **Charlotte's Chocolates** (Unit 1, Cavendish Arcade SK17 6BQ; ☎01298 214440).

Away from the town centre town at **F Redfern & Sons Ltd Farm Shop** (Harpur Hill SK17 9HT; ☎01298 25791) you can source a range of quality meat, poultry, eggs, cheese, cooked meats and pies. Traditional British handcrafted pies and steamed puddings, made using old-fashioned cooking methods and locally sourced ingredients, are specialities at **The Full Ladle** (Tongue Lane SK17 7LN; ☎01298 871896).

Buxton Farmers' Market is held on the first Thursday of every month from 10am to 3pm, except August, when it is generally held on the third Thursday, and in December, when there is usually an extra market just before Christmas. Both these and regular **Saturday Fine Food Fairs**, featuring both local and regional produce, take place in the Octagon at the Pavilion Gardens (SK17 6XN; ☎01298 23114). If you're in the area in October, watch out for the **Great Peak District Fair**, also at the Pavilion Gardens, which showcases some of the area's finest food and drink, plus various arts and crafts, all under one roof.

EATING OUT

FINE DINING

The Dome Fine Dine Restaurant
**University of Derby Buxton,
1 Devonshire Road, Buxton SK17 6RY**
☎ **01298 28345**
www.thedomefinedining.co.uk

Eat in the stunning setting of the University of Derby Buxton's showpiece campus. Meals prepared and served by students range from starters like Andalucian soup and tempura of oysters to main courses such as Derbyshire lamb and vegetarian crepes. Lunch is served Monday to Friday (two courses £10, three courses £12), and dinner on Thursday (four courses £18.50).

RESTAURANT

Columbine Restaurant
7 Hall Bank, Buxton SK17 6EW
☎ **01298 78752**
www.buxtononline.net/columbine

Local produce is the centrepiece of an à la carte menu that changes with the seasons, served in a cosy, intimate setting. Sample starters (from £4.60) are crab and salmon rissole and terrine of local game, while typical mains (from £11) are seared tenderloin of pork or fillet of wild sea bass.

The Old Hall Hotel
The Square, Buxton SK17 6BD
☎ **01298 22841**
www.oldhallhotelbuxton.co.uk

Formal à la carte dining in the elegant main restaurant, or informal meals in the cosy, intimate setting of the wine bar. Menu based on local produce where available, changes four times a year. Pre and post-theatre dining. Wine bar mains cost £10, à la carte £19 for two courses, £23 for three.

Kwei Lin Chinese Restaurant
**1 Lower Hardwick Street
Buxton
SK17 6DQ**
☎ **01298 77822**
www.kweilinbuxton.com

Wide variety of appetizers, soup, beef, chicken, seafood, sizzling and vegetarian dishes, plus a choice of six menus, served in a welcoming setting near Buxton's main shopping centre. Mains (vegetarian) start from as little as £4.60. Takeway service available.

Simply Thai Restaurant
**2–3 Cavendish Circus,
Buxton SK17 6AT**
☎ **01298 24471**
www.simplythaibuxton.co.uk

Fine, authentic Thai food made from quality ingredients, some direct from Thailand, served with a smile in a classy atmosphere. Huge selection of soups, starters, stir-fry, grilled and steamed dishes and vegetarian options, plus five set menus. Main courses start at around £7.50. Takeaway service available.

Michelangelo's Ristorante
1 Market Place, Buxton SK17 6EB
☎ **01298 26640**
www.michelangelosbuxton.com

Welcoming, family-friendly atmosphere, traditional Italian food and service with a smile. Extensive menu includes pizza (try the Inferno if you like them hot!), pasta, risotto, meat and fish dishes. Main courses cost from £5.25, 'happy hour' Sunday to Thursday features any pizza or pasta for £4.50. There is a 10% discount on takeaway service.

EATING OUT

CAFÉ

The Pavilion Gardens
St John's Road, Buxton SK17 6XN
☎ **01298 23114**
www.paviliongardens.co.uk

Revamped facilities include a light, spacious café on two floors, offering everything from traditional English dishes and a children's menu to home-made cakes and afternoon teas. Outdoor seating available on the Promenade, where visitors can make the most of warmer days. The contemporary ground-floor coffee and ice cream bar sells Bradwell's ice cream.

Beltane
8a Hall Bank, Buxton, Derbyshire SK17 6EW
☎ **01298 26010**
www.beltanebar.co.uk

Freshly made food at realistic prices, including daily specials and home-made cakes, in a relaxed family-friendly (high chairs and baby-changing facilities) atmosphere with wooden tables and chairs, comfortable sofas and a conservatory. Regular live music with late licence on Fridays and Saturdays. Real ales, rarer beers, wine and single malt whiskies are available.

Project X
Old Court House, George Street, Buxton SK17 6AY
☎ **01298 77079**

Stylish, licensed coffee shop and bar with chic, subtly lit interior offering a wide range of home-made snacks, bagels, paninis, cakes, hot and cold drinks, smoothies, cocktails and quality wines from around the world, including British varieties. Range of gluten-free puddings also available, and live jazz every Saturday evening.

The Devonshire Bakery
68 Spring Gardens, Buxton SK17 6BZ
☎ **01298 23405**

Fresh food prepared on the premises includes home-cooked breakfasts, snacks, sandwiches and light meals, including thick 'doorsteps' of toast made from the bakery's popular bread. Selection of hot and cold drinks, including speciality teas and coffees. Bustling, bright atmosphere and friendly service with a smile.

TEA ROOM

Hargreaves Edwardian Tea Rooms
16–18 Spring Gardens, Buxton SK17 6DE
☎ **01298 23083**
www.hargreavesgiftandcookshop.co.uk

First-floor, Edwardian-style café above a family-run china, gift and cook shop, with charming period atmosphere and food freshly prepared to order. Local produce sourced where possible. Menu ranges from full and budget breakfasts to clotted cream teas featuring home-made scones. Wide range of specialist teas, coffees and soft drinks. Children welcome.

No. 6 The Square Tea Room
The Square, Buxton SK17 6AZ
☎ **01298 213541**
www.no6tearooms.co.uk

Award-winning tea room in beautiful Georgian-style building that takes guests back to the genteel era of Jane Austen. All-day breakfast options include Derbyshire oatcakes with sweet and savoury toppings, while the main menu features light meals, pâtés, sandwiches, afternoon tea and cream tea. Dairy, gluten and wheat-free options available.

♨ Drinking

If you're looking for a true drinkers' pub rather than a restaurant, head for **The Swan** in Buxton's High Street (SK17 6HB; ☎01298 23278), where real ales include local brews and guest beers, and the busy social life includes darts, dominoes and quiz nights. Another popular venue is the bustling café bar **Beltane** (Hall Bank SK17 6EW; ☎01298 26010), where the emphasis is on food during the day, but more on drink in the evening. Expect to find beers from local microbreweries, plus live music every Thursday. Regular live music is also a feature at **The Eagle Hotel** (Eagle Parade, Buxton SK17 6EQ; ☎01298 73505).

If you fancy a pre-dinner or pre-theatre cocktail, either alcoholic or non-alcoholic, visit **Monk at Buxton** (Cavendish Circus SK17 6AT; ☎01629 581751), where you'll be served imaginative and unusual combinations of flavours in a lively, stylish setting. Or to enjoy a variety of beers and wines in a relaxed, convivial atmosphere, call in at **The George Potter Bar** in the Old Hall Hotel (The Square, Buxton SK17 6BD; ☎01298 22841), named after former owner Louise Potter's late husband. For a more traditional experience, venture out of town on the A515 road to Ashbourne, and you'll eventually reach the 17th-century **Jug and Glass Inn** (Ashbourne Road, Buxton SK17 0BA; ☎01298 84848), where you'll find fine ales, good food and en-suite accommodation; pets are also welcome.

① Visitor Information

Tourist information centre: Buxton Tourist Information Centre, The Crescent, Buxton SK17 6BQ, ☎01298 25106, www.highpeak.gov.uk, open daily.

Hospitals: Stepping Hill Hospital, Poplar Grove, Stockport, ☎0161 483 1010; Buxton Hospital, London Road, Buxton, ☎01298 214000; Cavendish Hospital, Manchester Road, Buxton, ☎01298 212800.

Doctors: Elmwood Medical Centre, 7 Burlington Road, Buxton SK17 9AY, ☎01298 23019; Buxton Medical Practice, 2 Temple Road, Buxton SK17 9BZ, ☎01298 23298; Stewart Medical Centre, 15 Hartington Road, Buxton SK17 6JP, ☎01298 22338; Goyt Valley Medical Practice, Chapel Street, Whaley Bridge SK23 7SR, ☎01663 73911.

Supermarkets: Waitrose, Spring Gardens Centre, Buxton, ☎01298 767469; Iceland, Spring Gardens, Buxton, ☎01298 72582; Morrisons, Bakewell Road, Buxton, ☎01298 24789; Co-op, Buxton Road, Whaley Bridge, ☎01663 732955; Tesco, Bridgemont, Buxton Road, Whaley Bridge SK23 7HT, ☎0845 677 9725.

Taxis: Ian's Private Hire, 15 Crossings Road, Chapel-en-le-Frith SK23 9RZ, ☎01298 814863; B & S Private Hire, 44 Fairy Bank Crescent, Hayfield, High Peak SK22 2HR, ☎01663 744887; High Peak Taxis, Stoneyland Drive, New Mills, High Peak SK22 3DL, ☎01663 744448; New Mills Cabs, 12 Bowden Crescent, New Mills SK22 4LN, ☎01663 746606.

FURTHER AFIELD

The Goyt Valley

The Goyt Valley, just to the west of Buxton, has sometimes been called the Dark Peak in microcosm. It has all the features of a typical gritstone valley – with brooding moors above, a deep valley filled by reservoirs and surrounded by forestry beneath, abundant wildlife and a fascinating human history. Once ruled by the wealthy Grimshaw family, who lived in Italianate splendour during the early years of the 19th century at **Errwood Hall**, the valley was also once the scene of industry, with local coal mines and even a gunpowder factory. And Goyt's Clough quarry was the birthplace of the mighty Pickford's removal empire, where the family started out as packhorse operators who led teams of packhorses across the bleak moors of the Peak District.

Nothing much remains of the glory which once was Errwood. The buildings were demolished in 1938 with the construction of the **Errwood Reservoir**, built to supply Stockport with pure Peakland drinking water. Only a few arches remain, set deep in the rhododendrons and azaleas of the Goyt Forest. But the poignant graveyard of the Grimshaw family and their servants still exists above the house, and the tiny circular shrine to Dolores de Bergrin, the much-loved companion and tutor to the Grimshaw children, still stands on the moors above. Today, Errwood Reservoir is the setting for a yacht club, and a popular place of resort for the people of nearby Buxton and district.

Path to the Errwood Reservoir and the Goyt Valley

The ruins of Errwood Hall

Fernilee Reservoir further down the Goyt Valley, was built in 1967, and submerged the site of the Chilworth gunpowder factory, which is reputed to have supplied gunpowder for use against the Spanish Armada in 1588.

Further downstream, the formerly industrial mill town of **Whaley Bridge**, is a convenient centre for exploring the beautiful Goyt Valley. The Peak Forest Canal, later linked to the Cromford Canal by the Cromford and High Peak Railway (now the High Peak Trail) has its terminus at Bugsworth (the old name for Buxworth), and is now once again very popular with narrowboat owners.

Although today the **Bugsworth Canal Basin** on the Peak Forest Canal at Buxworth, near Whaley Bridge, is a haven of quietness and beauty, it preserves the legacy of what was once a thriving industrial centre. It is the only surviving canal and tramway interchange in Britain, where the former **Peak Forest Tramway** linked up with the canal and later the railway, and was once one of the largest inland ports on the 3,000-mile national canal system. Colourful narrowboats are always to be found moored in the basin, and you can still see the kilns where burnt lime was prepared for over a century at the southern terminus of the late 18th-century Peak Forest Canal, for transport all over the country.

THE INLAND WATERWAY PROTECTION SOCIETY: Blackbrook House, Bugsworth Basin, Buxworth, High Peak, Derbyshire SK23 7NF; ☎01663 732493; www.brocross.com/iwps/. Entry: free; open daily.

Where to stay
There are two recommended options for accommodation whilst exploring the Goyt Valley. Self-caterers should check out **Cote Bank Farm** (Buxworth, Whaley Bridge

SK23 7NP; ☎01663 750566; www.cotebank.co.uk; £260–£560 for a week); two stone-built cottages near historic Bugsworth Basin. The 16th-century Old House once gave shelter to Charles Wesley and is the perfect romantic hideaway for couples. Cherry Tree Cottage, originally a hay barn, sleeps six. The farm also has a B&B option. Alternatively, quality bed and breakfast is on offer at **Springbank Guest House** (3 Reservoir Road, Whaley Bridge SK23 7BL; ☎01663 732819; www.whaleyspringbank. co.uk; B&B £28–£35 per person per night). Painstaking attention to every aspect of guests' comfort is the hallmark of this early Victorian guest house with many original period features. There are luxury, family, double and twin rooms, all with en-suite facilities on offer and local and free range produce is used whenever possible to cater for all diets, including vegetarian.

Food and drink

For Italian food, served the Italian way in the Goyt Valley, visit **Vito's Trattoria** (5 Market Street, Whaley Bridge, High Peak SK23 7AA; ☎01663 734333; www.vitostrattoria. co.uk) where you can expect a warm, Continental-style welcome from owner Vito Biasi and his staff. Options include starters ranging from mixed mushrooms with thyme, olive oil and garlic to mixed cold meats and olives, while mains (from £6.50) include spaghetti Bolognese, Italian meatballs, fresh filled pancakes, pizzas and specials featuring poultry, meat and fish.

Home-made hot and cold sandwiches, breakfasts and specials such as hot pot and meatballs, using locally produced meat and produce where possible, are on offer at **Babka**, Whaley Bridge (Old Road SK23 7HR; ☎01663 734419). A small deli counter sells cold meats, cheeses, chorizo and salamis, and orders totalling £10 and over qualify for free local delivery. **Whaley Bridge Farmers' Market** is held at the Uniting Church (Old Road SK23 7HP; ☎0845 129 7777) on the second Saturday of the month from 10am to 2pm.

Beer, wine and whisky connoisseurs are spoilt for choice in Whaley Bridge. **Cloud Wine** (Buxton Road SK23 7HX; ☎01663 734809; www.cloudwine.net) stocks both popular name brand and lesser known wines, lagers, beers and ciders, including international brands and bottled ales and a variety of spirits, including malt whiskies. Near the Peak Forest Canal terminus, **Goyt Wines Occasions** (Canal Street SK23 7LS; ☎01663 734214; www.goytwines.com) has featured in the *Guardian Food Directory* for the past two years and supplies an impressive variety of boutique wines and spirits, real ale recommended beers, handmade chocolates, ice cream and specialist coffees and teas. Other lines include quality glasses, Havana cigars, gifts, a Wine and Dine Club and regular tastings. If you prefer to visit a local pub, try the **Shepherd's Arms** (Old Road SK23 7HR, ☎01663 732384), close to Whaley Bridge railway station, which has a traditional tap room with an open fire and flagged floor, plus a welcoming lounge and small garden, and serves real ales, including guest beers.

LEEK, LONGNOR AND THE ROACHES

Leek is the capital of the Staffordshire Moorlands, a town centred on its cobbled market place and formerly famous for its silk and cotton factories, which were supported by William Morris of the Arts and Crafts movement (see Culture, p.55). Today it is perhaps best known for the large number and great variety of its antique shops. The town centre is watched over by the imposing 80ft/24m high Portland stone tower of the Nicholson War Memorial – known locally as 'the Monument'. Reputed to be the tallest tower in the country with four clock faces, it was built in 1925 by Sir Arthur and Lady Nicholson in memory of their son and other local men who died in the First World War. Brindley's Mill, the first mill to be built by the great canal pioneer James Brindley, is now a museum to his memory and nearby on the River Churnet is the Cheddleton Flint Mill, where flint was ground for use in the Potteries, and the popular Churnet Valley Railway.

As you drive north out of Leek on the A53 Buxton road, the skyline ahead is punctuated by some of the most spectacular rock formations in the Peak. These are The Roaches, Hen Cloud and Ramshaw Rocks, upthrusts of pink-tinged gritstone which tower over the plains and the glinting reflection of the Tittesworth Reservoir below, and offer wonderfully airy walking and climbing. Hidden in the depths of Back Forest to the north of The Roaches is Lud's Church, a mysterious chasm with links to the ancient alliterative poem of *Sir Gawain and the Green Knight*, and to secret services held by followers of John Wycliff in the 14th century.

Longnor is a former moorland market town which boasts that it was once more important than nearby Buxton, whose postal address used to be 'near Leek'. Longnor stands high on the ridge which separates the Dove and Manifold Valleys, so is an excellent centre for exploring both as well as the little-visited Staffordshire moorlands. The scale of charges on the old Market Hall (now a craft centre) in the cobbled village square gives an indication of Longnor's former importance and prosperity, and the village achieved fame as the original set for television's medical soap, *Peak Practice*.

WHAT TO SEE AND DO

Brindley's Mill
James Brindley – the so-called Father of Britain's canals – was an extraordinary character. And you can see where his amazing career began at **Brindley's Mill** at Leek, where he built his first water-powered corn mill in 1725. Restored in 1974, it is still a working mill and shows exactly where and how Brindley's extraordinary skill as the greatest engineer of his age developed. The adjoining **James Brindley Museum** has displays which illustrate the life and work of the great man, including one of his notebooks and the surveyor's level which was his principal tool in planning the

Leek

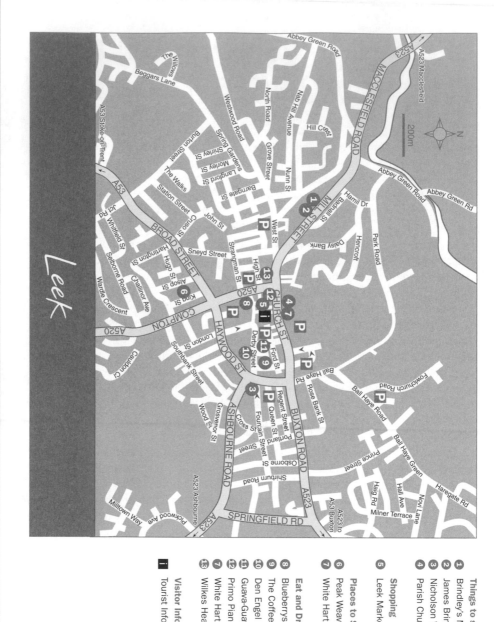

Things to see and do

1. Brindley's Mill
2. James Brindley Museum
3. Nicholson War Memorial
4. Parish Church

Shopping

5. Leek Market

Places to Stay

6. Peak Weavers Rooms & Restaurant
7. White Hart B&B

Eat and Drink

8. Blueberrys
9. The Coffee Clique
10. Den Engel
11. Guava-Guava
12. Primo Piano
7. White Hart Tea Room & Restaurant
13. Wilkes Head

Visitor Information

Tourist Information Centre

BRINDLEY'S MILL: Mill Street, Leek, Staffordshire ST13 8ET; ☎01538 483741; www.brindleymill.net. Entry: small admission charge; open 2pm–5pm, Sat, Sun/Bank Holidays; 2pm–5pm, Mon to Wed, 21 July to 27 Aug.

routes of the 3,000 mile canal network which he masterminded, and which was to transform the country and herald the start of modern Britain.

Tittesworth Water

Tittesworth Water reservoir, owned and managed by Severn Trent Water, is beautifully situated about 3 miles from Leek, with the dramatic rock towers of The Roaches as a dramatic backdrop. There is a well-appointed visitor centre, opened in 1998, which features a children's play area and adventure playground, a crafts and gift shop and an 80-seat restaurant, plus picnic and barbecue areas overlooking the water. A new feature is the Sensory Garden, a highly popular attraction which was designed by three Midland schools specifically for the benefit of the partially sighted and other people with disabilities. Tittesworth is also very popular with bird watchers and the reservoir supports a wide range of wildlife which can be observed from several hides by the water. It is well known for its trout fishing, which is available to the public either from the banks or by hired boats.

Brindley's Mill, Leek

TITTESWORTH WATER VISITOR CENTRE: Meerbrook, Leek, Staffordshire ST13 8SW; ☎01538 300400; www.stwater.co.uk. Entry: free but £1 charge for car park; open daily from 10am except Christmas Day.

The Churnet Valley Railway and attractions en route

The Churnet Valley Railway is a volunteer-run organisation which operates steam trains from the Cheddleton Railway Centre, a museum established in the mid-1970s by the North Staffordshire Railway Society, displaying artefacts from the original North Staffordshire Railway Company. The first passenger services run by the Churnet Valley Railway began in 1996, a 'push and pull' operation of a little over a mile between Cheddleton and Leek Brook Junction. In 1998, a southward 3¼ mile section between Cheddleton

CHURNET VALLEY RAILWAY: Cheddleton Station, Cheddleton, near Leek, Staffordshire Moorlands ST13 7EE; ☎01538 360522; www.churnet-valley-railway.co.uk. Entry: adults £9, children £5, seniors £7; open Sun, Mar–Sept, Wed, Jul–Aug and Bank Holidays (phone for times).

The Churnet Valley Railway

and Consall was reopened for passenger traffic, and the next extension, to Kingsley and Froghall, opened to traffic in 2001, giving a current operational length of about 5 miles. And you travel through one of the longest tunnels (531 yards/485m) on a preserved railway near Leekbrook Junction. Among the many other attractions along the route are the Cheddleton Flint Mill, the Churnet Valley RSPB Reserve and Froghall Wharf on the Cauldon Canal, with its adjacent historic lime kilns.

CHEDDLETON FLINT MILL: Cheddleton, Leek, Staffordshire ST13 7HL; ☎01782 502907; www.people.exeter.ac.uk/akoutram/cheddleton-mill/. Entry: free, but donations accepted; open 1pm–5pm weekends, phone to check Mon–Fri opening times.

Cheddleton Flint Mill is a fine example of a water mill which ground flint for the pottery industry in nearby Stoke-on-Trent. The site includes two water mills, a small museum, a period cottage, the Cauldon Canal and many other exhibits. The mill is dependent on public donations and is run by volunteers from the Cheddleton Flint Mill Industrial Heritage Trust, formed in 1972. Its aims are to preserve the unique mill complex and provide educational information concerning the historical development of the raw materials used in commercial pottery.

COOMBES VALLEY NATURE RESERVE (RSPB): Six Oaks Farm, Bradnop, Leek ST13 7EU; ☎01538 384017; www.rspb.org.uk. Entry and parking: free; open all year, dawn–dusk daily; visitor centre and toilets, 9am–5pm.

The RSPB's steep-sided **Coombes Valley Nature Reserve**, near Bradnop, 3 miles south east of Leek, is a great place to get close to nature. Although originally set aside for its ornithological interest – redstarts, wood warblers and pied flycatchers are typical breeding summer visitors – it claims to be about much

LOCAL KNOWLEDGE

Everyday objects such as bank notes and watches seem to vanish into thin air when Longnor-based magician **Chris Stevenson** is around. Regulars at Ye Olde Cheshire Cheese, where his wife Lynn is licensee and he is resident entertainer, tend to keep tabs on their possessions. An award-winning member of the International Brotherhood of Magicians, Chris now captivates audiences across the globe and has impressed celebrities such as American comedienne Joan Rivers.

The best thing about living in the Peak District: Living in a small village. You all know each other and everyone gets involved whenever there's a local event.

Favourite hangout: Castleton. We have a caravan and often take it there. Hills, great walking and pubs with good food and real ale. Heaven!

Best walk: Leave Longnor via Town End, cross the fields to Hollinsclough, past the school, out of the village and take the farm lane on your left that takes you around the base of Chrome Hill and Parkhouse Hill. Cross the road and follow the footpath up the field over the hill to Earl Sterndale. Stop at the Quiet Woman pub for a pint and a pork pie. Leave towards Crowdecote. From the base of High Wheeldon Hill, take the right-hand farm track past a house and at the first corner keep left. This takes you over the river Dove across the fields and up a steep track, back into Longnor.

Best view: Drive to the top of Crowdecote Bank, park, cross the road and gaze across the north end of the Dove Valley. Awesome.

Favourite takeaway: Longnor Chip Shop or the Indian Palace in Buxton.

Favourite pub: The Bull i'th'Thorn, Flagg. It's very old and comfortable with lots of character and good ale.

Secret tip for lunch: The George, Alstonefield. Excellent food, real ale and a real fire.

more than birds. This is a fine site for badgers – although you would be very lucky to see one – and the Coombes Valley also supports a wonderful variety of butterflies and wildflowers, including orchids in the spring. Or you could take a trip on the Cauldon Canal with the **Froghall Wharf Canal Boat Trips** which operate from Froghall Wharf. Here you can enjoy morning coffee, lunch or afternoon tea on board a traditional narrow boat as you gently navigate the picturesque winding Cauldon Canal, past the imposing remains of the lime kilns, in a $2^1/_2$ hour trip through the beautiful countryside of the Staffordshire moorlands.

> FROGHALL WHARF CANAL BOAT TRIPS: Foxt Road, Froghall, Stoke-on-Trent, Staffordshire ST10 2HJ; ☎01538 266486. Open 10am–dusk, Thurs/Sun mid-May to Sept; booking required.

Wet weather

Apart from Brindley's Mill, Leek's **Parish Church of St Edward the Confessor** is perhaps best known for its two Saxon cross shafts in the churchyard. The south aisle of the church has other Saxon cross fragments, mostly dating from the 10th century. The north aisle features a stained glass window by Edward Burne-Jones, which was made in the workshops of William Morris. His influence is also seen in the altar frontals made by the Leek School of Embroidery.

What to do with children

The children will love the **Blackbrook Zoological Park** at Winkhill near Leek, which is claimed to be the UK's largest bird park. You can take an avian tour of the world in the 37 acre park, going from the black swans of Australia to the secretary birds and flamingos of Africa in just a few steps. The Blackbrook Park has a proud record in its breeding programme of rare and endangered species, such as with the lesser flamingo and Maribou stork. Also at Blackbrook are many friendly animals for them to meet, including Red River hogs, kangaroos and several species of lemurs. The penguin exhibit opened recently, with an amazing underwater viewing cave.

> BLACKBROOK ZOOLOGICAL PARK: Winkhill, near Leek, Staffordshire ST13 7QR; ☎01538 308293; www.blackbrookzoo.co.uk. Open 10.30am–5.30am daily except Christmas Day.

Shopping

Leek has been the shopping and market capital of the Staffordshire Moorlands area for at least eight centuries, ever since Earl Ranulf of Chester was granted a charter to hold markets and fairs there in 1208. So we can be pretty certain that **Leek Market** has been held in the Market Square every Wednesday since then. There are also indoor markets at Leek on Wednesdays, Fridays and Saturdays, a **Fine Food Festival Farmers' Market** on the third Saturday of each month, and an **Antiques and Collectors' Market** held every Saturday.

Local legends – Lud's Church

Lud's Church, the setting of the Green chapel in *Sir Gawain and the Green Knight*

Deep in the woodlands of Back Forest, north-west of The Roaches in the Staffordshire Moorlands, there lies a deep and mysterious mossy chasm which is marked on the OS map as 'Lud's Church (cave)'. Actually, it is not a cave at all, but a huge natural landslip in the gritstone bedrock, which has created a winding fissure about 60ft/18m deep and only 20ft/6m wide at the top, and largely hidden in the trees. The name 'Lud' supposedly comes from the fact that it was used for illegal services by Walter de Ludank, a Lollard follower of the religious reformer John Wycliffe, during the 14th century. The story goes that the secret natural chapel was raided by the King's troops, and Walter's daughter was accidently shot dead. For many years, a statue (actually a ship's figurehead) supposed to represent Alice de Ludank stood high on the walls of the chasm, and she is still said to haunt the place.

But the legends of Lud's Church go back further than that. One of the earliest poems in the English language is *Sir Gawain and the Green Knight*, a 14th century Authurian alliterative poem by an unknown author which sets the finale of the somewhat gory tale of beheadings in a Green Chapel. This was identified as Lud's Church during the 1960s by an academic from Keele University, based on the medieval poet's detailed description of the area, and the north Midland dialect in which it was written. The description of the Green Chapel in latest translation of the text by the popular modern poet Simon Armitage (2007) seems a pretty fair description of Lud's Church:

> 'its walls, matted with weeds and moss,
> Enclosed a cavity, like a kind of old cave
> Or crevice in the crag...'

The best... PLACES TO STAY

HOTEL

Three Horseshoes Inn & Country Hotel

Blackshaw Moor, Leek ST13 8TM
☎ **01538 300296**
www.threeshoesinn.co.uk

At this family-run inn and country hotel the accommodation ranges from boutique-style standard bedrooms to luxury rooms with four-poster beds and whirlpool baths. Dine in the pub carvery, or brasserie, serving modern English food and Thai specialities, or Kirk's Restaurant.

Price: B&B from £75 for a double room.

FARMSTAY

Hurdlow Farm

Upper Hulme, Near Leek ST13 8TX
☎ **01538 300406**
www.hurdlowfarm.fsnet.co.uk

Set on a working family farm, Hurdlow Cottage is an 18th-century farmhouse offering self-catering facilities for six in a traditional country setting with scenic views. Open log fire and cosy, comfortably furnished bedrooms. Home-made sponge cake awaits on your arrival.

Price: £300 to £495 for a week.

Dove Valley Centre

Under Whitle, Sheen, Longnor SK17 0PR
☎ **01298 83282**
www.dovevalleycentre.co.uk

Special interest breaks and short courses focusing on the arts, rural crafts and conservation and self-catering accommodation in a sustainably converted 18th-century barn on a family-run, 50 acre upland farm.

Price: From £280 for a week.

B&B

Choir Cottage and Choir House

Ostlers Lane, Cheddleton, Near Leek ST13 7HS
☎ **01538 360561**
www.choircottage.co.uk

Multi award-winning accommodation in a quaint 17th-century stone-built cottage with many original features, once home to ostlers, then the village poor, and also in modern Choir House next door. Beautifully appointed en-suite rooms in pleasant setting close to the Cheddleton Canal.

Price: B&B £35 per person per night.

White Hart B&B

White Hart Tea Room, 1 & 3 Stockwell Street, Leek ST13 6DH
☎ **01538 372122**
www.whiteharttearoom.co.uk

Six en-suite, spacious bedrooms with modern facilities, including internet access, situated above what is believed to be Leek's oldest tea room. Home-cooked breakfasts incorporate locally sourced produce.

Price: B&B from £80 for a double.

SELF-CATERING

Paddock Farm

Upper Hulme, Leek ST13 8TY
☎ **01538 300345**
www.roachescottages.co.uk

Award-winning, family-run farmhouse holiday cottages with panoramic views over open countryside. Open-plan living in two cottages with stone walls and original beams, each sleeping up to six people. Across the courtyard, the Roaches Tea Rooms serve farmhouse breakfasts, cream teas and more.

Price: £295 to £695 for a week.

The best... FOOD AND DRINK

Staffordshire Oatcakes are a delicious local delicacy in this part of the Peak, where you'll also come across locally made cheese and real ales, organically raised meats and delectable heather, blossom and wildflower honey. The best local produce is also on sale at the monthly Festival of Fine Foods in Leek. There's a good choice of places to eat out, and you can sample either locally brewed real ales or a variety of Belgian beers in local bars and pubs.

▶ Staying in

For delectable food and drink ranging from cakes and cheese to pâté and pies, plus Italian specialities, try **Pronto** delicatessen in Leek (10 Sheep Market ST13 5HW; ☎01538 384445). You can also choose from a wide range of sandwiches, Italian salami, pastrami, home-cooked hams and pies made from meat sourced from the Peak District; there's also a hamper service. For locally made cheeses and locally brewed beers, head for **the Staffordshire Cheese and Beer Shop** at Cheddleton (Unit 12, Churnet Side, off Harrison Way ST13 7EF; ☎07971 808370). Handmade cheeses include The Staffordshire, a handmade, cloth-bound cheese, and Moorland oak smoked. Beers, made by Leek Brewery, range from Staffordshire Gold to Tittesworth Tipple. Traditional Staffordshire oatcakes, eaten in north Staffordshire, the Staffordshire Moorlands and The Potteries, are made to a secret recipe by **Povey's Oatcakes** of Biddulph (33 High Street ST8 6AW; ☎01782 511799) and are available at local shops, supermarkets and online at www.poveysoatcakes.com.

Several businesses in the area specialise in quality, locally reared meat and meat products. **Dovedale Traditional Beef** at Longnor (Ridge Farm SK17 0LF; ☎01298 83370) supplies traditional and rare breed beef, properly hung for traditional flavour, plus ready-prepared beef meals. In Butterton, **S Bagshaw & Sons** (Turnock House ST13 7TD; ☎01538 304294) specialises in lamb, beef, bacon and pork from animals raised on local farms. Organic lamb with a distinctive sweet flavour from animals reared on clover and herb-rich meadows is available from **Manifold Valley Organic Produce** at Reapsmoor (Rewlach Farm SK17 0LQ; ☎01298 84408). For rare breed pork, beef, lamb, home-cured bacon, speciality sausages and burgers, visit **The Threshing Barn** at Bradnop (Lower Lady Meadows Farm ST13 7EZ; ☎01538 304494). **Stoop Farm** at Hollinsclough (SK17 0RW; ☎01298 25494) produces beef and lamb as a member of the Peak Choice farmers' co-operative. Delicious heather, blossom and wildflower honey, mead, honey marmalade and beeswax can be sourced from **Daisybank Apiaries** at Longnor (Daisybank, Newtown SK17 0NE; ☎01298 83829).

In Leek, the **Festival of Fine Foods**, offering everything from cheese and cakes to home-made pies and locally farmed meat, is held in the Market Place (ST13 5HH; ☎01538 395589) on the third Saturday of the month, while the **Leek Moorlands Country Market**, offering a wide variety of locally produced foods and crafts, takes place every Wednesday at the Butter Market, from 8.30am to 3.30pm (ST13 5HH; ☎01538 308246; www.leek.staffordshirecountrymarkets.co.uk).

EATING OUT

RESTAURANTS

Peak Weavers Rooms & Restaurant
King Street, Leek ST13 5NW
☎ 01538 383729
www.peakweavershotel.co.uk

Award-winning restaurant and B&B accommodation in a 19th-century former convent, named after the industry which shaped Leek. Local, seasonal ingredients are sourced and prepared on the premises. The à la carte menu features items such as locally grown asparagus in June and Staffordshire venison in October. Starters cost from £3.50, mains from £9.95.

Primo Piano
10a Sheepmarket, Leek ST13 5HW
☎ 01538 398289

Friendly Italian restaurant in the centre of Leek with rustic décor and a convivial atmosphere. Large à la carte menu, and also pizza, pasta, steaks, fish, duck and chicken dishes and daily special. Mains around £10.50.

Guava-Guava
23 Getliffe's Yard, Leek ST13 6HU
☎ 01538 373344
www.guava-guava.co.uk

Relaxed Mexican and Latin dining in a chic contemporary setting, with breakfast, lunch and dinner menus and imaginative cocktail list. Classic and contemporary Mexican starters and mains, fish, grills, tapas and desserts available. Children welcome. Lunchtime mains start at £3.50 for soup of the day, dinner mains from £9.95.

GASTRO PUB

The Black Grouse
Market Square, Longnor SK17 0NS
☎ 01298 83205/83194

This Georgian inn, renovated to a high standard, offers meals in the rustic, oak-panelled bar and an elegant, more formal restaurant. Meals prepared from local produce, including vegetarian options, children's menu and Sunday lunch. Stylish accommodation also available, B&B from £70 per couple per night. A la carte main courses cost from £6.95 to £16.50.

CAFÉ

The Coffee Clique
16–18 Getliffe's Yard,
Off Derby Street, Leek ST13 6HU
☎ 01538 373132

Family-run coffee shop with internet access on two floors. In fine weather, has the feel of a summer house with sun shining through the glass roof. Locally sourced ingredients and many home-made items, such as soups, cakes, cookies and puddings. Other options include toasties, paninis, wraps, sandwiches and jacket potatoes. Free baby food is available and dogs are welcome downstairs.

EATING OUT

Longnor Craft Centre and Coffee Shop
The Market Hall, Longnor SK17 0NT
☎ 01298 83587

Warm, friendly coffee shop in the heart of Longnor, as part of a craft centre featuring work by local artists and artisans, including Fox Country Furniture. Home-baked cakes and scones, home-made soups, light lunches, local savoury oatcakes and ploughman's lunches, most using locally produced ingredients.

TEA ROOM

White Hart Tea Room and Restaurant
1–3 Stockwell Street, Leek ST13 6DH
☎ 01538 372122
www.whitehartttearoom,co.uk

Reputed to be Leek's oldest tea room, housed in Grade II listed, 16th-century premises. The majority of food is sourced from local suppliers and freshly cooked to order, including Staffordshire oatcakes, breakfasts, light meals, main meals, sandwiches, paninis, jacket potatoes, cakes and pastries and it is fully licensed. Evening meals are served from Wednesday to Saturday.

Roaches Tea Rooms
Paddock Farm, Upper Hulme, Leek ST13 8TY
☎ 01538 300345
www.roachestearooms.co.uk

Specialities include all day farmhouse and garden breakfasts, traditional home-cooked meals, Staffordshire oatcakes and locally sourced roast Sunday lunch. Home-made cakes and cream teas complemented by teas, coffees and cold drinks. Cosy up by the log burning stove in winter, or relax in the conservatory or on the patio in better weather.

🍸 Drinking

Real ale aficionados can choose from a range of locally named brews such as Cheddleton Steamer, Hen Cloud, Rudyard Ruby and Tittesworth Tipple, which are all available from **Leek Brewery** (Churnet Court, Cheddleton ST13 7EF; ☎01538 361919). The majority of its beers are bottle-conditioned, suitable for vegetarians and sold at farmers' markets in the area; cask beer is only made to special order.

In Leek, you'll find locally brewed real ales including guest beers, a real fire and regular live music at the **Wilkes Head** (St Edward Street ST13 5DS; ☎01538 383616), a cosy pub named after the 18th-century politician John Wilkes. The traditional Staffordshire market town may be the last place you'd expect to find a Belgian bar, but you'll discover an excellent one named **Den Engel** (The Angel) on Stanley Street (ST13 5HG; ☎01538 373751). Around 10 Belgian beers are on draught, and there are also bottled offerings and beers from British microbreweries. In fine weather you can sit out on the patio to the rear.

To the north west of Leek, you might come across an ivy-covered building that looks a tad familiar in the picturesque village of Longnor. **The Horseshoe Inn** (SK17 ONT; ☎01298 83262) appeared as the 'Black Swan' in the long-running ITV series *Peak Practice.* Dating back to the early 17th century, it offers real ales, a rotating guest ale and home-cooked food based on local produce. Another traditional hostelry offering a wide choice of food and drink, beer garden and Sunday carvery is **Ye Olde Cheshire Cheese** (High Street SK17 ONS; ☎01298 83218). You can also visit the 'Magic Room', where resident magician Chris Stevenson (see Local Knowledge, p. 221) keeps his collection of magic-related memorabilia. In nearby Crowdecote, **The Packhorse Inn** (SK17 ODB; ☎01298 83618) has a reputation for good beers, straightforward food such as fish and chips, traditional puddings and fine views. Children and dogs are welcome. In Sheen, the mellow, stone-built **Staffordshire Knot** dates back to the mid-17th century and has been sympathetically restored to retain its original character and friendly atmosphere. It has a good range of beers and food, including specials.

Guest ales from local microbreweries are on tap at **The Greyhound Inn** at Warslow (Leek Road SK17 OJN; ☎01298 687017), which serves home-cooked meals prepared from fresh seasonal produce, including specials. You'll also find a beer garden and access for disabled people (including toilets), and children are welcome. A range of real cask ales, including local brews, are on offer at **The Manifold Inn** at Hulme End (SK17 OEX; ☎01298 84537), a 200-year-old coaching inn and restaurant on the banks of the eponymous river. At Upper Hulme, near The Roaches and Leek, the 17th-century **Ye Olde Rock Inn** (ST13 8TY; ☎01538 300324) sells a good range of beers and has an extensive menu.

Well-kept beer and home-cooked food are a winning combination at **The Black Lion** Inn at Butterton (ST13 7SP; ☎01538 304232), an engaging 18th-century village inn on the edge of the Manifold Valley. Local brews, hearty pub food and a warm welcome can be found at **Ye Olde Royal Oak Inn** at Wetton (DE6 2AF; ☎01335 310287). Real ales, including ever-changing guest beers, plus meals cooked to order using local, seasonal ingredients where possible, are on the menu at **The Red Lion Inn** at Waterfall, Waterhouses (ST10 3HZ; ☎01538 308279). Also at Waterhouses, you'll find **Ye Olde Crown** (ST10 3HL; ☎01538 308204), a traditional village local with original stonework, beams and open fires on the banks of the River Hamps. Real ales, including guest beers, are served, and walkers are welcome.

ⓘ Visitor Information

Tourist information centre: Leek Tourist Information Centre, 1 Market Place, Leek, Staffordshire ST13 5HH, ☎01538 483741, www.enjoystaffordshire.com or www.staffordshiremoorlands.com, open daily.

Hospitals: Leek Moorlands Hospital, Ashbourne Road, Leek, ☎01538 487100; University Hospital of North Staffordshire, Princes Road, Stoke-on-Trent, ☎01782 715444.

Doctors: Health Centre, Fountain St, Leek ST13 6JB, ☎01538 381072; Moorland Medical Centre, Dyson House, Regent St, Leek ST13 6LU, ☎01538 399008; The John Kelso Practice, Park Medical Centre, Ball Haye Road, Leek ST13 6QR, ☎01538 399152; The Stockwell Surgery, Park Medical Centre, Ball Haye Road, Leek ST13 6QP, ☎01538 399398.

Supermarkets: Morrisons, Newcastle Road, Leek, ☎01538 399737; Farmfoods, Smithfield Centre, Leek, ☎01538 398508.

Taxis: JC Private Hire ☎01538 382045; Malkin's Taxis, ☎01538 386797; Taxico, ☎01538 387777 or 386666; Telecars, ☎01538 383383; Pearl's Private Hire, ☎01538 381404; A2B Private Hire, ☎01538 382100.

FURTHER AFIELD

Rudyard Lake Steam Railway

The 10¼ in narrow gauge **Rudyard Lake Steam Railway** just north of Leek takes you on a 3 mile return trip from the village of Rudyard to Hunthouse Wood, along the shores of Rudyard Lake. The 200-year-old reservoir is said to have been the source of the Victorian novelist Rudyard Kipling's name, after his parents had enjoyed a holiday there. All the steam engines sport Arthurian names, such as Excalibur, Merlin and King Arthur.

> RUDYARD LAKE STEAM RAILWAY: Rudyard Station, Rudyard, near Leek, Staffordshire ST13 8PF; ☎01995 672280; www.rlsr.org. Entry: adults £3.50, children £2; open daily 11am–4pm, school holidays and most Saturdays; 11am–4.20pm, Saturdays (Jul and Aug), Sundays and Bank Holidays.

Biddulph Grange Garden

You can travel the world, in a botanical sense at least, at the National Trust's **Biddulph Grange Garden** near Biddulph. The garden's Grand Tour will transport you from Italy, Egypt and China to the Himalayas via a journey of discovery through tunnels and pathways into gardens inspired by countries all over the world. Perhaps most famous is the Chinese Garden, whose design was inspired by the famous willow pattern plate.

> BIDDULPH GRANGE GARDEN: Grange Road, Biddulph, Staffordshire ST8 7SD; ☎01782 517999; www.nationaltrust.org.uk. Entry: adults £6.40, children £3.20; open 11am–5pm, Wed–Sun and Bank Holidays, 15 Mar to 2 Nov; 11am–4pm, weekends, 1 Mar–9 Mar and 8 Nov to 21 Dec.

An Easter train on the Rudyard Lake Steam Railway

Alton Towers

Thrill-seekers looking for that ultimate adrenalin rush will gravitate to the **Alton Towers theme park**, between Ashbourne and Uttoxeter. As Britain's premier theme park, Alton Towers claims to have a roller coaster for everyone. Here you can twist and turn, loop and swoop, speed and soar, all at terrifying speeds on rides with such significantly frightening names as Nemesis, Oblivion, Ripsaw, Submission and The Blade. More gentle, year-round activities at Alton Towers include the Cariba Creek Waterpark, which caters especially for children, the Alton Towers Spa and Extraordinary Golf.

ALTON TOWERS: Alton, Staffordshire Moorlands ST10 4DB; ☎0870 520 4060; www.altontowers.com. Entry: adults £29, children £22, family of four £81, family of five £98; open daily 10am, rides and attractions from 10.30am daily, 28 Mar to 1 Nov.

MACCLESFIELD AND MACCLESFIELD FOREST

It's no coincidence that Macclesfield's inner ring road is known as 'The Silk Road', nor its football team as the 'Silkmen'. During the 18th and 19th centuries, it gradually replaced Derby as the centre for the silk manufacturing trade in Britain, and the story of the growth of the industry is graphically told in the Silk Museum and Paradise Mill in Park Lane, where you can still see Jacquard handloom weaving taking place, and at the Heritage Centre in Roe Street.

Macclesfield is a convenient centre for exploring Macclesfield Forest, originally a medieval hunting forest and now largely submerged under conifers. But at places like the fine viewpoint of the Tegg's Nose Country Park and around the Trentabank and Lamaload Reservoirs, the forest is still a popular place for recreation, particularly walking and riding.

WHAT TO SEE AND DO

Macclesfield

Probably the best place to start a visit to Maccesfield is the **Heritage Centre** in Roe Street, which has displays featuring the town's living history, concentrating on the growth of the silk weaving industry. There are displays of silk costume from the 1830s until the present day, an award-winning audio-visual programme, a museum silk

The Heritage Centre, Macclesfield

THE HERITAGE CENTRE: Roe Street, Macclesfield, Cheshire SK11 6UT; ☎01625 613210; www.macclesfield.silk.museum. Entry: £4.25 adults, £3.75 concessions, children free; open 11am–5pm, Mon-Sat; 12pm–5pm Sun; 11am–4pm, Apr to Oct; 11am–5pm Sat, and 12pm–4pm Sun, Nov to Mar.

shop, and a restaurant. And you can visit the re-created Sunday School, which was built in 1814.

Your next stop should be the **Silk Industry Museum & Paradise Mill** housed in the old Art School in Park Lane. Here you can discover what life was really like working in Paradise Mill in the 1930s through children-friendly features and

SILK INDUSTRY MUSEUM & PARADISE MILL: Park Lane, Macclesfield, Cheshire SK11 6TJ; ☎01625 612045; www.macclesfield. silk.museum. Entry: £4.75 adults, £4.25 concessions, children free; open 11am–5pm, Easter to Oct, Mon–Sat.

Handloom weaving at Paradise Mill

no less than 26 still operational hand looms. There are also regular timed tours through the mill after an introductory video has set the scene.

A more traditional museum is the **West Park Museum**, set in one of Britain's earliest municipal parks in Prestbury Road. This excellent town museum was built and paid for by the entrepreneurs of the silk trade, and many of the exhibits from all

WEST PARK MUSEUM, Prestbury Road, Macclesfield, Cheshire SK10 3BJ; ☎01625 613210; www.macclesfield.silk.museum. Entry: free; open 1.30pm–4.30pm, Tues to Sun; 1pm–4pm, Nov to 31 Mar.

around the world, particularly Egypt, were brought back by silk family heiress Marianne Brocklehurst. The museum also contains, among its many paintings and local history exhibits, many works by the celebrated local bird artist, Charles Tunnicliffe.

CELEBRITY CONNECTIONS

Journalist and broadcaster **Jenni Murray OBE**, perhaps most famous as the regular presenter of BBC Radio 4's *Woman's Hour*, was born in Barnsley and now lives in a stone farmhouse in an idyllic location on the north western fringe of the Peak District. After attending Barnsley Girls High School, she graduated in French and Drama at Hull University, then began her long career with the BBC, initially at Radio Bristol, then on regional news at *South Today* and news analysis programme *Newsnight*, before joining *Woman's Hour* in 1987.

Jenni's love for the Peak District stems back to the days when her father often worked in Manchester. He would drop Jenni and her mother off on the moors and they would go for a walk. Particularly fond of Winnats Pass west of Castleton, which she has loved since her childhood, Jenni describes it as *'one of the most awe-inspiring places I've ever been to'*. She also appreciates the contrast between the limestone and gritstone scenery near Longnor. Jenni praises the Peak District as *'the most beautiful part of the country, because the hills are gentle in some parts and harsh in others'*. She considers herself very privileged to live in the area, and once declared: *'I shan't leave until I'm carried out of the house feet first and sprinkled on my field!'*

Around Macclesfield

For a breath of fresh air and outstanding views take the short trip out from Macclesfield to the **Tegg's Nose Country Park**. The wide-ranging views from the 1,246ft/380m summit of the park extend over the Cheshire Plain towards the white dish of the Jodrell Bank Radio Telescope and the shapely peak of Shutlingsloe, and there are many peasant walks with equally extensive views nearby.

TEGG'S NOSE COUNTRY PARK: Buxton Old Road, Macclesfield, Cheshire SK11 0AP; ☎01625 614279; www.cheshire.gov.uk/countryside. Entry: free; open daily all year.

Nearby is the **Macclesfield Forest Chapel** of St Stephen, which was originally built in 1673 and restored and rebuilt in 1834. This is the scene in August of the annual ancient ceremony of rushbearing, which goes back to the days when the floor covering of churches was provided by freshly cut rushes from the forest. The ceremony now attracts large numbers of worshippers, and the laying down of the rushes is seen as an act of spiritual renewal. This area also includes the highest point in the county of Cheshire at **Shining Tor** (1,834ft/559m), which overlooks the Goyt Valley to the east, and with extensive views south towards the shapely peak of Shutlingsloe (1,659ft/506m); sometimes rather ambitiously dubbed 'the Matterhorn of Cheshire'. Shining Tor is a favourite spot for hang-gliders and parascenders, who can often be seen riding the thermals from its crest like soaring eagles.

The name of the tiny village of **Wildboarclough**, in the shadow of Shutlingsloe, gives a clue to the former inhabitants of Macclesfield Forest. Like nearby Macclesfield, it once was home to several textile mills, some of which made carpets for the Great Exhibition in 1851. All that remains now of that industrial past is the imposing three-storey building which was the administration office of Crag Mill (now private), and which once served as the village post office.

Teggs Nose Country Park

Shining Tor summit, the highest point in Cheshire

The villages of **Bollington**, **Kettleshulme**, **Rainow**, **Pott Shrigley** and **Disley** are today mainly commuter settlements for Macclesfield, Stockport and Manchester, but at **Lyme Park**, on the northernmost tip of the area, you can get a taste of what the former Macclesfield hunting forest really looked like in the extensive deer park.

Lyme Park

Visitors to **Lyme Park** (National Trust), near Disley, may well recognise it as the setting for the television hit drama series from 1995, *Pride and Prejudice*. It served as Pemberley, the home of Mr Darcy in Jane Austen's famous novel, and the lake in front of the house was where Darcy (played by Colin Firth) took his notorious dip when meeting Elizabeth Bennet (Jennifer Ehle) for the first time. Actually, Lyme Park is a kind of blackened, northern Chatsworth, built in the then-fashionable 18th-century Palladian style for the Legh family, in whose hands it remained for 600 years. Like Chatsworth, Lyme is a treasure house of works of art, which include Mortlake tapestries, beautifully furnished rooms, and a nationally important collection of clocks.

Lyme Park was used as Pemberley in the TV dramatisation of *Pride and Prejudice*

Outside there is an attractive **Victorian garden** with sunken parterre, and an Edwardian rose garden with Jekyll-style borders, and an **Orangery** designed by Wyatt. The surrounding deer park is watched over by the turretted **Cage**, an 18th-century hunting tower, from where you may be lucky enough to spot the Peak's largest herd of red deer, which run freely alongside their fallow cousins.

Fishing

Danebridge Fisheries occupies a 2¼ acre spring-fed lake set in the Dane Valley near Winkle. The well-stocked, clear water is under 10 feet deep, and there is a fishing lodge with toilet and other facilities. Fish regularly caught here include rainbow and brown trout, blue and triploid, with an average weight of 2lbs.

LYME PARK: Disley, Stockport SK12 2NX; ☎01663 762023; www.nationaltrust.org.uk. Entry: house and gardens adults £7.70, children £3.80; house, restaurant and shop open 11am–5pm, 1 Mar to 9 Mar; 15 Mar to 2 Nov, except Wed/Thurs; park open 8am–8.30pm, Apr to 12 Oct; 8am–6pm, 13 Oct to 31 Mar.

DANEBRIDGE FISHERIES LTD: Pingle Cottage, Wincle, Maccesfield, Cheshire SK11 0QE; ☎01260 227293; www.go-fish.co.uk.

LOCAL KNOWLEDGE

Television presenter and radio broadcaster **Heather Stott** is a familiar face and voice to viewers and listeners throughout north-west England. As well as forecasting the region's weather every weekday morning on BBC Breakfast and BBC North West Today, she presents a morning show on BBC Radio Manchester. Heather and her family live in Macclesfield.

The best thing about living in the Peak District: Easy access to some of the most beautiful scenery in the country. I keep a horse in Pott Shrigley, and the riding around there is fabulous. Plenty of bridleways, spectacular views and friendly pubs. What more could you ask for?

Best kept secret: Wildboarclough Rose Queen Fete. Cragside Hall hosts it every year, and it's lovely. Wonderful plant stall, ice creams, coconut shy, sheep shearing, children's races and a fell run.

All that, plus delicious home-made cakes on the tea stall. Not even an English summer can take the shine off it.

Favourite haunt/hangout: Macclesfield Forest. You can walk the dog or ride the horse and it's different every time you go. No two days are the same.

Best view: From the top of Macclesfield Forest down over Trentabank Reservoir, or the view of Cheshire from Higher Ridgegate.

Best walk: From Trentabank car park all the way round Macclesfield Forest. There are lots of paths, and you can make your route as long or short as you choose.

Quirkiest attraction: Wincle Fete and Trout Run – every runner who completes the race gets a trout!

How to cope with the Peak's unpredictable weather: The only advice I can give is, if you want to know what the weather is doing – look out of the window!

Wet weather

Lovers of all things mechanical will enjoy the **Anson Engine Museum**, situated rather incongruously in the leafy countryside of Higher Poynton, Cheshire. This unusual and fascinating museum built on the site of the former Anson Colliery is one of the country's leading specialist engine museums. The award-winning museum houses a unique collection of over 200 gas and oil engines, many maintained in running order. The working engines range from early Crossley gas engines – including the first ever and largest running example of Crossley atmospheric gas engine – through to more modern diesels, including Mirrlees No. 1, the oldest diesel engine in the country. The museum also has a comprehensive display of local history items including photographs, maps, mementoes and keepsakes from the Vernon Estate and the former Anson Colliery.

> ANSON ENGINE MUSEUM: Anson Road, Poynton, Cheshire SK12 1TD; ☎01625 874426; www.enginemuseum.org. Entry: adults £4.50, children under 14 £2.50; open Easter to end Oct, Fri/Sat/Sun/Bank Holidays.

What to do with children

An exciting adventure playground will keep the children happy on a visit to **Lyme Park** (see above), and a series of events held throughout the year at the National Trust house are aimed specifically at younger visitors.

The best... **PLACES TO STAY**

HOTEL

Moorside Grange Hotel & Spa

Mudhurst Lane, Higher Disley SK12 2AP
☎ 01663 764151
www.moorsidegrangehotel.com

With a secluded moorland setting Moorside Grange has a relaxed country house feel complemented by modern facilities, including a health, fitness and beauty centre, pool and spa, Wi-Fi internet access, tennis and nine-hole golf. Accommodation includes suites and bedrooms with four poster beds.

Price: B&B around £90 for a double.

INN

The Stanley Arms

Bottom of the Oven, Macclesfield Forest, Near Wildboarclough SK11 0AR
☎ 01260 252414; www.stanleyarms.com

Seven luxurious en-suite double bedrooms with modern facilities in a sympathetically converted barn next to the Stanley Arms public house. Beautifully presented accommodation with antique furniture. Relaxed atmosphere, cask-conditioned real ales, good food and fine wines.

Price: B&B from £65 to £95 per room.

FARMSTAY

Harrop Fold Farm and Michael Moore Art School

Rainow, Macclesfield SK10 5UU
☎ 01625 828814
www.harropfoldfarm.co.uk

Award-winning B&B and self-catering accommodation on a 17th-century smallholding in an idyllic location.

Charming bedrooms with great character, antique beds and oak beams. 'A Taste of Cheshire' British Regional Food Weekends and residential and day art courses available.

Price: B&B from £40 pppn.

B&B

Common Farm B&B

Smith Lane, Rainow, Macclesfield SK10 5XJ; ☎ 01625 574878
www.cottages-with-a-view.co.uk

Both B&B and self-catering accommodation on a working hill farm with stunning views over the Cheshire Plain. Well-equipped accommodation, substantial farmhouse breakfasts.

Price: B&B from £30 pppn.

The Grey Cottage

20 Jackson's Edge Road, Disley SK12 2JE; ☎ 01663 763286

Grade II listed house dating from the late 17th century, beautifully appointed with antique furnishings. Lyme Park is on the doorstep.

Price: B&B from £32 pppn.

SELF-CATERING

Higher Ingersley Barn

Oakenbank Lane, Bollington, Macclesfield SK10 5RP
☎ 01625 572245
www.higheringsleybarn.co.uk

Quality self-catering accommodation for six in a tastefully converted and furnished 17th-century barn with oak beams, private gardens with paved patio, outdoor seating and ample parking.

Price: From £440 to £770 for a week.

The best... FOOD AND DRINK

Hill farms abound in this area, where there's a good choice of locally raised, organic, lamb, beef and pork and locally made ice cream in a range of tempting flavours. Eat out in everything from an elegant country house setting to an outdoor kiosk in Macclesfield Forest, or enjoy excellent pub food and real ales in out-of-the-way pubs.

▶ Staying in

Organically reared lamb, beef and pork from animals raised on clover-rich meadows to give excellent taste and quality is on the menu at **Organic on the Hill** at Wincle (Butterlands Farm SK11 0QL; ☎01260 227672). All cuts are available, including the farm's own recipe sausages and burgers. You'll find Organic on the Hill at **Macclesfield Market** every Friday and at various Farmers' Markets in the area. Half or whole lambs are also available from **Lamaload Lamb** at Rainow (Common Barn Farm, Smith Lane SK10 5XJ; ☎01625 574878). Ring ahead to collect from the farm gate or to arrange local delivery. Prime beef, lamb and pork raised on clover-rich pasture is also produced at Soil Association-registered **Cloverbank Organic Farm** at North Rode, Macclesfield (CW12 2NX; ☎01260 222907 or ☎07969 094079). The farm also hosts a Farmers' Market on the third Saturday of the month from 8.30am to 12.30pm, selling everything from chutneys and pickles to home-made puddings and pies.

For organic foods, gluten-free products, diabetic and health foods, visit **Fit as a Fiddle** in Macclesfield (108 Mill Street SK11 6NR; ☎01625 612553). If you fancy a slightly more indulgent treat, visit **Blaze Farm/Hilly Billy Ice Cream** (Wildboarclough, near Macclesfield SK11 0BL; ☎01260 227229), where you'll be able to sample creamy ice cream in all imaginable flavours, made from the farm's own milk. Choose from Double Dutch Chocolate, Ginger, Irish Cream, Pistachio and Almond, Turkish Delight and White Chocolate Mountain, to name but a few. You'll also find a friendly tea room, farm trail and paint-a-pot studio.

Macclesfield Country Market is held on the first Friday of every month (except January) at the Senior Citizens Hall, Duke Street (SK11 6UR; ☎01625 573483).

EATING OUT

FINE DINING

Shrigley Hall Hotel
Shrigley Park, Pott Shrigley, Near Macclesfield SK10 5SB
☎ **01625 575757**
www.barcelo-hotels.co.uk

Fine cuisine in a stylish, elegant setting serving award-winning food in a beautifully situated, 19th-century country house on a 262-acre estate with quality accommodation, 18-hole golf course and spa facilities. Evening meals served in the Oakridge Restaurant, which boasts scenic views. Table d'hôte menu: £29.50 per person.

RESTAURANT

Briscola Restaurant
88 Palmerston Street, Bollington SK10 5PW
☎ **01625 573898**

Smart Italian-style restaurant with relaxed atmosphere, welcoming everyone from families with children to couples and groups of friends. Pasta, pizza, à la carte choices and specials available, including children's menu. Mains cost from around £10.90.

Beasdales
22 Old Market Place, High Street, Bollington, Cheshire SK10 5PH
☎ **01625 575058**

Bistro-style dining in a cosy, intimate setting with friendly service in the heart of Bollington's conservation area. Menus are constantly evolving, but sample dishes could include starters such as grilled smoked haddock on crispy bacon mash or asparagus spears in smoked

salmon and mains featuring local lamb and beef. Mains from around £14.50.

Lajawaab Indian Restaurant
14 Jordangate, Macclesfield SK10 1EW
☎ **01625 618636**

Warm welcome, friendly and helpful service in this quality Indian restaurant with stylish modern décor and comfortable leather seats. Extensive, competitively priced menu includes mixed starters and a variety of curry options such as rogan josh, dopiaza and jalfrezi, as well as rice dishes, naan breads, poppadums and other side orders. Mains cost from £6 to £8.

GASTRO PUB

Sutton Hall
Bullocks Lane, Sutton, Macclesfield SK11 0HE
☎ **01260 252538**
www.brunningandprice.co.uk/suttonhall

No less than seven different dining areas can be found in this 480-year-old manor house, once family home to the Earls of Lucan (including the notorious sixth Earl, who disappeared after the murder of his nanny) and a former convent. The menu ranges from sandwiches and side orders to sumptuous mains, starting at £8.50.

Leathers Smithy
Clarke Lane, Langley SK11 0NE
☎ **01260 252313**
www.leatherssmithy.co.uk

This pub derives its name from 19th-century licensee William Leather and its former role as the village forge. With a scenic location with views of Ridgegate

EATING OUT

Reservoir, Macclesfield Forest and a country park, it serves imaginative main courses based on meat, fish and vegetarian options as well as sandwiches, baguettes and salads. Main courses average £8.

The Swan Inn
**Macclesfield Road,
Kettleshulme SK23 7QU
☎ 01663 732943**

Quality food from an interesting menu that changes frequently at this 15th-century whitewashed pub with wooden beams, stone fireplaces and a real fire within the Peak District National Park. Pork and beef sourced from Kettleshulme, lamb from Glossop. Guest beers served, walkers and families welcome. Outdoor patio seating. Mains cost from £10 to £18.

The Church House Inn
**Church Street, Bollington SK10 5PY
☎ 01625 574014**

Stone-built free house with cosy atmosphere created by beams, log fires and rustic decorations. Wide-ranging menu includes starters such as Bury black pudding and black tiger prawns, mains based on meat, game, offal and fish and vegetarian options such as wild mushroom and four cheese farfalle or stir-fry. Mains cost from £8.75.

The Ship Inn
**Barlow Hill, Wincle, Cheshire SK11 0QE
☎ 01260 227217**

Quintessential, unspoilt country pub with regularly updated menu based on fresh, local produce where possible, complemented by real ales, Belgian beers and fine wines. Pre-booking recommended in the restaurant, where a sample menu might include Aberdeen Angus steak or Gloucester Old Spot pork. Walkers and dogs welcome in the tap room. Mains cost from £11.95.

CAFÉ

The Coffee Tavern
**Shrigley Road, Pott Shrigley SK10 5SE
☎ 01625 576370**

Locally sourced food cooked on the premises in a former reading room and library. Options range from home-made cakes and scones to three-course meals, and among the popular mains are lasagne and steak and kidney pie. Popular with walkers and cyclists as well as local people. Closed Tuesday. Local crafts upstairs.

TEA ROOM

Peak View Tea Rooms
**Buxton Road,
Macclesfield Forest SK11 0AR
☎ 01298 22103
www.peakviewtearooms.co.uk**

Home-made food in a licensed tea room near the famous Cat and Fiddle pub on the A537 between Buxton and Macclesfield, with unrivalled views over the Dark Peak and Cheshire Plain. Options include sandwiches, jacket potatoes, all day breakfasts, cakes and puddings, plus soups, roast dinners, fish dishes and vegetarian specials. Open Thursday to Sunday.

🍺 Drinking

Timber beams, stone fireplaces and a real fire create a traditional ambience at **The Swan** in Kettleshulme (Macclesfield Road SK23 7QU; ☎01663 732943), where you'll find constantly changing guest beers and good food, plus a small beer festival every September. Surrounded by the excellent walking country of the Peak District National Park, families and walkers are welcome and there are two outdoor patio areas where you can sit in fine weather.

In the pretty village of Bollington, visitors really are spoilt for choice. Real ales, including guest beers, and a range of food are available at the low-ceilinged, stone-flagged **Cock and Pheasant** (Bollington Road, Bollington Cross SK10 5EJ; ☎01625 573289). Other facilities include a conservatory, patio and children's play area. **The Poachers Inn** (Ingersley Road SK10 5RF; ☎01625 572086) is a family-run free house with a welcoming feel, serving guest beers and home-cooked food. Warm yourself in the sunny garden in summer and by the coal fire in winter. Plenty of choice when it comes to real ales is on offer at the award-winning **Vale Inn** (Adlington Road SK10 5JT; ☎01625 575147), which also serves home-made food and has a garden that overlooks a cricket ground. Regular beer festivals and live music are also staged.

At Rainow, the 17th-century **Highwayman** (Macclesfield Road SK10 5UU; ☎01625 573245) enjoys sweeping views of the surrounding countryside and offers a selection of real ales and award-winning food, described as 'traditional English with a French twist'. Another traditional country pub with fine ales and home-cooked food is **The Rising Sun** (Hawkins Lane, Rainow SK10 5TL; ☎01625 424235). Idyllically situated, overlooking the Ridgegate Reservoir, Macclesfield Forest and a country park, the **Leathers Smithy** (Clarke Lane, Langley SK11 0NE; ☎01260 252313) serves a range of cask ales and imaginative food ranging from sandwiches to full meals. Also at Langley is the community-minded **St Dunstan Inn** (Main Road SK11 0BU; ☎07801 818868), thought to be the only pub bearing this unusual name in the UK. It's a traditional terraced inn, where regulars get to choose the guest beers.

When it comes to magnificent views, it's hard to beat the unrivalled vantage point of the **Cat and Fiddle Inn** (SK11 0AR; ☎01298 23364) on the A537 Buxton to Macclesfield road. England's second highest pub, it is popular with both passing motorcyclists and walkers. Another popular haunt for walkers bent on ascending the nearby conical peak of Shutlingsloe, known as 'The Matterhorn of Cheshire', is the cosy **Crag Inn** at Wildboarclough (SK11 0BD; ☎01260 227239), which boasts open fires, a selection of real ales and traditional food, including a popular Sunday carvery.

In Sutton, near Macclesfield, half-timbered, historic **Sutton Hall** (Bullocks Lane SK11 0HE; ☎01260 253211) has a constantly changing line-up of ales from small breweries around the country, as well as a mouth-watering menu. **The Hanging Gate Inn** (SK11 0LY; ☎01260 525238), has regular real ales, a seasonal craft range and other cask ales, plus everything from bar meals to an à la carte menu, as well as stunning views as far as Snowdonia and Liverpool Cathedral (on a clear day!) from the restaurant and beer garden. For a good choice of ales and home-prepared food, try **The Lamb Inn** (Hollin Lane SK11 0HL; ☎01260 252000). Real ales, home-made food and accommodation are also available at **The Ryles Arms** (Hollin Lane SK11 0NN; ☎01260 252244). Real ales, a choice of Belgian beers and fine wines are served at the **Ship Inn**, Wincle (Barlow Hill SK11 0QE; ☎01260 227217), a quintessential, unspoilt country pub which is also justly famed for its food.

ⓘ Visitor Information

Tourist information centre: Macclesfield Tourist Information Centre, Town Hall, Macclesfield SK10 1DX, ☎01625 504114, www.macclesfield.gov.uk, open daily.

Hospitals: Macclesfield District General Hospital, Victoria Road, Macclesfield, ☎01625 421000; Stepping Hill Hospital, Poplar Grove, Stockport, ☎0161 483 1010.

Doctors: Dr LKR Smith, Dr AK Moar & Dr GD Plant, 250 Park Lane, Macclesfield SK11 8AD, ☎01625 612999; Park

Green House Surgery, Sunderland Street, Macclesfield SK11 6HW, ☎01625 429555; Dr IME Kramer, 2 High Street, Macclesfield SK11 6UD, ☎01625 423692; Dr WPD Ford-Young, 50 Fallibroome Road, Macclesfield SK10 3LA, ☎01625 617300.

Supermarkets: Tesco, Hibel Road, Macclesfield, ☎0845 677 9455; Tesco, Exchange Street, Macclesfield, ☎0845 677 9449; Somerfield, Thornton Square, Macclesfield, ☎01625 421568; Sainsbury's, Cumberland Street, Macclesfield, ☎01625 503592.

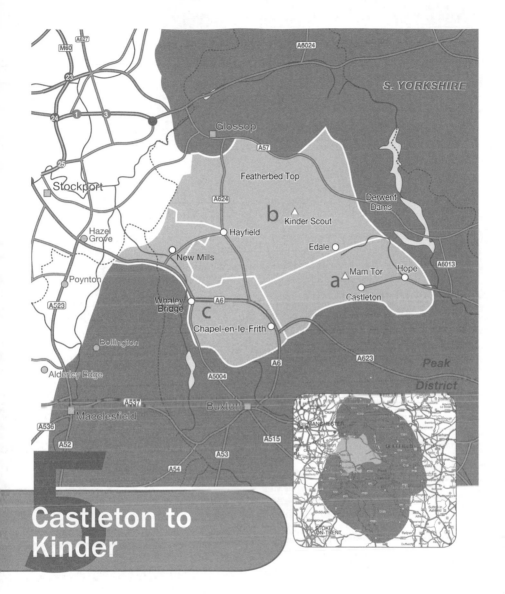

Castleton to Kinder

a. Castleton and the Hope Valley

b. Kinder Scout and Edale

c. The Sett Valley and New Mills

Unmissable highlights

01 Unravel the mysteries of the Devil's Arse, **the** alternative and original name for gaping Peak Cavern, Castleton, p. 250

02 Take an underground boat journey **like the** former lead miners in Speedwell Cavern, Castleton, p. 251

03 Enter the underground wonderland **of the** beautifully illuminated Treak Cliff Cavern, Castleton, p. 250

04 Delight in the beauties of Blue John, **the unique** semi-precious stone found in the Blue John Cavern, Castleton, p. 251

05 Become the king of the castle **at feudal Peveril** Castle, overlooking Castleton, p. 248

06 Be the master of all you survey **from the** commanding viewpoint of Mam Tor, above Castleton, p. 252

07 Climb the tortuous gradient **of the Winnats** Pass, west of Castleton, p. 251

08 See where the Pennine Way **mountain marathon** starts, at Edale, p. 259

09 Retrace the steps of the Mass Trespassers, at Bowden Bridge and William Clough, above Hayfield, p. 247

10 Wander along the dizzying Millennium Walkway, above the River Sett in the Tors, New Mills, p. 267

CASTLETON TO KINDER

Arthur Conan Doyle, creator of the world's most renowned detective, Sherlock Holmes, once described the countryside around Castleton: *'All this country is hollow. Could you strike it with some gigantic hammer, it would boom like a drum or possibly cave in altogether'*.

This is the Peak's caving capital, and while the 'wild' caves of the locality are the province of experienced cavers only, Castleton's four famous show caverns attract thousands of ordinary visitors wanting to enjoy the Peak's spectacular underground riches in comfort and safety. The show caves are all quite different, from the spectacular and brilliantly lit formations of Treak Cliff, to the unique experience of an underground canal trip at Speedwell and the awesome gaping void of Peak Cavern, thought to be the largest cave entrance in Britain and once the site of a subterranean village of rope-makers. Towering above the popular honeypot village are the imposing keep and walls of Peveril Castle, which gave the village its name and was constructed in the 11th century by William Peveril, the illegitimate son of William the Conqueror. The view from the castle is breathtaking in more ways than one, but well worth the steep climb up the winding path to reach it.

If you enter Castleton from the west, you will descend the spectacular, crag-rimmed Winnats Pass, whose name means 'wind gates' from the frequent gales which blast down its narrow defile. Also to the west of Castleton is the so-called 'Shivering Mountain' of Mam Tor, which overlooks the whole length of the beautiful Hope Valley to the east, and the village of Edale and the brooding southern slopes of Kinder Scout, the highest mountain in the Peak District at 2,088ft/636m, to the north.

Kinder Scout is an iconic hill for many reasons, not least of which is that it is the southern starting point of the country's greatest mountain marathon, Tom Stephenson's epic 270-mile Pennine Way, which winds up the backbone of England to the Scottish border at Kirk Yetholm. But Kinder Scout also holds a special place in the long fight for national parks and the right to roam across all Britain's mountains and moorlands. The pretty village of Hayfield lies in the western lee of Kinder, and was the starting place on 24 April 1932, for the legendary Mass Trespass across Kinder, which led to the eventual imprisonment of five ramblers who were arrested simply for walking on the mountain. Their brave action eventually led to the creation of the first national park here in the Peak in 1951, and eventually to the Countryside and Rights of Way (CROW) Act of 2000.

CASTLETON AND THE HOPE VALLEY

The undoubted attractions of **Castleton** make it one of the most popular tourist destinations in the National Park, so it is probably a place to be avoided on bank holidays or busy summer weekends. But it nevertheless repays several visits, because there are so many things to see and do in this bustling village, which spreads out at the foot of the crag on which stands **Peveril Castle**, one of the earliest stone-built castles in the country, and which gave the village its name. The **show caves** are the obvious attraction, and nowhere else in the Peak shows the subtly powerful forces of water on limestone than around Castleton. In addition to the showcaves, the area is popular with sporting cavers and Titan, the largest cavern yet found in our British hills, was recently discovered under the surface of pastures above Castleton by a team of local cavers.

The view from **Mam Tor**, one of the largest and highest Iron Age hillforts in the Pennines, takes in the length of the sylvan Hope Valley from its summit. It is interesting that the broad and beautiful valley takes its name from the ancient market centre of Hope, and not from the apparently more important settlement of Castleton at the western end of the valley. **Hope** is a historic village, and the parish church of St Peter, mentioned in *Domesday*, preserves an ancient Saxon preaching cross and two other foliated cross slabs which are thought to show the arms of a forester from the medieval Royal Forest of the Peak. A weekly livestock market still used to be held here until recently. Nearby **Bradwell**, under the bulk of **Win Hill**, is famous for its delicious ice cream and a high-precision engineering works which is hidden away behind its main street.

Close by at **Brough** are the remains and earthworks of the 1st-century Roman fort of *Navio*, which when excavated revealed a stone cist which may have been used to hold valuables. It is thought that the small fort was used by the Romans to defend their lead mining interests in the area.

WHAT TO SEE AND DO

Peveril Castle

There are many pleasant walks around Castleton itself, including the steep, stepped ascent from the Market Place to the ruins of **Peveril Castle**. This early stone keep was built by William Peveril, the bastard son of William the Conqueror, in the 11th century to administer the

PEVERIL CASTLE: Castleton, Hope Valley, Derbyshire S33 8WQ; ☎01433 620613; www.english-heritage.org.uk/eastmidlands. Entry: adults £3.70, concessions £3, children £1.90; open daily 10am–5pm, 21 Mar–30 Apr; 10am–6pm, May–end Aug; 10am–5pm, Sep–Oct; 10am–4pm Thurs to Mon, Nov–Mar. Closed for Christmas.

Peveril Castle

former Royal Forest of the Peak, and today as then, it commands extensive views up to Mam Tor and down the Hope Valley to Lose Hill and Win Hill. It was originally approached by a bridge across the Peak Cavern gorge.

Castleton's Caves

The show caves are the main attraction in Castleton, and as they are all quite airy and very well illuminated, sufferers from claustrophobia need not worry too much. The story of **Peak Cavern** (also known as the Devil's Arse) is particularly interesting because its huge, yawning entrance was the site of 'the village which never saw the sun'. A community of rope-makers lived in ramshackle cottages inside the vast entrance – said to be the largest natural cave entrance in Britain – and rope-making demonstrations are still occasionally held there.

Once inside the cave, you have to stoop to pass through the appropriately named Lumbago Walk before you enter to hear the amazing acoustics of the Orchestral Gallery (concerts are still sometimes held here), and the perpetual cascading water of Roger Rain's House.

PEAK CAVERN, Castleton, Hope Valley S33 8WS; ☎01433 620285; www.devilsarse.com. Entry: adults £7.25, concessions £6.25, children £5.25; open daily 10am–5pm, Apr–Oct; 10am–5pm weekends and school holidays and Mon to Fri outside school holidays.

Roger Rain's House in Peak Cavern

The entrance to Odin Mine, Castleton

The Devil's Arse

The awesome void of Peak Cavern – at 60ft/18m high and 100ft/30m wide, the largest cave entrance in Britain – was one of the original 'Wonders of the Peak', described by Charles Cotton in 1681 as the 'Inteftinum Rectum of the Fiend'. The place had been known locally as the Devil's or Peak's Arse since time immemorial, and in times of flood, the River Styx, which flows through the cavern (and Hades) and becomes Peakshole Water when it gushes out from the entrance, was said to be the Devil relieving himself. Victorian sensibilities saw the name changed to the much safer-sounding Peak Cavern, perhaps after Queen Victoria herself had visited the cavern during the early years of her reign. The controversial decision to change the name back to its original was taken by the owner, John Harrison, in the 1990s as a marketing ploy. It certainly attracts attention, and will surely amuse the children!

Treak Cliff Cavern, on the old, land-slipped and now disused road which led west out of the village, probably has the finest formations of stalactites and stalagmites, flowstones and illuminated pools. These include the stunningly beautiful Witch's, Aladdin's and Dream Caves, which includes the famous Stork formation, looking like the bird standing on one leg. The whole cave is a Site of Special Scientific Interest (SSSI), because of the beautiful deposits of Blue John which are

TREAK CLIFF CAVERN: Castleton, Hope Valley S33 8WP; ☎01433 620571; www.visitcaves.com. Entry: adults £7, concessions £6, children £3.60; open daily 10am–4.30pm, Mar to Oct; 10am–3.30pm, Nov to Feb.

found here. When you reach the surface again, you can actually polish your own piece of this semi-precious stone to take home with you, or buy a piece of jewellery from the shop.

The **Blue John Cavern**, at the very foot of the shifting, landslipped east face of the 'Shivering Mountain' of Mam Tor, has more visible veins of the semi-precious fluorspar, which is uniquely found in the Treak Cliff hill. There are no less than 14 recognisable varieties of Blue John fluorspar, all with subtly different colouration. Inside the Blue John Cavern, you will see examples of the some of the equipment of old lead miners, who first opened up these caves, before you descend on the guided tour which takes you into the Waterfall and Great Crystallised Caverns before you enter Lord Mulgrave's Dining Room, where his lordship is once believed to have entertained the miners.

Many peoples' favourite cavern, however, is the **Speedwell Cavern** at the foot of the spectacular Winnats Pass, which now once again carries the main road to the west towards Chapel-en-le-Frith. After a long descent down 105 steps, you reach the landing stage of an underground canal, where boats take you on an incredible journey by water into the heart of the hills. After passing the Halfway House, where the canal splits to allow on-coming boats to pass, you eventually reach the magnificent, cathedral-like cavern of the so-called Bottomless Pit, with its subterranean lake.

Treak Cliff Cavern

BLUE JOHN CAVERN: Castleton, Hope Valley S33 8WP; ☎01433 620638; www.bluejohn-cavern.co.uk. Entry; adults £8, concessions £6,children £4; open daily 9.30am–5.30pm, summer; 9.30am-dusk daily, winter.

Blue John Cavern

SPEEDWELL CAVERN: Winnats Pass, Castleton, Hope Valley S33 8WA; ☎01433 620512; www.speedwellcavern.co.uk. Entry: adults £7.75, concessions £6.75, children £5.75; open daily 10am–5pm, Apr to Oct; 10am–5pm daily, Nov to Mar.

The land slipped road below Mam Tor

Walks around Castleton

One of the most interesting walks from Castleton is the dramatic dry valley of the significantly named **Cave Dale**, which is entered by a very narrow fissure leading off from near the Market Square. It opens up into a steep-sided valley, with the usually unseen south face of the keep of Peveril Castle teetering on its brink.

The short walk up from the Mam Nick car park to the summit of **Mam Tor**, just outside Castleton, one of the largest and highest Iron Age hillforts in the Pennines, will reward you with one of the finest views in the Peak. The view at the top extends down the Hope Valley to the east, with the pimple-like summit of Win Hill prominent to the left. The now-paved ridgeway path to Lose Hill via Hollins Cross and Back Tor beckons nearer at hand, while across the verdant Edale Valley stands the brooding peak of Kinder Scout. Just across the road from the Mam Nick car park, an easy path leads to the fenced-off entrance to **Windy Knoll Cave**, where rhinoceros, bear and wolf bones dating from the end of the last Ice Age were found in the 19th century.

There are also a number of easy, riverside walks in the Hope Valley, although the more ambitious and experienced might like to attempt the ascent of **Win Hill** (1,516ft/ 462m) from Hope. This is another fine viewpoint, looking north across the twin arms of the Ladybower Reservoir and up to the heights of Derwent Edge, Kinder Scout and Bleaklow.

Useful maps of the local area can be picked up at **Castleton Visitor Centre** (Buxton Road S33 8WN; ☎01629 816558; www.peakdistrict.gov.uk) and plenty of walking routes are offered in its leaflet, *Walks around Castleton*.

Local legends – The story of Allan and Clara

In April, 1758, a well-to-do couple called at the Royal Oak Inn in Stoney Middleton to feed their horses. Their names were Allan and Clara, and as they waited for their horses, their hostess eavesdropped on their conservation. It seemed that they had eloped against Clara's father's wishes, to get married in the parish church of King Charles, King and Martyr at Peak Forest, which at the time was a kind of Derbyshire Gretna Green. By some quirk of ecclesiastical law, the incumbent of Peak Forest church did not demand banns to be read in advance and could grant marriage licences.

Clara and Allan set out for Castleton, where they stopped at one of the inns for breakfast, before setting out on the final stage of their fateful journey, up through the Winnats Pass and then to Peak Forest. In an adjacent room, a group of four uncouth lead miners already the worse for wear for drink, overheard their plans. The couple left the inn and headed towards the gloomy portals of the Winnats. Just as they entered the pass, the miners armed leapt out on them. After robbing them of £200 in money and valuables near the site of the present entrance to Speedwell Cavern, the miners clubbed them to death with pick axes and buried them nearby. The young couple were soon missed, and their horses were found, saddled and bridled, in the King's Forest near the Winnats. But it was to be many years later before two bodies thought to be Allan and Clara were found and were buried in St Edmund's churchyard at Castleton. The identity of their murderers remained a mystery until a series of strange, apparently accidental, events pointed the finger at the men who were responsible.

One of the miners bought horses with his share of the booty, but they all died in rapid succession, and he frequently said: 'I always have a beautiful lady with me – she rides on my horse'. The daughter of another of the miners was seen at church wearing a very rich silk dress, and people began to put two and two together. Some years after the horrendous deed, one of the guilty men fell from a precipice in the Winnats and was killed instantly. Another was mysteriously killed by a falling stone in the same place, and a third lost his reason and died in a miserable state having tried to commit suicide on several occasions. A fourth man was more successful in his death wish, and hanged himself. Finally, the horse-owning miner, after lying on his death bed for 10 weeks, eventually owned up to the crime, and admitted that it was he and his four friends who had robbed and murdered Allan and Clara. He added: 'she was the handsomest woman I ever saw', just before he died. In the words of an early 20th-century writer: 'though the hand of human justice did not reach these guilty beings, yet the hand of God found them out, even on earth'.

🌂 Wet weather

The **Museum of the Castleton Historical Society**, formerly in the village chapel, has been incorporated into the **Castleton Visitor Centre**, and features a range of exhibitions about village life through the ages. And the **parish church of St Edmund** in Castleton is an interesting place to visit on a wet day. Although extensively restored in Victorian times, in retains its 17th-century box pews and a dog-toothed chancel arch which echoes the decoration of the entrance doorway to Peveril Castle on the hill above, and may suggest they shared the same architect.

Hope's **Parish Church of St Peter** has a squat, broached spire dating from the 14th century, but one of its finest possessions is the stump of a richly decorated Saxon preaching cross in the churchyard near the south door. Inside the church, two foliated 13th-century cross slabs are carved with the arms of foresters – another reminder of the Royal Forest of the Peak, and the days when Hope was important enough to give its name to the whole of the valley.

What to do with children

Children will love finding the small Iron Age-themed icons to be found along the path up from the Mam Nick car park to the summit of **Mam Tor**. These range from a torc (metal collar) to a sword, and an Iron Age hut to a grinning face. Two downloadable **audio trails** have been developed by the National Trust and Peak Experience to help visitors explore this iconic tor. Each of the two tours has been developed with different audiences in mind, one for adults and one for children, but both help visitors to understand more about the unique history of Mam Tor.

The audio trail takes visitors on a journey from the Mam Nick car park through a series of stops as they climb the mountain. Both tours can be downloaded from the National Trust website (www.nationaltrust.org.uk/mamtoraudio) directly onto your MP3 player. They are also available from the Peak Experience website (www.peak-experience.org.uk), and the Castleton Visitor Centre.

 The best... **PLACES TO STAY**

HOTEL

Losehill House Hotel & Spa

Edale Road, Hope, Hope Valley S33 6RF
☎ **01433 621219**
www.losehillhouse.co.uk

Secluded hotel on the slopes of Lose Hill, with attractively appointed, contemporary en-suite bedrooms and suites. Spa facilities include an indoor heated pool, sauna, treatment rooms and outdoor hot tub.

Price: B&B from £135 for a double.

FARMSTAY

Dunscar Farm

Castleton, Hope Valley S33 8WA
☎ **01433 620483**
www.dunscarfarm.co.uk

Delightful 18th-century farmhouse on a working farm at the foot of Mam Tor. Prettily decorated bedrooms are en-suite or have private facilities and enjoy views across the Hope Valley. Traditional cooked breakfasts prepared on the farmhouse Aga.

Price: B&B £30 to £33 pppn.

The best... **PLACES TO STAY**

B&B

Underleigh House

Off Edale Road, Hope, Hope Valley S33 6RF; ☎ 01433 621372 www.underleighhouse.co.uk

Former 19th-century cottage and barn with tastefully converted accommodation, including a large and comfortable guest lounge. Full, vegetarian and smaller breakfasts are served in the charming beamed and stone-flagged dining room. Attractive garden and views.

Price: B&B from £40 pppn.

Bargate Cottage

Market Place, Castleton, Hope Valley S33 8WQ ☎ 01433 620201 www.bargatecottage.co.uk

Pretty 17th-century cottage in quiet, central location below Peveril Castle, overlooking Castleton's pretty village green. Comfortable en-suite bedrooms with modern facilities. Hearty breakfast served in a traditional dining room with oak beams and Derbyshire gritstone fireplace.

Price: B&B £30 pppn.

SELF-CATERING

Mullions

Pindale Road, Castleton, Hope Valley S33 8WU ☎ 01433 620257 www.peak-district-cottages.co.uk

Award-winning historic country property built in 1620, sleeping up to six people, with period features, oak beams, leaded windows, log fire and excellent views over Win Hill and Lose Hill. Stone-flagged floors and a Derbyshire gritstone fireplace add to its old world charm.

Price: £580 to £1,250 for a week.

Rushop Hall

Rushup Lane, Rushup, Near Castleton, Hope Valley SK23 0QT ☎ 01298 813323 www.rushophall.com

Individually designed self-catering holiday cottages renovated to a high standard, all with modern facilities, on a working farm with a variety of livestock, including alpacas and Highland cattle. Stabling for up to seven horses for visitors riding along the nearby Pennine Bridleway.

Price: £225 to £675 for a week.

The best... FOOD AND DRINK

Whether you have a sweet or savoury tooth, you'll discover plenty to whet your appetite here, from cold meats and olives and home-reared meat to award-winning ice cream. Opt for anything from fine dining to a 'special' on the menu at a local café, and look out for ghosts in some of the local hostelries as you sample everything from real ales to malt whiskies.

▶ Staying in

Traditionally baked bread, cakes and sandwiches made to order can be bought at **The Hope Chest** in Hope (S33 6RD; ☎01433 620072 or ☎07875 465219). You can also choose from up to 50 varieties of cheese, an array of cold meats and other speciality foods from the deli counter and olive bar. Free local delivery is available for self-catering accommodation, cottages, B&Bs and campsites. Home-reared Losehill lamb and beef and home-made speciality sausages and burgers are available at the family-run **Watson's Farm Shop** in Hope (Edale Road S33 6ZF; ☎01433 620223). The beef, mainly Aberdeen Angus or Hereford, is hung for at least three weeks to ensure the best possible flavour.

For more than a century, **Bradwell Ice Cream** has been made at Wortley Court, Bradwell (S33 9LB; ☎01433 620536) and has kept sweet-toothed customers satisfied with a tastebud tingling selection of flavours. Now on sale at local outlets, shops and supermarkets far and wide, the range now includes a Platinum Collection featuring such delights as chocaccino, cherry Bakewell, pannacotta with caramel and velvety vanilla. And at **Cocoadance** (S33 8WA; ☎01433 621334 www.cocoadance.com), based at idyllic Mam Farm, leased from the National Trust, quality chocolate and confectionery are created by award-winning Castleton-based chocolatiers David Golubows and Bridget Joyce. Not only can you buy their delicious products in many local shops, at farmer's markets and on the internet, you can also learn how to make chocolate yourself thanks to their regular Chocolate Experience workshops, held in a converted farm building.

EATING OUT

FINE DINING

Losehill House Hotel
Edale Road, Hope S33 6RF
☎ **01433 621219**
www.losehillhousehotel.co.uk

Light, healthy lunches, afternoon teas
and dinner based on locally sourced
produce are on offer in this chic
restaurant with superb views. Vegetarian
and other dietary requirements catered
for. Groups of up to 12 can enjoy the
private dining room with Arts and Crafts
fireplace and bay window. Table d'hôte
dinner costs £30 per person.

RESTAURANT

The Castle
Castle Street, Castleton S33 8WG
☎ **01433 620578**
**www.vintageinn.co.uk/
thecastlecastleton**

Reputed to be haunted by four spirits,
including a jilted bride, The Castle offers
roaring log fires, freshly prepared food,
real ales and diverse wines. Meals
served all day, including lunch, dinner
and Sunday lunch. Popular dishes
include braised lamb shank, five spiced
duck and ham hock. Lunch mains cost
from £5.95, dinner mains from £6.95.
Accommodation also available.

Gastro pub
The Bulls Head Inn
Cross Street, Castleton S33 8WH
☎ **01433 620256**
www.bullsheadcastleton.co.uk

Refurbished, family-run inn offering
a warm welcome in comfortable
surroundings, with leather sofas and
open log fires. Locally sourced food
catering for most tastes, both traditional
and more adventurous options, changing
regularly to reflect the availability of
seasonal produce. Sunday roasts and
special themed evenings, draught and
cask ales. B&B from £60 per room per
night.

The George Inn
Castle Street, Castleton S33 8WG
☎ **01433 620238**
www.georgehotelcastleton.co.uk

Quality, locally sourced food and fine
ales served in a relaxed, traditional
atmosphere. Sample starters include
peppercorn mushrooms, mussels and
Thai fishcakes, while among the mains
are honey roasted ham shank, lamb
shank, sausage and mash, steak and
kidney pudding and fish and chips.
En-suite accommodation also available.

CAFÉ

The Three Roofs Café
The Island, Castleton S33 8WN
☎ **01433 620533**

Quality food based on local produce,
including breakfast, lunch, teas and
early evening meals. Home-made pies,
locally made sausages with bubble and
squeak and vegetarian dishes such as
wild mushroom and cashew nut pasta
bake are on the menu. Home-made
cakes, desserts and clotted cream teas
also served.

⬛ Drinking

Cask ales and cosy open fires assure a warm welcome at **The Castle** in Castleton (Castle Street S33 8WG; ☎01433 620578), though you may also feel a slight shiver down your spine, as it is reputed to be haunted by no less than four ghosts! Stone-built and situated below historic Peveril Castle, **The Peaks Inn** (How Lane S33 8WJ; ☎01433 620247) has roaring log fires and a comfortable bar for walkers, plus real and guest ales and a traditional menu. A good range of ales and food can also be found at **Ye Olde Nag's Head** (Cross Street S33 8WH; ☎01433 620248), a traditional, family run former coaching inn, again with a real fire. Traditional hospitality in a convivial setting, plus real ales and a selection of malt whiskies are available at **The George** (Castle Street S33 8WG; ☎01433 620238), which has an outdoor seating area overlooking Peveril Castle and Mam Tor, while fine wines and draught and cask ales are also on offer at the **Bulls Head Inn** (Cross Street S33 8WH; ☎01433 620256).

Further down the Hope Valley at Hope, the 16th-century **Cheshire Cheese Inn** (Edale Road S33 6ZF; ☎01433 620381) serves real ales, including local brews, and pub meals, and has a beer garden to the rear. Fine cask ales, food featuring local produce and en-suite accommodation can be found at the **Poachers Arms** (Castleton Road S33 6SB; ☎01433 620380), while traditional ales and home-cooked food also feature at **The Old Hall Inn** (Market Place S33 6RH; ☎01433 620160). In Bradwell, **The Old Bowling Green Inn** (Smalldale S33 9JQ; ☎01433 620450) is a former coaching inn dating from the 16th century, with exposed stone walls, low-beamed ceilings and open fireplaces. Real ales include ever-changing guest beers and hearty, home-cooked food, made from local produce where possible, is on the menu.

ⓘ Visitor Information

Tourist information centre: Castleton Visitor Centre, Buxton Road, Castleton, Hope Valley S33 8WN, ☎01629 816558, www.peakdistrict.gov.uk, open daily, also includes the museum of the Castleton Historical Society.

Hospitals: Northern General Hospital, Herries Road, Sheffield, ☎0114 243 4343.

Doctors: Evelyn Medical Centre, Marsh Avenue, Hope S33 6RJ, ☎01433 621557.

Taxis: Corporate Services of Hope, Hope, ☎01433 620525; Ian's Private Hire, Chapel-en-le-Frith, ☎01298 814863.

KINDER SCOUT AND EDALE

Kinder Scout, the highest point of the Peak District, is the 15sq mile, 2,000ft/600m moorland plateau which dominates the landscape of the Edale valley and the northern Peak. It is also the southern terminus of Britain's toughest mountain marathon, the 270 mile Pennine Way, and the place where, over 75 years ago, the fight for national parks and the right to roam began.

Kinder is not a place for inexperienced walkers, and although comparatively modest in height, the weather conditions on it can change quickly and unpredictably, and the conditions underfoot are extremely hazardous. You shouldn't venture onto this hill unless you are a competent, fit and experienced walker, as many lives have been lost by those who have underestimated it. For those who can reach its 2,000ft plateau, the rewards are enormous, and include a string of weirdly carved summit tors, such as those known as The Woolpacks, Noe Stool and the Boxing Glove Stones, which have been eroded over eons of rain, wind and frost. Small wonder that the great British sculptor Henry Moore was said to have been inspired by these natural works of art.

WHAT TO SEE AND DO

Perhaps the best introduction to **Kinder Scout** is to follow the paved path of the official **Pennine Way**, which skirts around the southern slopes of the mountain and heads for Upper Booth and the easy ascent up the steps of **Jacob's Ladder**, an ancient packhorse route which leads up from a narrow packhorse bridge over a shoulder of Kinder. This leads to the ancient boundary marker known as **Edale Cross**. Alternatively, you could follow the broad path of the former main route of the Pennine Way over the famous log bridge and through **Grindsbrook Meadows** into the **Grindsbrook Gorge**, returning from the plateau into the village by the holloway known as the Sled Road.

Perhaps the highlight of Kinder's natural wonders is the 100ft/30m high waterfall known as **Kinder Downfall**, on its western escarpment overlooking Hayfield. This is the highest and greatest waterfall in the Peak and, under certain conditions, it exhibits the strange phenomena of blowing back on itself – when the water is thrown back by a strong westerly wind. There are many other shorter, family-length walks in the Edale valley, if you are not experienced enough to head for the heights. You will find information, maps and guides at The Moorland Centre in Edale (see below).

The village of **Edale** – more correctly Grindsbrook Booth – lies at the heart of the valley of Edale. Actually, Edale consists of five 'booths', which was the Tudor name for a cattle shelter, but Grindsbrook, the largest of these small hamlets, is the one now usually referred to as Edale village. **The Moorland Centre** (Fieldhead, Edale

Blow back at Kinder Downfall

S33 7SZ; ☎01433 670207; www.edale-valley.co.uk) is the natural starting point for the exploration of Edale and Kinder Scout. Opened by the Duke of Devonshire in 2006, the centre is housed in a circular, grass-roofed, fully sustainable building entered under a porchway with an artificial, recycled waterfall.

Activities

Situated in an idyllic spot at Rowland Cote, in the valley of the Lady Booth Brook on the southern slopes of Kinder Scout, the 157-bed Youth Hostel at Edale is also a dedicated **YHA Activity Centre** (Rowland Cote, Nether Booth, Edale, Hope Valley, Derbyshire S33 7ZH; ☎0845 371 9514; www.yha.org.uk) in one of the best known walking and adventure locations in the country. It's the perfect place to try activities such as caving, climbing, kayaking, canoeing, abseiling, orienteering and archery. Whether alone or part of a group or family, this is the place to have fun while you improve your outdoor skills.

LADYBOOTH EQUESTRIAN CENTRE: Nether Booth, Edale, Hope Valley, Derbyshire S33 7ZH; ☎01433 670205; www.ladybooth.co.uk.

The **Ladybooth Equestion Centre**, also at Nether Booth at the eastern end of the beautiful Edale valley, was established over 40 years ago and has a reputation as one of the best equestrian and pony-trekking centres in the area. With an abundance of bridleways and ancient packhorse routes in and around the Edale valley, it is also in a prime spot to enjoy the best of the Dark Peak scenery on horseback.

LOCAL KNOWLEDGE

Internationally respected woodworker **Robin Wood** lives and works in Edale. Originally a National Trust forester, he gave up the day job in 1995 to specialise in making bowls on a foot-powered lathe, recreating the medieval craft that had died out with the last practitioner, George Lailey, in 1958. Inspired by time spent in Scandinavia, Robin has now started teaching the skills of axe and knife work with his wife, Nicola.

The best thing or things about living in the Peak District: The diverse mix of people, from farm labourers and eastern European youngsters to artists, writers and doctors – all working together keeping the community alive.

The Peak District's 'best kept secret': Kinder Scout is empty after 5pm, and I don't know why, but nobody goes walking on a Monday.

Best thing to do on a rainy day: A walk around the north-western rim of the Edale valley, up Jacob's Ladder, through The Woolpacks and down either Crowden or Grindsbrook. Or sitting in front of the fire, carving wooden spoons.

Best view: Driving over Mam Nick, entering the Edale valley in the dark after being away and seeing the few scattered lights then the blackness and space of Kinder.

Quirkiest attraction: The 'broken road' in Castleton. The old A625 road across the face of Mam Tor kept slipping and being repaired until it was abandoned in the 1980s. Today it looks as if a giant has picked it up and torn it apart. Fantastic!

Favourite restaurant: For a nice meal in a relaxed atmosphere, the Monsal Head Hotel. For a special meal, Rowley's gastro pub at Baslow. I am still saving up to go to Fischer's Baslow Hall.

Favourite takeaway: The Raj in Chapel-en-le-Frith.

Favourite pub: Three Stags Heads at Wardlow or the Nag's Head in Edale.

Secret tip for lunch: Edale Station and the Penny Pot Café for panini and good coffee, or Grindleford Station Café – recommended for anyone who likes old-fashioned transport cafés.

261

Wet weather

There's not much to see or do in wet weather in the Edale Valley, but a visit to **The Moorland Centre**, at Fieldhead on the road running past the railway station, is always worthwhile. Talks are given and guided walks start from here during the season, and there is an excellent audio-visual show.

The Moorland Centre in Edale

The best... **PLACES TO STAY**

HOTEL

The Rambler Country House Hotel

Edale, Hope Valley S33 7ZA
☎ **01433 670268**
www.theramblerinn.com

A warm welcome awaits at this inviting country inn, with its traditional dining room, bar with wooden floors, brightly decorated accommodation and attractive gardens with outdoor seating and children's play area. Meals to suit all tastes and appetites.

Price: B&B from £38 pppn.

B&B

Stonecroft Country Guest House

Grindsbrook, Edale, Hope Valley S33 7ZA; ☎ 01433 670262
www.stonecroftguesthouse.co.uk

Charming Victorian-style house with many original features at the start of the Pennine Way, offering a taste of old-fashioned hospitality. Host Julia Reid also offers photography courses and an imaginative and varied breakfast menu.

Price: B&B from £70 per room per night.

CAMPSITES

Fieldhead Campsite

Fieldhead, Grindsbrook Booth, Edale, Hope Valley S33 7ZA
☎ **01433 670386**
www.fieldhead-campsite.co.uk

Situated in a convenient and scenic setting at the start of the Pennine Way, this well-equipped campsite is owned by the Peak District National Park Authority and is open 365 days a year. Facilities include modern showers, toilets and disabled access. There are separate fields for families and backpackers.

Price: from £3 to £5.50; vehicles from £2.50 to £5.

Upper Booth Farm & Campsite

Edale, Hope Valley S33 7ZJ
☎ **01433 670250**
www.upperboothcamping.co.uk

Located alongside Crowden Clough amid beautiful scenery, award-winning Upper Booth Farm provides facilities for tents (no caravans or large motor homes) in a relaxed, secluded setting. Pitches are limited, to maintain the quality and atmosphere. Camping barn also available.

Price: £3 to £4 pppn.

SELF-CATERING

Ollerbrook Cottages

Middle Ollerbrook House, Ollerbrook, Edale, Hope Valley S33 7ZG
☎ **01433 670083**
www.ollerbrook-cottages.co.uk

Two 17th-century traditional stone cottages in a tranquil setting in the heart of the Edale valley, one sleeping three people, the other accommodating five. Each beautifully decorated and comfortably furnished. Pretty cottage garden with sitting/eating area.

Price: £275 to £665 for a week.

The best... PLACES TO STAY

Greenacres Farm

Hayfield Road, Chinley Head SK23 6AL
☎ 01663 750373
www.greenacresbarn.co.uk

Traditional, detached stone-built barn sleeping four people, tastefully furnished and well-equipped, with a range of modern facilities. Open plan lounge with natural stone floor and large French windows. Sweeping views to the front, overlooking Cracken Edge. Within easy reach of the Pennine Way. Grazing can be provided for visitors' horses.

Price: £235 to £545 for a week.

UNUSUAL

Edale Mill

Edale, Hope Valley S33 7ZE
☎ 01628 825925
www.landmarktrust.org.uk

Former 18th-century cotton mill bought by The Landmark Trust in 1969, restored and divided into seven apartments, one of which is rented out as a holiday let. An irresistible blend of luxury and Puritanism, it is set in attractive communal grounds and sleeps up to four people, with parking nearby.

Price: From £360 for a week.

The Old Nag's Head in Edale, the starting point for the Pennine Way

The best... FOOD AND DRINK

When you stop off to sample hand-pulled ales and home-cooked food at **The Old Nag's Head** in Edale (Grindsbrook Booth, Hope Valley S33 7ZD; ☎01433 670291), don't be surprised to see ghostly figures in airmen's uniform. During the Second World War, an RAF bomber crashed on Kinder Moor, and the bodies of the dead crew were carried down to the pub. The Nag's Head is also popular with walkers setting out to tackle the Pennine Way, which starts just outside the front door. Families, walkers and dogs are all welcome at this 16th-century pub, which has oak beams and open fires in winter.

You can also enjoy a relaxing drink in the stylish bar of **The Rambler Country House Hotel** (Edale, Hope Valley S33 7ZA; ☎01433 670268).

ⓘ Visitor Information

Tourist information centre: The Moorland Centre, Fieldhead, Edale, Hope Valley S33 7SZ, ☎01433 670207, www.edale-valley.co.uk, www.peakdistrict.gov.uk.

Hospitals: Northern General Hospital, Herries Road, Sheffield, ☎0114 243 4343.

Doctors: See Castleton (p. 258).

Taxis: Corporate Services of Hope, Hope, ☎01433 620525; B&S Private Hire, Hayfield, ☎01663 744887.

THE SETT VALLEY AND NEW MILLS

The bustling market town of Chapel-en-le-Firth advertises itself as 'the Capital of the Peak', and is situated on a ridge surrounded by hills. The cobbled Market Place, where a cattle market was once held, runs above and parallel to the main street, and stands at a lofty 776ft/236m above the sea. It is complete with a Market Cross, village stocks dating from the Cromwellian period, and a number of ancient inns. An open-air market still takes place every Thursday.

New Mills traces its history back to the 13th century, when the first corn mill was established on the River Sett. Later in the 18th century, the textile industry found the conditions at New Mills ideal for cotton production, and more water-powered mills were built. A total of five 'new mills' were built around The Torrs, an impressive sandstone gorge which runs through the centre of the town, on the banks of two rivers, the Sett and the Goyt.

When the cotton industry was coming to an end by the early years of the 20th century, the buildings fell into disrepair and the whole area became overgrown and uncared for. During the 1990s, however the Torrs Riverside Park – known as 'the park under the town' – was created to provide a place for relaxation and recreation, and the New Mills Heritage Centre was opened. The spectacular Torrs Millennium Walkway was opened in 1999, and is an award-winning footbridge soaring high above the side of the gorge.

WHAT TO SEE AND DO

Chapel-en-le-Frith

Church Brow, a steep, cobbled street leading off Market Street, has been likened to Gold Hill in Shaftesbury, Dorset, famous for the television Hovis advertisement. Like Gold Hill, it is lined with attractive cottages in a delightful, completely unplanned fashion. The town derives its unusual name from a chapel of ease originally built in a clearing in the Royal Forest of the Peak in the 13th century (*frith* is Norman French for forest). A reminder of those far-off days is still provided in the churchyard of the present **parish church**, which has an unusual dedication to St Thomas à Becket (see *Wet weather* below). A gravestone known as the **Woodcutter's Grave** displays a carving of an axe and the initials P L, and is thought to mark the resting place of a 13th-century forester from the Royal Forest. But Chapel's church is best known as the scene of one of the most horrific incidents of the Civil War. A group of 1,500 Royalist Scottish prisoners captured at the Battle of Preston in 1648 were imprisoned in the church for 16 days, and before their eventual release, 44 men had died in terrible conditions which must have resembled the infamous Black Hole of Calcutta.

Chapel Brow, Chapel-en-le-Frith

In later years, Chapel-en-le-Frith has played an important role in the development of the motor car. The **Ferodo works** west of the town were founded by local man Herbert Frood (the name of the company is a close anagram of his surname), who developed a brake block for horse-drawn carts before turning his attention to motor vehicles. He originally invented a brake lining for buses, and he later provided brakes for cars as well. The Ferodo works now produce brake linings for vehicles all over the world.

New Mills and The Torrs Riverside Park

The **Heritage and Information Centre** in New Mills is on the cobbled track leading down into The Torrs, the dramatic gorge above which the town is perched. Inside the centre, a magnificent model of the town as it was in 1884 – the year in which the Union Road high level bridge over The Torrs was built – with an accompanying commentary, describes the growth of industrial New Mills. The later growth of engraving and printing industries and the development of New Mills as a town are also described in vivid detail.

The **Torrs Riverside Park** – the so-called 'Park under the Town' – provides access to an area of spectacular natural beauty which includes mills and the ruined foundations of mills and weirs situated in the bottom of the gorge. The mill-builders were attracted to the gorge of the River Sett at the end of the 18th century by the potential of its water power. An awe-inspiring highlight of The Torrs is the amazing, award-winning **Millennium Walkway**, constructed at a cost of £525,000 in 1999. It clings like a silvery spider's web to the massive

NEW MILLS HERITAGE AND INFORMATION CENTRE: New Mills, High Peak, Derbyshire SK22 3BN; ☎01663 746202; www.newmillsheritage.com. Open daily 11am-4pm, Tues–Fri and weekends.

retaining wall of the 1867 Midland Railway line on a sharp bend 90ft/27m above the rushing waters of the River Sett. Although the walkway is wide and well-railed, you still need a good head for heights to traverse its length – but it's an inspiring example of modern engineering grafted onto an outstanding example of 19th-century work. It won the small projects category in the British Construction Industries Award, and even featured on a national postage stamp.

Torr Weir in the Riverside Park is the first community-funded hydro-

The Millennium Walkway in the Torrs, New Mills

TORRS HYDRO NEW MILLS: 90 Market Street, New Mills, High Peak SK22 4AA; ☎01663 898070; www.torrshydro.co.uk. Entry: phone for appointments.

electric scheme in the country. A 2.4m diameter, 70kW reverse Archimedes screw – nicknamed 'Archie' – was installed at a cost of £226,000 by Water Power Enterprises in 2006 and is now run by the Torrs Hydro New Mills company. It should generate 242,000KWh (or units) of electricity annually. A share of the revenue from the scheme will help Torrs Hydro achieve its aim to help regenerate the community and to promote the environmental sustainability of New Mills. Although not open to the public, interested parties can call in advance for an appointment.

The Torrs path and the Millennium Bridge links with the **Sett Valley Trail** along the old railway track to Hayfield and the Goyt Way, a long-distance route linking the Manchester conurbation with the Goyt Valley and the Peak District National Park, and the bridge provided the last link in the 225 mile **Midshires Way**, between the Ridgeway National Trail in Buckinghamshire and the TransPennine Trail at Stockport.

☔ Wet weather

The Georgian exterior of the parish church of **St Thomas à Becket** in Chapel-en-le-Frith, conceals a mainly 14th-century interior. Inside the church, there are some fine box pews, Flemish-style chandeliers, a 13th-century stone coffin and several memorials, including many to the Bagshawe family. The most famous of these was William Bagshawe who was a well-known evangelist during the Restoration, and known as 'the Apostle of the Peak'. **St George's Parish Church, New Mills** was built in the early 19th century on land donated by Lord George Cavendish, the youngest son of the fourth Duke of Devonshire. It is built in the Gothic revival style, surmounted by an embattled tower complete with pinnacles and a spire. New Mills only became an ecclesiastical parish in 1844; before that it was a chapel of ease to All Saints, Glossop.

LOCAL KNOWLEDGE

Following a career as a lecturer in Environmental Management at Sheffield Hallam University, the late **Sir Martin Doughty** (1949 – 2009), who lived in New Mills, developed his expertise and interest in nature conservation alongside landscape and access work as Chair of The Peak District National Park Authority. He held a wide range of key roles in the public and voluntary sectors, including a spell as Leader of Derbyshire County Council from 1992 to 2001. Martin was also a board member for the Countryside Agency from 1999 to 2005, and was Chair of English Nature before being appointed Chair for Natural England. He was knighted in 2001 for services to local government in Derbyshire, and was awarded Honorary Doctorates from Sheffield Hallam University in 2002, Cranfield University in 2005 and the University of Derby in 2006.

Best thing about the Peak District: Enjoying the best of both worlds. Living here, you have stunning scenery and wildlife on your doorstep, but are close to major cities like Manchester and Sheffield.

Best kept secret: Mountain hares in their white winter coats on Bleaklow in February and March. The Peak is the only place in England where you can see them.

Favourite haunt: The Moors for the Future Centre at Edale,

Best thing to do on a rainy day: Put good waterproofs on, get outside and ignore the weather.

Favourite activity: Bird watching.

Best view: From 'Bigstone' on Ollersett Moor (SK037842) across to Peep o-Day and all points east.

Best walk: Snake Summit to Edale via the Pennine Way or, preferably, across the Kinder plateau. Most importantly, this walk can be done using public transport.

Favourite restaurant/pub: The Barrel Inn at Bretton, near Eyam. It stays open on Sundays for a late lunch, normally serving food from 12 noon until 8.30pm, and has an open fire, hand-pulled real ales and meals using local, fresh produce.

CELEBRITY CONNECTIONS

Television presenter **Tess Daly**, best known as **Bruce Forsyth's** co-host on BBC's *Strictly Come Dancing*, was born in Stockport, Cheshire, grew up in Birch Vale near Hayfield, and was a pupil at New Mills Community School. Married to fellow presenter **Vernon Kay**, she attributes her down-to-earth attitude to life to her solid, loving upbringing in the Peak District with parents Vivian and Sylvia, and is determined to create a similarly stable background for her young daughter, Phoebe.

Tess began her career as a model at 17, when a model scout handed her a leaflet in Manchester and she was subsequently signed up by an agency. After living and working in France and New York, where she made the most of the *Sex and the City*-style social life in Manhattan, she launched her television career in 1999. Her first assignment was to host the 'Find Me a Model' competition on Channel 4's *The Big Breakfast*. She has since presented *The National Lottery: This Time Tomorrow*, *Just the Two of Us* with Vernon and won the BBC's *Children in Need* version of *Strictly Come Dancing*.

What to do with children

For young visitors to the **New Mills Heritage Centre** (see above), there is a reconstruction of a coal mine tunnel to crawl through, and they'll love the 'fly-on-a-wall' experience of walking across the **Millennium Walkway** in The Torrs below.

The best... **PLACES TO STAY**

INN

The Waltzing Weasel
Inn

New Mills Road, Birch Vale SK22 1BT
☎ **01663 743402**
www.w-weasel.co.uk

Quintessential English Inn built around 400 years ago, with views of Kinder Scout, Lantern Pike and surrounding hills and moors, and situated next to the Sett Valley Trail between Hayfield and New Mills. Single, double and family rooms, all with en-suite facilities, including two ground floor rooms with wheelchair access.

Price: B&B from £85 for a double.

The Old Hall Inn

Whitehough, Chinley SK23 6EJ
☎ **01663 750529**
www.old-hall-inn.co.uk

En-suite accommodation (three double rooms and one twin single), including a large room with a balcony overlooking the garden beyond are available at this family-run, 16th-century inn in the heart of prime walking country. Sweeping views of the surrounding countryside and home cooking focusing on food sourced from local suppliers.

Price: B&B from £70 for a double.

FARMSTAY

Slack Hall Farm

Castleton Road, Chapel-en-le-Frith SK23 0QS; ☎ 01298 812845

Just one mile from Chapel-en-le-Frith, this 17th-century farmhouse is situated on a working dairy, beef and sheep farm, with sweeping views over the surrounding countryside. An ideal base for walking and touring, it has spacious en-suite bedrooms with colour television and tea/coffee making facilities. Overnight grazing for horses available.

Price: B&B from £35 pppn.

B&B

High Croft Guest House

**Manchester Road,
Chapel-en-le-Frith SK23 9UH**
☎ **01298 814843**
www.highcroft-guesthouse.co.uk

Edwardian country guest house set in 1½ acres of gardens next to Chapel-en-le-Frith golf course and Combs Reservoir. Scenic views and excellent walking on the doorstep. Tastefully furnished en-suite bedrooms, spacious and comfortable sitting room, log fires, elegant dining room and extensive breakfast menu.

Price: B&B from £38 to £53 pppn.

SELF-CATERING

Fox Hall Barn Cottage

Kinder Road, Hayfield SK22 2HS
☎ **01663 745090**
www.stilwell.co.uk

Situated in the heart of Hayfield, at the foot of Kinder Scout, this well-equipped Grade II listed stone cottage sleeps two, and dates from the early 16th century. Set in attractive, mature gardens with summer house, it is full of character, with oak beams and mullioned windows, and comfortably furnished in traditional country style.

Price: From £240 to £310 for a week.

The best... FOOD AND DRINK

Small producers in this corner of the Dark Peak can supply everything from locally raised meat and traditional bacon to Continental sausages, pancetta and sheep's milk. Local delis also satisfy even the most demanding palate with a range of eat-in and takeaway foods. If you're dining out, tuck into a traditional Derbyshire oatcake or farmhouse breakfast, or opt for Italian or Chinese. You can also enjoy a selection of ales close to where the famous Kinder Mass Trespass began in 1932.

▶ Staying in

Home-reared beef, lamb and pork and home-produced bacon, sausage, eggs and sheep's milk can be sourced from **New House Farm**, Chapel-en-le-Frith (The Wash SK23 0QL; ☎01663 750647 or ☎07837 875261). All products are available at the farm gate or delivered locally. For fully matured and hung Dexter beef and lean Texel lamb, contact **Paradise Farm** in Chapel-en-le-Frith (Ashbourne Lane SK23 9UF; ☎01298 814650 or ☎07775 511498). You'll also be able to buy traditional and Continental sausages, bacon, pancetta and hams from local rare breed pigs and honey.

Authentic Italian coffee and mouth-watering foods ranging from home-made cakes and quiches to cooked meats and pork pies are on sale at **In a Pickle**, Chapel-en-le-Frith (Market Street SK23 0HP; ☎01298 816555). This deli also has a small coffee shop where you can enjoy eat-in breakfasts, lunches, home-made cakes and hot and cold drinks.

🍺 Drinking

In the centre of Hayfield, the **Royal Hotel** (Market Street SK22 2EP; ☎01663 742721) has original oak panels and pews and open fires in winter, and serves real ales, including locally brewed options, plus bar snacks and meals. On Kinder Road, near the quarry where the famous Mass Trespass began back in 1932, is **The Sportsman Hotel** (SK22 2LE; ☎01663 741565), a family-run hostelry that serves a range of ales, food and accommodation and has a friendly atmosphere; dogs are welcome.

Wholesome food, fine ales, scenic views of the valley beyond and outdoor seating are on offer at the **Lamb Inn**, Chinley (Hayfield Road SK23 6AL; ☎01663 750519). At Whitehough you'll find the historic **Old Hall Inn** (Chinley SK23 6EJ; ☎01663 750529), a family-run 16th-century inn offering good food, a range of cask ales from around the country and a selection of malt whiskies, wines and lagers, plus quality accommodation. In New Mills, the stone-built **Pack Horse Inn** (Mellor Road SK22 4QQ; ☎01663 742365) has a traditional bar with open fire, an imaginative choice of guest beers and recently added restaurant serving food.

EATING OUT

RESTAURANT

CoCo's Ristorante and Pizzeria
**20a Market Street,
Chapel-en-le-Frith SK23 0HH
☎ 01298 813180**

Classic Italian cooking in a chic, contemporary setting, including starters, mains, risottos, pizza, pasta, fish and specials, using locally sourced ingredients wherever possible. Private parties can be accommodated in an upstairs room, and a takeaway service is also available.

Imperial Palace Chinese Restaurant
**142 Buxton Road,
Furness Vale SK23 7PH
☎ 01663 745777**

Friendly Chinese restaurant with good selection of dishes based on chicken, beef, fish, seafood and vegetarian options, with large round table for parties of up to 14 people. Takeaway service available. Closed Mondays. Vegetarian mains (eat in) from £3 to £4, chicken and beef (eat in) £7.50, seafood (eat in) £9.50 and fish at market price.

GASTRO PUB

Beehive Inn
**Combs, High Peak SK23 9UT
☎ 01298 812758
www.thebeehiveinn.co.uk**

Warm and welcoming atmosphere whatever the season, with roaring open fires in winter and flower-filled garden in the summer, in an idyllic location in the hamlet of Combs. Extensive selection of starters, mains and desserts, including special menus at Christmas and Valentine's Day, plus Menu Rapide served Monday to Friday noon to 2pm and 6pm to 7pm. Two courses cost £5.95, three courses £6.95.

CAFÉ

Stocks Café and Bistro
**4–6 Market Place,
Chapel-en-le-Frith SK23 0EN
☎ 01298 814906
www.stockscafeandbistro.co.uk**

Traditional home-cooking using fresh, local produce served in a relaxed atmosphere with indoor and outdoor seating in Chapel-en-le-Frith's historic Market Place. Specials change daily, but favourites like meat and potato pie, traditional Derbyshire breakfast, veggie breakfast and filled Derbyshire oatcakes are staples. The café has a firm commitment to environmental values, including recycling and composting.

ⓘ Visitor Information

Tourist information centre: New Mills Heritage and Information Centre, New Mills, High Peak, Derbyshire SK22 3BN, ☎01663 746202, www.newmillsheritage.com, open daily Tues–Fri and weekends.

Hospitals: Stepping Hill Hospital, Poplar Grove, Stockport, ☎0161 483 1010; Buxton Hospital, London Road, Buxton, ☎01298 214000; Cavendish Hospital, Manchester Road, Buxton, ☎01298 212800.

Doctors: Thornbrook Surgery, Thornbrook Road, Chapel-en-le-Frith SK23 0RH, ☎01298 812725; Sett Valley Medical Centre, Hyde Bank Road, New Mills SK22 4BP, ☎01663 743483.

Supermarkets: Co-op Supermarket, Eccles Road, Chapel-en-le-Frith, ☎01298 814292; Londis, Thornbrook Road, Chapel-en-le-Frith, ☎01298 812527; Morrisons, Market Street, Chapel-en-le-Frith, ☎01298 814434; Co-op Supermarket, Church Street, New Mills, ☎01663 741301.

Taxis: High Peak Taxis, New Mills, ☎01663 744448; New Mills Cabs, ☎01663 746606; Mike's Taxis, New Mills, ☎07984 495245.

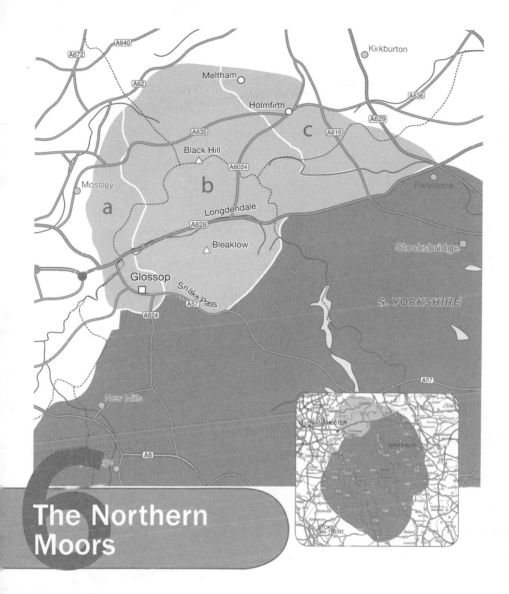

The Northern Moors

a. Glossop

b. Longdendale, Bleaklow and Black Hill

c. Holmfirth and Meltham

Unmissable highlights

THE NORTHERN MOORS

The northern moors of Bleaklow, Black Hill and Saddleworth are the nearest thing the Peak District comes to a real wilderness. Mile after mile of desolate peat moorland stretches north across the aptly named Bleaklow and on to the even more appropriately named Black Hill, inhabited only by the hardy moorland sheep and the occasional determined human 'bog-trotter'.

The only breaks in the forbidding chocolate-brown peat moorlands are the Snake Pass, at 1,600 feet (500m) the highest road pass in the Peak, which carries the A57 Sheffield–Glossop road to the south; and Longdendale in the north, which takes the A628 Sheffield–Manchester road over the remote Woodhead Pass. Reservoirs like those at Dovestone, Yeoman Hey and Greenfield in the Greenfield Valley above Uppermill fill some of the moorland valleys, and the windswept expanse of the Chew Reservoir, 1,600ft/500m above the sea on Dove Stone Moss, is the highest in the country.

Sizeable human settlements are found only on the eastern and western fringes, where the moors slope down to the lowlands. The former textile town of Glossop to the west has more of the feel of a Lancashire mill town than Derbyshire about it. The original settlement is known as Old Glossop, but the modern town was mainly laid out in the 19th century by the eleventh Duke of Norfolk who owned large shooting estates in the area, and named it Howard Town. Road names, such as Norfolk Square, Howard Park and Norfolk Street, still reflect this past ownership. Over to the east of the moors, the compact mill town of Holmfirth also had its industrial past, as did Meltham, but today Holmfirth and district is forever associated with the longest-running television comedy in Britain, Roy Clarke's *Last of the Summer Wine*, which has been shot in this locality for over 40 years.

GLOSSOP

Glossop's beautiful setting at the foot of the Snake Pass on the western edge of the Peak has earned it the title of 'The Gateway to the Peak'. The original settlement on the Glossop Brook is still known as Old Glossop, an attractive area with some fine 17th and 18th-century cottages clustered around the Market Square and Cross. But it was the Romans who first discovered the strategic importance of Glossop, guarding as it did the western approaches to the lead riches of the Peak. The ancient trackway which winds up from Old Glossop over the Snake Pass is known as Doctor's Gate and follows the line of the Roman road which linked the fort of Navio at Brough in the Hope Valley with that of Melandra, now almost surrounded by a housing estate in the Glossop suburb of Gamesley, to the west of Dinting Vale.

The plentiful and powerful water supply from the bleak moors to the east of the town meant that the cotton industry developed rapidly here during the early years of the Industrial Revolution. At one time, the town had no less than 46 mills in operation, and they were a major employer of local labour. The full story of Glossop's fascinating past is told in the excellent Glossop Heritage Centre, and the bustling town centre hosts an indoor market in the colonnaded Market Hall every Thursday, Friday and Saturday.

A short distance down the A6016 is the village of Hadfield, which doubled as 'Royston Vasey', the North Country village inhabited by some very bizarre characters in the cult BBC2 television comedy sketch show, *The League of Gentlemen*, which was first broadcast in 1999. *The League of Gentlemen* was mainly filmed in and around Hadfield, but it also featured Glossop, Marsden, Mottram and the Hope Valley as backdrops. But hopefully, you will no longer find Tubbs and Edward Tattsyrup behind the counter of the local shop...

WHAT TO SEE AND DO

The starting point for any exploration of Glossop is the **Heritage Centre**, in Henry Street, which also supplies the *Explore Glossop Guide,* a set of self-guided trails around the town. The Heritage Centre was created by local enthusiasts and shows the way that the town, its setting and its people have developed through history. In addition to a well-stocked shop, the recently refurbished **Art Gallery** upstairs houses a large collection of original paintings and prints offered by local artists for sale.

The centre's permanent exhibition features an authentic Victorian kitchen and numerous historical costumes. The strong influence on the town's economic and social structure made by the Dukes of Norfolk and the Victorian mill-owners are emphasised, and regularly changing

GLOSSOP HERITAGE CENTRE: Bank House, Henry Street, Glossop, Derbyshire SK13 8BW; ☎01457 869176; www.glossopheritage.co.uk. Open 10am–4pm, Mon to Sat, year round.

exhibitions illustrate specific aspects of the town's development and local subjects of general interest – from natural history, arts and crafts, sporting activities, schools, family history, to local history and the influence of the railways.

There is an interesting local history trail around the original settlement of **Old Glossop**, along the banks of the Glossop Brook which runs through the centre of the old village. This attractive area has some fine gritstone cottages grouped around the Market Square and Cross. The parish church is Norman in origin and has an 18th-century sundial.

The Cross at Old Glossop

CELEBRITY CONNECTIONS

Acclaimed for her cutting edge creations ranging from pagan to punk, internationally renowned fashion designer **Dame Vivienne Westwood** OBE was born Vivienne Isabel Swire in Tintwistle, near Glossop, in 1941. Her mother, a former weaver in local cotton mills, and her father, from a family of shoemakers, ran a sub-post office in Tintwistle after the war. Vivienne attended Glossop Grammar School (now Glossopdale Community School) before the family moved to north-west London in the late 1950s.

Always interested in dressing in distinctive style, Vivienne adapted her school uniform to copy the then fashionable pencil skirt and sewed many of her own clothes. After leaving grammar school at 16, Vivienne briefly studied fashion and silversmithing at Harrow Art College, but left after a term because she felt her working class background wouldn't be conducive to a career in art. She worked in a factory, trained to become a primary school teacher and married her first husband, Derek Westwood, in the early 1960s, though the relationship was short lived. Vivienne subsequently met rock band manager **Malcolm McLaren** and finally began designing in earnest in the early 1970s, when she showcased her innovative fashions in his shop on London's famous King's Road, which she still owns.

Vivienne's initial 'punk style' designs bristled with safety pins, razor blades, bicycle and lavatory chains and spiked dog collars and were sported by bands such as the notorious, McLaren-managed **Sex Pistols**. Famed for combining traditional elements of British design with more outlandish features, her unique creations are instantly recognisable across the globe. In 2007, Vivienne was honoured by her old school, when Glossopdale Community College named one of its houses, Westwood, after her.

Glossop

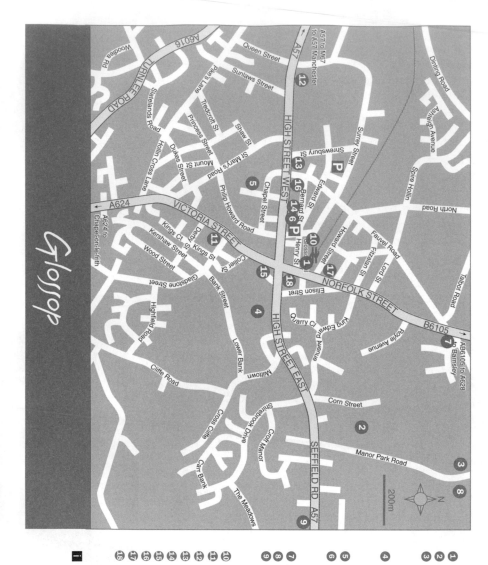

Old Glossop is also the starting point of the **Doctor's Gate** footpath, named after the Dr Talbot who re-discovered this medieval paved packhorse route, which leads up through rough moorland to the Snake Pass and Pennine Way between Kinder Scout and Bleaklow.

NOTE: The Doctor's Gate route should only be attempted by experienced and well-equipped walkers.

A short walk from Glossop town centre is **Manor Park**, set in 60 acres of gardens, woodland and lakes, and offering crazy golf, putting, bowling and tennis, as well as a miniature railway and children's playground. **Howard Park** off Park Crescent is named after the landowning Dukes of Norfolk and features their symbolic stone

The Church of All Saints, Old Glossop

lions and a statue to the memory of the Wood family, who donated the park to the town in 1888. Although smaller than Manor Park, it is equally pleasant, and features among other attractions an ornamental lake, an arid garden and a wildflower meadow. Howard Park is also the home of the beautifully restored **Victorian Swimming Pool**.

The earthworks of the Roman fort of **Melandra Castle** are situated at Gamesley, 2 miles west of Glossop town centre on the A626. It was built in the last quarter of the 1st century AD, commanding high ground above the River Etherow and a fine view

Looking down on the Snake Pass

towards the jaws of Longdendale. Excavations have revealed walls, a shrine and the fort headquarters and the whole site is now landscaped to provide parking and picnic areas.

Wet weather

The **Glossop Heritage Centre** (see p. 278) is the best place to visit when the heavens open, but a happy hour or so could also be whiled away in Glossop's interesting shops, mainly centred around the elegant Norfolk Square. Enjoy one of **John Mettrick's** wonderful freshly made sandwiches bought from his award-winning butcher's shop in the High Street (see *Staying in* below) – that's after you've had a good browse through the comprehensive stock held at **George Street Books.**

GEORGE STREET BOOKS: 14–16 George Street; ☎01457 853413; www.georgestreetbooks.co.uk.

What to do with children

The Victorian Swimming Pool in Howard Park, or the **Glossop Leisure Centre** (High Street East, Glossop SK13 8PN; ☎01457 842272; www.highpeak.gov.uk/leisure/glossopLeisureCentre/), should keep energetic children occupied, especially on a gloomy day. Alternatively, try the **Halcyon** in Hadfield (Rear of 101 Station Road SK13 1AR; ☎01457 853713), a welcoming venue where you and the children can unleash your creative talents and paint a pot, as well as enjoying a coffee, tea, freshly squeezed orange juice and a variety of snacks.

GLOSSOP SWIMMING POOL: Dinting Road, Glossop, Derbyshire SK13 7DS; 01457 851618; www.highpeak.gov.uk/leisure/glossopPool. Entry: adults £2.80, juniors £1.70, over-50s £2.10; open daily; ring for details.

LOCAL KNOWLEDGE

Television and radio presenter **Andy Crane** lives near Glossop with his wife Caroline, who teaches locally, three daughters, four chickens, two cats, a dog, a rabbit and a guinea pig. Now news anchor for Manchester's local television station Channel M, he grew up in the city and began his television career as the BBC's late afternoon children's continuity announcer with puppet co-host Edd the Duck. He also presented *Top of the Pops* before leaving the BBC in 1990 to work on other radio and television projects. As well as his day job at Channel M, Andy also presents a Sunday afternoon show on BBC Radio Manchester, when his guests always comprise a politician, a singer-songwriter and a comedian – an interesting mix!

The best thing about living in the Peak District: If I turn left out of my front door, I'm in the National Park. If I turn right, I'm 15 miles from Britain's second city. This is a fantastically beautiful part of the country, right on Manchester's doorstep.

Favourite haunt/hangout: Home. I'm out working so much, there's nothing I like better than sitting in with Caroline, a good meal and a bottle of red wine on a Saturday evening.

Favourite activity in the Peak: Walking with Caroline, our daughters and the dog. We don't mind going out if it rains, we just pull on the waterproofs and get out there. My children's enthusiasm for walking in the Peak District seems to be directly related to the weather conditions. Snow or sun, they're very keen. When it's wet, it's usually just Caroline and myself.

Favourite walk: We tend to go on a different one each time, but we particularly like the circular walk from Castleton up Winnats Pass and back down by the caverns, the ridge walk at Mam Tor and Coombes Rocks at Charlesworth.

Favourite view: The Hope Valley from Mam Tor, where the scenery folds out in front of you – superb.

The Snake Pass

The A57 Snake Pass between Ladybower and Glossop is well-known to motorists from wintertime weather warnings. In times of prolonged snow, it is usually the first of the trans-Pennine routes to close – and the last to reopen. The reason for this is that the route is one of the highest major trunk roads in the country, reaching a height of 1,680ft/512m at the Snake Summit on Featherbed Moss, between the moorland massifs of Kinder Scout and Bleaklow. Actually, this section of the road is usually clear, but when the road descends into Lady Clough, huge cornices of snow and ice can build up on the surrounding moorland escarpments, threatening to, and often actually, avalanching across the road.

The Snake gets its name not from the winding nature of its route as many people seem to believe, but from the twisting serpent at the head of the coat of arms of the Cavendish family from Chatsworth, which owns much of the surrounding moorland. The Cavendish family were the major shareholders in the trust when the road was constructed as one of the last turnpike roads in the country, linking Manchester and Sheffield, in 1821. The only habitation on the Snake Pass is the remote Snake Inn, which was built as a posting house at the same time as the turnpike. The first landlord was John Longden, who was also a Methodist preacher and held regular prayer meetings there. Regular prize fights were once held in the field below the inn.

The Snake Pass Inn, the only building on the Snake Pass

The best... **PLACES TO STAY**

HOTEL

Wind in the Willows

Derbyshire Level, Glossop SK13 7PT
☎ **01457 853354**
www.windinthewillows.co.uk

Early Victorian country house hotel situated in five acres of open countryside in the Peak foothills. Oak panelled rooms, traditional furnishings and open log fires create a peaceful, relaxing atmosphere. All bedrooms are individually styled, with antique furniture and personal touches. Home-cooking served in the charming period dining room.

Price: B&B from £65 for double room.

FARMSTAY

White House Farm

Padfield, Glossop SK13 1ET
☎ **01457 854695**
**www.thepennineway.co.uk/
whitehousefarm**

This 18th-century farmhouse on a working farm combines traditional hospitality with modern-day comforts. Ideal stopover for walkers tackling the Pennine Way.

Price: B&B from £20 pppn.

B&B

Avondale

28 Woodhead Road, Glossop SK13 7RH
☎ **01457 853132**
www.avondale-guesthouse.co.uk

Edwardian house with elegant period dining room and well-kept en-suite accommodation, each with a table top fridge as well as other modern facilities. Freshly cooked English breakfast, porridge in winter and other lighter options.

Price: B&B from £30 pppn.

Woodlands

Woodseats Lane, Charlesworth, Glossop SK13 5DP
☎ **01457 866568**
www.woodlandshighpeak.co.uk

Set in mature gardens with attractive views. Mostly en-suite, prettily decorated accommodation (one room with private bathroom). Guest lounge and conservatory, where full English or lighter breakfasts, prepared using local produce, are served.

Price: B&B from £60 for a double room.

Wayside Cottage

106 Padfield Main Road, Padfield, Glossop SK13 1ET; ☎ **01457 866495**
www.wayside-cottage-online.co.uk

Sleep in the room where Oliver Cromwell is alleged to have stayed during his brief visit to the High Peak in this select B&B accommodation dating from the 17th century. Original beams, exposed stonework and antique furniture all add to its old world charm.

Price: B&B £60 per room per night.

SELF-CATERING

Rowan Tree Cottage

22a Old Cross, Old Glossop SK13 7RX
☎ **01457 858786**
www.rowantreeglossop.co.uk

Double-bedroomed listed cottage in pleasant gardens situated in the picturesque village of Old Glossop sleeping two to four people. Small private courtyard with outdoor furniture.

Price: £136 to £254 for a week.

The best... FOOD AND DRINK

Award-winning meat, quality fruit and vegetables, fresh fish, speciality deli fare and handmade chocolates are among the goodies in store in Glossop. If you want to eat out, there's a reasonable choice of restaurants, gastro pubs, cafés and tea shops. For real ale connoisseurs, the town has two microbreweries and a range of traditional pubs.

▶ Staying in

For a wide variety of gourmet foods ranging from antipasti to olives and pâtés to pasta, call in at **Praze Fine Foods**, Glossop (High Street West SK13 8AZ; ☎01457 860916). Food is sourced locally where possible, with cream and eggs sourced from a supplier a mile away, and locally made tzatziki. There's also a good selection of cheese and wine.

Locally reared and slaughtered meat, plus a wide range of associated meat products, including traditional and more unusual sausages, are on sale at multi-award-winning **J W Mettrick & Son**, a family-run butcher's shop on High Street West, Glossop and Station Road, Hadfield (SK13 8BH; ☎01457 852239). Produce includes bacon, gammon, beef, chicken, turkey, game, High Peak lamb raised just a few miles away and pork. In the past, Mettrick's has been named Best Butcher in England, Best Local Retailer and in BBC Radio 4 Food & Farming Awards. John Mettrick (see *Local Knowledge*, p. 293) has also appeared on BBC TV's *Ready, Steady, Cook* and *Kill It, Cook It, Eat It* and been acclaimed as Local Food Hero in Derbyshire's Annual Food and Drink Awards. Before its recent facelift, the Hadfield shop also starred as Hilary Briss's butcher's shop selling its 'special sausages' in the BBC comedy series *The League of Gentlemen.*

Quality fruit and vegetables, much of it sourced from growers in nearby Cheshire and Lancashire, are available from another family business, **Sowerbutts Greengrocers**, Glossop (High Street West SK13 8BH; ☎01457 852520). Other lines include dairy products from nearby Holmfirth, freshly made coleslaw, fresh herbs, fresh fruit salads and freshly squeezed orange juice, and several varieties of English apples are sold when in season. There is also an online ordering service with free local delivery.

For a selection of fresh fish, visit **David Bradley** fishmongers (High Street West SK13 8AZ; ☎01457 854349), and to finish off your meal with a touch of pure self-indulgence, you'll find luxury hand-made chocolates at **Simon Dunn Chocolatier** (High Street West SK13 8AZ; ☎01457 866666).

EATING OUT

RESTAURANTS

Dowds Restaurant
**110–112 High Street West,
Glossop SK13 8BB**
☎ **01457 855444**

Sample modern British fare from an evening menu which changes monthly and includes regular special offers, in an intimate atmosphere. Typical starters include crab cake with avocado ice cream and orange and ginger dressing, mains such as whole lobster with fondant potato and fresh asparagus. Two courses from the table d'hôte menu costs from £15.50.

Restaurant at 54
**54 High Street West,
Glossop SK13 8BH**
☎ **01457 861054**

Modern European cuisine in a pleasant setting. Sample starters include pan seared mushrooms in garlic cream sauce and artichoke and salami salad with parsley oil, while typical mains are grilled Derbyshire rump steak au poivre or pan-roasted Loch Duart salmon. Puddings include Eton Mess. Starters cost from around £4.50, mains from around £7.50.

Va Bene
12 Norfolk Street, Glossop SK13 8BS
☎ **01457 863333**
www.va-bene.co.uk

Authentic Italian cuisine served in a stylish, contemporary environment.

Extensive menu encompasses appetisers, starters, pasta, risotto, pizza, meat, fish, poultry, salads and side orders. Children are very welcome: they have their own menu and can make their own small pizza, while all the family tuck into a 24-inch version! Mains cost from around £9.95.

Kinnaree Thai Restaurant
**46–50 High Street West, Glossop
SK13 8BH**
☎ **01457 865168**
www.kinnareethai.com

Modern Thai cuisine in a bright, welcoming first-floor restaurant. Extensive menu includes starters, soups, salads, Thai curries, chicken, pork, beef, duck, seafood and vegetarian dishes, plus set meals, including a vegetarian option. Takeaway service with free delivery for orders over £8 within 3 miles of Glossop. Mains cost from £4.50 (vegetarian), £6.35 (beef).

Rainbow Bistro
The Basement, 14a High Street East (Smithy Fold), Glossop SK13 8DA
☎ **01457 865990**

Colourful décor and service with a smile in this basement bistro. Fresh local produce is a feature of the menu, which at lunchtime includes hot and cold sandwiches, baguettes, jacket potatoes and omelettes. Evening meals range from steaks and swordfish to pork in apple brandy and stilton and vegetable crumble. Evening mains average £14 to £15.

EATING OUT

GASTRO PUB

The Bulls Head
**102 Church Street,
Old Glossop SK13 7RN
☎ 01457 853291
www.bulls-head.co.uk**

Said to be the oldest pub in Glossop, the modern Bulls Head is prized for its Indian cuisine, prepared by chefs trained on the famous 'Curry Mile' in Rusholme, Manchester. Look out for Coronation Street stars and other celebrities tucking into dishes from its extensive menu. Starters cost from £1.50, mains from around £6.

CAFÉ

The Chocolate & Coffee Shop
**6 Henry Street, Glossop SK13 8BW
☎ 01457 864604
www.thechocolateandcoffeeshop.co.uk**

Country-style café with wicker chairs and stylish décor offering home-cooked food, light meals and a huge array of home-made cakes and puddings, ranging from coffee and walnut cake to chocolate cheesecake. Savouries include cheese and onion pie, crumpets, jacket potatoes, quiches, soup and sandwiches. Extensive use of local produce, including cooked meat from Mettrick's.

TEA ROOM

Woodlands Tea Room
**Woodseats Lane, Charlesworth, Glossop SK13 5DP
☎ 01457 866568
www.woodlandshighpeak.co.uk**

Friendly welcome, good service and fresh, local food when available are priorities at Woodlands, where savoury options range from cold and toasted sandwiches to soup, hot meals and daily specials. Sweets include chocolate fudge cake, dessert of the day and fruit cake, plus home-made scones and Victoria sponge. Outdoor seating in attractive garden in fine weather.

⫏ Drinking

Two microbreweries flourish in Glossop:

- The **Globe** – High Street West SK13 8HJ; ☎01457 852417; www.globemusic.org; based at the rear of the pub of the same name.
- The **Howard Town Brewery** – Hawkshead Mill, Hope Street, Old Glossop SK13 7SS; ☎01457 869800; www.howardtownbrewery.co.uk.

At **The Globe**, the main brews are Amber, Comet, Eclipse and Sirius, while special one-off lines are brewed for beer festivals. You'll also find real cider and British bottled beer, regular live music, vegan food and a garden to the rear. **Howard Town Brewery** supplies more than 100 outlets with brews inspired by local names, such as Bleaklow, Wrens Nest, Dinting Arches and Glotts Hop, plus seasonal beers.

If you're in search of a traditional drinkers' pub, visit the **Crown Inn** (Victoria Street SK13 8HY; ☎01457 862824), which has two snugs with real fires and a pool/games room, plus old images of Glossop's fascinating past. A stone's throw from the railway station, the **Star Inn** (Howard Street SK13 7DD; ☎01457 853072) is a real ale lover's paradise, with a range of beers and real cider. You'll also find wooden floors, scenes of old Glossop on the walls, and a tap room served through a hatch.

In Old Glossop, the early 17th-century **Bull's Head** (Church Street SK13 7RN; ☎01457 853291), thought to be the oldest pub in Glossop, is now a curry and guest house as well as a pub, but retains a bar, tap room and games room and serves a good selection of real ales. Its lively social calendar includes regular jazz and quiz nights. Nearby, **The Queen's Arms** (Shepley Street, Old Glossop SK13 7RZ; ☎01457 862451) serves draught beers and lagers, wines and food ranging from light bites to full meals. For real ales and a friendly atmosphere, visit **The Peels Arms** in Padfield (Temple Street SK13 1EX; ☎01457 852719), which has a cosy snug/games room where customers can play pool, darts and dominoes; walkers and dogs are welcome. Another traditional hostelry serving cask beers and home-cooked food is the **Bulls Head** at Tintwistle (SK13 1JY; ☎01457 853365).

In Mossley, you'll find a selection of real ales and food at the **Britannia Inn** (Manchester Road OL5 9AJ; ☎01457 832799) and the **Dysarts Arms** (Huddersfield Road OL5 9BT; ☎01457 832103). The **Rising Sun** (Stockport Road OL5 0RQ; ☎01457 834436) has scenic views of the Tame Valley and Saddleworth Moor, a wide range of vodka and malt whiskies and stages regular live music. Another pub with an interesting location is the **Tollemache Arms**, fondly known as the 'Tolley' (Manchester Road OL5 9BG; ☎01457 834555), situated where the recently restored Huddersfield Canal crosses the main road.

ⓘ Visitor Information

Tourist information centre: Glossop Tourist Information Centre, The Heritage Centre, Bank House, Henry Street, Glossop SK13 8BW, ☎01457 855920, www.glossoptouristcentre.co.uk, open daily Mon–Sat.

Hospitals: Shire Hill Hospital, Bute Road, Glossop, ☎01457 866021; Stepping Hill Hospital, Poplar Grove, Stockport, ☎0161 483 1010.

Doctors: Howard Medical Practice, Howard St, Glossop SK13 7DE, ☎01457 854321; Manor House Surgery, Manor St, Glossop SK13 8PS, ☎01457 860860; Lambgates Surgery, 1–5 Lambgates, Hadfield, Glossop SK13 1AW, ☎01457 869090; Dr AJ Dow, Cottage Lane Surgery, 47 Cottage Lane, Gamesley, Glossop SK13 6EQ, ☎01457 861343; Simmondley Medical Practice, 15a Pennine Road, Glossop SK13 6NN, ☎01457 862305.

Supermarkets: Tesco, Wren Nest Road, Glossop, ☎0845 677 9299; BKG Marketing, Gamesley, Glossop, ☎01457 855879.

Taxis: A2B Taxis, Glossop, ☎01457 855411; Goldline Taxis, Glossop, ☎01457 857777; New Line Taxis, Glossop, ☎01457 861111; Padtax Taxis, Glossop, ☎01457 854360; Shadow Taxis, Glossop, ☎01457 862000.

LONGDENDALE, BLEAKLOW AND BLACK HILL

Alfred Wainwright, doyen of walking guide authors and the writer of the best-selling *Pennine Way Companion*, was not exactly enamoured with Bleaklow, Black Hill or Longdendale. '*Nobody loves Bleaklow*', he wrote. '*All who get on it are glad to get off*'. And he continued: '*Black Hill is well named. The broad top really is black. It is not the only fell with a summit of peat, but no other shows such a desolate and hopeless quagmire to the sky*'.

And Longdendale didn't fare any better at the hands of the curmudgeonly old Lakeland fell-wanderer. He dismissed it as '*a mess*'. That rather grumpy assessment of the highest and wildest parts of the Peak (which Wainwright never liked anyway) was more than a little unfair. Bleaklow and Black Hill offer the experienced hillwalker a wilderness experience which the more popular hills like Kinder Scout or the Eastern Edges cannot match. This is the country of the well-equipped and experienced hillwalker – affectionately and with good reason known in these parts as a 'bogtrotter'.

The boggy summits of Bleaklow and Black Hill, over which the Pennine Way undertakes one of its toughest legs, are separated by the deep, reservoir-filled trench of Longdendale, which winds up from Tintwistle (pronounced 'Tinsel') to the 1,512ft/461m summit of Woodhead Pass at Fiddler's Green and on to Dunford Bridge. When they were constructed in the mid-19th century, the five reservoirs which flooded Longdendale – the Woodhead, Torside, Rhodeswood, Valehouse and Bottoms – were the largest stretch of man-made water in the world. They were the genius of engineer John Frederick Bateman, and at their height, contained a staggering 4,000 million gallons of fresh Pennine water, destined for Stockport and Manchester.

The hamlet of Crowden-in-Longdendale is the only sizeable settlement in the valley, and is now the site of a Youth Hostel run jointly by Rotherham Borough Council and the YHA. Crowden Hall, the Tudor-style manor house of the Hadfield family, was demolished in the interests of water purity in 1935. While the Woodhead road and Longdendale reservoirs altered the surface appearance of the Pennines, the 3 mile Woodhead Tunnel to the east and, further north, the Standedge rail and canal tunnels, burrowed far beneath them. Many navvies suffered during their construction, and 28 who perished in a cholera outbreak at Woodhead in 1849 are remembered in the tiny chapel of St James in Longdendale.

WHAT TO SEE AND DO

Standedge Tunnel

The Standedge Tunnel on the Huddersfield Narrow Canal at Marsden is the highest (643ft/196m above sea level), longest (3¼ miles/5,029m) and deepest (636ft/194m) canal in the country. The project was started in 1794 at the height of 'Canal Mania' and took 17 years to complete. The **Standedge Tunnel and Visitor Centre** at Tunnel End, Marsden is a great introduction to the **Huddersfield Narrow Canal**, a waterway of great contrasts, ranging from tranquil countryside to dramatic mills. You can actually have a go at 'legging' through a tunnel, like the old canal navigators did, in the centre, and see how the canal was excavated through the heart of the Pennines.

The trip on a glass-roofed guided narrow boat actually into the mouth of the Standedge Tunnel is a real step back in time, as you sit back and wonder at the work which went into this major feat of 18th-century engineering. You have the choice of a 30-minute excursion into the

STANDEDGE TUNNEL AND VISITOR CENTRE: Tunnel End, Waters Road, Marsden HD7 6NQ; ☎01484 844298; www.standedge.co.uk. Entry: adults £4.50, children £3.50, concessions £4, one-way ticket £10; open 10am–5.30pm, 15 Mar to 2 Nov, closed on Mon except Bank Holidays. For trips through tunnel (Wed/Fri) book at least three days in advance: call ☎ 0113 281 6860 or email enquiries.yorkshire@britishwaterways.co.uk.

tunnel, or the more adventurous may like to consider the three-hour trip right through the 3¼ mile tunnel (Wed and Fri only) all the way to Diggle on the other side of

A trip on a glass roofed narrow boat through the Standedge tunnel

LOCAL KNOWLEDGE

Avid botanist turned award-winning butcher **John Mettrick** was born in Glossop. After graduating with honours in botany at Leeds University, he returned to join the family business. John – voted 'Local Food Hero' in the 2007 Derbyshire Food & Drink Awards – and brother Steven jointly run J W Mettrick and Son, and supply locally raised meat, prepared in their own abattoir and sold in their shops in Glossop and Hadfield. Voted England's Best Butchers Shop in 2004/5, Mettrick's has won numerous regional and national accolades. John has appeared in television series such as *Ready, Steady Cook* and *Kill It, Cook It, Eat It*.

Best thing about living in the Peak District: Being surrounded by 'th'ills'. I never noticed them until I returned after university. I remember standing at the top of Kiln Lane in Hadfield and thinking 'Wow!' as I looked towards Longdendale.

Best kept secret: Old Glossop, with its Celtic cross, quaint cottages, Mossy Lea and Manor Park.

Best thing to do on a rainy day: Visit the Pavilion Gardens at Buxton and one of its specialist fairs or keep dry in the conservatory.

Favourite activity: Bird watching. I've logged species such as merlin, ring ouzel, hen harrier and my favourite, the kingfisher.

Best view: From the top of Redgate towards Longdendale. If you walk up towards Bettenhill you can see the Snake Pass in front and Mottram Church behind.

Best walk: The Longdendale Trail. It's a good length and the children can take their bikes.

Favourite restaurant: Va Bene, Glossop. Italian cuisine using local produce, and the children can make their own pizza.

Favourite takeaway: Raj Gourmet, Glossop. Voted the Best Curry House in the High Peak.

Favourite pub: The Pack Horse Inn, Hayfield. Voted the Best Dining Pub in the North West.

Secret tip for lunch: Byways, Bakewell. Excellent, home-cooked food and very friendly.

the hill. The really fit might even like to consider the walk 'over the top' across Castleshaw Moor and Close Moss, using the Standedge Trail to get back to Standedge.

Walking

Venturing on to the high moorlands of **Bleaklow** or **Black Hill** requires good waterproof equipment, boots, and map and compass, and the knowledge of how to use them. It is **not** recommended for inexperienced walkers. The 270 mile **Pennine Way** crosses the area from south to north, but despite recent path improvements, such as the paving slabs (recycled from former mill sites in the surrounding towns) which now mark the route from the Snake summit and across Black Hill, this is not a route for the ill-equipped or inexperienced. Bad weather can sweep in very quickly and unexpectedly on these hills, and it's very easy to get lost in misty conditions.

Approaching the Standedge Tunnel

The peaty summit of Bleaklow

GLOSSOP SAILING CLUB: Club House, Torside Reservoir, Longdendale, High Peak, Derbyshire; ☎0161 427 4864; www.sail-glossop.org.uk. Entry: prices on request; club racing takes place on Sun, Easter to Dec; Wed evenings, May to Aug.

Easier walking can be had around the many reservoirs which dot the moors, such as at **Dovestove**, in the Greenfield Valley, or **Torside** in Longdendale, both of which have sailing clubs.

On the water

Glossop Sailing Club offers excellent sailing on Torside Reservoir, with 160 acres/65 hectares of safe enclosed water surrounded by the attractive hills of Longdendale. The reservoir benefits from prevailing south-westerly winds blowing up the open valley and a large sailing area, more than a mile from end-to-end, offers challenging competition for experienced helmspeople, as well as a friendly and supportive environment for newcomers to the sport. The club also offers wind-surfing, kayaking canoeing, and training by Royal Yachting Association (RYA)-qualified instructors.

The **Dovestone Reservoir Sailing Club** is also affiliated to the RYA, and welcomes families and individuals new to sailing or experienced. It provides training and coaching for adults and young people to enable them to develop skills towards taking part in the club racing programme.

DOVESTONE RESERVOIR SAILING CLUB: Club House, Dovestone Reservoir, Greenfield, Saddleworth, Oldham; ☎0161 682 4393 or ☎07974 651014; www.dovestone.fsnet.co.uk. Entry: ring for prices and opening times.

There's also fishing and water-skiing on the **Bottoms Reservoir** (contact United Utilities Group at Haweswater House, Lingley Mere Business Park, Great Sankey, Warrington WA5 3LP; ☎01925 237 000 or ☎01925 237 066; www.unitedutilities.com for details).

🏃 What to do with children

A good way for the family to enjoy some of the wildest hills in the Peak is to park at Torside Reservoir, opposite the sailing club, and take the **Longdendale Trail**, which follows the level trackbed of the former Great Central Railway line, through the valley. This route is also now part of the **TransPennine Trail**, which also links with the E8 European Long Distance Path from Liverpool to Hull.

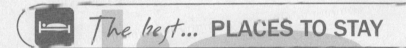

🛏 *The best...* PLACES TO STAY

INN

The White Hart

**51 Stockport Road,
Lydgate, Oldham OL4 4JJ
☎ 01457 872566
www.thewhitehart.co.uk**

Award-winning 18th-century inn with 12 en-suite rooms named after local dignitaries, with deluxe bathrooms and free internet access. Sweeping views in fine weather towards Manchester and the Cheshire plain. Room service, including full brasserie and restaurant menus, during normal kitchen hours.

Price: B&B £127.50 for a double.

B&B

The Old House 🥾 🏠 🍴

**Woodhead Road,
Torside, Glossop SK13 1HU
☎ 01457 857527
www.oldhouse.torside.co.uk**

Comfortable B&B accommodation, including two-day package for walkers tackling one of the toughest stages of the Pennine Way. Facilities include some en-suite rooms, guest lounge, drying room, a packed lunch service and evening meals. Sweeping views over the Longdendale Valley. Bunk barn sleeping 12 also available.

Price: B&B from £25 per person per night.

The best... FOOD AND DRINK

Staying in

Everything from a bakery to a butchery and fish to fresh vegetables is available from **The Pantry** at the Rams Head Inn (Denshaw, Saddleworth OL3 5UN; ☎01457 874802; www.ramsheaddenshaw.co.uk). You'll also find a delicatessen, drinks cabinet, hampers and gifts, pre-prepared dishes and seasonal lines. Many of its products, including a wide selection of cheeses, meats, pies, jams, pickles and pâtés, are sourced from Yorkshire and Lancashire, and breads, cakes and puddings are baked on the premises.

EATING OUT

GASTRO PUB

The White Hart
51 Stockport Road, Lydgate, Oldham OL4 4JJ
☎ **01457 872566**
www.thewhitehart.co.uk

Dining to suit all tastes is on offer at this scenically situated pub on Saddleworth Moor. Typical pub mains include grilled Barnsley lamb chop (£15) and beer battered haddock (£12.50), while restaurant mains range from pork fillet to poached halibut steak. A three-course restaurant menu with coffee costs £19.95.

The Rams Head Inn
Denshaw, Saddleworth OL3 5UN
☎ **01457 874802**
www.ramsheaddenshaw.co.uk

Multi-award winning, 450-year-old inn with log fires, fascinating memorabilia and fresh, imaginative food based on seasonal produce. Game, seafood and steak are particular specialities. Also home to 'The Pantry', with quality food and drink on sale and a coffee shop. Typical mains include roast wild mallard (£10.95) and pan-fried wood pigeon (£9.95).

ⓘ Visitor Information

Tourist information centre: Marsden Information Point, 20–26 Peel Street, Marsden HD7 6BW; ☎01484 845595, open Wed–Sat and Tues afternoons.

Hospitals: A&E, Huddersfield Royal Infirmary, Acre Street, Huddersfield, ☎01484 342000; Calderdale Royal Hospital, Salterhebble, Halifax, ☎01422 357171.

Doctor: Marsden Health Centre, Victoria Street, Marsden HD7 6DF, ☎01484 844332.

Supermarket: Spar, 113 High Street, Uppermill, Oldham OL3 6BD, ☎01457 871910.

Taxis: See Glossop (p. 290).

HOLMFIRTH AND MELTHAM

The countryside around Holmfirth and Meltham is inevitably associated with the long-running television comedy *Last of the Summer Wine*, first shown on BBC1 in 1973 and now broadcast in more than 25 countries. It's thought to be the longest-running comedy television programme in Britain and the longest-running television sitcom in the world. Mostly filmed in and around Holmfirth, the plot centres around three old men who despite their years, refuse to grow up. The original trio consisted of Bill Owen as the scruffy Compo, Peter Sallis as the deep-thinking Clegg, and Michael Bates as authoritarian Blamire. Brian Wilde joined the cast as the war veteran Foggy when Bates left and later, Frank Thornton joined as the ex-police officer Truly. Another constant character has been the fearsome battleaxe Nora Batty (played by the late Kathy Staff), with her famous wrinkled stockings, the object of Compo's thwarted desire.

Like so many other Yorkshire towns, Holmfirth was founded on the textile, and particularly the woollen, industry. The proximity of the vital ingredients of soft-wool moorland sheep and the fast-flowing rivers to power the impressive mills, which still bear testimony to the town's long tradition of producing some of the world's finest woollen yarns and cloths, made the location ideal. Somewhat incongruously, Holmfirth was once also the Hollywood of Yorkshire, as the local firm of Bamforths, probably most famous for their saucy seaside postcards, produced some of the earliest movie films in the country here. A reminder of those glamorous days of the Silver Screen is the celebrated Holmfirth Picturedrome in Market Walk, built in 1910 in the Art Deco style. Holmfirth still has a thriving artistic community, which includes the landscape painter Ashley Jackson, whose gallery is on the Huddersfield road; the CragRats Theatre, housed in a former mill building on the Dunford Road, and a couple of very fine secondhand bookshops.

The mill complex in the village of Meltham, in the far north of the area, was the former site of Jonas Brook and Brothers, a silk manufacturing business which employed over 1,000 workers during the late 19th century. The goat's head crest of the philanthropic Brooks family can still be seen on the old mill office building and their arms are also emblazoned on St James Church, in Meltham Mills. The factory site was eventually taken over by David Brown Tractors, and is now home to the fascinating David Brown Tractor Museum.

WHAT TO SEE AND DO

Like or loathe the programme, you can't avoid taking the *Last of the Summer Wine* trail while you are in Holmfirth. Next door to the famous and instantly recognisable venue of **Nora Batty's Steps** (complete with a pair of Compo's wellies!), you can tuck into some delicious home-cooked cakes and cream teas at the **Wrinkled Stocking Tea Rooms**, which is also home to the *Last of the Summer Wine* **Exhibition**, just off the Huddersfield Road. Here you can relive the unlikely adventures of the terrible threesome, trace some of the venues which were used, and meet some of the other memorable characters from the long-running television comedy.

Nora Batty's Steps next to the Wrinkled Stocking Tea Rooms

LAST OF THE SUMMER WINE EXHIBITION AND THE WRINKLED STOCKING TEA ROOM: 30 Huddersfield Road, Holmfirth HD9 2JS, ☎01484 681408; www.summerwineexhibition.co.uk or www.wrinkledstocking.co.uk. Entry: adults £2, children free; open daily 11am–4pm; 11am–3pm, 1 Nov to 28 Feb, closed Tues.

In the town centre, which is characterised by its steep cobbled streets and ginnels, io **Sid's Café**, the scene of the hatching of so many plots by the leading characters of Compo, Clegg and Foggy. The 10 mile **Summerwine Magic Tour** leaves from here in a 21-seat minibus, and during a 45-minute journey visits many of the film locations used by the television series around the Holme Valley.

SUMMERWINE MAGIC TOUR: Summerwine Leisure, 7 Wadman Road, Scholes, Holmfirth HD0 1QZ, ☎01484 687231; www.summerwine.tv. Entry: adults £6, children £3; daily Sat–Thurs.

Walking

The **Holme Valley Riverside Way** is an easy 6 mile linear walk through the valley, linking Holmfirth with villages like Honley and Netherthong, while the **Holme Valley Circular Walk** covers 24 miles from Berry Brow near Huddersfield, but is easily divided into 13 shorter sections.

Choose a fine, clear day for your visit to the **Holme Moss View Point**, on the Woodhead road out of Holme village. At 1,733ft/525m above the sea, the views from the car park here are breathtaking, extending for many a mile across West Yorkshire to Huddersfield, Holmfirth and the distant, steam-belching cooling towers of the Ferrybridge and Drax power stations in the Vale of York. The 740ft/225m needle-like mast of the nearby **Holme Moss BBC TV transmitter** often threads the scudding clouds, but it brought colour television to vast areas of the north when it opened in 1951. Local people still tell of the fearful crash when it was felled by a build-up of ice during the winter of 1969.

Sid's Café as featured in *The Last of the Summer Wine*

On the water

The **Pennine Moonraker** is the only narrowboat operating on the Uppermill section of the Huddersfield Narrow Canal. It is operated by Saddleworth Canal Cruises, who have been hiring canal

SADDLEWORTH CANAL CRUISES: 7, Alva Road, Oldham OL4 2NS; ☎0161 652 6331; www.saddleworth-canal-cruises.co.uk.

boats and organising holidays for many years. The Dobcross to Ashton section of the Huddersfield Narrow Canal reopened in 2001 after being closed for half a century, and the Moonraker offers a unique and entertaining experience of life on the canal.

Wet weather

If you're an unrepentant 'Tractor Boy', then the **David Brown Tractor Museum** in the mill buildings at Meltham is worth a visit. It is home to a large selection of new and used tractors, technical drawings, records, photographs and David Brown Tractor Club memorabilia.

DAVID BROWN TRACTOR MUSEUM: Spink Mill, Huddersfield Road, Meltham HD9 4AN; www.dbtc.co.uk. Open Sun, Mar to Nov, ring for details of opening hours and prices.

LOCAL KNOWLEDGE

Artist **Ashley Jackson** was born in Penang, Malaysia in 1940. His evocative paintings of brooding moorlands have been exhibited worldwide and have become synonymous with Yorkshire. Since opening his first gallery in 1963, he has become one of the country's most successful watercolour painters. He is perhaps best known for his television series *A Brush with Ashley*, and his current gallery is located on Huddersfield Road, Holmfirth.

Favourite haunt: The Wessenden Valley, which is so wild and beautiful. When you stand at the top of Wessenden Head, you feel you could spread your arms out like wings and swoop down the valley.

Best thing to do on a rainy day: Walking on the moors with my old boss Ron Darwent through the mist and rain, and hiking across Black Hill.

Favourite activity: Being an ambassador for Yorkshire and its Pennines. I am extremely proud of my adoptive home and wherever I travel, I extol its virtues. Everyone should visit us at least once in their lifetime.

Best view: From the top of Holme Moss (Black Hill to the walkers), looking across to Leeds.

Best walk: Around Digley Reservoir, with my family. It takes around three quarters of an hour at a leisurely pace.

Quirkiest attraction: Standedge Tunnel, Marsden, where you can ride on a narrow boat on the Huddersfield Canal and call in at the visitor centre and café, as well as taking a look at where the where the railway and water cross.

Favourite restaurant: The Three Acres at Shelley, Huddersfield. Quality food, but be warned to save a space for desserts.

Favourite take away: Compo's Fish and Chips at the top of Parkhead, Holmfirth. You can eat in or takeaway.

Favourite pub: The Elephant and Castle, Hollowgate, Holmfirth: a traditional pub full of characters and no pretensions.

Best place to paint or sketch: All the views around Holmfirth provide inspiration that has influenced my every brushstroke, so it's hard to choose one specific location. I love them all.

🏃 What to do with children

There are two easy circular walks around the **Digley Reservoir** to the south-west of Holmfirth, the shorter of which is ideal for families with younger children, just over a mile long and running through woodland and fields. For those with older children, this walk can be extended to nearly 5 miles by taking a wider loop across open moorland with spectacular views. The walk around **Blackmoorfoot Reservoir** north of Meltham is accessible to wheelchairs and very popular with birdwatchers.

Digley Reservoir

🛒 Shopping

There are many galleries and bookshops in Holmfirth, including that of the internationally respected watercolourist **Ashley Jackson** in Huddersfield Road. Ashley specialises in capturing moody Pennine landscapes, and many of his pictures and prints are on view and for sale in his gallery. And you may well meet the artist himself.

Holmfirth is also well-known for its second-hand bookshops, which include the **Daisy Lane Bookshop** (Daisy Lane, Towngate, Holmfirth HD9 1HS; ☎01484 688409; open daily) and the **Tollhouse Bookshop** (32–34 Huddersfield Road, Holmfirth HD9 2JS; ☎01484 686541; open Mon–Sat), just round the corner from Nora Batty's House.

ASHLEY JACKSON GALLERY: 13–15 Huddersfield Road, Holmfirth HD9 2LJ; ☎01484 686460; www.ashley-jackson.co.uk. Entry: admission to gallery by appointment only; open daily.

The Ashley Jackson Gallery, with the artist himself

🎭 Entertainment

The tiny **CragRats Theatre** in Dunford Road, Holmfirth (HD9 2AR; ☎01484 691323; www.cragratstheatre.com; ring for details of performances), was converted by a group of enthusiasts from a former cotton mill. It now stages a comprehensive programme of shows, professional and amateur, and also has a fine restaurant as part of the complex.

The **Holmfirth Picturedrome** in the centre of town (Market Walk, Holmfirth HD9 1DA; ☎01484 689759; www.picturedrome.net; ring for details of performances) is a gem of Edwardian architecture, built in 1910. A range of rare and unusual films are shown here, and then the seats are removed for a programme of live music shows. The Picturedrome recently won funding for a thorough restoration, which should restore it to its former Art Deco glory.

The best... **PLACES TO STAY**

INN

The Huntsman Inn

Greenfield Road, Holmfirth HD9 3XF
☎ **01484 850205**
www.the-huntsman-inn.com

With a scenic setting above Holmfirth, the Huntsman offers luxury en-suite accommodation, including a honeymoon suite with jacuzzi, close to superb walking and sightseeing country. Continental or full English breakfast prepared to order.

Price: B&B from £60 for a double.

B&B

Sunnybank

78 Upperthong Lane, Holmfirth HD9 3BQ; ☎ **01484 684857**
www.sunnybankguesthouse.co.uk

Quality accommodation surrounded by two acres of wooded gardens close to the centre of Holmfirth. En-suite bedrooms furnished to a high standard with modern facilities, including Wi-Fi internet access.

Price: B&B from £30 pppn.

The Old Co-op

96 The Village, Thurstonland, near Holmfirth HD4 6XF; ☎ **01484 663621**
www.theoldco-op.com

Comfortable and charming 19th-century stone built house, offering quality accommodation in a quiet location. Breakfast, incorporating local produce, is served in the oak beamed dining room, which also has a wood burning stove. Tiered garden with pleasant views.

Price: B&B from £33 pppn.

SELF-CATERING

Lane Farm Holiday Cottages

Lane Farm, Holme HD9 2QF
☎ **01484 682290**
www.lanefarmcottages.co.uk

Well-appointed stone cottages, each sleeping six, on a working sheep and beef farm. Open views towards Holme Moss, ample parking in cobbled courtyard and shared patio and garden.

Price: From £300 to £575 for a week.

Mytholmbridge Studio Cottages

Mytholmbridge Farm, Luke Lane, Holmfirth HD9 7TB
☎ **01484 686642**
www.mytholmbridge.co.uk

Contemporary, spacious, open plan 18th-century barn conversion featuring original beams, well-equipped kitchen and comfortable accommodation for up to four or up to six people. Private garden and plenty of parking.

Price: £200 to £400 for a week.

UNUSUAL

Nora Batty's Cottage

28 Huddersfield Road, Holmfirth HD9 2JS
☎ **01274 603750**
www.nora-batty.co.uk

Get a true *Last of the Summer Wine* experience by staying in this shrine to Nora Batty, furnished as she would have approved. Packed with memorabilia, signed photographs of the cast and props used in filming the popular television series.

Price: £270 to £625 for a week.

The best... FOOD AND DRINK

Around Holmfirth you'll come across a wealth of quality delicatessens and farm shops, plus quality dairy products ranging from crème fraiche to cottage cheese and yoghurt to ice cream, plus a food and drink festival every September. You can dine out at everything from stylish brasserie to a tea room celebrating *Last of the Summer Wine's* famous battleaxe Nora Batty, played by the late actress Kathy Staff. Locally brewed beers abound in a choice of traditional pubs, many serving food featuring local produce.

▶ Staying in

Delicacies ranging from cooked meats to speciality cheeses and more exotic offerings such as chilli jam and Thai jelly can be sourced at **Beattie's Delicatessen & Coffee Shop** in Holmfirth (Towngate HD9 1HA; ☎01484 689000). You can also buy olives, roasted vegetables, vinegars, pesto, freshly ground coffee and speciality teas, plus takeaway sandwiches and pastries. Home-baked items, meats, cheese and dairy products, preserves and fruit and vegetables from around the world are among the wide selection of foods on offer at **Taylor's Food Store** at Honley, Holmfirth (Meltham Road HD9 6DP; ☎01484 661682).

Home-reared beef and own-brand jams are among the hand-picked produce on sale at **Hinchliffe's Farm Shop** in Netherton (Netherton Moor Road HD4 7LE; ☎01484 661231), which prides itself on its commitment to sustainability, healthy eating and animal welfare. Its award-winning butchers make everything from traditional pies and pasties to pork, Cheddar and chive sausages from organically reared meat and are particularly renowned for their pork pies. The farm also boasts an open farm with a range of unusual birds and animals such as alpacas, kune kune pigs, rheas (flightless birds from South America) and silkies (Asian poultry) and you can also eat locally sourced breakfast, lunch or dinner at **The Old Farmhouse Restaurant** (☎01484 668949), where regular events include jazz nights, gourmet and wine tasting dinners and cookery demonstrations.

Quality dairy products such as cream, fromage frais, crème fraiche, cottage cheese, soft cheese, yoghurt, butter and ice cream are available from **Longley Farm** in Holmfirth (HD9 2JD; ☎01484 684151). You can also enjoy one (or several) of the dairy's 20-plus flavours of home-made ice cream, from unusual damson to perennially popular vanilla, just half-a-mile away at **Longley's Ice Cream Parlour**, Huddersfield Road, Holmfirth (HD9 3JH; ☎01484 681252), where other Longley specialities such as Yorkshire curd tart are on sale.

Holmfirth Farmers' Market is held at the Market Hall, Huddersfield Road (HD9 3JH; ☎01484 223730), on the third Sunday of the month, from 8am to 2pm. And if you're in the area in September, look out for the annual **Holmfirth Food & Drink Festival**, which celebrates the best of foods from around the world and includes a food market with stalls throughout the town and cookery demonstrations.

EATING OUT

FINE DINING

CragRats Brasserie
**Sheffield Road, Near Hepworth,
Holmfirth HD9 7TP
☎ 01484 683775
www.cragratsbrasserie.com**

Elegant fine dining restaurant and bar with scenic views, serving a modern British menu based on fresh, local produce where possible. Emphasis on friendly, attentive service. Menu includes sandwiches, Sunday lunch and a Brasserie Special featuring locally sourced, seasonal dishes (two courses £16.95, three courses £19.95), plus à la carte.

The Olive Branch
**Manchester Road, Marsden HD7 6LU
☎ 01484 844487
www.olivebranch.uk.com**

Family-run restaurant in the scenic Colne Valley, with a warren of snug rooms, open fire and decked outdoor area overlooking Marsden Moor Estate. Locally sourced produce used wherever possible, including beef from Hartshead Meats, Mossley. Sample mains include confit leg of duck and grilled native lobster tail, from £13.95.

RESTAURANT

Number 11
**11 Huddersfield Road, Upperbridge,
Holmfirth HD9 2JR
☎ 01484 688811
www.11rb.co.uk**

Well-presented English, Mediterranean and Caribbean food prepared fresh to order using produce from local suppliers, served by a friendly team in a modern, stylish setting. Daily specials, vegetarian and coeliac options. Mains include sirloin steak, pan-seared duck breast or chicken, Caribbean curried goat and Caribbean vegetable curry. Two courses cost £16.95, three courses £19.95.

Les Caveaux
**11a/11b Victoria Square,
Holmfirth HD9 2DN
☎ 01484 689003**

Tapas restaurant with more than 45 dishes on offer, ranging from pan-fried Valencia almonds and king prawns in filo pastry to seafood and chorizo paella and Mexican beef burrito with cheese. Mains include sea bass fillet, Cornish crab and chicken stroganoff. Average price for meal, including drinks, is around £24 per person.

Harrow's Restaurant
**11 Victoria Street, Holmfirth HD9 7DF
☎ 01484 688764
www.harrowsrestaurant.com**

Smart ground-floor café bar and flag-stoned, spacious cellar open for lunch and dinner (early evening in wine bar). Hot and cold ciabattas and bagels, light lunches, early bird and full à la carte menus. Typical mains include pan-fried chicken with mousseline stuffing, confit of duck glazed with honey and canon of new season lamb (from £10.95).

Carniceria Café Bar and Restaurant
**3 Victoria Square, Holmfirth HD9 2DN
☎ 01484 681568
www.thenookholmfirth.co.uk**

A blend of the best of traditional British cuisine and the authentic taste of the

EATING OUT

Mediterranean, redolent of summer holidays in the sun. Friendly, informal atmosphere, good selection of wines, spirits, beers and lagers. Choice of tapas, from £2.75, or mains such as halloumi cheese and roast pepper parcels and seared beef fillet, from £9.50.

Cinnamon Lodge Indian Restaurant
4 Holmfirth Road, Meltham HD9 4ES
☎ **01484 851777**
www.cinnamonlodge.co.uk

Contemporary Indian cuisine in a chic setting, seating up to 140 people. Both traditional favourites and speciality recipes aimed at more adventurous diners are on the extensive menu. Takeaway service available. Specialities include Cinnamon Amchor, featuring pieces of chicken or lamb in creamy mango sauce, and start at £5.75.

Mozzarella's
23 Peel Street, Marsden HD7 6BW
☎ **01484 845511**
www.olivebranch.uk.com

Cheerful Italian restaurant and takeaway, sister business of The Olive Branch. Large range of speciality breads, starters, salads, bakes, pastas, risottos, grills, mains, side orders and puddings, complemented by wines from around the world. Mains cost from £6.50.

Mustard and Punch
6 Westgate, Honley, Holmfirth HD9 6AA
☎ **01484 662066**
www.mustardandpunch.co.uk

Enjoyable dining in an understated, comfortable setting. Varied, imaginative menus complemented by a large choice of wines and beers. A la carte starters include black pudding and queen scallops chowder, while typical mains are pan-roasted guinea fowl, rib-eye steak and medallions of monkfish. Starters cost from £5.50, mains from £15.50.

GASTRO PUB

CragRats Café Bar
Dunford Road, Holmfirth HD9 2AR
☎ **01484 691393**
www.cragratscafébar.com

Seasonal, locally sourced and organic food is on the menu at this stylish venue. Food ranges from light bites to full meals, with starters (from £4.95) such as Thai spiced prawn cakes and organic Caesar salad and mains (from £12.95) from organic buffalo burger to Black Sheep Ale battered haddock.

The New Inn
Manchester Road, Marsden HD7 6EZ
☎ **01484 841917**
www.newinnmarsden.co.uk

British food with a modern twist and real cask ales are served here, where Wednesday night is 'pie night', offering home-made options such as steak and onion pudding and Whitby fish pie, while Thursday night is 'steak night'. Restaurant mains include slow-roasted Gloucester Old Spot pork belly and handmade merguez sausages and start at £8.95.

EATING OUT

CAFÉ

Café & Crafts @ Penny Lane
14c Daisy Lane, Holmfirth HD9 1HA
☎ 01484 688151

Home-cooked food sourced from local suppliers with a varied menu reflecting the seasons and customers' tastes. Open for all day breakfasts, lunch, specials and afternoon tea, including cream teas featuring home-made scones with local cream and jam or the famous Yorkshire 'fat rascal'. Local crafts on display on the ground floor.

Miss s'l le nieuce [pronounced Miscellaneous]
27 Hollowgate, Holmfirth HD9 1HA
☎ 01484 689846
www.holmfirthgifts.co.uk

Family-run café serving light meals, sandwiches, baguettes, ciabatta and paninis using bread baked on the premises, cakes, scones and flatbakes. Selection of coffees, speciality teas, hot chocolate, cold drinks and Yorkshire cream tea special.

Sid's Café
4 Towngate, Holmfirth HD9 1HA

A 'must' for all fans of the long-running BBC television series *Last of the Summer Wine* where customers hide behind green and white gingham curtains to sample teas, snacks and souvenirs in an instantly recognisable venue associated with the vintage comedy. You'll spot plenty of famous faces in the cast photos lining its walls.

TEA ROOM

The Wrinkled Stocking Tea Room
30 Huddersfield Road, Holmfirth HD9 2JS
☎ 01484 681408
www.wrinkledstocking.co.uk

Traditional home-baked hot and cold food and speciality cakes in another setting which pays homage to the sartorial idiosyncrasies of the curler-crowned battleaxe, Nora Batty, played by the late Kathy Staff, in *Last of the Summer Wine*. Local produce used where possible to create culinary specialities such as Yorkshire parkin and lemon drizzle cake.

🍺 Drinking

For a wide range of beers supplied by national and local brewers, visit the **Farmer's Arms** in Holmfirth (Liphill Bank Road, Burnlee HD9 2LR; ☎01484 683713), which also serves home-cooked food at lunchtimes and evenings. There is a warm and welcoming atmosphere and regular folk nights. Eight real ales feature in the well-stocked bar at **The Nook Real Ale Bar (Rose & Crown)**, (Victoria Square HD9 2DN; ☎01484 683960), which hosts traditional pub games, poker, live music and an annual beer festival. Home-cooked food, including the 'Nook Burger' and traditional Sunday roasts is served all day, and The Nook is also planning to open its own four-barrel brewery.

Real ales and home-prepared food can also be found at the **Foxhouse Inn** (Penistone Road HD9 2TR; ☎01226 762536) and the **Sycamore Inn** (New Mill Road HD9 7SH; ☎01484 683458). The Sycamore also hosts regular quiz and live music nights, a summer golf society and a 'muddy boots society' for keen walkers. Walkers (and dogs) are also welcome in the hospitable bar at **The Huntsman Inn** (Greenfield Road HD9 3XF; ☎01484 850205), which has a traditional air, with a selection of beers and an open fire. Food is served at lunchtime and in the evening, and all day Friday and weekends.

Just outside town on the Holme Moss road, frequently changing guest ales and food ranging from sandwiches to full meals are on offer at **The Fleece Inn** at Holme (HD9 2QG; ☎01484 683449), which boasts a cosy coal fire and welcomes walkers. Situated in a picturesque location near Ingbirchworth Reservoir, **The Fountain Inn** at Ingbirchworth (S36 7GJ; ☎01226 763125) is a former 17th-century coaching inn with a cosy, yet elegant interior. Real ales and food made from fresh local produce is served, and there are regular quiz and theme nights.

ⓘ Visitor Information

Tourist information centre: Holmfirth Tourist Information Centre, 49–51 Huddersfield Road, Holmfirth, Yorkshire HD9 3JP, ☎01484 222444, www.holmfirth.tic@kirkleesmc.gov.uk, open daily.

Hospital: A&E, Huddersfield Royal Infirmary, Acre Street, Huddersfield, ☎01484 342000; Calderdale Royal Hospital, Salterhebble, Halifax, ☎01422 357171.

Doctors: Elmwood Health Centre, Huddersfield Road, Holmfirth HD9 3TT, ☎0844 4771772; Meltham Village Surgery, Parkin Lane, Meltham, Holmfirth HD9 4BJ, ☎01484 850638; Meltham Group Practice, 1 The Cobbles, Meltham,

Holmfirth HD9 5QQ, ☎01484 347620; Honley Surgery, Marsh Gardens, Honley, Holmfirth HD9 6AG, ☎01484 303366; Oaklands Health Centre, Huddersfield Road, Holmfirth HD9 3TP, ☎01484 689111.

Supermarkets: Co-op, Market Street, Holmfirth, ☎01484 688611; Morrisons, Station Road, Meltham, ☎01484 850921.

Taxis: Holme Valley Private Hire, Honley, ☎01484 663160; Holme-Time Private Hire, Honley, ☎01484 666321; Honley Private Hire, ☎01484 661144; Oak Taxis, Upperthong, ☎01484 683450; Shaws Private Hire, ☎01484 684777; Town & Country Private Hire, Thongsbridge, ☎01484 687805.

INDEX

C

G

H

I

J

K

L

This first edition published in Great Britain in 2009 by
Crimson Publishing, a division of Crimson Business Ltd
Westminster House
Kew Road
Richmond
Surrey
TW9 2ND

A catalogue record for this book is available from the British Library

ISBN: 978 1 85458 467 0

The author and publishers have done their best to ensure that the information in *The best of Britain: Peak District* is up-to-date and accurate. However, they can accept no responsibility for any loss, injury or inconvenience sustained by any traveller as a result of information or advice in this guide.

Printed and bound by Mega Printing, Turkey

Series editor: Guy Hobbs
Layout design: Nicki Averill, Amanda Grapes, Andy Prior
Typesetting: RefineCatch Ltd
Cover design: Andy Prior
Picture editor: Holly Ivins
Production: Sally Rawlings
Town map design: Linda M Dawes, Belvoir Cartographics & Design and Angela Wilson, All Terrain Mapping, using source material from Ordnance Survey.
Regional map design: Linda M Dawes, Belvoir Cartographics & Design and Angela Wilson, All Terrain Mapping, using source material: © Maps in Minutes™/Collins Bartholomew, 2009.

This product includes mapping data licensed from Ordnance Survey® with the permission of the Controller of Her Majesty's Stationery Office. © Crown Copyright 2009. All rights reserved. Licence number 150002047.

Acknowledgements
The authors would like to thank the staff of Visit Peak District and Derbyshire in Buxton, who helped with both information and pictures.

Help us update
While every effort has been made to ensure that the information contained in this book was accurate at the time of going to press, some details are bound to change within the lifetime of this edition: phone numbers and websites change, restaurants and hotels go out of business, shops move, and standards rise and fall. If you think we've got it wrong, please let us know. We will credit all contributions and send a copy of any *The Best of Britain* title for the best letters. Send to: The Best of Britain Updates, Crimson Publishing, Westminster House, Kew Road, Richmond, Surrey TW9 2ND.

Photo credits

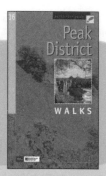